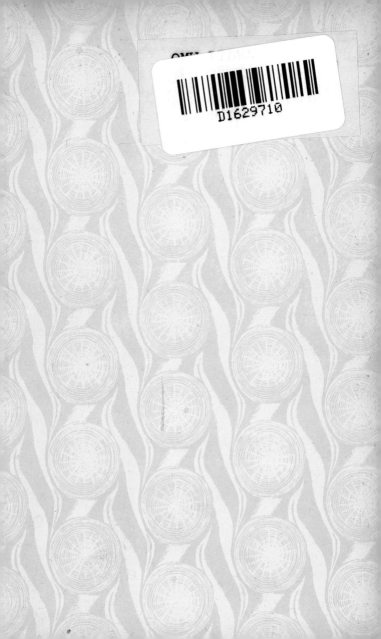

Everyman, I will go with thee, and be thy guide,
In thy most need to go by thy side.

084902
20.7.70

This is No. 943 of Everyman's Library. A
list of authors and their works in this series
will be found at the end of this volume. The
publishers will be pleased to send freely to all
applicants a separate, annotated list of the
Library.

J. M. DENT & SONS LIMITED
10–13 BEDFORD STREET LONDON W.C.2

E. P. DUTTON & CO. INC.
286–302 FOURTH AVENUE
NEW YORK

EVERYMAN'S LIBRARY
EDITED BY ERNEST RHYS

ESSAYS & BELLES-LETTRES

THE GEORGIAN LITERARY SCENE
BY FRANK SWINNERTON

FRANK ARTHUR SWINNERTON, born
12th August 1884. Office boy to Hay
Nisbet, newspaper publishers, March 1899;
clerk to J. M. Dent & Co., 1901–7;
reader to Chatto & Windus, 1909–26.
Sole book reviewer to the London *Evening
News*, 1929–32. Principal novel reviewer
to the *Observer* since April 1937.

THE GEORGIAN LITERARY SCENE

FRANK SWINNERTON

LONDON: J. M. DENT & SONS LTD

PREFACE

WHEN his novel, *Angel Pavement*, was included in the series, Mr J. B. Priestley recorded his debt to Everyman's Library, and most interestingly described his first boyhood acquaintance with it. If the suggestion had been made to him in boyhood that in thirty years' time one of his own books would adorn the galaxy, he would have found it incredible. My case resembles Mr Priestley's in the sense that my century and a half of Everyman, collected since 1906, has been a continuous source of knowledge and delight; but my association with the Library is even longer than his, and to myself is of the utmost importance. It goes back to days when no such series was in existence. I must have been one of the first half-dozen people in the world to know that it was so much as contemplated.

In 1906 I was what was called 'confidential clerk' to Mr Hugh Dent, and as Mr Hugh Dent's association with his father was as close as it was loyal I thus stood at one remove only from the Chief himself. I saw the tentative lists of books which it was thought might fittingly open the series. I knew which of them were chosen and which deferred, and sometimes why. I handled proofs of these adventurous choices. I harried printers and editors. I checked the letterings upon the early dustcovers. And, as did the other members of the staff, I awaited breathlessly the zero hour at which the whole fifty volumes would burst simultaneously upon the world. It was decidedly exciting.

Everyman's Library is now calmly accepted as an institution. It is known through two hemispheres. Its riches have long been a recognized boon to students. You will find it present as a matter of course in every kind of home, from the luxury flat to the advertised seaside or riverside shack where, in repellent words, they 'sleep six.' And, in consequence, nobody remembers how sensational was the first news of the series, the first sight of the books, and the first tremendous sale which they enjoyed. From within, it seemed as though we were besieged by storming enthusiasts who wanted the books we had, the books we should have in the next two or

three batches, the books newly published which the enthusiasts wanted to buy for a shilling. We ran out of stock and
out of print; we reprinted, bound, and supplied in a delicious
frenzy; we drove stationers, printers, and binders to a speed
which we ourselves believed to be impossible. I think even
Mr Dent was impressed by several major book-trade miracles.
His employees certainly were. They all worked like ants in
a disturbed nest. And while they worked to supply the first
fifty volumes the second fifty volumes were being editorially
assembled for the production of a second terrific wave. It was
like an avalanche. Such publishing, I feel sure, had never
previously been known.

At that time I was twenty-two years of age. My days were
as full as could be of publishing; but my evenings were full of
reading, writing, theatre-going, and—as I have told elsewhere
—of immature distant observation of the world of literary men.
Bernard Shaw, Gilbert Chesterton, Hilaire Belloc, and H. G.
Wells were for me the great contemporary figures. Wells had
one day called at Dent's about two early books, *The Wonderful
Visit* and *The Wheels of Chance*, which the firm had published
back in the old century; Chesterton arrived late one evening
with a Dickens preface for Everyman's Library which he would
not entrust to me because I could not make a ready-money
exchange. The others I saw only upon the platform. I did
not emulate any of these writers, for I never was either a
dramatist or a publicist. The writing I did in the evenings
was the writing of novels and literary criticism. But the men,
their idiosyncrasies, their ideas, and their debates, were to me
the absorbing interests of the time.

As the years passed, I had two further sources of acquaintance with writers. One was a position as publisher's reader to
Messrs Chatto & Windus, the other was a literary start upon
my own account. In 1909, a year before King George V came
to the throne, I published my first novel. Three others followed before Mr Martin Secker asked me to write a critical
study of George Gissing for his series of Modern Monographs;
and I think it must have been the writing of this book—for
the biographical portion of which I found it hard to obtain
material—that crystallized a natural opinion which I have held
ever since. It is that the authors of books should ever be
traced and found in their books, and that all really interesting
interpretation of literature—whatever the dilettanti may say
—is humane.

What I have said above expresses the astonished delight which my juvenile self would have felt at the inclusion of a book by Frank Swinnerton in Everyman's Library. It also indicates the angle from which *The Georgian Literary Scene* approaches modern literature. The book, historical and biographical as it is, has a deliberate informality of tone. It contains sketches, portraits, and illustrative episodes. But it is primarily a criticism; and as such, although time may prove my judgment to be wrong, it is seriously offered. I have taken advantage of the publication in Everyman's Library to revise and prune the text, and in this process have eliminated one or two writers whose work was more or less perfunctorily treated in the original version. The book, I believe, has been thereby improved. It remains, however, unchanged in its verdicts upon both men and tendencies; and if it provokes disagreement I hope that is because, whatever its faults of taste and execution, it has some vitality of its own and a standpoint which cannot be gainsaid.

F. S.

1938.

The following is a list of the works of Frank Swinnerton:

NOVELS. *The Merry Heart*, 1909; *The Young Idea*, 1910; *The Casement*, 1911; *The Happy Family*, 1912; *On the Staircase*, 1914; *The Chaste Wife*, 1916; *Nocturne*, 1917; *Shops and Houses*, 1918; *September*, 1919; *Coquette*, 1921; *The Three Lovers*, 1923; *Young Felix*, 1923; *The Elder Sister*, 1925; *Summer Storm*, 1926; *A Brood of Ducklings*, 1928; *Sketch of a Sinner*, 1929; *The Georgian House*, 1932; *Elizabeth*, 1934; *Harvest Comedy*, 1937.

OTHER WRITINGS. *George Gissing, a Critical Study*, 1912; revised edition, 1924; *R. L. Stevenson, a Critical Study*, 1914; revised edition, 1924; *Women* (anonymous), 1918; *Tokefield Papers*, 1927; *A London Bookman*, 1928; *Authors and the Book Trade*, 1932; *The Georgian Literary Scene*, 1935; *Swinnerton: an Autobiography*, 1937.

Mr Swinnerton has also edited *Fiction* in Nelson's Modern Anthologies, 1937; and a new edition of Arnold Bennett's *Literary Taste*, 1937.

CONTENTS

CHAPTER I: INTRODUCTORY

I

AT the risk of beginning this book with a repulsive truism, I must remark that authors are born very untidily. They do not live, as they should do, from century to century, or from reign to reign, but rise as and when they will, and do their work unwinkingly regardless of the historian. Even Shakespeare himself—although Chaucer, who died neatly in the last weeks of the fourteenth century, might have shown him a better way—lived in two centuries and in two reigns.

But historians have their own methods of dealing with such rebels. They long ago decided that Shakespeare was an Elizabethan, and so he remains to this day. It is a convenient and justifiable assumption. Equally justifiable, it seems to me, for brief reference, is the description of Congreve, Farquhar, Vanbrugh, and Wycherley as 'Restoration' dramatists and equally convenient the term 'Augustan' as applied to the characteristic literature of the reign of Queen Anne. 'Commonwealth' and 'Regency' are also pleasant and suggestive economies for the historian of manners. But two subsequent major labels, both misleading in themselves, give an arbitrary tidiness to the births, deaths, and works of innumerable celebrated authors as diverse as the ills of mankind.

The first of these labels is that of the original 'Georgian' period with which this book has no concern. England was ruled, from 1714 to 1830, by four successive kings named George. Anything built or written at some time in the eighteenth century was 'Georgian.' Johnson, Horace Walpole, Sterne, Cowper, Fanny Burney, Burke, Gibbon, and Collins were all 'Georgian.' You could also call Lamb, Keats, and Hazlitt Georgians if you wished. As for Queen Victoria, whose name forms the second of these labels, she lived (she was born in 1819) and reigned (from 1837 to 1901) so long that whole generations of writers came and went while she indestructibly occupied the throne of her country.

No wonder historians, triumphant at their success with Shakespeare, and misled by the overwhelming embrace of the Georges and Victoria, assumed thenceforward that centuries and reigns and literary types marched together. In face of Queen Victoria's long reign, we all know what a jovial person means when he indicates by a single word smugness, stuffiness, wool-work, industrialism, moral strait-lacing, or whatever it is he most dislikes. But the historian and the jovial person are alike making a grand mistake. Just as smugness was to be found elsewhere than in England during the nineteenth century, and just as it lives on in that very scorn of the Victorians upon which scorners set such value, so literary types fall with extraordinary diversity far outside the widest limits of the descriptive term. And individual writers, already smiling at the critic who arrives with an Aristotelian formula, become positively ribald if the critic begins to classify by era.

The reason of their mirth becomes clear as soon as we try to apply the Edwardian name with precision. King Edward VII had so short a reign—only from 1901 to 1910—that there was barely time in it for Bernard Shaw, H. G. Wells, Joseph Conrad, Arnold Bennett, and a few more Victorian-born writers to shoot into decided prominence; and their real fame has been post-Edwardian. Shaw's best work, for example, was written in Victorian days; his triumph at the Court Theatre (the audience there, he once retorted to a questioner, was not an audience but a congregation) was Edwardian, but his deification, after much fruitless abuse in War-time, has been entirely a matter for post-War seekers after a new Grand Old Man.

Again, Wells conversed selectly with his uncle as long ago as 1895, and besides writing his greatest short stories and scientific romances before Queen Victoria's death he had reached *Anticipations* in 1901. Nevertheless, *Tono-Bungay*, his masterpiece, was published in the very last year of King Edward's lifetime, and the height as well as the decline of his reputation as a novelist is purely Georgian. Bennett's *Clayhanger* was published after the accession of King George. And although his best work was done earlier, Conrad's success with *Chance* came as late as the spring of 1914.

The word 'Edwardian,' accordingly, has no such general and acceptable meaning for any of us as the word 'Victorian.' When used—by those who are themselves, amusingly enough, Victorian by birth and Edwardian by first literary effort—as a term of discrimination and disparagement, it fails. But the object of its use is clear. The object is to suggest that Shaw, Wells, Conrad, and Bennett are out of date. It would be very convenient for those fashionable since 1920 if they could appropriate the

Georgian name to themselves. It would justify that exclusiveness to which they have attached much importance in the recent past. But all the same there is something juvenile in the plan, as if not very pleasant and nurse-bred children showed a familiar kind of ill-breeding. We seem to see the new little band of brothers and sisters crowding the windows and doorway of a first-class English railway carriage, and pretending that the carriage has been reserved for them. 'Full up, full up!' they cry, to Shaw and the other elderly and less elderly trippers. 'Plenty of room for *you* in the old third-class, Edwardian, coach.' Not very agreeable children; a good deal worried (like minor royalties) about precedence and congenital superiority.

II

Now King George V ascended the throne in 1910. And it was in or about that year, you will remember, that (on the authority of a much-admired woman novelist) human nature underwent a remarkable change. Human nature, at bottom, had been recognizably similar under Victoria and Edward. Philosophers had gone so far as to suppose it unchangeable. One of them, indeed, wittier than the rest, had said that the more it changed the more it remained the same. But no sooner did King George come to the throne than (if we are to believe our novelist) human nature disobeyed every known law. It must have done this, I suspect, in order to give some friendly assistance — almost a nudge—a sort of preferential nudge—to the literary historian. For in or about 1910 we entered the period of time which is now universally described as, not 'modern,' but 'modn.'

I do not believe that human nature changed in 1910, unless it can be said to change every twenty or thirty years. Perhaps it does that? Or is it only fashion that changes? Modernity, at least, is almost as old as history; and there have always been two opinions of it. For example, and to take superficial details only, I find that in the eighties of last century, much as the discovery may astonish those who regard youth as an exclusively modern phenomenon, there was something widely known as 'the revolt of youth.' How 'modn' that sounds! How almost incredible! Yet young women of the eighties shocked their parents by all sorts of uncouth doings, from fencing and boxing to travelling on the tops of omnibuses. In Mayfair at the same time the most fashionable accomplishment of all was the ability to play the banjo. Still in Queen Victoria's day, men and women of birth were 'almost ostentatiously' going into trade, and noble ladies were opening millinery shops in the West End just as if they belonged to the new poor. Shortly before the end of Queen Victoria's reign, young women were using cosmetics for facial decoration; cigarette-smoking was notably on the increase; smart dinner parties were no longer given at home, but in hotels and restaurants; and the week-end habit was in full swing. All this forty and fifty years ago, as a part of the normal development of fashion. Has there been, in manners, so abrupt a change since then as to constitute proof of a change in human nature?

It is true that the Georgian period has had its own peculiarities. At the opening of it the general tempo of life everywhere was visibly quickening. The telegraph, the telephone, the automobile had all helped to break up old ways. Wireless telegraphy had been effectively used at sea; the moving picture was in being; the phonograph had given way to the gramophone; the whole world had with marvel begun to look up into the skies at machines that flew. These things were simple indications that the imagination of the human race had been captured for a time by the fruits of that scientific genius which had been increasingly active since the middle of the nineteenth century. They foreshadowed most of the preoccupations of later years. They seem in retrospect very threatening as well as very wonderful. But they were the result of earlier research, earlier experiment, earlier learning, and earlier irresistible movement towards the kind of world amid which we now live.

Nor was this all; for the successive Education Acts of 1870, 1891, and 1897 had produced in England a state of almost universal literacy which was then considered a step towards the democratic millennium. Halfpenny newspapers had made the reading of news and views a matter for every breakfast table in the land, a daily feast of excitement, hotter and hotter as competition forced editors and contributors towards ever greater licence. And there was news in these papers, even then, provocative enough to make men thump tables and lose tempers, and to make women argue and lecture and go to prison. Although education had not greatly improved their intelligence, it had without doubt increased group consciousness in these men and women; and popular newspapers were very powerful, not so much in initiating ideas or movements, as in spreading infection far and wide, and in agitating half-developed minds into a state of foaming anger.

In the political world, after a good many years of Tory rule (rule, that is, by those with possessions and privileges who none the less have their disinterestedness also), and after a humiliating war in which general after general had lost his military reputation, the Liberal party in 1906 had been returned by a tremendous majority of voters. The Liberals, or democratic reformers, were no longer politically the most advanced body in the House of Commons (there were a few Labour members), but they were a body which in Victorian days would have seemed revolutionary; and they used their power to propose greater taxation of the rich, health insurance for the poor, and other progressive legislation tending to equalize distribution of wealth in the British Isles. The measures thus introduced were rejected by the House of Lords, which represented in its own eyes national stability and in the eyes of eager partisans of the other side the wellnigh indestructible bulwark of privilege; and the wildest feelings were roused throughout the country. In 1910, accordingly, another election was fought entirely upon the question whether the House of Lords should or should not in future be able to check the designs of the people's elected representatives. This election also was won—not without loss—by the Liberals; but the Liberals—in turn—those defenders of the Rights of Man —were terribly assailed by advocates of Women's Suffrage who once and for all destroyed the legend that women were a mystical cross between angels and slaves. Tempers at this hour, the beginning of King George's reign, were unusually hot.

But these things again were only signs of the times; they were the open results of a general tendency which had been long maturing. What may for conciseness' sake be called the democratic idea had taken possession of men's minds. The idea was not merely political; it was social. The long moral acquiescence of a nation which took its good manners from a widowed queen and her circumscribed court had been ending in the last twenty years of Queen Victoria's lifetime; and at her death everybody realized that it had gone for good. It had been ending because the old dominance of the landed gentry in England had passed, because wealth had grown and spread to the middle classes, because the franchise had been extended so as to bring into the electorate all sorts of people who had earlier been excluded, because of the rise of compulsory literacy, and because of the fall of class barriers. Respect for the upper classes had been undermined; the self-complacence of the bourgeoisie had taken its place; in turn the self-complacence of the bourgeoisie was being attacked; and finally the dominance of man was being assailed by that new feminist arm—physical force.

In literature, since literature, when it is not actively leading that thought, reflects so much of the common thought of the time, the consequences of this unrest were profound. The Victorian tradition in letters was represented only by a few surviving old men and women. There were not many of them. George Meredith and Algernon Charles Swinburne had both died in the year before King George's accession. Alfred Austin, who had been chosen poet laureate in the 'naughty nineties,' according to the gossip of that time as 'the least of evils,' was one of Time's laughing-stocks. Robert Bridges was still unknown to the majority. Thomas Hardy had just succeeded to the post of literature's Grand Old Man recently vacated by Meredith; and although he was still to achieve immense fame as a poet, so that his reputation may be said not to have reached its climax until about 1920, his work as novelist had been long done.

Professor Saintsbury and Edmund Gosse represented the elders in multifarious literary criticism, the one with gathering veneration, the other as a busy social figure, while A. C. Bradley represented them in criticism on the loftier levels. Theodore Watts-Dunton survived, largely as one who had seen Swinburne plain (it was thought, none the less, that his oversight had been detrimental to Swinburne's poetic talent) and as one who had contributed many columns of material to *The Athenaeum* in days when space was of no moment. Buried in the tomb which he had erected over the remains of Gladstone, the original Grand Old Man of English reverence, John Morley watched with gloom the decay of authority. Hardy was the only surviving 'giant'; and although the legend of giantism persisted it did so with difficulty. The convention by which belittlement of great men was discouraged on the ground that we were 'too near' to judge them wisely ('Stand away! Stand away!' cried the guards of fame) was yielding to a newer convention by which great men could at least be focused as soon as they were dead. Giants were smaller; and a small giant is an anomaly. It is also an anachronism, for although year by year some literary or political or economic figure is raised a little above the crowd by a few admirers, admirers quickly tire of supporting an idol, and when dropped the idol of a year or two looks positively dwarfish.

The true Edwardians, it seems to me, who represent the tumultuous charge of Liberalism passing over the country between 1906 and 1910 were G. K. Chesterton and Hilaire Belloc, with the Victorian William Watson as a sedate and unheeded singer of Liberal songs far from the battlefield. Chesterton and Belloc, both men of genius, were carried to renown by this glorious charge. With their colleague Charles Masterman, they spoke and wrote everywhere, cutting and slashing and waving large banners of purple and gold. But when the charge had spent itself, Belloc and Chesterton were somehow cut off from their fellows. They both worked indefatigably during the Georgian age. But they were not of it. Something happened to their bugles. Instead of sounding triumphantly a further charge, these instruments uttered nothing but the retreat. It has accordingly been left to others to lead both Liberalism and literature down steep places into the sea. Chesterton to the end announced that the true revolution was the counter-revolution; but he lost pace with the times, and will have to wait for immortality until liberty is reborn. Belloc devotedly rewrites history. He will probably be 'edited' in a hundred years' time, when his propagandism has become archaic, and when his extraordinary ability will shine like the jewel it is.

So much for the truly pre-Georgian writers. These were the men who had their roots in the past. They were entirely surrounded either by Victorianism or by Medievalism. It was enough for them to picture their own fixed world, or to criticize contemporary history in terms of former history. Chesterton and Belloc demanded the return of Merrie England; Hardy lived most richly in Napoleonic or forgotten rural days; Morley was lost in Gladstonian grandeur; the critics I have named, having celebrated, the one his father, and the other his cellar, were happiest with old books. It was time that other voices should be heard. They were heard.

The voices said little of the past. They were very clear voices, and they spoke of the present in scathing terms, and of the future as an opportunity for shattering the world and remoulding it nearer to the heart's desire. The present, it appeared, was bad; and it must be changed. But England had had writers in Victorian days who had criticized the ugly and industrial present; none more strongly than Mrs Gaskell, Charles Kingsley, Disraeli, and George Gissing. William Morris, alternatively, had dreamed of idyllic clodhoppers in endless medieval narratives and prophetic visions. All these writers were now outmoded; the new criticism was something different in style from all they had attempted. On the one hand it worked through irresistible raillery; on the other through what was at that time a quite shockingly fearless vein of speculation. 'Shaw and Wells,' said an old newspaper editor to me one day, 'we've never treated as "literature," but always as cranks.' It was the pre-Georgian voice that spoke. In pre‑Georgian days, 'literature' was 'serious' or it was 'light'; it was not effervescently destructive with a seriousness that shamed solemnity. Shaw and Wells came among the respectable with whips, scorpions, the extruded tongue, and an agitating suggestion that men and women were not wicked, but only stupid and smug. How unlike were these weapons to the Old Testamentary lamentation and exhortation of Carlyle: 'Woe! Woe! Unless ye repent——' How unlike to the nostalgic buglings of Chesterton and Belloc: 'Oligarchy! The Church! Medievalism!' It is not surprising that readers of plays and novels were disconcerted and rather annoyed by the new methods. But of course fascinated, also, and drawn to attend to what was so indignantly denounced by the effete, and delighted by a sense of their own 'modernity' in cultivating the latest frightfulness in moral criticism.

In those days, as in these, the play and the novel were the chief recreation of those who consider themselves cultured. And at the beginning of the Georgian age it was the correct thing to see or read Shaw's plays and to read Wells's books. It was the correct thing because it was, comparatively, a new thing. It was the fashion. The fashion in the eighties had been all for the now much-maligned three-volume novel. Having been replaced by the fashion of Stevenson and his imitators, and in turn by the fashion of the knowing and vigorous work of Rudyard Kipling, it had gone democratic. Besides Shaw and Wells, the public was attending to Arnold Bennett's closely studied engravings of provincial society, to John Galsworthy's dramatic vignettes of capital and labour and the dying bourgeoisie, and to the work of young men and women who had been influenced, in chief, by the spirit of the time as exemplified in the work of these elder leaders.

But then, as now, the spirit of the time worked in more than the immediately observable and immediately popular way. Just as I have said that you cannot fit authors into centuries and reigns, so you cannot without distortion fit them into schools and groups. In the nineties of last century, for example, which are for ever labelled with the names of Wilde and Beardsley, George Gissing was producing his sombre and powerful novels; Conrad and Wells were both active; Ibsen's plays had been translated and were being very widely read; Israel Zangwill and Kipling were the popular successes. In the nineteen hundreds, when Utopias were rife, and the present over-development of scientific education had already begun, Francis Thompson's selected poems were the success of their year, Granville-Barker wrote *The Marrying of Ann Leete* and collaborated in the writing of *Prunella*, while Kenneth Grahame's *Wind in the Willows* was published and a new poetic dramatist named John Masefield followed his historical novel, *Captain Margaret*, with *The Tragedy of Nan*. There was a stirring among young writers which made as much ferment as the current stirring of young writers appears to do. It may not now seem to us a stirring of pure gold, but at least there were bubbles of modernity in the crucible.

It may give some indication of the variety of writers whose work was watched with interest at the beginning of King George's reign if I mention what was at the time a periodical of great importance to observers of literary tendencies. This, *The English Review*, edited by Ford Madox Hueffer, was an impressively non-commercial monthly. It was first published as for the month of December 1908; and during its life under Hueffer's control it was, I think, the most valuable literary journal in the country. The earliest contributors to *The English Review* included some who will not come into our review of Georgian letters. But among the elders should be mentioned Thomas Hardy, Henry James, W. H. Hudson, R. B. Cunninghame Graham, Maurice Hewlett, Vernon Lee, and Lowes Dickinson. Bernard Shaw, as far as I know, was never a contributor.

In a generation rather younger, contributors included Joseph Conrad, John Galsworthy, Arnold Bennett, H. G. Wells, Norman Douglas, C. E. Montague, Violet Hunt, John Masefield, and H. M. Tomlinson. Conrad was not yet a success, in spite of the fact that his first book, *Almayer's Folly*, had appeared in 1895 and *Nostromo* in 1904. Galsworthy was already the author of *A Man of Property*, *The Silver Box*, and *The Country House*. Bennett's *The Old Wives' Tale* had been the talk of 1908. Wells's *Tono-Bungay* began to run as a serial story in the first number of *The English Review*. Norman Douglas and H. M. Tomlinson were quite unknown, unless some curious person had chanced upon Douglas's pamphlet, *The Herpetology of the Duchy of Baden*, and unless readers of *The Morning Leader* had noted Tomlinson's

articles in that newspaper.   Parts of *The Sea and the Jungle*
were published in *The English Review*.   Montague was the chief
leader-writer on *The Manchester Guardian* as well as the dramatic
critic who wrote about Manchester theatrical productions, but
outside Manchester he had no literary reputation until he published *A Hind let Loose* in 1910.

To these names were gradually added those of writers still
younger, the first of the distinctively 'Georgian' names.   I
instance Harley Granville Barker, who at the age of thirty was
considered the hope of the English theatre, Walter de la Mare,
W. W. Gibson, Gilbert Cannan, Edward Thomas, and D. H.
Lawrence.   The youngest contributor to the earliest numbers
of *The English Review* who survives to astonish the publishing
seasons was Percy Wyndham Lewis.

There are omissions, of course, both from my list and from the
complete list of contributors to this excellent journal.   No editor
can be more than catholic.   And any list of authors much admired at the beginning of the Georgian era would be partial which
did not include the names of Hilaire Belloc, Maurice Baring,
E. V. Lucas, and G. K. Chesterton.   Rudyard Kipling was in
the doldrums, partly because his politics were unpopular in the
decade following the Boer War, and partly because his later work
was inferior to the work by which he became famous.   Arthur
Symons was at the height of his reputation as poet and critic.
Robert Hichens was a writer of importance.   Sir Arthur Pinero
was in those days always called—rather defiantly, it seemed,
and by those who were uneasy at the rising Shaw—'England's
greatest dramatist.'   J. M. Barrie was the leading figure in the
theatre.   Hall Caine and Mrs Humphry Ward had become
occasions for ribald comment.   William de Morgan had ceased
to surprise as an example of reanimated Victorianism, although
he still published novels of notable volume.   Sir Arthur Quiller-
Couch, who became King Edward Professor of English Literature
at Cambridge in 1912, stood out from the wreck of the picturesque novel.   Robert Bridges (poet laureate in 1913), Lord
Alfred Douglas, William Watson, Laurence Binyon, Stephen
Phillips, Alfred Noyes, and John Davidson were all well known
as poets, however much opinions might differ as to their gifts.
Somerset Maugham and Rudolf Besier were rising popular
dramatists.   Eden Phillpotts, 'Elizabeth,' W. B. Maxwell, May
Sinclair, Charles Marriott, and John Buchan had all distinctive
reputations in the novel.

As will be seen at once from the enumeration, not all these

writers have been fortunate enough to hold their high place of that hour in the literary opinions of to-day. Fashion is always changing, and names go up and down very oddly, even in the minds of those whose taste is catholic rather than exclusive. If I were writing a purely critical study, I might omit some of these names altogether. To do so would be to give a wrong impression of the period which I am trying to sketch. In this introductory section I want to show, however superficially, which writers were 'established' in the year of the king's accession, which writers had still to make their reputations, and which writers were as yet engaged in preliminary scrawlings at school and in the nursery. The writers not named above were for the most part preparing for the great assault. They had not been heard of outside their own homes or their own small societies for mutual aid.

IV

But surely there were in 1910 at least dim notions of some critical standards by which any writer whatsoever could be judged? There were. There were severities of judgment in the rising generation which equalled those of the present day. Gilbert Cannan, in particular, was demolishing all the older writers as they are still being demolished; but some of these older writers are like the man in the song, of whom it is said that 'he's dead, but he won't lie down,' and they are still with us, dead but not forgotten, in some extraordinary manner more alive than those who assail them, more provoking, more ante-diluvian, and at the same time more essential than ever as Aunt Sallys to critics armed with ever-new weapons of destruction.

For it must be admitted that the critics of to-day are provided with a more elaborate critical apparatus than any enjoyed by their predecessors. In 1910 there were, as probably there are now, cheap editions of Aristotle's *Poetics*, Longinus *On the Sublime*, Lessing's *Laocoon*, and Coleridge's *Biographia Literaria*. But modern aesthetic criticism, with its new and baffling terminologies, was young. Benedetto Croce was on the horizon, but no more; Professor Irving Babbitt did not publish his *New Laocoon* in England until 1911. A. C. Bradley was considered the last word in the criticism of poetry and of Shakespeare's plays; Professor Dowden was the last long word on Shelley; Georg Brandes the last word on everything. Psycho-analysis was unheard of by the majority of English writers, and accordingly the application of post-Freudian methods and terms to the study of the minds of writers was unconsidered. We had to make do, the youngest of us, as well as we could, and in spite of some very haughty Aristotelians, with the light of nature.

Meanwhile all these writers were at work producing in excellent faith books which were felt to be more or less good, or more or less interesting. Not equally good, not equally interesting, but all possessed of some quality which justified their contemporary existence. Occasionally it was a social quality in the authors, more often it was an air of originality or profundity or just plain enjoyableness in the work. Some writers were fashionable, some were unfashionable; some had the suffrages of ordinary people (but most people were at that time ordinary), one or two made an impression upon those who pride themselves upon their exclusive taste. Is not that the history of books and their appraisement in all ages? There were 'the few' and 'the many' then, as now; and only the extremely democratic tone of the leading writers of 1910, who were democratic in manners and sympathies as well as in scholastic theory, kept literary snobbery at bay. The fight was then against professors who felt that 'literature' had mysteriously ceased in 1850; it was waged by those who desired greater liberty for everybody.

Perhaps, most of all, they desired liberty for themselves, but what they wanted was freedom from library censorship and freedom from dramatic censorship. More than anything else, they wanted a distinction made between the possible unpleasantness of work that shocked because it was too literal and the approved pruriency of work that was shocking by innuendo. And they wanted the novel and the play to be taken seriously. They were not, they said, telling tales to keep old men from the chimney-corner, but were all for the making of a better world by means of free criticism and prophetic vision. Finally, they insisted that art meant something more than pretty pictures and photography. Because they were entertaining, even when most serious, they captured the public. First of all, they captured the young, and then they captured the old. The stolid they never captured, because the stolid are always found in the last ditch, reading old numbers of *Punch* and playing follow my leader.

The young were all for seriousness. They were also all for iconoclasm. But the young have an endless capacity for reverence and a bottomless self-doubting, the first being the outcome of the second. And high above all fights, marked by everything that makes an author respectable in English life, sat one man. His years were many; his work was considered too rare for ordinary readers; his disinterested devotion to art had been lifelong. To read his books appreciatively was to prove oneself both intelligent and of fine taste; and to share his aesthetic ideals was to feel that one moved upon the same plane as a master-craftsman who was also a master-critic of the art he practised. Although crabbed professors who 'taught' literature might fidget at an approach to their subject wholly different from their own, even they at last were forced to acknowledge that if literature was in truth an art the secrets of it were best revealed by an artist obviously too good for the multitude. For these reasons, and for the reason that he had a very distinguished irony and great dignity, the writer I have described rose slowly to extraordinary eminence. He could not be the Grand Old Man (the post was held by Thomas Hardy); but he could be, and was, appointed Grand Literary Panjandrum of the Time. His position was lofty; it had been unsought; and it was deprecatingly relished by its holder. In the early years of King George V no critical voice had as subtle a power as that of Henry James.

CHAPTER TWO: ARTFUL VIRTUOSITY

'He makes it, somehow, such a grand, possible affair.'
'Ah, well, if he makes it possible!'
'I mean especially he makes it grand.'

The Wings of the Dove.

I

HENRY JAMES was not born a Panjandrum. He became one as the result of longevity, taste, and sustained technical virtuosity, but especially of longevity. He hardly knew himself to be a Panjandrum, for he was very modest, rather a snob, and quite unreadable by many of his fellow-creatures. He was born at Albany, New York, on 15th April 1843. His grandfather, an Irishman whose great commercial success in that city is still commemorated in the name of a street, left considerable estate to be divided among numerous heirs; his father—Henry James senior—was an unworldly mystical theologian whose devotion to Swedenborg was such that he always travelled with his own set of the Master's works. Henry was the second son, a year younger than William, the philosopher, and the second of five children.

To dismiss the father of Henry James, as I have seemed to do above, as 'an unworldly mystical theologian' would be very unjust to a man of abnormal mental ingenuity. The published portraits of him do not perhaps prepare us for the revelations of his son by which he becomes one of the most amusingly lovable characters outside fiction; but they do show the calm height of his noble head, the protrusive habit of his eyes (which seem not unlike those of his second son), and an unmistakable disinterested benevolence which shines from the whole countenance; and all these points mark him as an exceptional creature. He was a philosopher who was also a Christian; apparently, too, he was not only witty in himself, but the cause that wit was a natural activity in his family. The atmosphere of the James household was shot through and through, that is, with a gaiety and kindness allowing unlimited humorous reference to the father's 'ideas' (it was supposed to be Mrs James's word); while based, nevertheless, upon respectful affection. With what relish does his son, after referring to the senior Henry James's attachment to Swedenborg, add concerning this philosopher that 'in reply to somebody's plea of not finding him credible our parent had pronounced him, on the contrary, fairly "insipid with veracity"!'

The little boy was much appreciated by his father, who took him freely upon various journeys, even, on one occasion, to the daguerreotyper's, where the two Henrys were photographed side by side, the boy with his hand upon his father's shoulder, charming, modest, and wondering, the man kind, bland, and confidently at peace with his faith. But the education of the James children, if free, according to Henry James senior's wish, was also, in formal particulars, irregular. As Henry describes his own share of it, in that great autobiography, *A Small Boy and Others*, it was so haphazard, so much an experimental setting of the boy to tasks which proved uncongenial, and taking him away from them, so much a confusion of New York city and country life with impulsive travels in Europe, that the reader wonders how in the world such a bewildered child learned anything at all. And yet might not such an education have offered a perfect development to a master-novelist? 'Simply everything,' says Henry James, 'simply everything that should happen to us, every contact, every impression and experience we should know, were to form our soluble stuff; with only ourselves to thank should we remain unaware, by the time our perceptions were decently developed, of the substance finally projected and most desirable.'

No priggishness was allowed, for 'we were bred in horror of conscious propriety, of what my father was fond of calling "flagrant" morality' and 'our father . . . only cared for virtue that was more or less ashamed of itself'; but as time went on Henry James reached a kind of philosophical justification of a trait which coloured the whole of his life and work. 'One way,' he says, 'of taking life was to go in for everything and every one, which kept you abundantly occupied, and the other way was to be as occupied, quite as occupied, just with the sense and image of it all, *and on only a fifth of the actual immersion.*' In thinking of Henry James, do not forget that the second way was his own.

From Albany to the city of New York, where the Jameses lived down town, and where William and Henry haunted such theatres as there were and endlessly attended the church services of every denomination; and from New York back to Albany, where innumerable cousins, male and female, came to stay and

play; and from Albany to London and Paris, these children
passed in a rich process of picking up impressions. Here and
there they acquired some book knowledge, William, the elder,
ever a leader in that department, while Henry, given to what
he frankly calls 'pedestrian gaping,' and less pragmatically absorbed in rationalizing the universe, made do with his sensations
and intuitions. 'I had but one success, always—that of endlessly
supposing, wondering, admiring; I was sunk in that luxury.'

II

In the evenings, while William made drawings—he was in the
early stages of his artistic period—Henry also imitatively drew;
but he did something else as well, which threw a long finger out
towards the practice of the future craftsman. 'I sacrificed,' he
says, 'to the dramatic form with devotion—by the aid of certain
quarto sheets of ruled paper bought in Sixth Avenue for the
purpose; . . . grateful in particular for the happy provision by
which each fourth page of the folded sheet was left blank. When
the drama itself had covered three pages the last one, over which
I most laboured, served for the illustration of what I had verbally
presented. Every scene had thus its explanatory picture, and
. . . I thought, I lisped, at any rate I composed, in scenes. . . .
Entrances, exits, the indication of "business," the animation of
dialogue, the multiplication of designated characters, were things
delightful in themselves—while I panted toward the canvas on
which I should fling my figures.'

And so the Jameses went to Europe; and for Henry the plunge
into astonishing older lands was like a plunge into a dream. In
later years he went through his period of impatience with the
English, only, in the end, to take them permanently to his heart;
but now he was the instinctive artist, the 'votary and victim of
the single impression and the imperceptible adventure, picked
up by accident and cherished, as it were, in secret.' He could
only absorb and absorb, dreaming, listening, storing. 'I recall
in particular certain short sweet times when I could be left alone
—with the thick and heavy suggestions of the London room
about me, the very smell of which was ancient, strange, and impressive, a new revelation altogether, and the window open to
the English June and the far-off hum of a thousand possibilities.
I consciously took them in, these last, and must then, I think,
have first tasted the very greatest pleasure perhaps I was ever
to know—that of almost holding my breath in presence of certain

aspects to the end of so taking in. It was as if in those hours that precious fine art had been disclosed to me.'

That precious fine art was to be still further practised a little later, when the party travelled to Paris and this inveterate gazer and wonderer learned more consciously the lesson of art which was to dominate his creative life. Here, 'with plot thickening and emotion deepening steadily, . . . we mounted the long, black Rue de Seine—*such* a stretch of perspective, *such* an intensity of tone as it offered in those days; where every low-browed vitrine waylaid us and we moved in a world of which the dark message, expressed in we couldn't have said what sinister way too, might have been "Art, art, art, don't you see? Learn, little gaping pilgrims, what that is!" Oh, we learned, that is we tried to, as hard as ever we could, and were fairly well at it, I always felt, even by the time we had passed up into the comparatively short but wider and finer vista of the Rue de Tournon, which in those days more abruptly crowned the more compressed approach and served in a manner as a great outer vestibule to the Palace. Style, dimly descried, looked down there, as with conscious encouragement, from the high, grey-headed, clear-faced, straight-standing old houses—very much as if wishing to say "Yes, small staring *jeune homme*, we are dignity and memory and measure, we are conscience and proportion and taste, not to mention strong sense too: for all of which good things take us—you won't find one of them when you find (as you 're going soon to begin to at such a rate) vulgarity.'

After such saturation and injunction, and some less ecstatic experiences in Switzerland and Germany, William James decided to be an artist, and studied with William Hunt, in whose studio John La Farge was the only other pupil, although Henry James was also thoughtfully to be found there. And when William James declared suddenly for Physical Science, and went to Harvard University to study it, Henry had already reached a sense of his artistic destiny. Law, which was put to him as a possibility, and which he read for a year, had no lure. 'I didn't want anything so much as I wanted a certain good (or wanted thus supremely *to* want it, if I may say so). . . . What I "wanted to want" to be was, all intimately, just *literary*.'

III

He became 'literary,' at first not venturing very far or high (his first work seems to have been a translation from Mérimée, and he never attempted poetry), but modestly, as at all times, underestimating the originality of his own mind. The James family moved to Cambridge; acquaintance followed with Charles Eliot Norton, at that time editing *The North American Review*; and Norton accepted Henry James's first timidly submitted manuscript. E. L. Godkin, also, whose control of the newly established New York *Nation* was a matter of international fame, encouraged the young writer by printing his criticisms. Finally he had the fortune to make a lifelong friend of William Dean Howells, who read his earliest fiction with enthusiasm and bought some of it for *The Atlantic Monthly*.

He was launched; and he hastened to London, 'drawn by the sense of all the interest and association I should find.' This was in 1869, when he was twenty-six. He settled at first in Half Moon Street, off Piccadilly, in a couple of dusky ground-floor rooms the walls of which were hung with glazed coloured plates from the Christmas numbers of *The Illustrated London News*; and he began in earnest to explore the town. For choice, his company was imaginary. He was 'more and more aware of the "fun" (to express it grossly) of living by my imagination and thereby finding that company, in countless different forms, could only swarm about me.'

Thus the dreaming, gazing little boy had become a dreaming, gazing young man who preferred the delights of his own mental labyrinth to those of general society. He was in the old world, upon 'haunted, holy ground,' remote, a spectator. He was happy. Thenceforward his way of life was settled; and he was to know little change in it for over forty years.

He was 'just literary.' During a long stay in Paris he made the acquaintance of Ivan Turgenev, who was the grand third of his literary influences (the earlier influences had been Hawthorne and Balzac); and from Turgenev he learned in long conversations how Turgenev wrote novels, and how novels should be written. Crucial conversations. And when he published *Daisy Miller*, which still ranks very high among short stories written in English, he achieved a distinguished reputation with the critical public. It was his most interesting and original tale in this period, the scenes laid in Switzerland and Italy, with which countries he was familiar, and the American type new, baffling, and presented with suggestive detachment.

Daisy Miller was first published in 1879, when Henry James was thirty-six. Fron 1874-5, in which years he wrote *Roderick Hudson*, he was continuously productive. Book followed book

with great rapidity, sometimes a novel, sometimes a volume of
short stories, sometimes in a single year as many as three books
of one sort and another. He was a critic, too; and it is a remarkable fact that when he was not travelling or writing novels
he was in a style of the utmost grace describing the places he had
visited, or analysing with much fastidious insight the qualities of
some classic novelist, such as Balzac, or George Sand, or Flaubert, or Turgenev. What a happy manner of life for one who
aspired above everything else to be 'just literary'!

In those days he was less impressive in appearance than he
was to be in old age. He mixed, it is clear, with the select few
whose main interests were in art and letters; but as a quiet,
bearded man, his head ever slightly cocked, as if he were listening
and reflecting, who came and went with an air of shyness and
elaborate self-deprecating solemnity, and not at all as the
literary 'lion' he was afterwards to be. He was even considered
a trifle portentous, and the memories of him which appear in
such typical books as the autobiographies of Evelyn Sharp and
Arthur Waugh are unflattering. Evelyn Sharp recalls a time in
her friendship with Henry Harland when James came to tea,
'and Harland, for once losing his sense of humour in the presence
of one whom he always referred to as "mon maître," took me
aside to say in an impressive whisper, "He says he has *heard* of
your fairy tales!" This was the occasion on which we sat in
dumb humility while the famous American walked up and down
the room seeking the word he wanted for the completion of his
sentence. I am sure we all knew the word, but the sacrilege
that would be implied in our intrusion upon his mental travail
by mentioning it was undreamed of. It was, of course, an immense honour to have been invited to worship at the shrine; but
the atmosphere cleared pleasantly when he left.'

Once, late in life, our author returned to the United States for
the sake of writing an immense impression of the land he had
deserted. But for the most part he was in London or the
English country, in an apartment in town or staying at the
Reform Club, or living in the beautiful old house which he had
discovered in a corner of Rye. Here, in that charming little
hillside town in Sussex from which the English Channel has
drawn back a couple of miles in the last two or three centuries,
he lived from 1897 to the end. He aged, he corresponded volu-
minously, he gradually received all those signs of respect which
in England are accorded to literary survivals of the approved
social variety, and his art grew ever more elaborate, more

scrupulous and wordy, and for those who relish its quality, more wonderfully engrossing. He became a naturalized Englishman early in the European War, and died on 28th February 1916.

IV

It was once irreverently remarked, by a non-Jacobean too ready with historical analogy, that there were three Henry Jameses—James the First, James the Second, and the Old Pretender. That last, with its implications, was never true; but the suggestion held just enough malice to make it effective. Like other writers, Henry James had his three periods, in the first of which irony did no more than temper ingenuousness, in the second of which the emotional problems of travelling Americans were replaced by the doings of imaginary famous authors and other odd characters, and in the third of which every wizened theme was so dwelt upon, and turned, and manipulated, as to yield its last and finest shade of ironic meaning. The progress between these periods was natural, and in each of them the author was keeping pace with his own development. He was writing from young manhood until the age of seventy-two. During the whole, roughly, of that half-century he believed strongly that it was the finest thing in the world to be an artist and to write novels which were works of art.

I have used the term 'works of art,' and I want now to remind the reader that when Henry James thought of art he thought in terms of pictures, and not in terms of modern aesthetics. He was very much the professional artist, the man who assesses the value of a work of art according to the degree in which it may be said to be 'done.' When he spoke critically of novels he always used words such as one might hear in a studio when two painters were speaking intimately of a picture. But while, with a little study, he probably could have understood the phrases adopted by living aesthetes from physics and psycho-analysis, he would not have felt it necessary to use them. A book had 'composition,' 'tone,' 'values,' 'colour,' and 'form.' It might have had such qualities as 'foreground' and 'middle distance.' But it never had a moral; and it never took heed of such things as 'rhythm' or 'planes' or the 'sub-' or 'super-conscious.'

He began by writing critical reviews, and his first fiction consisted, as Hawthorne's did, of short stories. The earliest novel of which he thought well enough to include it in his collected works was *Roderick Hudson*. This is a book about a detached young American who conceived an admiration for the work of a young sculptor and offered him the chance of studying the antique in Rome. The sculptor, Roderick Hudson, jumped at his chance; but although he was engaged to a good girl in New England he fell in love in Italy with a wayward and enigmatic young woman of a kind always more fascinating to a novelist than to his readers. The young woman having been disposed of matrimonially—under the threat that if she did not marry the Prince Casamassima her mother and father would inexplicably disclose the fact of her illegitimacy — Roderick forsook his friends, lost his talent, and at last was killed in a mountain storm. The detached young American was in love with his protégé's sweetheart; but this young lady preferred to cherish her memory of authentic emotion, and the end of the book lies in shadow.

The American, which followed, carries us a stage farther in the history of our author's development. It is the story of a man who had made a sufficient fortune in his own country, and who coolly determined to marry a beautiful French widow. The widow's relatives, including an all-powerful mother from the English aristocracy, at first permitted the suit; but presently they decided against the American, sent his young fiancée to a convent, and defied him when he threatened disclosure of a frightful family secret. He burnt the evidence of this crime, from pride, and all was as before.

The third novel is about a lovely young American girl who was enriched by her uncle's will. She was so simple-minded as to be led into marriage with a dilettante egoist, whom she ultimately left after discovering that the marriage had been 'arranged' by her husband's former mistress, the mother of his daughter. There are two sick men who die in this book, both of them American, whimsical, wise, and kind; and there is a quiet, persistent, but unfailingly considerate American lover who turns up again at the end. The book is called *The Portrait of a Lady*, and it is the first in which one of those beautiful, tranquil old English houses in the country the imagination of which James so adored makes its appearance.

The fourth novel was *The Princess Casamassima*, one of the worst books by a good writer that I have ever read. It is about a youth of the lower orders (his mother had murdered a man, and he had been brought up by a sempstress and an old fiddler, both Thackerayan figures), who joined a revolutionary

organization, was given some unspecified piece of assassination to
do, and committed suicide. He was by trade a bookbinder,
infatuated with the notion that he was of noble birth; and the
Princess Casamassima, who first appeared as a *femme fatale* in
Roderick Hudson, still works her wicked will upon the young and
impressionable, without so much as stirring a hair of the reader's
head.

These four books may be said to represent James's first period
as a novelist. They were essays in what Hawthorne called
'psychological romance.' They have in common the distinction
of a very simple style of great dignity. They are about small
groups of characters who are saved from insipidity by unusual
conversational gifts and by a pervasive air of secret drama. In
the case of the first three, the chief male character is a cool
spectator of the events dramatized, not unmoved by these events,
but powerless to stay them, hardly at all, effectively, a participant in the action. This was a device, but a significant device.
The author deliberately chose to employ a single male character
as chorus, in order to exercise his own peculiar combination of
intimacy and detachment. He could thus be in the book and
out of it, without in the least sacrificing his own independence.
Later on, the bachelor chorus was to be discontinued; but a
chorus, in the shape of a single abnormally sensitive person or a
number of gossips who could speculate and scrutinize and comment at large, there was to be to the end.

I will not follow the ungracious and usually inaccurate habit of
some critics, who speak of characters being lifted bodily from
other books; but I cannot help believing that in these early
novels of Henry James, exquisite to me as they are, the people
derive (no more) from certain types in books by Hawthorne and
Turgenev and Balzac. That, in fact, they are as much 'just
literary' as their author. The Bellegardes, in *The American*,
for example, are Balzac; but the travelling Americans, and in
particular the constant Mary Garland, in *Roderick Hudson*,
might well have entered James's pages from corners of *The
House of the Seven Gables*, or from one of the exquisite tales of
Turgenev with which the author must by now have been very
familiar. They are not copies; the author's explanations of
them have profundity; but the characters themselves are
ethereal. Perhaps the books altogether were nothing but Henry
James's lovely prolonged play; perhaps each of them was something of which he was the godlike creator and the happy,
interested, tremendously aware and relishing spectator. 'It is

not my impulse,' said a character in *The House of the Seven Gables*, 'either to help or to hinder; but to look on, to analyse, to explain matters to myself, and to comprehend the drama.' And James: 'My identity for myself was *all* in my sensibility to their own exhibition, with not a scrap left over for a personal show.'

v

In the composition of these books, as in the composition of many of Henry James's books, one notices a very odd circumstance. It is that the concrete is often a matter of great difficulty. I do not mean the sort of detail about which novel-readers write triumphantly to the newspapers, such as the right railway station for Paris, the right omnibus number for Richmond, and so on; for such matters interested Henry James not at all. 'The station,' 'the onmibus,' and 'the train' would ever be sufficient for him. I mean points of greater moment. In the author's mind there was to be 'a something' that forced Roderick Hudson's wayward young woman to marry when so clearly she did not want to. There was to be 'a something' in the history of the Bellegarde family which should enable Newman unavailingly to frighten them. There was to be some sort of secret society, and some sort of disagreeable job for the hero to fail to perform, in *The Princess Casamassima*; just as the mystifying divorces in *What Maisie Knew* had to be conducted 'somewhere' and 'somewhen' outside the book's obvious theme, and (most amusing of all) some odd and unmentionable small article of commerce upon which the family fortune had been built had to figure in *The Ambassadors*. Just what these things were, James's speculative intelligence, his endless habit of wondering and supposing, did not tell him. In his early books he tried to invent practicable 'somethings'; and so we have in *Roderick Hudson* an illegitimacy, in *The American* a scrawled message from a dying man to the effect that his wife is killing him, and in *The Princess Casamassima* a desperate effort to give conspiracy a kind of tangible convincingness. But as time went on James either pooh-poohed the matter altogether, as he managed to do (with the aid of what Maisie could not possibly be expected to know) in *What Maisie Knew*, or carried off his ignorance with a high hand, as in *The Ambassadors* where there is an almost feverish questioning from which, although severely

pressed, the possessor of the knowledge escapes with a promise
—never kept—that he will reveal the nature of the article at a
later date.

'Is there a business?'
'Lord, yes—a big, brave bouncing business.   A roaring trade.'
'A great shop?'
'Yes—a workshop; a great production, a great industry.   The
concern's a manufacture—and a manufacture that, if it's only
properly looked after, may well be on the way to become a monopoly.
It's a little thing they make—make better, it appears, than other
people can, or than other people, at any rate, do.' . . .
'And what *is* the article produced?'
Strether looked about him as in slight reluctance to say; then
the curtain, which he saw about to rise [the two are in a theatre]
came to his aid.   'I'll tell you next time.'   But when the next
time came he only said he would tell her later on . . . 'Unmentionable?   Oh no, we constantly talk of it; we are quite familiar and
brazen about it.   Only, as a small, trivial, rather ridiculous object
of the commonest domestic use, it's rather wanting in—what shall
I say?   Well, dignity . . .'

And so on.   Like his father, Henry James enjoyed 'the strongest instinct for the human and the liveliest reaction from the
literal.'   But James's great exemplar, Balzac, would have re-
minded our friend that such reaction from the literal may result
in the vagueness of the bluffer.   Balzac certainly would have
explained the nature and use of the article; he would probably
have gone farther and described its manufacture and its sales
organization, and if he had done that he might well have supplied
us in good faith with details of the firm's costs, earnings, and
profits over a period of years.

The truth was that James did not know what sort of thing
would force a spirited young woman into marriage with a man
she despised, or what sort of secret might or might not frighten
an old French family into permitting the marriage of their
daughter and sister to an outsider, or how divorces were managed, or what kind of small article—or indeed what kind of
large article, other than a literary article—might be manufactured with immense profit in the United States.   These
things did not interest him otherwise than as pretexts for psychological conflict or a gathering of people upon the stage of his
imagination.   He pretended not to care about inconvenient details; but in reality he could not be bothered to take any steps to
find out what he should have known, because in all things he
preferred to puzzle out explanations, rather than to step outside
his study and into the world of practical affairs.   'Something

. . . the money comes from . . . somewhere . . .' His experience of life was extraordinarily restricted.

As long as he could bring transatlantic types to Europe and show them the extreme gentility of the old world, full of princesses and other titled people, and lovely old English houses and good breeding, he had a distinct place among American writers. But when he grew tired of such things, and became absorbed in the purely literary life, he tended to write about writers and the occult—two difficult and unpopular subjects. Some of his shorter stories in this vein, it is true, are among his most famous, and one or two of them are very good indeed. But they are stories for a small public; and while the small public invariably thinks itself a choice public most authors, however select, hanker after general applause. James was really, I think, at the end of his resources as a writer of long, straightforward stories of character when he published, without success, in 1890, at the age of forty-seven, *The Tragic Muse*. No wonder that he was at this period in something like despair. No wonder he wrote to W. D. Howells—as late as 1895—that 'I *have* felt, for a long time past, that I have fallen upon evil days—every sign and symbol of one's being in the least *wanted*, anywhere or by any one, having so utterly failed. A new generation, that I know not, and mainly prize not, has taken universal possession. The sense of being utterly out of it weighed me down, and I asked myself what the future would be.'

The future was to be brighter, for James must in those years have been feeling his way towards what proved to be his natural and ultimate vein. Within two years of writing that despondent letter to Howells he had published both *What Maisie Knew* and *The Spoils of Poynton*. He had found—or had perfected—a new, highly characteristic manner. And the manner provoked comment. Was it, or was it not, due to his venture into the habit of dictation? He said that dictation had no effect at all upon his style; others said that it was responsible, at the very least, for increased verbal artifice. However that may be, the rise of Henry James to a peculiar and personal rank among novelists— that subtle ascendancy to which many distinguished writers never attain—began in 1897. His remoteness from common life ceased to hamper him: it became, instead, one of the literary miracles of the age. *The Spoils of Poynton* is still a contribution to the technique of prose fiction which can be studied with advantage. Until we reach *The Ambassadors*, that fine flower of the Jacobean novel, it is his best work in the long story.

The Ambassadors was written before *The Wings of the Dove*, although it was published later. It is superior both to *The Wings of the Dove* and to *The Golden Bowl*. The former book is very long, and the author considered it a failure. 'The thing in question,' he said in a letter, 'is, by a complicated accident which it would take too long to describe to you, too inordinately drawn out, and too inordinately rubbed in. The centre, more-over, isn't in the middle, or the middle, rather, isn't in the centre, but ever so much too near the end, so that what was to come after it is truncated. The book, in fine, has too big a head for its body.'

More than that, it has a body too big for its substance. A journalist—still a writer, you see!—is in love with a young woman largely dependent upon a wealthy aunt. He is too poor to marry, and the two meet in Hyde Park on the sly. A dove who is something of a pigeon, and fabulously rich, comes from America to England, and falls in love with the journalist. He is induced to pay some court to her, and his sweetheart goes so far as to assure the dove that there is no understanding between them. However, when the dove dies of a mysterious and al-most operatic complaint (a sort of world weariness), and leaves the journalist a legacy, he and the young woman whom he loves fail to approximate their scruples over the result of what has been in fact a sordid deception, and the novel sinks. No amount of casuistry upon the author's part can purify the atmosphere of this degraded book, which is without spirit and point.

In the same way, if the story of *The Golden Bowl* were told of ordinary bourgeois people it would be seen to rely upon the practicable plot that an Italian sponger has married money, that his discarded mistress reappears and re-establishes her attractive-ness to him, and that his wife, scenting the difficulty, manages to bring the husband back to her side. The symbolism of the golden bowl is adventitious; the manipulation by which the mis-tress of the young husband becomes her lover's mother-in-law is quite artificial. But whereas *The Wings of the Dove* has, as I see it, no redeeming feature, *The Golden Bowl* has great beauty in many of its aspects, and in particular in the relationship between father and daughter. No other novelist could so delicately and so entirely without mishap have created the illusion of a relation-ship unselfishly loving and protective such as Maggie and her father feel for each other. In some respects this relationship is the most beautiful thing in any of Henry James's books, illus-trating, as it does, to perfection, his enchanting sympathy with the disinterested. As a piece of composition the book is marvellous; and as a presentation of idealized love it has nobility and exquisiteness. What a pity, therefore, that the tale upon which it is built should have been—and should have been allowed to remain—commonplace!

The Spoils of Poynton is similarly mean at its heart. It arose from a dinner-table anecdote; and is about the squabble between mother and son as to a houseful of art treasures collected by the mother and her husband before the latter's death. The son has become engaged to an obstinate and tasteless creature to whom his mother takes an instant dislike. Although she realizes that her son is legally the possessor of the treasures, the mother surreptitiously removes the bulk of them to her cottage. The struggle between mother and (by representatives) her prospective daughter-in-law is ferocious and prolonged; but in the end the daughter-in-law wins the battle, the treasures are restored, and the house which they thus readorn is immediately afterwards destroyed by fire.

The virtuosity of *The Spoils of Poynton* is extraordinary. The book is maintained by the smallest, most voluptuous hints of what the actual treasures are, and there are but five characters in it. But while these characters, presented with great brilliance, contribute with precision and in due proportion to the drama, coherence as well as richness is assured by a familiar Jacobean device. This device is the one by which a single character presents an abnormally sensitive mind, at times baffled (but that is for the further artful purpose of elucidation through clarifying analysis) and at times miraculously lucid, to the whole intrigue; and in *The Spoils of Poynton* the mind is the mind of a girl tempted into greater concern with the matter by the prospect that she may herself hereafter possess the treasure by a reversionary marriage with the combative son.

Henry James, jubilant at his discovery of this theme, replies to possible criticism of his use of such a heroine as his prime co-ordinator. He says: 'It is easy to object of course "Why the deuce then Fleda Vetch, why a mere little flurried bundle of petticoats, why not Hamlet or Milton's Satan at once, if you 're going in for a superior display of 'mind'?" To which I fear I can only reply that in pedestrian prose, and in the "short story," one is, for the best reasons, no less on one's guard than on the stretch; and also that I have ever recognized, even in the midst of the curiosity that such displays may quicken, the rule of an exquisite economy. The thing is to lodge somewhere at the heart of one's complexity an irrepressible *appreciation*, but where a light lamp will carry all the flame I incline to look askance at a heavy.'

The light lamp; the comic muse; James had no sort of gift for tragedy. He was an ironist, some will think from natural coldness of temper, but perhaps from a too-sensitive dread of personal suffering. If you live apart from life, as he did, you cultivate a delicious acuteness of mind; but you lose actuality. *The Spoils of Poynton* is rich comedy; but it is only tolerable so long as one regards it as artificial, as a marvellous *performance*. The assumptions upon which the performance is based are appallingly gross.

The Ambassadors is an entirely different case. A young American, son of a manufacturer of the unspecified article— 'Unmentionable? Oh, no, we constantly talk of it; we are quite familar and brazen about it'—has been too long in Paris. His masterful mother has sent her tame editor, who may in time be her second husband, to bring the boy home. The editor, in company with a rather morose friend, makes the trip. He convinces himself that the boy is living an entirely moral and admirable life in innocent relation with a French married woman. He lingers on in Paris. In this act he renews his youth, and is made to see the boy as fruitfully enjoying what he regards as his own lost opportunity. But the morose friend sends home messages less pacificatory than his own; a further detachment of the family arrives in Paris; there are many complications; the boy's relationship with the Frenchwoman is revealed as less innocent than it has seemed. And our poor editorial traveller and ambassador is faced with the knowledge that his return to America and to his employer is both unavoidable and undesirable. He ruefully makes preparations to depart.

That very crude and over-simplified outline does shameful injustice to a novel which I consider as of almost the first order in comic literature. It is consistently comic, and upon a high plane; rich in scene and dialogue, in atmosphere, detail, and implication. Technically it is the work of a master in his own craft; and unless one is very prejudiced against the arch and elaborate manner of Henry James, with its rather puffing alternative sentences and its persistent avoidance of the direct, I do not see how one can fail to admire it. It is the most excellent complete example of the Jacobean method as outlined in the abstract of his unfinished novel, *The Ivory Tower*, where he says, in reference, of course, to *The Ivory Tower*, and not to *The Ambassadors*: 'By the blest operation this time of my Dramatic Principle, my law of successive Aspects, each treated from its own centre, . . . I have the great help of flexibility and variety; my persons in turn, or at least the three or four foremost, having control, as it were, of the Act and Aspect, and so making it *his* or making it *hers*.'

If a novelist could be great by virtue of his devotion to his art, Henry James would be a great novelist. He gave to the writing of novels a fastidiousness and a conviction of the importance of his task which was new and strange in English fiction although it was not new in France or to Turgenev. Whatever the great English novelists may have been, they had no conception of the novel as something to be executed within a frame, to be 'composed' in the painter's sense, with what Henry James called 'shades' and 'the lovely art of foreshortening,' and that impressionistic vagueness in the distance about which I have already written. James had this conception.

He had another excellence, which is explicitly stated in a letter which he wrote in 1884 to Alphonse Daudet. He there said: 'J'estime pourtant qu'il n'y a rien de plus réel, de plus positif, de plus à peindre, qu'un caractère; c'est là qu'on trouve bien la couleur et la forme.'

From character, in this specialist sense, which he regarded as the essential basis of the novel, and form, of which he was to become a master, the Jacobean novel springs. 'Form alone takes, and holds and preserves, substance—saves it from the welter of helpless verbiage that we swim in as in a sea of tasteless tepid pudding. Tolstoy and Dostoevsky are fluid puddings, though not tasteless, because the amount of their own minds and souls in solution in the broth gives its savour and flavour, thanks to the strong, rank quality of their genius and their experience.' And, finally, in revolt from Wellsian improvisation: 'Any illustration of anything worth illustrating has beauty, to my vision, largely by its developments.' 'There is to my vision, no authentic, and no really interesting and no *beautiful*, report of things on the novelist's, the painter's, part unless a particular detachment has operated, unless the great stewpot or crucible of the imagination, of the observant and recording and interpreting mind in short, has intervened and played its part—and this detachment, this chemical transmutation for the aesthetic, the representational, end is terribly wanting in autobiography brought, as the horrible phrase is, up to date.'

In these four quotations may be found the artistic theory of Henry James so far as the novel is concerned. Character, development, form, and experience. His form was increasingly

expert and satisfying; the development (he once deprecatingly
referred to his own practice as 'embroidery,' and in his case
'delightful dissimulation' was unquestionably among 'the refinements and ecstasies of method') became virtuosity of an
extreme kind.   But he was inferior at the very core of the
novelist's art.   His characters, although material for endless
and most exquisite speculation, and although he liked to imagine
them as aristocrats of the spirit (as well as, sometimes, aristocrats by birth), were cheats, liars, adulterers, and simpletons
without grandeur.   One's final impression of them is that of
commonness.   The explanation of this, in my judgment, is that
James was prevented by timidity from ever having more than
a superficial acquaintance with men and women who were not
writers.   He had no practical experience of the world; for where-
ever he went upon its surface he was alone, and his thoughts were
of art and artists, craft and craftsmanship.   He could, and did,
watch strangers; he had a delightful life of speculation as to the
ways and thoughts of all except the poor and unrefined; but
unless you are ready to suffer by and through experience you do,
it seems to me, content yourself with the second-hand.   James
did not want to suffer.

Why, then, has he been so powerful an influence upon the
Georgian writers?   I think because no writer who lives in
England to a great age (no writer, at least, who is willing to
cultivate the literary *ton* of his period) can fail to gather the
prestige of continued practice in his craft.   I think because
James could never have been accused by any other writer of
being false to his own artistic standards.   But beyond and above
these reasons I think he had his influence because nobody had
ever done so well, and with such grace and elaborateness, such
skill and such subtlety, the thing that he did.   He took a little
story and a small group of characters; he made a picture; he
made a drama; he made a continuously developing narrative.
The picture was for beauty's sake; the drama was for suspense;
and the narrative was for all the artfulness and interest and delight he took in the practice of his craft.   If only the people in
these books had been interesting James would have been a great
novelist; but as it is he is in every other respect the finest craftsman among Victorian novelists; and the man nowadays who
could write novels as well as Henry James, after learning a little
more than he did about what really goes on in the world, would
stand a good chance of being canonized (in a literary sense)
about the year 2000.

CHAPTER III: TEACHERS

All that we have lived on up till now has been the remnants of the revolutionary dishes of the last century, and we have been long enough chewing these over and over again. Our ideas demand a new substance and a new interpretation. Liberty, equality, and fraternity are no longer the same things that they were in the days of the blessed guillotine; but it is just this that the politicians will not understand, and that is why I hate them. These people only desire partial revolutions, revolutions in externals, in politics. But these are mere trifles. There is only one thing that avails—to revolutionize people's minds.

HENRIK IBSEN.

I

WHEN, in 1895, Henry James complained to William Dean Howells that 'a new generation, that I know not, and mainly prize not, has taken universal possession,' he was saying what every writer who sees himself neglected by the fashion feels impelled to say. He was in the midst of literary movements with which he had, and could have, no sympathy. There were the romantics, such as Gilbert Parker, Stanley Weyman, and Anthony Hope, who were all for post-Stevensonian charades. There were the so-called Kailyarders, such as J. M. Barrie, Ian Maclaren, and S. R. Crockett, who were being arch about the Scottish scene and the Scottish character. There was Rudyard Kipling, of whom James despaired as he came 'steadily from the less simple in subject to the more simple—from the Anglo-Indians to the natives, from the natives to the Tommies, from the Tommies to the quadrupeds, from the quadrupeds to the fish, and from the fish to the engines and screws.' There was the Dead Sea Fruit school, sentimental and cynical, with which the nineties are now usually associated. And finally, there was the New Drama.

The New Drama was as far as possible from Henry James's comfortable reticence. It was imported from Northern Europe, and was unpopular, but it aroused great controversy. Although in Victorian days English novelists and preachers had criticized the social system, they had never mentioned the unmentionable. The New Drama not only mentioned it, but insisted upon it. W. S. Gilbert had laughed at corruptions and hypocrisies in a

dozen comic operas; the New Drama seriously arraigned corruption and hypocrisy and called men to judgment. It attacked
the morals of the respectable, and showed those in high places
intriguing for power, sweating the poor, transmitting venereal
disease, hiding sins, and hushing up scandals. It announced that
'all our spiritual sources of life are poisoned, and that our whole
bourgeois society rests upon a soil teeming with the pestilence of
lies.' It went thoroughly into the question of the unmarried
mother, offering her, not as a wanton and a shame, but as a
problem of character and the product of social conditions. The
woman with a past became a stock figure; the woman with a
future not exclusively matrimonial and subservient was pictured
as something other than a freak of nature. When one such
woman was asked, at the end of the first act of a play by Ibsen,
what *she* would do in our society, she brought down the curtain
by answering 'I will let in fresh air.' Her words might have
been taken as a motto by all New Dramatists; for in their plays
all that was generally accepted as good, proper, and desirable
was brought into the light of day and shown to be considerably
affected by moth. How could Henry James, to whose art a
stable world of conventions and prosperity was an essential
background, possibly approve of such boisterousness, such raw-
ness, such ugly blurtings-out of things better hidden, better
murmured? Fresh air was the last thing he wanted.

It is sometimes objected to the plays of Ibsen—and it was
objected to them as long ago as the nineties—that they are
provincial. But as a social critic the provincial writer has always an advantage over the writer reared in a great city. He
has been a member of a society known as a whole; because a small
society has few secrets, cause and effect are more easily to be
observed and confirmed in it; the writer's practical acquaintance
with the social system is a part of his nurture. To the metro-
politan-born person, whose horizons are potentially wider, but
whose conceptions of society, once he steps outside the life of his
immediate circle, are vaguer, the provincial often appears crude.
If his manners are rough, and if his taste in clothes is peculiar,
there is no limit to the amusement which he may give the metropolitan; but it is usually the provincial writer who has something
to say about society, while the metropolitan, who knows very
little about any society but that of his own circle, perforce concerns himself with manners. James was a metropolitan by
choice. When plays of the kind written by Ibsen in his last
period are condemned as provincial it may be replied that they

are criticisms of society, robust with knowledge gained in a provincial upbringing, and deliberately restricted in scene for the sake of dramatic economy.

Ibsen's plays arrived late in England. That they arrived at all is largely due to the enthusiasm of a young Scottish dramatic critic named William Archer and a young Irish dramatic critic named George Bernard Shaw. Archer, who never grew old, but always looked rather parsonically Victorian, long-faced, and with thin, plastered hair, was one of those curiously non-priggish reformers who began to flourish in the eighteen-eighties (Havelock Ellis was another of them), and who did such disinterested work in the cause of what they believed to be the truth. Shaw, newly arrived in London, hailed from Dublin, where poets, dramatists, politicians, and inexhaustible talkers are common phenomena.

II. GEORGE BERNARD SHAW

GLORIA [*Sweeping round at him again.*] What gifts were you born with, pray?
VALENTINE. Lightness of heart.

You Never Can Tell.

Shaw was born on 26th July 1856. He was the youngest of three children, and the only boy. His father was a wholesale corndealer, and his mother was the daughter of a country gentleman named Gurly. Having quite early in life established his independence by a refusal to go to church, young Shaw had some schooling of the ordinary kind then available; and at the age of fifteen became a clerk in the office of a land agent, where he proved himself so clear-headed that he was soon made cashier and accountant. Clear-headedness, Shaw discovered, is rare. But he was so modest that his advancement seemed to him to be due to something else—something later remarked by Cleopatra:

CLEOPATRA. No, no: it is not that I am so clever, but that the others are so stupid.
POTHINUS. [*Musingly.*] Truly, that is the great secret.

It is the way in which genius first explains its own superiority to the rest of mankind.

Within a year, Shaw's mother and sisters left Dublin, the mother to teach music in London and the sisters to make their own careers. Shaw for a time stayed where he was; but when he was twenty he too left Dublin for London. He never recovered from this plunge; for he fell in love with the English (as Henry James did), and has been explaining them to himself ever since.

Shaw first noticed, and was baffled by, the fact that the English have a habit of ignoring everything but what they wish to see. It is the primary act of good breeding in England, and is disconcerting to strangers. Also, at that time, the English had not been shaken by a few events which have occurred since; they were calm, prosperous, perhaps rather complacent. Shaw's admiration was thus of the exasperated kind which shows him to have fallen in love with the people in spite of his better judgment.

His judgment told him that England was in a muddle morally and industrially. It told him that the English were smug, comfort-loving, half-asleep. Their terrible incuriosity affronted him. And yet from that day to this Shaw has given his life to the English, wooing them with all the blandishments of insult (of which he is a master) and the charm of his incessant wit; until the English, at first ignoring him, have been successively amused by a jackanapes, stimulated by a humorous, truth-loving scourge, enthralled by an original dramatist beside whom all other dramatists were tame, annoyed by a schoolmaster who lectured while bombs were being dropped, eager to be friends again, in the English way, as soon as the row subsided; and at last are a little impatiently proud of an octogenarian chatterbox. Shaw's wooing of Britannia was successful years ago; but he was too modest to believe it. While Britannia waited with reserved amorousness for his embrace, Shaw, like John Tanner, kept on talking. He is still talking. He has never known when to kiss.

But in his early days he was serious enough in his wooing. The England to which he came in the eighteen-seventies was an England drowsy with prosperity, yet stirring with anarchy. Its typical citizens believed that the best form of government was one which interfered as little as possible with the world as it then was. *Laissez-faire.* Let well (or ill) alone. The English were Christians or Rationalists and Utilitarians; but in any case they were largely materialists. Even young people of the day were engaged in reading John Stuart Mill, Malthus, Ingersoll, Darwin, Spencer, and Tyndall, all of whom, whether Christians or Agnostics, had conducted animal, vegetable, or mineral research, and all of whom, whatever they might say about the Primal Cause and the Unknowable, had unsettled the religious beliefs of their readers.

Shaw's religious beliefs, long his own, were not unsettled by what he now read.   But when he was barely a man he had one or two shocks of another kind.   First of all, he heard Henry George speak, and was converted to Socialism; and secondly he read the *Kapital* of Karl Marx, and was converted to revolutionism.   He formed a friendship with Sidney Webb, who, although an unimpressive public figure and a poor speaker, possessed an acute and well-stored brain, and was able to see in Shaw an ideal intellectual foil and partner.   He also made the acquaintance of Edward Carpenter and Henry Salt, whose idols were Thoreau and Whitman, and through whose influence he became a Shelleyan, a Vegetarian, and a Humanitarian.   He learned to declaim against hanging, flogging, and anything known as sport.   He began to dress as a Simple-lifer; he went without an overcoat and wore astonishing woollen gloves; he stood at street corners upon soap boxes and harangued loiterers. From the point of view of the average Englishman, Shaw was in a fair way to become a crank.

In 1884 Shaw weighed 142 pounds.   His height, without shoes, was six feet one inch.   He was lean, pale-faced, bearded, rather ginger, with blue-grey eyes and small hands.   Upon a soap box he may well have looked eight feet tall, and of course far above the heads of such men as gathered to listen.   To look down upon an audience is to feel mastery of it: hence the soap box, the platform, and the stage.   Shaw has always been above his audience. He does not know what passes in the minds of individual listeners.   He did not become a crank, because he had great humour and great shrewdness, and he was very ambitious.   But he was confirmed by his soap-box altitude in a truly aristocratic contempt for democracy, 'the last refuge of cheap misgovernment.'   He threw over the respectable bourgeois, agnostic, and materialistic thinkers who in adolescence had impressed him. Altruism, he found, had higher, colder reaches than theirs; and upon the whole he preferred the nobility of Shelley and the passionate economics of Marx to their philosophy of the merely good and useful.   Also, whether by reading Samuel Butler at this time or not I do not know, he found reason to reject, not evolution, but the Darwinian theory that variation of species was due to blind accident.   Lamarck, many years before, had suggested that variation arose from a 'sense of need' or the impulse towards improvement; and this suggestion, so brilliantly reinforced by Butler in *Life and Habit*, has always had for Shaw an irresistible charm.   Blind accident was the horror of his life; a world in which nothing was ever attempted because all was hopelessly evolutionary would have been, for him, intolerable. Since he, Shaw, wanted to make a new earth, that was proof that man had arisen through the desire of lower forms of life to 'better themselves.' He felt that even the amoebae must have had their Shaws, working towards a higher excellence.

Another discovery he made was Woman. To his surprise, the young, consciously intellectual and revolutionary women of that era were greatly drawn—as they would be to-day, or at any time—to a handsome and talkative young Irishman, attractively rufous, and with a baffling habit of turning to nonsense any approach to a Very Serious Subject Indeed. They came closer, fascinated by his eloquence and charm; and Shaw, at first not quite understanding the possessive aim of these ladies (possessiveness being a non-Shavian trait, and thus outside his comprehension), kept on talking and edging away in perfect good humour. At length he was compelled to realize his own attractiveness; and, just as he had explained in Cleopatra's way clear-headed superiority to others, so now, in his modesty, he sought to explain biologically what most men would smirkingly have set down, in Gissing's phrase, to 'sexual prefulgence.' Shaw is a natural ascetic. Not himself, but some strange general necessity, he thought, must cause these women to mistake his laughing eloquence for wooing and come a-wooing in earnest. He began to long for the peace which equality of the sexes would give him; and so threw his weight into the campaign for women's rights and the development of women as rational creatures.

Shaw had started with a combination of Irish clear-headedness and English humour that made him different from all other men. He had inherited a love of music and an exceptionally accurate ear. He had discovered the revolutionary music of Wagner and the revolutionary theory of class war propounded by Marx. He was a Lamarckian or Butlerian evolutionist because any action not dictated by the intelligence was abhorrent to him. When, presently, he discovered the revolutionary drama of Ibsen, so vigorous, so critical, and so moral, he was again deeply impressed; and when at last (although this did not happen until much later) he read *Beyond Good and Evil*, and found in that work the first expression of Nietzsche's doctrine of the Life Force, he felt that he really understood everything that was to be known about the world of men. The Life Force was the phrase he needed to crystallize his belief in purposeful evolution. It was the phrase he needed to explain the behaviour of those women whose intellectualism was but a prelude to wooing. He adopted it.   To the roles of economist, vegetarian, revolutionary, musician, and reluctant lover, he added that of prophet and philosopher.

While first living in shabby gentility in London he had written some novels; but although these novels are highly readable, and full of effective dialogue, they were neither overwhelmingly excellent nor acceptable to the publishers of the time.   Accordingly they made no appearance in book form.   The young Shaw, baffled to fight better, turned from novels to art criticism, music criticism, and finally to dramatic criticism.   This was for the purpose of earning a living.   For diversion and training, as well as for the love of argument, he joined all sorts of debating societies, spoke in public, formed a large circle of acquaintances, and in his own words was 'up to the neck in the life of his time.' He should have said that he was in the life of his time 'from the neck upwards.'

III

Shaw says he has nothing of a voice; but he knows how to produce it.   When he speaks, his Irish accent, and still more his Irish intonation, captivates the English ear.   He seems to sing. Moreover, few men think as clearly and adroitly as he does or can express themselves as clearly and adroitly as he can.   He is a first-class debater.   Whenever I have heard him in debate, he has triumphed because he knew perfectly well what he was saying and doing.   That is a terribly rare accomplishment in a public speaker.

From the time when he first spoke to an audience, Shaw has lived in the eye of the world as few men other than leading actors and politicians do.   He has had little or no private life as the ordinary citizen knows it.   His job has been to reform mankind, and he has been about his task day in, day out, from morning to night, from the day, fifty years ago, when he first heard Henry George speak.

How has he done it?   By means of plays, prefaces, lectures, and pamphlets; by means of earnest sincerity presented with such a flow of nonsensical high spirits that it passed often enough for provocative folly.   New readers, coming in these days to Shaw's writings, cannot possibly understand what was the effect of those writings at the time of their first appearance.   'It is peculiar to original genius,' says Coleridge, 'to become less and less striking, in proportion to its success in improving the taste and judgment of its contemporaries.'   And Shaw's alleged love of paradox, now cheapened in its undergraduate gown of the inverted obvious, was in fact the disconcerting candour of the child in Hans Andersen's story of *The Emperor's New Clothes*. It is no longer novel; some of the arguments which now pass for truisms seemed in those olden days, to the sedately muddle-headed, the sheerest acrobatics; and furthermore Shaw has all his life belittled his own gifts. He has done what Jack Point promised when he told Wilfred Shadbolt that he would 'teach thee all my original songs, my self-constructed riddles, my own ingenious paradoxes; nay more, I will reveal to thee the source whence I get them.' Shaw has told the world that his ideas were derived from Wagner, Ibsen, Samuel Butler, and Nietzsche, and that his characters were stolen from Dickens. There is not a word of truth in all this. The cast of his mind, his mingling of kindness with an impatience of fools, his mingling of sense and nonsense, is altogether natural and peculiar. He has that intellectual simplicity to which all ideas are, as it were, foreknown. He had written in the manner of Ibsen before ever reading Ibsen; Wagner was a fellow-revolutionary; Nietzsche merely gave him the formula, the phrase, necessary for the expression of his own views, Samuel Butler had almost privately written down thoughts long familiar to Shaw.

> Whatever in those climes he found
> Irregular in sight or sound
>   Did to his mind impart
> A kindred impulse, seemed allied
> To his own powers, and justified
>   The workings of his heart.

It is true that Dickens—and also Bunyan—showed him how characters, to entertain, must have objective consistency, how they must be broadly outlined and self-explanatory (what E. M. Forster calls 'flat'), and how if seen with exultant and exaggerative humour such characters are manipulable at will by the expert dramatist. It is true that Nietzsche at his best throws off ideas so instantaneously convincing that a superficial reader believes them to be his own inspirations, and a modest one the teachings of a master (but Freud and other great men have the same instant convincingness), and that the idea of the Life Force was due for revival when Shaw gave it dramatic expression. It is equally true that Ibsen, once his work was known, must have influenced any man already determined to express moral ideas in dramatic form. But Shaw's real impetus came from something else.

I said just now that Shaw was a first-class debater. I think the real reason why he became a dramatist was that when as a young man he spent his evenings in debate he always found the opposition so weak that he longed to take both sides—all sides—himself, just to show how a case should be conducted. Most of his plays are dramatic debates, interspersed with farcical incidents. The brilliance of the conversation may at times blind us to some lethargy of invention; but we have often in retrospect a little discomfort when we realize that only a scuffle or some desperate turn has brought to an end arguments which, uninterrupted, might be going on to this hour. Shaw can always think of something more to say; he is never at the end of the matter, so that he has to write long and very eloquent prefaces to his plays to incorporate all that he has not been able to say in the plays themselves, or all that has occurred to him on kindred subjects since the plays were written; and he has several times cruelly over-estimated, in prefaces as in the theatre, an audience's power of continuous attention. But in spite of all this the plays conquered because they were so much more amusing and interesting and stimulating than any other plays of their period; and it is necessary that this fact should be recognized before all others.

They did not conquer without difficulty. Although Shaw was known as a writer and pamphleteer and speaker, he was regarded by theatrical managers as a hopeless investment for them. Cursed as theatrical managers always are with the belief that only cretins pay for stalls in theatres, these men had marked him down as one doomed for ever to Sunday evening performances to the loud-voiced intellectual snobs of the Edwardian Stage Society. But they were wrong; and when the public, in disgust at everything associated in its mind with the humiliations of the Boer War, threw over its old literary favourites, the way was opened for Shaw and other new figures. They stepped forward.

Shaw was enabled to do so because a young actor named Harley Granville Barker and a young impresario named J. E. Vedrenne had joined forces in leasing the Court Theatre in Sloane Square, Chelsea. Here were given some matinée performances of *Candida*, with Barker in the role of Marchbanks; and here, too, other plays, by Galsworthy, St John Hankin, John Masefield, and Barker himself, were intermingled with a host of plays by Shaw. Since Ireland was prominently in the news, Shaw's Irish play, *John Bull's Other Island*, was given its first London production. It created a furore.

The play, which flattered and ridiculed English and Irish alike, made everybody laugh. It made everybody feel that he was thinking hard and wisely about politics and human nature. Instead of being 'buffoon' and 'charlatan,' Shaw became with all the politically minded *bourgeois*—who are the really stupid English (the rest of the community being not so much stupid as ingeniously idle)—'a queer fellow—quite a genius in his way.' He had reached the public. Young men and women, the modest equivalent in those days of our black-hatted or bare-headed devourers of Dunne, Jeans, Lawrence, Huxley, and Freud, had for years taken him very seriously indeed. They had discussed him, over nuts and barley water, over red ties and straggly beards; and had resolved long ago that it was proper to be 'modern' in the Shavian way. But after the success of *John Bull's Other Island* everybody was 'modern' in the Shavian way. For the first time English theatre audiences saw plays which presented, not a situation twisted for the sake of arousing superficial excitement or amatory prowess, or for the sake of driving home for the millionth time some creaky moral obsolete in every place but the theatre, but the fantastic world of a social and political revolutionary. Whatever the artistic faults of the Shavian drama, these plays did without any question change theatre-going from a habit to an event. At their worst they seemed endless; at their best they roused and rewarded the audience as oxygen revives the cellar-dweller.

Shaw's fame grew and grew. He was more and more successful. True, even after the accession of King George V he was arraigned by dramatic critics on the ground that he could not write a play; but he was generally admired as a man of extraordinary gifts. His more recent reputation, which at the time of his seventieth birthday verged upon idolatry (but fashions pass quickly nowadays), is a Georgian acknowledgment of his virtual creation of the Georgian mentality out of nothing.

IV

THE DEVIL. . . . The truth is, you have—I won't say no heart; for we all know that beneath all your affected cynicism you have a warm one——

Man and Superman.

The plays seemed to the generation that first saw them the most ruthless of destructive humours. We, being more ruthless than Shaw (who could not hurt a fly and who would hurt a man, even a fool and an opponent, only because he could not see or hear him), find them gentle. At first they emphasized the *rentier's* moral obligation to invest his money in untainted concerns, or laughed at the difficulties of a lover who in spite of every Shavian device could not get rid of a supplanted mistress, or showed what a shock a modern girl might have if she found that her mother, a self-made woman, lived comfortably on the proceeds of continental brothels. Or they told the world that poets have their dreams and clergymen of upright character their mystical weaknesses, or that a supposed ne'er-do-well has his code of honour, or that a brigand would be as much a slave to Ellen Terry as any dramatist, or that you have only to put on a false nose and talk a lot of nonsense to bring sanity into a situation hitherto impossible. The first three of these plays were labelled 'unpleasant.' One of them was found by the British Dramatic Censorship so distasteful that its public performance was forbidden altogether.

But it was not the themes of the plays that upset all who objected to Shaw. It was their verbal irreverence. Now what they said, but the nasty way they said it. To a people accustomed since the death of Dickens to a serious treatment of serious matters, a mocking attitude towards morals, parents, and respectability was abhorrent. Yet here parents were made such crass humbugs that it would have been impossible to honour them. Marchbanks, instead of being a defeated seducer, left the theatre without a stain upon his character. Dick Dudgeon seemed almost to have been ready to sacrifice himself because he had an idea in his head, and not because (which would have been quite comprehensibly in accord with stage convention) he was romantically in love with a married woman. They were queer stuff: were they 'art'?

Art was a new thing in literature; it was usually associated with those who

> walked down Piccadilly
> With a poppy or a lily
> In their medieval hands,

and there was nothing at all aesthetic in Shaw. Nor had these plays 'dignity and memory and measure,' in Henry James's sense. But then Shaw had said of James that 'his intellectual fastidiousness remains untouched by the resurgent energy and wilfulness of the new spirit. It takes us back to the exhausted atmosphere of George Eliot, Huxley, and Tyndall, instead of thrusting us forward into the invigorating strife raised by Wagner, Ibsen, and Sudermann.' He did not want to write

like Henry James or Oscar Wilde, like Pinero and Henry Arthur
Jones. Instead, he wanted, apparently, to make jokes in very
bad taste at the expense of mothers and fathers, and rake up
a lot of disagreeable stuff about slums and brothels, and libel
young English womanhood. Such a man could safely be left
to the dramatic critics.

But what then? The dramatic critics were in the position of
all critics who are governed by formula and who are called upon
to deal with a writer who acts upon his own assumption that
'the golden rule is that there is no golden rule.' They laughed
in the theatre; and then—it is always done—they went away
and wrote every time that Shaw had written another play which
(a) was not a play, and (b) was inferior to its predecessors from
the same agile pen. In this way they kept the theatre sweet
for adaptations from the Palais Royal and the lighter or heavier
production of others.

We cannot do what contemporary critics did, for Shaw cannot
now be budged from his place among the stars. But we can at
least agree that the earlier plays were less entertaining than the
plays of Shaw's maturity, and that they were inferior in everything except genius to the plays that thousands of well-educated
young writers of to-day can produce. But they were the prentice
work of a born dramatist, a man to whom talking and writing
(with him the acts are almost inseparable, so much has his
writing the ideal conversational quality of emphatic lucidity)
were the most enjoyable of all occupations. All the characters
in these plays were bursting with talk. As characters they may
have been rough and not unfamiliar; but when they talked they
were reanimated with original life.

Arms and the Man, a farcical comedy, is the best of all his
plays in the respect that it is the simplest and clearest of them.
It is based upon a good comic theme, and it deals with that
theme dramatically and without excursions. The scene is a
house somewhere in the Balkans, a district which came into the
news in the mid-eighties with the first Balkan War; and there
are only half a dozen characters in the play. All of these
characters are original, from the sentimental, untruthful girl
Raina and her brave but self-deceiving fiancé to the practical
Swiss who puts everybody and everything to rights and meets
his matrimonial fate with philosophy. The whole play has a
natural and happy development from its opening passages; and
it is full of little surprises that are heightened because one sees
them an instant before they occur. The play is in consequence

extraordinarily effective in the theatre. It is more effective now than it was when Shaw, taking his call after the first performance, and in reply to a solitary booer, said politely: 'I quite agree with you, sir. But what are we among so many?' Not only has it become more pointed, so that every point may be said to make itself, but its wisdom is more immediately appreciated. That is what emphasizes its classic quality and gives one the sense of enjoying and praising a work that has lived through its own generation and found continued life in ours.

Arms and the Man shows that Shaw had abandoned realism for ever. His sole connection with it henceforward was to be a persistent anti - romanticism. Where the realist coolly and fatalistically shows the inevitable sequence of events—Ibsen in his social plays is a realist—Shaw leaps hither and thither among solemn follies and makes them ridiculous. He shows in this play, with a glee akin to that of Molière, the absurd impulse to lie and to pose which is dominant in men and women. And, instead of allowing the lie to persist, and even to triumph, as a realist might justifiably have done, he makes every lie achieve the ignominy of ludicrous exposure. That is an unmistakable mark of comic genius, and in the field of farcical comedy *Arms and the Man* remains unequalled in Shaw's work.

Bright and amusing though it is, *You Never Can Tell* has no theme to carry the delightful nonsense. Parents, those butts of Shavian and post-Shavian drama, are made to look absurd—the guying of mothers was a part of the campaign for youth the results of which did not please too well the author of *Too True to be Good*—children are pleasantly unruly and impertinent; young lovers quickly reach an understanding. But false noses, ludicrous discomfitures of the irascible, waiters whose sons are famous barristers, and fun about a dental chair do not quite carry the play beyond hotch-potch. Perhaps for the first time in his plays Shaw allows us to notice his inability to distinguish between what is good and what is not so good in his own work.

Much better and wiser, and more characteristic of the author's mind, are the two moralities, *Candida* and *The Devil's Disciple*, in which the chief characters illuminate what Dean Inge calls the 'absolute values' of goodness, beauty, and truth. They do right from a natural impulse to do right. The two plays illustrate another of Shaw's beliefs, comprehension of which is much overlaid in the minds of those who refer to themselves as 'my generation.' This belief is in the power of virtue. Candida and Dudgeon are both—like Shaw—self-sufficient and

self-sacrificing; but they are able to sacrifice themselves without
weakness and without heroics because they are both above fear
and temptation.   The plays in which they figure are not those
which have most impressed the public (although George Jean
Nathan has long distinguished *Candida*, and many people piously
suppose it an attempt of the Life Force to put Barrie's ink into
Shaw's pen); but they show that behind all bravura his spiritual
assumptions are quite as simple as those of his own Joan of Arc,
and not unlike them.   The machinery of both plays is adequate,
but not inspired; both have some amusing sketches of character;
both are still easy and agreeable to read or see in the theatre.
But it is because they express with such veracity the positive
Shavian conception of personal virtue and personal strength
that they are important.   In my opinion they are, with *Arms
and the Man* (because of its classic quality) and *Man and Superman* (because of its richness), the best of Shaw's dramatic works.
They have not had anything like the influence of *Man and
Superman*.

Owing to the fact that the whole of *Man and Superman* is
hardly ever seen upon the stage, but only the more farcical flight
of John Tanner, embodiment of his creator's coyness and
garrulity, from the boa-constrictor Ann, many theatre-goers
believe that the Superman is Woman.   The fundamental
seriousness of Shaw in this play, and the extraordinary beauty
of the interlude in hell, are alike ignored, and the play as performed is only a joke in three acts.   Hence its popularity.   Shaw,
meaning to help along the mind of the race, has roused in
beholders of *Man and Superman* nothing but laughter and
concupiscence.   It is a misfortune, and one for which he cannot
have been in the very least prepared.   Among those who neither
see plays nor read them, but who rely entirely upon hearsay for
their news of wisdom, he has contributed to the modern man's
sense of helplessness before the predatory Female.   That was
not his design.   Nor was it his design that *Man and Superman*
should be thought of as a sort of Clo Graves farce, like *Mother of
Three*.   But without the interlude this play, as performed, is
hardly more than a feast of back-chat.   What is it, indeed, but
the picture of a liar and a gossip, a concealed marriage between
two other young people, and a collection of discomfited elders?
Ann Whitefield, resolved (at the bidding of the Life Force) to
marry her true mate, John Tanner, succeeds in spite of his wild
motor journey to escape her, his capture by brigands, and his
protestation to the last that he will not succumb.   To most

people there is nothing more in the play than that. Is it not a weakness in Shaw that he should have to supplement his farce with an explanatory play, a preface of great length, and a whole collection of maxims under the title of *The Revolutionist's Handbook*?

You would never convince him of that; and it is quite true that as a whole, with interlude, revolutionary postscript, and a brilliant jumble of preface which darts from Don Juan to the duel of sex, from Shakespeare to politics, from Bunyan to art for art's sake (art for art's sake does not stand a dog's chance), it is an epitome of Shaw's genius. If this were the only work of its author to survive a cataclysm it would still provide laborious delvers with materials for treatise after treatise concerning Shaw. The preface illustrates in perfection his belief that 'effectiveness of assertion is the Alpha and Omega of style'; the four-act play betrays the beginning of his break-up as a dramatic craftsman; the *Revolutionist's Handbook*, a medley of opinions, is in itself proof of the opulence of a talent calculated to stretch the covers of any book; and the complete work is so full of life, thought, argument, and eloquence that it shows the author (now at the height of his powers) as an original and creative genius of first-class importance in modern letters.

Man and Superman belongs to the twentieth century. It was published in 1903. Since that time Shaw has written many plays, one at least of them a very ambitious attempt to express the philosophy of his old age. This, *Back to Methuselah*, is so long that one would have to emulate the ardent Wagnerite in order to see the whole of it performed in the theatre. I have not seen it. I can judge it only from the printed text, which is disappointing. The play begins in Eden, and it ends far in the future, when life has become as humourless as it always seems to do in imaginative pictures of an ideal state. In this play Shaw is very serious indeed. The brilliance of *Man and Superman* is left far behind. But while the play is no doubt packed with wisdom it is less entertaining, and therefore less successful, than others which the author undertook with less serious purpose. Much more excitement was caused in the theatre world of London by a later, very slight, and extremely comic peep into the future called *The Apple Cart*.

The Apple Cart was one of the author's most successful plays. It was successful in spite of a perfect rage of condemnation on the part of the dramatic critics. These odd persons declared that Shaw had betrayed the cause of democracy, and gone back

upon all the lessons of his own earlier teaching. But they were
wrong: Shaw had never been a democrat. He has always been,
politically, something of a realist. And if a dictatorship will
give mankind a chance of escaping from the dead weight of
democratic doctrine he will support a dictatorship, whether that
dictatorship be upon the Russian or the Italian model. His
question is: 'Will it work?' So in *The Apple Cart* he made a
dictatorship work. He so much enjoyed the knockabout portions
of the play that he affronted once again, as he had always done,
the uncommonly serious. But he did once again what he has
so often done—he made people angry; he made them argu-
mentative; he stirred the sluggards by means of a little charge
of dynamite. That has been his strength as a political thinker,
and his strength as a lively dramatist—the power to make ideas
amusing. As to the ultimate truth or otherwise of his ideas
the critic of his work, it seems to me, has no concern. *The Apple
Cart*, although far below Shaw's finest plays, has a life of its own.
Not one of its critics has the talent to write anything a tenth
part as stimulating.

Many Shavians believe that the author's masterpiece is *Saint
Joan*. I do not. The play is an admirable essay in the dramatic
chronicle form invented anew by John Drinkwater with *Abraham
Lincoln*, and continued by him with *Robert E. Lee*, *Mary Queen
of Scots*, and others. It has many beauties. It is very exciting.
It is shot through and through with Shaw's unsurpassed lucidity.
But it owed its popularity to the fact that respectable people,
long shy of a revolutionary who was also an irreverent, found as
they thought a new seriousness, a new faith, in an author whom
they longed to admire because he was getting so old; and it was
praised by dramatic critics because the hour had struck and
Shaw was due for acclaim. Such gratification as was felt at the
thought that he had given up teasing arose from ignorance of
the author's mind. If these same thankful stalwarts of conventional faith had studied *The Devil's Disciple* and *Candida*,
and if they had listened to William Poel's delightful performance
of Father Keegan in *John Bull's Other Island*, or better still if
they had read with attention any large stretch of Shaw's criticism
of other authors, they would have known that throughout his
life, whenever he cared to do so, he has employed an almost
divine gift of understanding the good, the simple, and the
unpretending. Because he has been so much a propagandist
he has been forced to attack ideas the virtue of which he has
well known, but he has never been a blind man. Having been

wound up, as it were, to talk for twenty-four hours a day, he has
had no opportunity of listening to anybody but himself; that
has been his public performance, and it is due to that public
performance that his name is known to more human beings than
the name of any other living author, not excepting Wells.   But
nobody could talk so much as Shaw without becoming familiar
with his own performance, and while still perfectly able to startle
and anger millions of stupid people—merely by pressing the old
button—he has not passed the age of eighty without the restorative refreshment of quietism.   He could as well have written
Saint Joan in 1903 as 1923 if he had wished; but in 1903 he was
busy upon something else.

Shaw is *not* a reformed character.   He never will be.   He is
Shaw.   And he has always recognized the value of work by other
authors, even though it was work antipathetic to him.   He has
sat devotedly in the uncomfortable seats of innumerable
theatres and perceived and remembered the talents of actors and
actresses struggling with bad small parts.   He has been ever a
chivalrous opponent.   He has been so kind to those less kind
than himself as to be beset mercilessly by spongers and favour-
hunters.   He has been modest, polite, and considerate to strangers whom he could have eaten (had he been omnivorous) out of
hand.   These traits are worth pondering in connection with his
genius.   They can be set beside his notorious self-advertising,
which in comparison with the laborious and pointless self-
advertisement of a hundred modern quack-authors is positively
reticent, and which was always undertaken as publicity for his
ideas as well as publicity for himself.   And while it is true that
he has made his characters say and do many things upon the
stage with the sole object of raising a laugh—as in my judgment
he was entitled to do—he has never written any work with the
sole object of exhibiting the wonders of G. B. S.   As nearly as
possible, he is a selfless, a disinterested author who has worked
for the destruction of error; and for him the whole business of
any writer worth his salt (apart from those 'artists' for whom he
professes such contempt and has in fact such respect) is that of
arousing from sleep or lethargy the God or the Will in mankind.

V. HERBERT GEORGE WELLS

The Owner of the Voice you must figure to yourself as a whitish
plump man, a little under the middle size and age, with such blue
eyes as many Irishmen have, and agile in his movements and with
a slight tonsorial baldness—a penny might cover it—of the crown.

His front is convex. He droops at times like most of us, but for the greater part he bears himself as valiantly as a sparrow. Occasionally his hand flies out with a fluttering gesture of illustration. And his Voice (which is our medium henceforth) is an unattractive tenor that becomes at times aggressive. Him you must imagine as sitting at a table reading a manuscript about Utopias, a manuscript he holds in two hands that are just a little fat at the wrist. The curtain rises upon him so. But afterwards, if the devices of this declining art of literature prevail, you will go with him through curious and interesting experiences.

H. G. WELLS, *A Modern Utopia.*

Shaw once described himself as a 'revolted bourgeois.' He might equally well have used the phrase 'intellectual revolutionary,' for his aim has always been to hold a bunch of carrots before the nose of civilization, and not at all to flatter workers into the belief that they are the salt of the earth. He has never been a democrat. Wells, on the other hand, although never a believer in votes for all, has been and is still much more a man of the people than Shaw. His father, instead of being a wholesale corndealer, was a retail shopkeeper. His mother for some years was a domestic servant, then lady's maid, and finally housekeeper in a big house in Sussex. Gardening, cricket, shopkeeping, and service are the soil from which Wells's much more personal Socialism sprang in the first instance. As a boy he had to touch his cap to the idle rich; he listened restlessly (but with an excellent memory) to the unctuous conversation of ladies' ladies and gentlemen's gentlemen; and he and his brothers were all enslaved as apprentices to linen-drapers through his mother's pathetic wish that they might at any rate wear black coats and collars and look like second-rate gentlefolk.

He was born at Bromley, in Kent, now a London suburb, on 21st September 1866. His birthplace was a small room over his father's persistently unprosperous shop (originally established for the sale of glass and china, but used also for the sale of cricket bats, balls, and other odds and ends); and before he was fourteen he was tried as a shop assistant. After one or two false starts he spent two years as apprentice to a draper in Southsea; and when desperation drove him to flight he was lucky enough to find a friend and employer in the head master of the Midhurst Grammar School. In 1884 he applied for and obtained a scholarship as a teacher-in-training at the Normal School of Science (afterwards the Royal College of Science) at South Kensington.

This meant that he would have just over a pound a week to live on while he explored the marvels of human knowledge. 'He

was a passable-looking youngster of eighteen, fair-haired, in-
differently barbered,' says Wells of Mr Lewisham; 'he wore
ready-made clothes, his black jacket of rigid line was dusted
about the front and sleeves with scholastic chalk, and his face
was downy and his moustache incipient.' And 'he kept himself
in London' (this is no longer Mr Lewisham, but Hill, in *A Slip
under the Microscope*) 'on his allowance of a guinea a week, and
found that, with proper care, this also covered his clothing allowance, an occasional waterproof collar, that is; and ink and
needles and cotton, and such-like necessaries for a man about
town.'

To the three years of active learning, arguing, and prentice
writing which he enjoyed at the School of Science can be traced
the experience upon which Wells has drawn in composing first of
all his scientific romances, then his sociological criticisms and
forecasts, and finally his novels of contemporary life. He was
an ardent debater; he for a time edited the school magazine and
wrote for it; and although in the examination finals for June
1887 he was 'slaughtered,' so that he left without taking a
degree, his active, incessantly curious mind had found its range
and direction. He was to be the first scientific novelist in
English literature.

Before he became a novelist he had read an extraordinary
variety of books. He had held two posts as assistant master,
one of them under the father of A. A. Milne (who was one of his
pupils). He had taken his degree as Bachelor of Science. And,
at the age of twenty-four, he had married for the first time.
Within five years he had found his marriage a hampering failure,
had been divorced, and had married again.

This second marriage, to Amy Catherine Robbins, was a
turning point in his life. Mrs Wells was a great woman, who
to the end of her life was the staunch ally and helpmeet of her
husband. Without her aid, as he has more than once admitted,
Wells could not have produced anything like the amount of work
he has done. She was for years his secretary; she typed his
manuscripts, corrected his proofs, did much research, dealt with
difficult and disagreeable correspondents, and acted as hostess in
both London and the country to a multitude of visitors of every
kind and colour. With her encouragement, Wells from the first
wrote steadily and with increasing confidence and success. He
began with journalism and short stories; then, as soon as he had
written one book, he wrote as if by magic a dozen others.
Actually in two years he published nine works of fiction; and

since the nineties not a year has passed which has not seen one, two, three, or four new books of his. No wonder that he was famous before he was thirty! And no wonder that although he is ten years younger than Shaw he has seemed for the last forty years to be equally a one-man arsenal of new and explosive ideas!

Apparently inexhaustible brilliance is shown in the rapidity with which Wells works, in his extraordinary gift for assimilating facts, in the swift ease with which he communicates to the simplest mind the results of his observation and reflection. Nobody alive can compare with him in this unceasing and always stimulating fertility. Although some of his books have been less acceptable than others to critical judgment, he has always been the champion surprise packet of the literary world. And while, having written so many books, 'mood after mood of the one mind within him,' he has by now fully revealed the range and degree of his intellect, no man could confidently prophesy what new aspect of cosmic activity he will next choose to analyse.

Naturally this versatility and fecundity have resulted in great popular success. That is unfortunate for his present fame. But they have done something else; they have brought a charge that since he is always 'at it' he must constantly be changing his ground. Nothing could be more untrue. He has been, on the contrary, particularly consistent. He has always wanted the World State and all that the World State involves. He has wanted the abolition of kings and privileges. He has wanted a new type of aristocracy, the severely self-disciplined Samurai. His views of details may have varied with the increasing awareness of different facets in the universal kaleidoscope; but in the main his constructive ideas have been the same from quite early days. That is noteworthy.

What gives critics the excuse for suggesting waywardness is that Wells has from time to time taken up different *instruments* and let them fall. He took up the Fabian Society; but when he found that the Fabian Society was more Fabian than international, and that it preferred its own Shavian corner in ideas to any ideas that he could bring in from outside, he dropped it. He took up the League of Nations; but when he found that the League of Nations would do nothing to advance his own view of internationalism he dropped that, too. He took up the Labour Party, hoping that he could instil into it some of his knowledge and faith in a scientific future; but when he found that the Labour Party was a nest of private vanities and personal ambitions, wedded to class warfare, and incapable of non-political conceptions, he dropped it. He is not, and never has been, a political democrat. He has never been, in the strict sense, a Socialist ('I was never at any stage a loyal party man,' says Remington). But he has been willing to take any path that might bring him to his goal; and only when he found the paths leading to dead ends has he retraced his steps in order to get once more upon his own road. There is no inconsistency here, but only an excess of faith in the power of the Wellsian mind to dominate the hesitations and self-importance of other men.

He has always been a lively and vigorous host. His social contacts have been innumerable. Scientists of every order, politicians of every party, his fellow-writers in every genre, philosophers, labourers, painters, actors, lawyers, and civil servants of every description have all come within his immediate purview. Hence the thumbnail sketches scattered through his work of all sorts of odd types. He has gone here and there about the earth and in the air, always active, always alert, always storing observation with those quick eyes, that astoundingly rapid mind, and talking, talking with that witty, exaggerative tongue. There is hardly an Englishman of note whose personal experience Wells has not explored, whose character he has not assessed, whose brain and temper he has not enlivened. There is hardly a reader in the world to whom he has not opened new vistas of entertainment, understanding, indignation, and the millennium.

He has not Shaw's platform gift; he does not always enjoy the support of experts in this or that kind of learning which he surmounts with his seven-league boots. But after he has passed, and after the dust has settled, many an expert has scratched his head, swept together the ruins of his hobbyhorse, and (to adapt a popular advertisement) has murmured 'That's Wells, that was'; while many a common man hitherto baffled by jargon or old hypocrisy has seen the world afresh as if by the brilliant passage of a meteor. To say that Wells has been always right, or always fair, or always subtle, would be to risk exaggeration; but to undervalue the influence of so impetuous a force upon changing social conceptions would be the merest futility.

VI

It might be thought from this, by those who do not know him, that Wells personally resembles a hurricane. He does not. Shaw may bring with him a breeze of some force; but Wells would enter any room, and shut the door behind him, as quietly as you or I would do. If you were a very young and modest person, who had failed to catch his name, you would see a not very tall but rather stoutly built man with a brown face and very blue eyes. You would hear a hoarse little voice which, although not at all like the solemn squeak of many English intellectuals, is pitched high and is not incapable of surprising shrillness. Your first impression would be of a very friendly and easy manner. You would notice small birdlike jerks of the head. At last you would see that the very blue eyes were darting here and there with great quickness, and that they were full of amusement and mischief.

If you had quite distinctly heard the name of the newcomer, were conceited, and furthermore knew all and more than all about the celebrated Mr H. G. Wells, your response would be different. You would first of all be surprised and possibly disappointed by the absence of glitter, carriage, *empressement* in so famous a man. All your preconceptions would be disconcerted. You would be paralysed by the feeling that what you had to say could not by any means be made to interest this all-knowing, restless, and unimpressible person. You would feel helpless, would say stupid things, would fall haughtily silent. Or you might find yourself embarked upon a conversation amusing, indeed, but on your side strained, never comfortable, never quite natural because you could never overtake Wells's inventiveness and quickness of epithet, and on consideration a failure. There are some people who are absolutely unable to talk to him, not from awe, but from constraint. Sinclair Lewis, for example, otherwise hard to check, and in spite of almost idolatrous admiration, is tongue-tied. Lewis needs an evening: Wells gives nobody an instant.

The truth is that his quickness of mind carries him to the end of a sentence long before a tongue that requires room in language can make the same journey. Really to converse with him one should be as quick as he, as fluent, and as little devoted to those scrupulousnesses of verisimilitude which delay the lumbering talker. Perhaps one should be a very adroit woman. Or, if less gifted, one should trust to his kindness, for Wells is a great sufferer of fools. He is so kind that one has but to be simple and receptive to evoke his affectionate consideration. But he is very impatient of the long story or the aggressive or pompous manner.

At his best, he is the most richly amusing raconteur I know.

He improvises; he invents; he mimics (not with precise accuracy of intonation, for which his voice is unsuited, but with irresistible sense of character); and he laughs and teases all the time with the greatest spirit. He does everything with spirit. Whether he is dancing, or playing at cards or hockey, charades, or the many-ruled (and I may say constantly and even momentarily re-ruled) ball-game of his own invention, he is hotly and energetically active all the time. I think he begins to write a book as if he were playing a game, and with the same enthusiasm; but there is this difference between his play and his work, that the former is a relaxation, whereas the latter originates in a really passionate desire to change the world, so that those who are born into it may be healthier, wiser, and happier than they have ever been.

Change! That is the keynote of his character. He cannot be content with what is. I recall visiting the late Sir Harry Johnston shortly after Wells had spent a week-end at St John's Priory. Now Sir Harry, although one to whom (as to the infant Nelson) fear was unknown, had some of the idiosyncrasies usually linked with the traditional old maid. Having quelled the fiercest of savage warriors and penetrated the most intimidating of jungles, he spoke like a little old woman and clung to rule and habit like a recluse. And when I saw him he was still palpitating from the Wellsian week-end. He had proposed, it seemed, a scrupulously unscrupulous game of croquet upon his beautiful lawn. But to his horror he found the lawn by no means sufficient for Wells's game of croquet. The entire garden, thorough bush, thorough brier, had been called into requisition. The world itself would not have been too wide for its range. In two twinks, Sir Harry's sedate game of croquet had become a mixture of golf and steeplechase.

I instance this because it shows Wells's hatred of all that is cramped in life. It also illumines his dislike of the petty viciousness of croquet as that game is usually played. As Alice in Wonderland used a flamingo and a hedgehog for mallet and ball, Wells took all spitefulness from the most quarrelsome of pastimes by letting air into it, and converted the game into both an open contest and a planned campaign. Change and plan; plan and change. Not without significance that Schema of Mr Lewisham's! If he had not had this eager desire for change, Wells might have remained a draper's assistant all his life; and if he had not had this intense love of planning he might have remained a writer of romances and tales without ever giving the world new visions of sanity and order. Nay, without the desire to make mankind healthier and happier by means of air and light and space, education and hygiene, change and plan, he might long ago have lost his own zest for life and gone without reluctance to his quiet grave. As it is, he may live another twenty years, still vividly interested in the human scene and its rectification. I continue to find in him at every turn the boy who knew the life suffered by Kipps and Polly; the chalky young schoolmaster of *Love and Mr Lewisham*; the waterproof-collared student at the School of Science, arguing and spasmodically swatting and learning to see Victorian men as but a stage in the progress towards something more admirable; the novelist of escaping workers who in early days took bicycles, and then cars, and aeroplanes, and at last trips to Labrador and Utopia, in order to get away from the distracting pressure of daily life; the novelist of careers and inconvenient passions; the novelist who breathed life into a history of the world that all could understand; and, within and above all these, the very natural, sensitive, nonsensical, affectionate, quick-tempered human being who was born over seventy years ago in a little room above his father's shop in Bromley. He is many other things, as those who do not know him can tell you in detail, and indeed as his books will show; but behind the celebrated writer and the ready talker, the not perfectly cogent moralist, the publicist and the open conspirator, is a much more endearing person, full of fun, kindness, and simplicity, a man who if he is not really Mr Polly himself, is at least of the Polly clay and the lovable Polly fantasy.

VII

I've read an average share of novels . . . and I've found the restraints and rules of the art (as I made them out) impossible for me. I like to write, I am keenly interested in writing, but . . . do what I will I fail to see how I can be other than a lax, undisciplined story-teller.

Tono-Bungay.

When Wells wrote *The Time Machine, The Wonderful Visit, The War of the Worlds, The Invisible Man,* and their companions, he was doing something which had never been done before, and which has never been done since with the same vivid freshness. Picture to yourselves the shock to readers of those days of a rush of new inventions, simple to us now, but then so novel and so startling; and imagine how they must have roused the attention of the age. Here was a man who put posers—scientific

posers—with the facility and enjoyment of a child; who said
'Why?' 'What if——?' 'How?' 'Suppose——?' about all
sorts of things that people found they wanted to know. It was
prodigious. Jules Verne had taken boys on conducted tours
under the sea, and to the moon; but he had creaked as he did so.
This new man's quickness allowed no time for creaks; he bubbled
with new notions, and they were notions to which other minds
jumped just an instant late. And as they jumped, so Wells jumped
again—in a different direction. He asked a thousand questions.
He has always asked questions—odd, irreverent questions, such
as those that Uncle Ponderevo asked about history. Do you
remember?

'Don't want your drum and trumpet history—no fear! Don't
want to know who was who's mistress, and why So-and-so de-
vastated a province; that's bound to be all lies and upsy-down
anyhow. Chaps who did it didn't clearly know . . . What I want
to know is, in the Middle Ages Did they Do Anything for House-
maid's Knee? What did they put in their hot baths after jousting,
and was the Black Prince—you know the Black Prince—was he
enamelled or painted, or what? I think myself, black-leaded—very
likely—like pipe-clay—but did they use blacking so early?'

I need not say that Ponderevo's point is one that Wells himself
makes about drum-and-trumpet history; or that Wells himself
has an eloquent passage in *The World of William Clissold* to the
effect that the scholars who so tidily arrange history into systems
—the Feudal System and the Manorial System, and even the
Capitalist System—are dealing in artificial lozenges with no
relation at all to the casual sprawl of events as they occurred.
That is not what I want to show. It is that Wells's mind is, and
was, a questing mind, ever in search of the things that are not in
encyclopaedias. He was doing this when he wrote the scientific
romances. He is still doing it. To him, any fact is a starting
point for speculation. 'Why?' 'What if——?' 'How?'
'Suppose——'

What if an angel came to earth? What if a man experimented
with the fourth dimension and could as readily visit and contemplate the future as the past? What would he see? How
would he make the journey? What if a man could make himself invisible? And so on. He could treat the subject seriously
and at the full stretch of his mind, as he did in *The Time Machine*,
still the most striking, though not the most charming, of the
books of this general type. Or he could treat it fantastically,
as he did in *The Invisible Man*, where the unfortunate creature

who had discovered a practicable formula for invisibility could not retranslate himself to opacity, though he perished with cold and hunger. Or as plain farce, as in *The Stolen Bacillus*, where an anarchist swallowed in mistake for cholera germs something that would bring out blue patches upon his skin. Or as whimsy, as in *The Inexperienced Ghost*; or as tract, as in *The Wonderful Visit*; or as sensational thriller, as in *The War of the Worlds*. There seemed no end to the subjects or the approaches to them; and while it could be said with force that such themes were not strange to the mind of any boy born poor, who had only imaginings to set between himself and the dreariness of drab circumstance, the themes were given new vitality, they were made more novel, more credible, by the scientific detail, the bright inventiveness of a mind ruthlessly active and coolly amused at its own power.

Concurrently with the scientific romances, Wells was writing novels not very much outside the manner of his period, but noteworthy because of their personal humour and increasing richness. They were simple narratives, long and short, of events in the lives of very simple-minded people. The first of them was the tale of Mr Hoopdriver, the draper's assistant with a bicycle, who went for a cycling holiday and became for the time being a knight-errant. There was also the more autobiographical, but still indulgent, story of *Love and Mr Lewisham*, in which a boy, a schoolmaster, fell idyllically in love, became a student at the Royal College of Science, went to a fraudulent séance (so, you may remember, did Mr Parham, in one of Wells's latest fantastic tales), met at the séance his early sweetheart, married her, and had his trials and quarrels until a stronger feeling checked the strain and ended the book with a rosy glimpse. A little later there was *Kipps*, in which a draper's assistant inherited money and entered society and ran away from his intellectual fiancée to marry the domestic servant he had always loved and build a house and lose his money and settle in life as a shopkeeper again. Finally, as the supreme example of this sort of book, there was *Mr Polly*, the story of a little shopkeeper who set fire to his shop, ran away from his wife, and found a nice cosy widow who kept an inn to which all sorts of odd visitors came, and lived happily ever after.

All these books belong to the same order. All are fairy stories, and all are about 'simple souls.' All were written, not merely as relaxations, but because one side of Wells's genius, the happiest side, has kinship with the comic genius of Dickens, his favourite author. Whenever Wells is amused, he is happy and inventive. The living figures in his books are all comic characters, fantastic, talkative, simple, phonetically colloquial, seen with what used to be called 'open pleasantry,' but seen none the less with keenness and precision. Teddy Ponderevo, Polly, Chaffery, Kipps, Chitterlow, having amused us as we read, persist in our imaginations. We love them. When Wells is serious, he is expository; he does not create. We lose the character in the exposition; and this, I think, is why, as novels, all but the two best books in the serious and discursive manner must remain unsatisfactory. That is not to be said of the simple soul novels.

What is to be said of them, and of the early romances, is something else. It is that they were all written in an easy narrative form untrammelled by those shackles to which the rising authority of Henry James presently condemned romancers. In the nineties and early nineteen-hundreds, people who wrote books thought little of 'art' and 'form' and 'composition.' They found the writing of books 'fun,' and not a stern tussle with refractory material. We have changed all that now. We have even gone rather too far in the other direction, for any author who writes less to exhibit than to amuse himself is regarded from the distance, by the immaculate, as a prostitute. But, when Wells began to write, things were so different that he was allowed, unreproved, to enrich our literature with several artless works of genius which still give delight to all but the aesthetically unco' guid.

As a consequence, Wells never learnt how to write a novel which was a work of art. When advised of this, he bluffs after the manner of the defendant in an English law court, charged with libel. This defendant answers the charge by saying that the words were never uttered, or alternatively that they do not bear the meaning put upon them, or again alternatively that they are in fact true, and legitimate comment. Wells, charged with being unaesthetic, replies that he never said he was, and alternatively that the aesthetes can't prove it, and anyway, Yah! This seems to me, coming from Wells, to be entirely justifiable. The rules of art need revision, so as to include the work of Wells. Any suggestion that they are as fixed as those horrid wire cages which are put over box trees in the shape of peacocks, foxes, and the like, seems to me to beg the whole question. The rules of art are not made by edicts; they are developed from the practice of artists; and if they cannot admit of provision for such a book as *Tono-Bungay* they ought to be stretched; for *Tono-Bungay*, illustrating as it does the form and pressure of the time in which it was written, is one of the great modern novels, and will be so appreciated after a century's variations of aesthetic dogmatism. But I must not pause here to dwell upon *Tono-Bungay*, for it belongs to a later stage in the author's development.

VIII

I see about me a great multitude of little souls and groups of souls as darkened, as derivative as my own; with the passage of years I understand more and more clearly the quality of the motives that urge me and urge them to do whatever we do . . . Yet that is not all I see, and I am not altogether bounded by my littleness. Ever and again, contrasting with this immediate vision, come glimpses of a comprehensive scheme, in which these personalities float, the scheme of a synthetic wider being, the great State, mankind, in which we all move and go, like blood corpuscles, like nerve cells, it may be at times like brain cells, in the body of a man.

A Modern Utopia.

Having written the scientific romances, and having begun to write novels, Wells at the turn of the century found himself working in a new field. He had been a young schoolmaster, a young scientist, a journalist, a writer of romances, and a novelist; and now his increasing range of knowledge led him ever farther into speculation. It was speculation directed by the schoolmaster and the scientist in him; for his interests lay in the everyday world of that time and the future. For him the first step in the 'New Republicanism' of which he became the champion was 'to reject and set aside all abstract, refined, and intellectualized ideas as starting propositions, such ideas as Right, Liberty, Happiness, Duty, or Beauty.' He was a Darwinian; he knew that the world was to be more and more dominated by inventions and practical ideas; and he wanted to breed good citizens who would create a world in which order replaced present chaos. First of all, therefore, it was imperative that he should make up his mind as to the most probable developments of the near future. He did this, and wrote *Anticipations*.

I need not say that many of Wells's anticipations have proved accurate. The book is here to demonstrate the fact. From my point of view it is more interesting to realize that *Anticipations* was but a first step in the clarification of Wells's own mind. He went on to imagine what kind of world it was that he and his fellow-reformers were striving to create. He dared to formulate his idea of a practical Utopia. That was much more difficult. It was so difficult that he made a number of false starts in the writing of the book, and at last took refuge in a hybrid literary form — half essay, half tale — that excellently suited his gifts. And as a bridge between *Anticipations* and *A Modern Utopia* he wrote another book, called *Mankind in the Making*, in which he discussed elaborately the problems of eugenics and education.

The three books, taken together, represent the character of Wells's interest in the world and the human species. Later books in the same vein—and here I include such works as *The Outline of History*, *The Science of Life*, and *The Work, Wealth, and Happiness of Mankind* — have been educational. And whatever their positive qualities they have been undertaken deliberately as stop-gaps, with no pretence to much more than utilitarian purpose. They have been written because Wells felt the instructional need of such books; and the *History* was written only after he had failed to persuade other men, whom he considered better qualified than himself for the task, to undertake it. But all exhibit what I believe to be the same character. They are concerned with a practicable civilization of the future, and a civilization which has grown directly out of our present ways. They concentrate upon inventions, social order, education; they have little concern with aesthetics or what is called the psyche. And they are so simply expressed that any man of ordinary intelligence can read them with understanding. That is a quality due to the journalist in Wells. He is readable. It has been made a matter of reproach against him. He is said to have betrayed culture to the Philistines. It should rather be said that he has introduced the Philistines to a culture larger than that of the Dons.

It is the desire to teach, to expound, that is behind all Wells's serious work. He does not like a vague world, or one that has unexplored beauties; and for him the scientific mind is the best type of mind. By science and through science, he thinks we shall get a world that better men and women than ourselves may inhabit. How, therefore, looking to the future, could he do anything but create Utopias in which orderly but apparently unmerry people are identified by their thumb-prints and dominated by a highly organized State, what time they travel at immense speeds, do everything that can be done by means of machinery, and so manage their sanitation that with the fly and mosquito every familiar loveliness of our world, the world of the poets and merrymakers, has been expunged? It would not be true to say that, like other Republican theorists, Wells had banished laughter and beauty from the State; indeed, he specifically refers to these indications of the human spirit. But when he talks of beauty he never carries conviction, and his ideal world, in spite of every persuasive effort, and in spite of the fascinating ingenuity of parts of his analysis, remains, as all Utopias do, a place from which one hurries back to one's own fireside with relief.

Why is this? One explanation is that Wells has more courage than we, in that he is not in revolt against machinery, but is determined upon subduing it to the service of man. Another, which I am bound to speak of, is that in spite of every gift he is deficient in that kind of imagination which even those of us who are not poets do strangely share with the poets. It seems to me that Wells, with all his quickness, all his power, all his vivid inventive habits of mind, has no true sense of beauty in art or in life. Even love, in his books, never moves us; every one of his busy scientific heroes, interrupted in full flight of research or political activity by what he terms an 'urgency,' has an affair with a woman, but as to emotion there is no sign of it, and as to beauty of relation there is so little that we quite coldly estimate the duration of the urgency and the affair. Wells is interested in other matters. He is interested in getting things done. He will work for a cause, for the improvement of the world, for the instruction of mankind in essential knowledge. But save in so far as it is useful to one or other of those ends he is indifferent to beauty. He is a prose writer. He is at his best in books where he is nearest his own time and his own people. His best novels are *Tono-Bungay* and *Mr Polly*, which are both rich with the very texture of life itself. His best expository books are also novels—*The Undying Fire*, *The New Machiavelli*, and *The World of William Clissold*; and they are the best because the first is passionate and the two others are less expository than exploratory of the author's always original and interesting mind and experience.

IX

Art is selection and so is most autobiography. But I am concerned with a more tangled business than selection. I want to show a contemporary man in relation to the state and social usage, and the social organism in relation to that man.

The New Machiavelli.

The above quotation reveals the fact that by the time he wrote *The New Machiavelli* Wells had heard from Henry James. The two, indeed, had long been friends; and James was full of admiration (but never quite of approval) for the younger master. By now, James, Joseph Conrad, and Ford Madox Hueffer had all brought the gospel of art into Wells's life. They had all groped for the precise word with which to express the finest shade of thought and feeling and drama. But while Wells was rather impressed with the men and their gospel, his response to the cajolery of the artists was only fitful, and at last became less a response than an impatience. He wanted to write well. He had written well. The writing of *The Time Machine*, for example, is full of quality. He had been quick to see and praise the talent of Conrad; he respected James; he must have been entertained—who has not been?—by Hueffer. But what he wanted to do was to get *himself* upon paper; and the search for words and phrases that should have just so much value and meaning (kinetic and potential in Arthur Ransome's phrase), and not a hairbreadth more or less, seemed to him a waste of valuable energy and time. Where did it lead?

Furthermore, he was not interested—he never had been interested—in the novel of situation. All James's relish for situation, and all the delicacy of James's poise in dealing with situation, left Wells wondering why on earth any man should think it worth his while to tell so feeble a story at such length, and with such gloating. It was life, the life about him, in the busy streets, and in the little houses he had known, and in offices and laboratories and committee rooms all over the world, that had value for his mind. And even then only value in respect of what was being done with it all, and how the people were planning their lives and work, and making false steps and adjusting themselves to new jobs and new exciting conditions. When there was so much real life, and when so much needed voicing and changing, how could one sit down to write a made story, with however great a finesse?

Once he had finished *Kipps*, Wells was done with fairy stories. He had no longer any need of them. In his own case, the story had come true. He was at the height of his powers, and his reputation was tremendous. His success was popular and unquestioned. And about him was this intricate and absorbing world of workers and employers, inventors and politicians, and a new generation of free-thinking men and women who were none of these things, and business men and advertisers and newspaper proprietors, and graft, and drudgery, and exploitation, and opportunity, all waiting to be expressed, all waiting to be

used as material for fiction.   By 1908, so far as any man can be
said to do such a thing, Wells was living more fully in the life of
his day, and was more generally informed as to all its ramifica-
tions, than any other English novelist has ever been.   No wonder
Tono-Bungay is such a full book.

But, to return to the art of the novel, nothing but a full book
could have served the purpose of this one.   To use an artificial
story would have been to waste all sorts of material in which
Wells was deeply interested.   Moreover any visitor to Wells's
library will notice one row of books which bears all the signs of
constant reading: it is the row of Dickens's novels.   There can
be no doubt at all that when he began to plan *Tono-Bungay*
Wells thought *David Copperfield* was a very great novel indeed.
He used the form of the pseudo-autobiography with deliberation,
as the one in which most freedom was allowed for the introduc-
tion of innumerable details of contemporary life, and the one
in which such details could best be related to a select group
of characters and a milieu with which he was thoroughly acquainted.   'I want to show,' he said, 'a contemporary man in
relation to the state and social usage, and the social organism in
relation to that man.'   While we may wish that largeness of
conspectus could have been more intimately associated with
fineness of concept, we cannot without eccentricity deny to
Tono-Bungay its importance both as a social picture and as a
development in the craft of novel-writing.

Henry James did not deny either of these things.   Writing to
Wells about the second of the great pseudo-autobiographic
novels, *The New Machiavelli*, he said: 'I have read you then, I
need scarcely tell you, with an intensified sense of that life and
force and temperament, that fullness of endowment and easy
impudence of genius, which makes you extraordinary. . . .
Your big feeling for life, your capacity for chewing up the
thickness of the world in such enormous mouthfuls, while you
fairly slobber, so to speak, with the multitudinous taste—this
constitutes for me a rare and wonderful and admirable exhibition.'   But he added (and it is for the sake of the addition that
I quote this passage): 'I make remonstrance . . . bear upon the
bad service you have done your cause by riding so hard again
that accurst autobiographic form which puts a premium on the
loose, the improvized, the cheap and the easy. . . . There is, to my
vision, no authentic, and no really interesting and no *beautiful*,
report of things on the novelist's, the painter's part unless the
great stewpot or crucible of the imagination, of the observant

and recording and interpreting mind in short, has intervened and played its part—and this detachment, this chemical trans- mutation for the aesthetic, the representational, end is terribly wanting in autobiography brought, as the horrible phrase is, up to date.'

This criticism—for it must be admitted that James's mind was like the mills of God—sums up all or nearly all the objections to the Wellsian novel. The weakness of the method is better seen when one contemplates the repetitions or variations that followed *Tono-Bungay*. The stories told in these books are different; and yet the more they differ the more they emphati- cally remain the same story—the story of the man with a job to do, a marriage, an affair, a flight; the whole involved in a richly and consummately sketched chiaroscuro of the social and intellectual life of England between 1880 and 1930. *Tono- Bungay* is the best of these books because it was the first pressing of the grapes. It is a really amazing picture, furthermore, of the change that occurred in English life between the author's childhood and his maturity. It is contemporary history. Its vigour never fails; its detail, both domestic and social, is exact and sufficient. It is absorbingly interesting; it was a genuine attempt to present a modern man at something like full length in spite of every moral convention of the time.

It is also the best, however, because of another feature, not apparent in its successors: it is the only sociological novel of Wells's in which there are comic characters in any way to be compared with those in the humorous novels. He has always been most at ease in writing about poor and half-cultured people; he understands and loves the simple souls among them, and understands and loves rather less the cupidity, the inquisitive- ness, and the bad manners of the not so simple. They are, as it were, in the hollow of his hand. He perceives the significance of every gesture they make, and every glance they cast. He can be kind to them — sometimes mercilessly kind — ribald, indulgent without sentimentality, Dickensian and more than Dickensian because more economical in illustration, beautifully suggestive in phonetics or in phrase. In dealing with poor people he is an artist. Personally, I think that in this field he has no equal.

X

Fashions change more quickly than manners, manners more quickly than morals, morals more quickly than passions, and, in general, the conscious, reasonable, intellectual life more quickly than the instinctive, wilful, affectionate one. The dramatist who deals with the irony and humour of the relatively durable sides of life, or with their pity and terror, is the one whose comedies and tragedies will last longest. . . . Fashionable dramatists begin to 'date,' as the critics call it, in a few years.

G. B. SHAW, *Dramatic Opinions.*

Between them, Shaw and Wells have done more than any other writers to create what may be called the modern attitude towards morals and civilization in general. Not towards aesthetics, because for both of them art has been of less urgent importance than the propagation of ideas and opinions. Each has stood upon his rostrum and said: 'You're all wrong. You have a world in which there is disease, poverty, dishonesty, and a huge mass of filth and corruption. The way in which you are to cure this is not the way of religion as it is taught in any church, or by any existing party in the political world; it is the way of common sense, determination, and a planned future. If you want a better world, you must will it. Believe in no more humbug: it is all about you, and it is ruining the earth. I will show you that most of your accepted ideas are humbug, and I will mock at those ideas or flout them, so that they will be seen of no worth. I will show you what men are, and what they might be if only they would make up their minds to work for a better and wiser world in which all could share in the rewards of that wisdom and that improvement.'

And so, while Shaw laughed sentimentality and romance off the stage in his plays, and teased the English for their slowness and pomposity and self-infatuation, and made parents ridiculous and only the young wise and bold, and demanded a new aristocracy of supermen, Wells, ever more impatient of levity than Shaw (whom he once, as a young man, described as 'giddy'), looked ahead and planned a clean and orderly future in which certainly there would be no place for Shaw's unnecessary beard and Shaw's irrepressible, irrelevant brilliance, and celebrated the new youth and the open conspiracy to revolutionize the world, and demanded a new intellectual aristocracy of Samurai who would lead mankind by way of 'love and fine thinking.' And the chief thing about both of them was that they addressed millions of men and women never before educated by the State by way of plays and novels which all could hear and read with delight. In this lay their novelty. There had been novelist-teachers before Wells, but none with his grasp of general ideas coupled with scientific training and the eager brilliance of his invention and improvisation. Other dramatists before Shaw had dared to be outspoken (but that was long ago), and had shown the world as something in which not all was love and adultery; but there had been none to whom blue books were child's play and the English simultaneously a laughing-stock. Ideas, ideas, ideas, they were in the heads of all the young Edwardians and early Georgians. Shaw and Wells, Wells and Shaw; Chesterton and Belloc and Wells and Shaw—the seeds of disbelief in accepted morals and manners were sown by Wells and Shaw, while Belloc and Chesterton fought a gallant but losing fight against the forces of science and economics, machinery and the future, incandescence and destruction.

I say 'destruction,' for Wells and Shaw had need to be destroyers. 'Let it burn,' says Caesar in *Caesar and Cleopatra.* And when Theodotus cries wildly: 'Will you destroy the past?' he answers: 'Ay, and build the future with its ruins.' It may be that the future will be built upon the ruins left by Shaw, and that it will resemble the future planned by Wells—this remains to be seen; but it is the case, and naturally the case, that the generations influenced by the two men should first of all seize upon what was destructive in their philosophies. The young, having learnt from Shaw that their parents were fools, proceeded to treat them as fools. The young, having learnt from Wells that young people should be bravely and nobly free from restraint, became, as they believed, bravely and nobly free from restraint. To humility in face of all authority succeeded conscious defiance of every authority. To the hypocrisy of romantic virtue succeeded the pretence of frank, honest sincerity which is such a nuisance to others when it is paraded. I do not think Shaw likes the new freedom. He may do so; but I do not think he likes it. He is himself too fastidious to care for the spiritual vulgarities of the current hour, and he has cried out against them. But that he first spread in influential form the ideas upon which they are based I have no doubt whatever. I do not think Wells likes the new and self-constituted intellectual aristocracy. He may do so; but it has a very aristocratic manner, and is not so much leading mankind to wise freedom as trying to corral it for the political ends of slavery; so that I cannot suppose him content. But that he first spread in influential form the ideas upon which this new intellectual aristocracy has consciously based itself I have no doubt whatever.

CHAPTER IV: CATHOLIC LIBERALISM

I

They looked backwards to old enlightenment and forwards to
new prejudices. . . . They hoped—but it may be said that they
hoped for yesterday.

G. K. CHESTERTON, *A Short History of England.*

I HAVE called this chapter 'Catholic Liberalism'; but indeed
that is a mere label, for I propose to speak of Belloc and Chesterton, not as Catholics or Liberals, or as Catholic Liberals or
Liberal Catholics, but only as writers. If I felt I could do so
without impertinence, I should use that name, 'The Chester-
belloc,' which Shaw invented to cover the common identity of
the two; but while there are many liberties I will allow myself
there is one, the use of a stranger's Christian or nickname, which
I feel bound to leave to the less squeamish. The truth is that
I have no personal acquaintance whatever with these two
ornaments of our age.

Probably young people now can hardly imagine how Shaw,
Wells, Chesterton, and Belloc stood out from their fellows
and argued among themselves for the enlightenment of extraordinarily mixed audiences. Wells, being no speaker, largely
contented himself with printed argument; the others were as
happy face to face as they were in column. Sometimes Shaw
would debate with Chesterton, and sometimes with Belloc:
once, I recall, he debated with Chesterton while Belloc took the
chair and rang an infuriating bell; upon another occasion he met
Belloc in the large Queen's Hall, when an audience of three
thousand people heard these two discuss the question whether
a Democrat who was not also a Socialist could possibly be a
Gentleman, and came away with the problem unsolved after
two hours of resolute hard hitting. The admiration between
these men was not that of the literary nest, but that of the
battlefield or the ring; and I think it fair to say that if any one
of them wrote or spoke of another it was as an opponent whose
nose at all costs must be struck and struck hard. This was
especially true of Belloc; for while all felt a tenderness for
Chesterton, none—engaged in a battle for self-preservation—
had the smallest tenderness for Belloc, and none, certainly,
received quarter at his hands.

One reason for the love of Chesterton was that while he fought he sang lays of chivalry and in spite of all his seriousness warred against wickedness rather than a fleshly opponent, while Belloc sang only after the battle, and warred against men as well as ideas, for the love of fighting and the pleasure he took in what might be called the deployment of the intellect. Another was that Chesterton could be distracted by a joke or an absurdity, whether it occurred to his own mind or to the mind of his foe, while Belloc was a master of the divagation or parenthesis, and never lost his place in an argument. But a third, and very important, reason was that it was often supposed that Chesterton might have been convinced if only Belloc had not stiffened him with recalcitrance. As the front legs of a performing horse are supposed to be the leaders (for Front-Legs works the head and ears), so in the monstrous animal conjured up by Shaw's conception of the Chester-belloc Belloc had the teeth and claws, while the warm and jovial heart belonged to Chesterton. The public said 'G. B. S.' and 'G. K. C.': it said neither H. B. nor H. G. W.

Belloc's aggressiveness may have been due to the fact that he had served in the French artillery before ever he went to the university; or it may have been due to the fact that his college at Oxford was Balliol, which at that time—I know nothing of the present day—produced men deeply assured of their own superiority to other men; or it may have been due to the fact that he is a casuist, to whom the views of others are the mere rough material for destructive analysis. Whatever the cause, however, he was a most disconcerting and angering opponent, who had ever an impudent answer for hecklers and a severe thrust for the one who stood nearest upon the platform. These were a few—by no means all—of the differences between Chesterton and Belloc as they were seen by those who disagreed with both; and they will serve to introduce us to some details of the life of the elder and more pugnacious of the two.

II

'No,' said I, 'I have no land, and not even the power of which you speak. I am really, though moderately, poor. All that I get I earn by talking in public places in the cold weather, and in springtime and summer by writing and by other tricks.'

H. BELLOC, *Esto Perpetua*.

Joseph Hilaire Pierre Belloc was born on 27th July 1870, at La Celle, Saint-Cloud, a suburb of Paris. He was the son of a

French barrister, Louis Swanton Belloc; and his mother was Bessie Rayner Parkes, daughter of Joseph Parkes, an English politician and the historian of the Chancery Bar of England. I do not know at what date Belloc left France for the first time; but he was educated at the Oratory School, Birmingham (a city in which his maternal ancestor, Joseph Priestley, was once a dissenting minister).   On leaving school he served as a driver in the 8th Regiment of Artillery at Toul, Meurthe-et-Moselle, and when he left the service in 1892 he went to Oxford.   At Oxford he became a Brackenbury History Scholar, and in his final History Schools in 1895 he took first class honours.   That is a fact which should be kept in mind.

He published his first book, a collection of verses, in 1895, and in the two following years he enriched the literature of nonsense with *The Bad Child's Book of Beasts* and *More Beasts for Worse Children*.   He then revealed another gift with a book called *The Modern Traveller*, and began that series of historical and biographical studies which forms his greatest contribution to library catalogues with books on Danton and Robespierre.   In 1902 he became a naturalized British subject.   In 1904 he published the first of his satiric novels, *Emmanuel Burden*.   In 1906 he not only acted as chief book reviewer for *The Morning Post*, but was elected Liberal M.P. for South Salford.   Four years later, although unsupported by party funds, he again won an election for the same constituency (this time as an independent candidate), but in the second election of 1910 he refused to stand, and from that time has had no further connection with official politics.   His work on *The Morning Post* ceased in 1910; his most important political book, *The Servile State*, was published in 1912; and for two years (1911-13) he was head of the English literature department at the East London College.

At the outbreak of the European War he acted as commentator upon military operations for *Land and Water*, and thus perhaps for the first time impressed the large reading public with his extraordinary powers of lucid communication.   Week by week a sceptical and badly shaken public read Belloc and was re-converted to faith by his unfaltering certainty, his logic, and a literary skill in that department second to none.   'However powerful, native, sympathetic to his hearer's mood or cogently provable by reference to new things may be a man's idea,' said Belloc in 1889, 'he cannot persuade his fellow-men to it if he have not words to express it.   And he will persuade them more and more in proportion as his words are well chosen and in the right order, such order being determined by the genius of the language whence they are drawn.' Belloc himself persuaded the British public not only by the genius of their language but by the genius with which he used it. He gave them a weekly draught of new life, new clarity, new nerve. The war period was the period in which his influence stood at its highest point.

III

I still have very clearly in memory the appearance of Belloc as I first saw him. He must have been slightly over thirty, not very tall but very broad-shouldered and with that fine head cocked at its usual considering angle. He bent over a small table, smiling, his big white shirt-front bulging; and he surveyed the congregated Fabians as if they were simple-minded children to whom he was unfolding the wonders of the universe. In fact he was explaining, among other things, with much salt, a few of the fallacies which lay fatally behind the principles of their own movement. He was confident, gay, rich in lively asides or extravagant alternative phrases. He made everybody laugh— that was intended—as his tongue played with the words of triumphant ridicule; and having made them laugh he slew them. Never was there such a Fabian slaughter.

I recall him at another time, also at a Fabian meeting (and a public one, for I was never a Fabian), speaking rather quietly, and somehow less confidently, at the Memorial Hall in Farringdon Street. I think he had been severely attacked at a previous meeting: at any rate he had papers with him, and may have been reading or carefully speaking from notes. And so low did he hold his head that somebody, hoping to disconcert him, called from the back of the hall: 'Speak up!' There was a hush at the interrupter's cheek; but Belloc, lifting his head, only smiled, and like lightning answered the affront. The fluty French voice, rather high-pitched but never otherwise than pure and fluent; the French 'r' that is very nearly a 'w'; the arrogance which his former modest demeanour had concealed—all rose. He called out: 'It's all wight: I'm only talking to myself.' The interrupter's brief advantage was destroyed; and the lecture proceeded with increased animation on the speaker's part.

Belloc is no longer the same young and triumphant man of those early days. He is stouter, more preoccupied. The keenness of his face has roughened, and his colour is deeper. Having grown small side-whiskers, he would look like John Bull if he did not look like a French parish priest. His black cloak and low-crowned black felt hat increase the priestly effect, and I do not think that Belloc has ever lost pride in the fact that he was born a Frenchman; but there is none the less a good English look to him which also, I hope, he would not disclaim.   He is more considerate of fools than he used to be.   He reads Trollope at nights, and spends much time at his home in Sussex, where he writes more histories and biographies in praise of the Catholic Church, but no more accounts of his journeys in France or North Africa or of the Four Men who made such songs of good wine and good ale and the Sussex inns.   Alas that it should be so!

IV

If you cannot find him, and Fleet Street looks lonely and forsaken, then be sure he has been spirited away to some solitary place by his wife, the keeper of his business conscience, to finish a book for which some publisher is angrily clamouring.   For 'No clamour, no book,' is his maxim.

A. G. GARDINER, Prophets, Priests, and Kings.

Gilbert Keith Chesterton's life corresponded with Belloc's in no particular.   He was not born a Catholic; he became a convert.   He was not born in France, but in the London district of Kensington, which is as much associated in the popular mind with respectability as Chelsea and Bloomsbury are associated with aesthetic affectation or Tooting with the inexplicable gibes of professional humorists.   He was born in 1874.   He went to St Paul's School, London, and did not go to a university.   Nor did he engage in any military training; but instead attended classes at the Slade School, tried office life without success, and first began writing for the press by reviewing books on art for Robertson Nicoll's monthly magazine *The Bookman*.   From reviewing books on art he passed to reviewing books upon all subjects; and in 1900, when he was twenty-six, he passed from reviewing books to publishing them.

The earliest title-pages to bear his name were those of *The Wild Knight*, a collection of poems which included a poetic drama notable for its brevity, and *Greybeards at Play*, a collection of rhymes inscribed to 'E. C. B.' (long subsequently, of course, the author of *Trent's Last Case*) after this fashion:

He was, through boyhood's storm and shower,
  My best, my nearest friend;
We wore one hat, smoked one cigar,
  One standing at each end.

These books were followed in the autumn of 1901 by a collection of reprinted essays called *The Defendant*; and from that time Chesterton was what is called an author, in contradistinction to a journalist. But he remained a journalist to the end of his life. Many of his books are made up of material which has first appeared in periodicals. Others were written because publishers insisted. His journalism was never absent from the London press, and it remained to the last months of his life as vigorous as ever it had been. To his constant lecturing I have already referred. What profligate expenditure of energy for one who was born a poet!

It was in *The Daily News*, when that paper was edited by A. G. Gardiner, that Chesterton made his earliest reputation. He used to write in its columns upon all manner of books and other pretexts. A single sentence would be enough to set him at work with an antithesis or proposition that brought the stars into Fleet Street and light into many dark places. Gardiner, his former editor, in an affectionate sketch printed in *Prophets, Priests, and Kings*, pictures the young journalist as he was in those days. 'You may track him,' said Gardiner, 'by the blotting-pads he decorates with his riotous fancies, and may come up with him in the midst of a group of children, for whom he is drawing hilarious pictures, or to whom he is revealing the wonders of his toy theatre, the chief child of his fancy and invention, or whom he is instructing in the darkly mysterious game of "Guyping," which will fill the day with laughter. "Well," said the aunt to the little boy who had been to tea with Mr Chesterton, "well, Frank, I suppose you have had a very instructive afternoon?" "I don't know what that means," said Frank, "but, oh!"—with enthusiasm—"you should see Mr Chesterton catch buns with his mouth."'

Charles Masterman, another friend, and one who in old days was as inseparably linked with Belloc and Chesterton as Athos himself was linked with Porthos and the priestly Aramis, has told me how Chesterton used to sit writing his articles in a Fleet Street café, sampling and mixing a terrible conjunction of drinks, while many waiters hovered about him, partly in awe, and partly in case he should leave the restaurant without paying for what he had had. One day—I do not know whether Chesterton was present or absent—the head waiter approached Masterman. 'Your friend,' he whispered admiringly, 'he very clever man. He sit and laugh. And then he write. And then he laugh at what he write.' It has always been essential to Chesterton that he should be amused by what he wrote, and by what he said in public. I have heard him laugh so much at a debate that he gave himself hiccups for the rest of the evening.

In early days he was very nearly as big as he afterwards became, but whereas in mature years his much-thinned hair straggled untidily, like a blown wisp of steam, it was then solid and well brushed. A feature of it was a Whistlerian white plume in the centre; and anybody who sees an old photograph of Chesterton will there find the plume as neat and trim as brush could make it. Presently he grew more like Porthos; and then like Dr Johnson; and at last like that portrait by Velasquez of Don Alessandro del Borro which is at present to be seen in Berlin. His gigantic aspect became a matter of common reference. The story of the man who gave up his seat to three ladies was associated with him. Finally a serious illness contracted his figure and forced him to live less strenuously than he had done. He went to Beaconsfield, in Buckinghamshire; and there he lived until his death, blind to the greatness of Disraeli, who took the name of the town as his title when he became a lord, but by no means blind to the forces of tyranny and the mischiefs wrought in the modern world by stupidity and exactitude.

Upon the public platform he swayed his large bulk from side to side; but he did not gesticulate. His speech was prefaced and accompanied by a curious sort of humming, such as one may hear when glee singers give each other the note before starting to sing. He pronounced the word 'I' (without egotism) as if it were 'Ayee,' and drawled, not in the highly gentlemanly manner which Americans believe to be the English accent, and which many Englishmen call the Oxford accent, but in a manner peculiar to himself and either attractive or the reverse according to one's taste (to me attractive). As he talked, and as he invented amusing fancies, he punctuated his talk with little breathless grunts or last gasps of laughter, so that he gave the impression—what with the drawl and the breathless grunts—of speaking very slowly indeed. He also gave the impression of speaking without any effort whatever, without raising his voice, or becoming intimidated by his audience or by lack of material to fill the time allotted to him, or feeling anything but sweet charity towards all those—even Jews, politicians, and sophisticates — whom he felt compelled to denounce. To those, accordingly, who care more for character than for opinion, more for talent than for fashion, Chesterton remains one of the great figures of our time. For the rest, and for those easily made impatient by his habit—they call it 'trick'—of antithesis, he was merely an ingenious and snort-provoking creature. He certainly lived behind the times; but whether that is a sin or only a misfortune I shall not now attempt to determine.

v

The explanation of the progressive failure of Belloc and Chesterton to impress younger sceptics is that both were forced by faith to become, in a sense, defendants. They attacked the trend of modern society towards mechanization as severely as any other writers whatsoever. But they did so from the stand-point of the Catholic Church. They said that the world was in a very bad way; but they both insisted that it was once—in the Middle Ages—in a very good way. Belloc, in a really masterly short work called *The Servile State*, published in 1912, established the fact that slavery is a familiar condition of European life. It is his argument that slavery was destroyed by Christianity, and that until the end of the Middle Ages, it had ceased to exist in the West. He believes, and so did Chesterton, that all the ills of modern England arise from what followed the dissolution of the monasteries by King Henry the Eighth. If Henry, says Belloc, had done as he intended, and kept in his own hands—the hands of the Crown—the property taken from the clerical body, the country would have had a happy future. Henry was not strong enough to keep his appropriations; he found the rich men of his day too powerful for him, and was forced to hand over the greater part of the spoils. Hence the violent inequality of wealth and power in England out of which grew from the sixteenth century onwards the evils of Capitalism. Hence, in process of time, the inevitability of the servile state, to which all parties by one path or another have led and will lead the people of England.

It is not my business to comment upon the truth or otherwise of this theory; but there can be no question as to the clearness and power of the book in which it is outlined. And there can be no doubt, I think, that possession of such a view of history has prevented Belloc and Chesterton from capturing the imagination of generations increasingly influenced by scientific and mechanical theory and practice. It is one thing to say that the world is wrong—every reformer agrees that the world is wrong—but when, instead of proceeding to say that the world can be set right by something new, a man says that it can only be set right by a return to something old, he is thrown into a defence of the past. And the past, as Chesterton admitted, is no easy subject. 'I can make the future as narrow as myself; the past is obliged to be as broad and turbulent as humanity.' Both Belloc and Chesterton have had to rewrite history for purposes of propaganda amid incessant interruptions both from dryas-dusts and from ribalds who have not believed a word of what they say. Men who attack the present are always sure of support; men who contrast the present with the delights of an improved future society may be scorned as unpractical idealists, but they cannot be confounded by texts or refutations; men who insist that at some past time an ideal state existed may be challenged by the proven inability of that ideal state to with-stand aggression, and they will certainly be floored by extracts from some old charter or pipe roll or antique letter which de-molishes the whole structure they have so ingeniously erected.

That is what has happened to Belloc and Chesterton. Belloc deliberately, and Chesterton with misgiving, have set up a version—in Belloc's case a series of detailed versions—of what happened in England long ago. It has not been accepted by Protestants, scientific historians, or sceptics. Belloc has gone farther. He has told us in several books how the French Revolution arose, succeeded, and failed (the early chapters of his *Danton* give the clearest exposition of the events preceding the Revolution which I have ever read, but I do not know if they are reliable); he has in one book of *Miniatures of French History* told us what must have happened in France at various crucial points from 599 B.C. to A.D. 1914. He has traced the history of warfare in England. His mind has played over the entire history of Europe, and he has expressed himself as to that history with a certainty and I imagine a consistency which ought to have satisfied every reader. But he has not satisfied every reader. Every reader can relish the style in which Belloc tells his story; but every reader, in spite of the charm and certainty of the narrative, feels that Belloc is a partisan, bent upon proving a case. It is nothing new in historical writing; if the case is the popular case it will be swallowed gladly; but when it conflicts with the case as presented by every Whig and Protestant historian, or with the case as overwhelmingly demonstrated by the ironist Gibbon, it is suspect from the start.

Now Belloc adores Froissart. He owes much to the gar-gantuan historical method of Rabelais. He believes that legends and ballads are better authorities than pipe rolls. He has used his imagination in describing battles (for which he has a peculiar gift and fondness), political intrigues, and religious and economic influences as to which there are or are not written records. The results have been controversial. I need not dwell upon the horrid pursuit of A. F. Pollard whenever Belloc writes upon the Tudors; nor upon that description of the campaign of Evesham in 1265 for which he gave as his chief authority the chronicle of Matthew Paris, who died in 1259. All I need say is that in a scientific period a man who sets out to prove upon general philosophical grounds that such and such events must have been caused in such and such a way, and in that only, must expect to be challenged by all to whom his major premiss seems arbitrary. And that a man who writes history as if it had just happened under his eyes, in a scene as familiar to him as the palm of his hand, and for the glory of the Catholic Church, must expect to be smothered with dust brought directly from the Record Office.

VI

I am sure that most of us would find the Middle Ages an occasion for—it is the 'modn' word—disgust, if we were transported back into them. Belloc would not do so. Belloc, it seems to me, would have been a very happy man if he had been born in the days when disputatious scholars went from university to university upon the Continent and argued for their bread. He still has the hardiness to sail his own boat across the English Channel in a fog; and a life that gives him wine to drink, brains to test, and a soul to shrive will ever be a good life for him. Chesterton I see as one less hardy, but as one, nevertheless, to whom eating and drinking and good talk were as well conducted from the floor as from a modern chair. Neither Belloc nor Chesterton ever had anything of the funereal sleekness of the 'modn' aesthete, the silence, the self-engrossed aloofness, the lack of good fellowship, the pinched assumption that humour is not humour unless it is concerned with sexual symbols. Yet neither Belloc nor Chesterton ever had the dreary boisterousness of the boon companion. Each was born an original.

When Belloc wrote *The Path to Rome* he was following a recognized literary road—the writer of charm going alone upon a trip among strange people, laughing, learning, and then posing a little before the world. Stevenson had done just such a walk through the Cévennes, and his book about the journey had greatly pleased the sentimentalists. Earlier in history, Laurence

Sterne had also told the story of his travels in France rather better than Stevenson, and had pleased even those who were not sentimentalists. And so Belloc knew what he was doing when he took this path and set down his account of what happened to him *en route*. But, miraculously, he avoided sentimentality; there was in him a certain robust and boyish courage and simplicity which, although he could chaff the reader and at times do a little bragging of one sort or another, gave *The Path to Rome* a character of its own. It remains Belloc's best long book, and the one by which most of his admirers would wish him first to be known. It is a tale of dangers run, and fears acknowledged, of hours enlivened by nonsense and accidentally good or evil meals. It is a chronicle of moods, a picture of mountains and forests and small towns, a traveller's tale, an enchanting monologue, and anything else the reader fancies. And it is the early work of a man who could already do anything he wished with his pen.

That, indeed, is one of Belloc's weaknesses—that he has always been so much a master of his pen. He has been too versatile for the mind of the public that prefers repetition. And furthermore it has sometimes been difficult to discover at what point the serious Belloc yields to the extravagant Belloc; for in the grand manner which he often uses an able and humour-filled writer must often check himself sharply lest he guy his own grandeur. Let any reader take Belloc at his most serious, and then turn to his satirical novel, *Emmanuel Burden*: it will be found that *Emmanual Burden* contains passages, despite its satirical character, which strongly resemble Belloc at his most serious, and barely exceed the sonorousness of his more rhetorical mood. That does not happen in so finished and consummate a work of irony as *The Mercy of Allah*, of course; but *The Mercy of Allah* is extremely mature, whereas *Emmanuel Burden*, being experimental, shows the author's mind more fitfully playing between anger and pity, and reveals the danger to a stylist of the power to burlesque all styles, including his own.

Even so, Belloc is a more persistent and sustained writer than Chesterton, who was best in short flights. To take one single work of his as an example, *The Flying Inn* is a laborious and aimless extravaganza, spoiled by the author's inability to keep upon one plane and by his uncertainty as to the particular plane he is occupying. But the lyrics in it, and single episodes or paragraphs where inspiration has caught up the pen and made it caper, are sufficient to make *The Flying Inn* a book known to every man of humour in England. It would seem to have been an effort upon Chesterton's part to write a modern Peacockian novel; but his was a rambling wit and not an incisive one, and the resemblance between *The Flying Inn* and the scholarly Peacock's *Melincourt* is in favour of the older book in all except the poetical passages.

But if we compare a book such as *The Flying Inn* with the volumes of Father Brown stories we can see how admirably the Chestertonian genius is fitted to colour with magic the slightest tale. Whether we observe how a crime can be committed by a postman because nobody sees a postman (or any other quite familiar figure) entering a block of flats; or hear the steps of the tall man who is the guest to the waiters and a waiter to the guests and uses his opportunity to steal all the fish knives and forks of the 'Twelve True Fishermen'; or imagine the velocity of a hammer flung from a church tower upon a villain below, we are taken entirely away from the world we live in and into a world of dreams and strangeness. And we are taken, not because the events are strange in themselves, but because the author mesmerizes us with the aid of the genius which he conceals up his sleeve. It is the literary genius, and nothing else, which effects the mesmerism; for the charm of *The Hammer of God*, for example, would vanish if the story were told by any other writer.

These two men have exhibited greater skill in dialectical writing than any of their contemporaries excepting Shaw. They have both enjoyed the gift of writing with peculiar simplicity and beauty, and the utmost clearness. But when it comes to what they have written, it must be said that Belloc is governed by his passion for propositions; and that Chesterton was governed by his passion for antithesis. Belloc says 'I shall show; I shall prove; I shall establish.' He will show that the French Revolution turned upon and was conditioned by its military history. He will prove that Robespierre, a weak man, did not create the Terror, but resisted it and was unwillingly driven by others. He will establish that the dissolution of the monasteries in England in the sixteenth century was the beginning of the industrial revolution and the Capitalist system. But he will not convince us about the French Revolution or about Robespierre or about the dissolution of the monasteries for at least three reasons. The first of these reasons is that we already hold other views (the basis for which he ignores in spite of all clamour) as to the events; the second reason is that his style, being authoritative, is unfitted for persuasion; and the third reason is that despite every ingenuity he is unable in the communications he makes to fulfil the promise he has given. The third reason is the fatal reason.

Chesterton in the same way made propositions; but they were less peremptory and less serious than Belloc's. He did not say 'I shall show.' He said: 'There is one metaphor of which the moderns are very fond; they are always saying, "You can't put the clock back." The simple and obvious answer is "You can." . . . There is another proverb, "As you have made your bed, so you must lie on it"; which again is simply a lie. If I have made my bed uncomfortable, please God I will make it again.' But nobody, reading these remarks, can fail to make sufficient retorts to them; and the soundness of Chesterton's opinion is lost in a fritter of nonsense.

Now what can we do about such men? All who enjoy debate and the flexible use of thought and language must delight in their adroitness. All who can stand outside the stream of current opinion must observe how many ideas of virtue and value continually appear in their work. But when all is turmoil, as it is to-day, it is too much to expect that the occupants of a back-water will receive any acknowledgment of their literary genius. They may even be regarded as old gentlemen doing whatever is the nautical equivalent of fiddling while Rome burns. For this reason I think it will not be until Belloc and Chesterton have been dead for half a century that their gifts — finally separated for ever from their views and resistances — will again be fully realized and acknowledged. How great those gifts are, in my opinion, could only be stated in terms which would seem at this time extravagant.

CHAPTER V: FANCY FAIR

I

VENABLES. . . . You Scots, Mrs Shand, are such a mixture of the practical and the emotional that you escape out of an Englishman's hand like a trout.

What Every Woman Knows.

IT cannot have escaped the notice of those who have been commended by Desmond MacCarthy as 'alert, original men and women' that, so far, the only true-born Englishman to find a place in this book is H. G. Wells. I emphasize the fact, however, in view of constant generalizations as to the English character. We began our sketch of the Georgian literary scene with an American who became an Englishman only at the end of his life. We then continued with an Irishman and two men who are half-French. As the chapters follow, it will be found that an extraordinary number of English writers are Americans, Frenchmen, Scotsmen, Irishmen, Welshmen, Jews, South Africans, Australasians, and Poles. Let us look at our first Scotsman.

I suppose that Scottish invaders are outnumbered by the Irish, but I have not counted the two classes, and I must not stay to do so. The most celebrated Scots authors, apart from two kings who belong to earlier times, have been Hume, Adam Smith, Smollett, Boswell, Burns, Scott, Carlyle, Macaulay, Susan Ferrier, Dr John Brown, William Black, and R. L. Stevenson; and it must be admitted, I think, that with the exception of Boswell all these writers—some of them very wrongly—are at the present moment estimated less highly than they have been in the past. Hume is never read; Adam Smith (whose economics are too simple for our intricate days) has received his quietus; Smollett has always been underrated, except by Robertson Nicoll; Burns as an original writer was rather blown upon in the Henley-Henderson edition of his works; Scott, to my horror, is found dull; Carlyle, that admirable dramatist and rhetorician, has been daubed with the stigma of sexual chilliness or worse, and has been buried in a six-volume biography; Macaulay is the most traduced genius in English literature, since every Jack-in-the-box feels safe in accusing him of mud-slinging; William Black (although Justin McCarthy once witheringly dismissed Hardy as his inferior) and Susan Ferrier are alike forgotten; and

Stevenson is waiting for Robert Lynd to set him on his legs again. The truth is that Scotland is out of the literary fashion.

That does not mean, of course, that Scottish authors remain unread. But it does mean that their names are less freely canvassed than of old. For one thing, ours is a day when reserves are suspect; and we have it on the authority of a Scots writer that whereas 'the bolder Englishman (I am told) will write a love-chapter and then go out, quite coolly, to dinner, such goings-on are contrary to the Scotch nature; even the great novelists dared not. Conceive Mr Stevenson left alone with a hero, a heroine, and a proposal impending (he does not know where to look). Sir Walter in the same circumstances gets out of the room by making his love scene take place between the end of one chapter and the beginning of the next.' But that is only half the story. The Scots, being fundamentally sensual people, who would go raging mad if they allowed free rein to their emotions, long ago imposed severe restraints upon themselves, and became grave, cold, and haughty. Their domestic affections have always been strong; between those affections and the world they have interposed a barrier of pride and silence. This defence is rarely pierced from without; but, from within, the old Scottish character may be said to leak in a kind of superficial tenderness and sentiment.

Furthermore, there is a complacency about the Scots which is curiously combined with modesty. It is less objectionable to others than Yorkshire and Lancashire self-satisfaction, because it goes quietly deeper. Some men are troubled at the thought that others may be cleverer than they; the Scotsman has no such qualms. If he is humourless, it does not occur to him; if he is humorous, he has such playfulness of mind and such ingenuity of tongue that the problem is immediately dissolved and dispersed. Self-righteous the Scots may be, and it is a fault; but they are among the few people in the world who perceive and are amused by their own complacency, and who make jokes about it for the amusement of others. If they also stuff their emotions into the dark cupboard of the mind, and laugh and cry over the few remnants which have escaped concealment, we who are not Scotsmen can always bring our ever-ready contempt to the scene and dismiss the Scots as thrifty sentimentalists who make fortunes out of these by-products.

It was Stevenson who began the last Scottish revival. He told the world about a little Scots boy, and about a young man travelling about the world and charming everybody, and about the delights of make-believe; and in his hands Caledonia did not seem so stern and wild as had been supposed. It seemed a place where delightful children fancifully played in bed, or by the fireside, or out upon the hills; and English readers, who are always made to cry by anything about Ireland, thought that Scotland was nearly as touching, and somehow less harrowing and melodramatic than the sister isle. So at the end of the eighteen-eighties booksellers could not circulate tales of Scottish life fast enough to please their eager patrons. At that time Augustine Birrell wrote in a weekly review that 'what has happened so often before is happening now. Everybody is reading *A Window in Thrums* and *Auld Licht Idylls*. The instantaneous popularity of these two books,' continued A. B., 'is a beautiful thing. It is Faith's Restorative, for if it does not annihilate the doctrine of the Universal Depravity of the Human Race, it goes a long way to justify a belief in their Final Restoration. The author has conceded nothing to the public taste. May he never do so! Of sentiment, that odious onion, not a trace is to be found in these sweet-smelling pages.'

A Window in Thrums and *Auld Licht Idylls* were not the only Scottish tales of that era; but they were the first essays in a new kind of book that immediately became the rage. They made Scotland not only charming but quaint. They enjoyed the applause of such pundits as Birrell, who as you have seen thought them free from sentiment; and they went nevertheless directly home to the bosoms of men and women who judged with their hearts. And the author of these two books, who, without expecting to do so, had set a new fashion and created a new literary genre—the 'kail-yard' or cabbage-patch novel—was a very small, quiet, pale Scots journalist named J. M. Barrie. He was unknown in London, not yet thirty years of age, the first Scotsman to take the town since Stevenson. And although there were soon imitators of the new fashion who drove it at last into commonplace, Barrie himself went on to show that he had learnt more at his mother's knee than old memories of Thrums.

II. JAMES MATTHEW BARRIE

The horror of my boyhood was that I knew a time would come when I must give up the games, and how it was to be done I saw not. . . . I felt that I must continue playing in secret.

Margaret Ogilvy.

James Matthew Barrie was born at Kirriemuir, Forfarshire, on 9th May 1860. He was his parents' second son, but his elder brother died while Barrie was very small, and from that time Barrie was the apple of the family eye. Kirriemuir was a tiny place; the Barries were poor; and the little boy had plenty of occasion for story-making. He was quick to imagine himself any kind of character he created in his fancy; and that is a habit which lasted well into late life, for in his last years he often spoke to audiences less as J. M. Barrie than as some ghost, or fantastic figure of the past, whose opinions for the time he appropriated. And he began to write stories before he was twelve years old. His first full-length novel was completed and offered to a publisher in the year before he went to Edinburgh University. It was rejected, with the assurance, nevertheless, that the author was 'a clever little lady.' That was a shock. For a time the impulse to write novels was checked.

But a literary life was the one for which Barrie pined; and as soon as he was able to do so he obtained a position as leader-writer on a Nottingham newspaper; and while he was there he began to send sketches, articles, and stories to the London press. It took him eighteen months to get his work accepted; but at last the first of the *Auld Licht Idylls* caught the attention of Frederick Greenwood, then editor of *The St James's Gazette*, who took it and asked for more. 'There came to me,' says Barrie, 'as unlooked for as a telegram, the thought that there was something quaint about my native place.'

Something quaint! That was exactly the key for which this talent was waiting. He hastened to get more and more memories of the Kirriemuir of past days from his mother. 'Now my mother might have been discovered, in answer to certain excited letters, flinging a bundle of undarned socks from her lap, and "going in for literature"; she was racking her brains, by request, for memories I might convert into articles, and they came to me in letters which she dictated to my sisters.' And when the articles had been published in sufficient number there arose the thought that they might be collected together into a book, and so make a bid for wider fame and fortune. *Auld Licht Idylls* was the result.

There was a slight difficulty about this, because publishers did not share the view of Frederick Greenwood as to the merits of the sketches of Scottish life. But at last a brother Scot, William Robertson Nicoll, a man whose nose for talent was to the end of his life uncannily sure, 'found a wy,' and the book was published. So was *A Window in Thrums*. So was *When a Man's Single*. And so, two years later, was *The Little Minister*. Now

The Little Minister differed from its predecessors in having a really old-fashioned and melodramatic story. It was a tremendous success; and it was dramatized, and had another tremendous success as a play. By this time Barrie had already begun to write original plays; and after Toole had produced one small skit on Ibsen which he had written he became the author of *Walker, London.* When a little over thirty he was well known both as novelist and dramatist, and equally successful in both fields. From that time forward he could do nothing but add and add and add to his fame. The novels ceased with *Tommy and Grizel* in 1900, although a few later pieces of fiction appeared. But the plays went on, from *The Professor's Love Story* in 1895; *Quality Street, The Admirable Crichton*, and *Little Mary* in 1903; and *Peter Pan* in 1904; to *Dear Brutus* in 1917, *Mary Rose* in 1920, and—a final flowering—*The Boy David* in 1936.

III

MYSELF. I had a letter the other day from an old friend of mine. She said: 'I don't envy you anything except knowing Barrie.'
BARRIE. [*Gravely.*] Then she'd better not meet him.

When he was a young man, portraits used to appear at times in the press which showed a little pale face, a tiny moustache, and an enormous brow. I am under the impression that in those days brows were worn high; and Barrie's was both high and broad. As time passed his face filled out and grew less pale, more full of character, more full of melancholy; and the brow somehow less conspicuous. But then Barrie's whole appearance was inconspicuous, for he must have been one of the smallest writers who ever lived. He gave the impression of being very broad in the shoulder; he cared nothing at all for dress; and his little figure in general passed unnoticed as he walked along the street. Quite different from Shaw, who, being tall and thin, strides along in woollen gloves and without an overcoat as if he were in training for a London to Brighton race. Quite different from Wells, who radiates a sedate cheerfulness and, when he sees you from afar, is immediately full of the mock insult he will deliver at meeting. Quite different from anybody else, as one would expect. Totally different from the impression which might be formed of the author of a Barrie play. Smoking a great big pipe, in winter wearing a half-buttoned great-coat and hard felt hat, he (unlike the late Hall Caine, who could not help being spectacular) expected to pass unnoticed,

and seemed unconscious of his surroundings. He was not unconscious. He was merely not self-conscious.

In company he was silent—unless cricket was mentioned, when
silence departed from him, and he was filled with great eloquence.
On the subject of cricket he was invincible. I remember one
cold day some years ago—an English cricket team was at the
time touring Australia—that I felt a touch on my arm, and
turned to find that Barrie had caught sight of me and stopped.
We had barely spoken; and the cold was such that the tears in
our eyes were far from being those of sentiment; when a newsboy
passed, shouting 'Test Match Clozer Play.' With incredible
alacrity, Barrie deserted me, drew a penny from his pocket, and
grabbed a paper, into which he completely disappeared for
several minutes. On another occasion, a friend of mine was
invited by another friend to join Barrie and himself at lunch.
My friend did not know Barrie very well, and tried his hardest
to find a topic upon which Barrie would open his mouth. At
last, in despair, he spoke of something that interested himself
—cricket. He had no further difficulty, except that (he is a
loud-voiced man) of making himself heard.

IV

'Sometimes his emotion masters him completely, at other times
he can step aside, as it were, and take an approving look at it!'

Sentimental Tommy.

Besides being the first Scotsman, Barrie is the first sentimentalist to figure in our panorama of the Georgian literary
world. It was all very well for Augustine Birrell to say that
there was no sentiment in *Auld Licht Idylls* and *A Window in
Thrums,* for we know he meant that these books are free from
gross appeals to our lachrymal glands. He could hardly have
repeated his commendation after reading *The Little Minister*
and *Sentimental Tommy.* One either reads the later novels
with an all-indulgent smile or tear, or one fidgets, or one breaks
into stentorian curses. To explain why this is so I should have
to write a great tome on the nature of life and the value of
differing interpretations of human nature. I am sure that no
reader wishes this.

But I will try to make a distinction. Shaw says that men are
self-deceiving humbugs, and that women are the instruments of
what he calls the Life Force. Wells says that in a clean and
orderly universe men and women would lead sexually common-

sense lives, but that the men of to-day who plan great advances in science have their work seriously interfered with by the intrusion of sexual affairs. He is never voluptuous in describing these affairs. If he had been, he would have had little trouble with watch committees and censors. It is because he tried to justify freedom of conduct on grounds that upset Christian ethics that he had his black and prosperous days of 'banning.' Henry James saw men and women as strange oblique minds— not bodies—touching each other, glancing off, endlessly swimming in extraordinary comprehensions which common readers do not share. Belloc and Chesterton have hardly at all concerned themselves with men and women as men and women; both being born allegorists and dealers in fantasy. But to Barrie women were tender motherly creatures and men were their little boys.

To an age taught to ridicule parents (I do not say that it is wrong to ridicule parents), this conception appears so thoroughly preposterous that Barrie's sincerity is suspect. A wrong conclusion. The book he wrote about his mother—it is called *Margaret Ogilvy*—is both affecting and sincere. The relationship pictured in it is quite sufficient (even without the Freudian gloss) to account for the turn of all Barrie's work. She was his sweetheart. It was a joke in his family that every heroine he drew was but another portrait of her; and none more teasingly and complacently accepted the identification than the mother herself. But few now wish to believe in the tender motherly woman; and most of us feel that the boy who will not grow up is a trifle emasculated.

That is one aspect; here is another. By some dispensation, each one of us carries in his heart a little ideal self-portrait. Whatever we do has somehow to be adjusted to this picture; and whether we are aesthetes who regard our taste as too fastidious for toleration of the second-rate, or whether we are proud of being amusing, or whether we picture ourselves as loving—and loved by—all dear little things, or as disillusioned, or as pillars of moral indignation, or whether we are so clever that we get right round behind these fantasies and reach a state of what looks to others very much like nonentity, we keep the ideal portrait as a sort of model. Now to play to a model, or to imitate oneself, is sentimentality. It is self-consciousness in action. We have a lot of it nowadays tricked up as intellectual anger, disgust, or contempt for the familiar; but in its simple form it is sentimentality as Barrie illustrated it in *Sentimental Tommy*.

Tommy Sandys, you will remember, could move himself to tears by a kind of impersonation of somebody or something heroic or pathetic or romantic, and at other times could 'step aside, as it were, and take an approving look' at his own emotion. Barrie's sentimentality was this sentimentality. To those who are sentimental in other ways it is a source of acute discomfort. But just as egoists are mordant observers of the foibles of other men, sentimentalists, while observing themselves with pleasure, do not entirely spare the rest of mankind. In his three best plays, *The Admirable Crichton*, *Dear Brutus*, and *The Twelve-Pound Look*, Barrie was almost cruelly critical of those who are neither mothers nor little boys. It may be said that these plays are sentimental; they do not, it may be, go to the very bottom of the human mind. But they are amusing, astringent, and pointed. Each presents, in the guise of a simple situation, a parable from nature.

The Admirable Crichton, the first of them, depicts the experiences of a small party wrecked upon an island without inhabitants. Immediately, a change in the relationship of the various members of the party begins. The man who, in a state where privilege is all-powerful, is a butler, assumes command; the others find their own level. Only when rescue is achieved does the old order re-establish itself, and all, ironically, is as before—but not quite as before. *Dear Brutus*, written some years later, collects a number of unsatisfied men and women upon Midsummer Eve, all of whom believe that if—something other than what they have—could be theirs they would be happy; and gives them, in a fairy wood, a chance to realize their dreams. The melancholy result—so salutary, so convincing, and so saddening to the beholder—is shown to be that if they could all have what they hanker for they would be no better satisfied than they now are.

> The fault, dear Brutus, is not in our stars,
> But in ourselves, that we are underlings.

Finally, *The Twelve-Pound Look* is about a professional typist, once a wife, who had left her vulgar husband years before, and had been divorced by him. In the play, she is by chance engaged by the quondam husband to type letters of thanks for congratulations upon a new honour, is recognized by her husband, and pressed by him to tell the name of the man for whom she has sacrificed her position. She answers that there was no man, but that her liberty was of more value than anything he could give her. When assured by the husband that he is now worth a quarter of a million pounds, she answers that he is worth no more than twelve pounds, the sum she has paid for her typewriter and liberty. Husbands are warned to beware of the 'twelve pound look' upon their wives' faces; and indeed this same look is discovered before the end of the play upon the face of the wife's successor.

These plays are not the work of a man who is well content with the world as it is; but they are the work of a man who demurely presented his ideas in the form of parables. They are not the work of a man with abounding energy, such as Shaw, but of one who sat quietly in his chimney corner turning over the disillusions of a lifetime and giving them this wry little twist to make them tolerable to himself. The same ideas, treated grimly or exuberantly, might be more impressive, but they would not be more profound.

Treated grimly, they would strike most audiences as fairly bitter; treated with fancy, as at present, they may appear more bitter still. Certainly, with all their fancy, they are not happy plays. Beautifully neat as they are, so that in public performance every shade is retained and a wealth of what Pooh-Bah called 'corroborative detail' of the theatre added, they read, especially the acid introductory stage directions, as unsmiling comments upon a world that is past helping. If, as I believe, the charm and the stealthy and subtle humour are no more than superficial—the play of a mind that works best in the darkness; but a subtle mind, even where it avoids the full implications of its own discoveries—they illumine very particularly the nature of the talent, I think the genius, from which they rise.

This genius is expressly a Scottish genius, one which never dares to regard literature (I grant the exception of Burns) as a field for the display of emotion. Except for superb passages in *The Heart of Midlothian*, I do not recall any Scottish prose writing in which the author's imagination is allowed to range free. Always, with Scottish writers, either timidity or restraint or some personal or thematic hobble keeps them from attempting grandeur or the grandiose. It is if as they all said 'Let me first of all be safe.' That is not what they say, of course; it is only what they seem to say; but the effect is the same. The effect is that there is always measure alike in the work and in our response to it.

I say this of Barrie's finest work, which I take to lie in the three plays just described. Only in the case of one play of his

can the response be called unmeasured; and this play unfortunately is the one by which he is always judged. *Peter Pan*, the
children's entertainment which is less a play than a portmanteau
of games and insights, has given the utmost pleasure to many
children and many adults for more than thirty years.   Lines
from it, remembered from the past, are as familiar to grown-up
children as are lines from the Gilbert and Sullivan operas.   And
yet as one recalls *Peter Pan*, and its admitted charms for many,
one does, I think, hesitate.   Although there has been no entertainment for children which approaches it in popularity in the
whole of modern theatrical history, and although it has contributed greatly, I surmise, to the decline and fall of the English
Christmas pantomine, there is in *Peter Pan* something approaching an exploitation of the child mind.   As it entertains, so it
deceives.   When Peter says that 'to die will be an awfully big
adventure,' he makes me shudder.   When he demands to know
whether the audience believes in fairies, and poor over-excited
tots thunder out their applause, I wonder whether Barrie is a
human being or a demon.   For I do not think that Barrie
himself believes in fairies.

This you will say is a moral criticism.   So it is.   But surely it
also suggests why I believe *Peter Pan* to have its fair share of
mawkishness.   It is to entertain the children; that is agreed.   So
was *Alice in Wonderland*.   And yet *Alice in Wonderland* contains not the smallest hint of sentimentality.   It is genuine gold
throughout.   There is not the smallest hint of sentimentality in
any one of the Gilbert and Sullivan operas, which are genuine
gold throughout.   *Peter Pan* is sentimental.   For this reason
Barrie's work is at the present time seriously undervalued by
many who, if they knew the major plays and the early books
of Kirriemuir sketches, would recognize in it a positive contribution to modern letters.

V. ALAN ALEXANDER MILNE

In conclusion, I must distress my friend J. M. Barrie (who gave
me a first chance) by acknowledging my great debt to him.   It
would be more polite to leave him out of it, but I cannot let him go.

A. A. MILNE, Preface to *First Plays*.

It would also be more politic on my part, in writing of A. A.
Milne, to omit reference to Barrie; but I, too, cannot let him off.
Barrie was here first, and Milne would have been Milne if Barrie
had never lived (make no mistake about that); but there are

such parallels between the two that I want to introduce Milne here and now, instead of waiting until, in a manner of speaking, he is old enough to enter the book as a full-grown author.

Alan Alexander Milne was born on 18th January 1882. His father was the schoolmaster whose preparatory school in Kilburn has already been mentioned; and Milne's association with modern writers began early. Those who are amused by such accidents will be glad to know that there is reproduced in the *Henley House Magazine* a photograph which shows H. G. Wells as a wispy young assistant master, and Milne as a ringleted child of about eight years old. He later went to Westminster School, and then to Trinity College, Cambridge. At Cambridge he edited *The Granta*, and upon returning to London he immediately became a contributor to *Punch*. He was sub-editor of *Punch* for eight years, and left the staff to fight in the line during the European War.

Punch, therefore, is the key to Milne (or it has been assumed to be the key by those who think keys are derisory symbols). In its pages he made his first reputation; and his initials were familiar during several years to every reader of the paper. They appeared week by week at the end of the lightest of trifles, in which nonsense had such wings that the solid-minded could not in those days entirely distinguish it from silliness. They did not appear in connection with the smaller quips filling each tiny corner, or in connection with his more arduous sub-editorial labours. Few people realized that the trifling A. A. M. was in fact a very hard-working journalist, with no time at all to indulge his fancy for the luxury of play-writing. But the War, as we know, changed all things; and while other subalterns forgot horrors in games of chance or by writing poetry Milne began in leisure hours to produce the plays upon which his heart was set. He is thus a War-time and post-War dramatist, and his second reputation has been made in the post-War theatre.

Finally, it is now nearly twenty years since *The Times* announced that a son had been born to the Milnes; and in the interval the name of Christopher Robin Milne has long been as familiar to thousands of readers as that of Peter Pan. And having written, to please himself, a number of poems and stories for and about Christopher Robin, Milne presently published some of the poems in a book, and thus made his third reputation, that of a writer of verses for and about the children of pleasantly circumstanced parents in two hemispheres.

Three reputations made in a quarter of a century—unless we

call them four, on account of *The Red House Mystery*; and as many reputations, of course, to be assailed by all who find the combination of lightness of heart with love of virtue an anachronism in the modern sceptic world.   I think it must be said that to the 'modns' Barrie and Milne are the least acceptable of all modern writers.   Why this is so I have shown in the case of Barrie, and I shall presently show in the case of Milne.   Meanwhile I am going to ask what kind of man is the author of *The Day's Play*, *Michael and Mary*, *The Red House Mystery*, and *When We Were Very Young*.   Although some critics think that one should take no heed of the author in estimating the quality of his work, that is not my notion; and in Milne's case the relation of man to work is especially interesting.   Our judgment of that work, I agree, should not depend upon the author's moral character; but whether we mean to do so or not we do react to the personality of any author whose work we read, and far too many critics believe that because they like or dislike a mental attitude they are in fact dispassionately assessing a talent.   As a boy in one of Milne's plays puts it: 'Why are you the devil of a fellow if you like drinking whisky, and the devil of a prig if you don't?'   Or in other words, why are you the devil of an artist if you write about prostitutes, and the devil of a literary prostitute if you don't?   'The gentleman,' says C. R. W. Nevinson, 'cannot be an artist.'   One of the half-truths; for an artist may be a gentleman.   But even if it were true, it is equally true that art is no concern of that shoddy cynic, the man of the world.

Milne is so far out of the literary fashion that he failed to detest his parents.   His parents had previously failed to ill-treat and misunderstand him.   He failed to detest his school and his schoolfellows.   He failed to have furtive adolescent sexual misadventures which left him with burning hatred of all females and an illicit love for some fellow-male.   He married early, and his marriage failed to be a failure.   He had one son, who failed to disappoint or to hate him.   And his life has failed to be disagreeable in every particular, perhaps because he has failed to be as unpleasant as possible to every person he met.   As the same boy whom I quoted a moment ago tells his young wife: 'I'm respectable.   That's what's the matter with me really.'   And the young wife sympathetically adds: 'Public School, University, and M.C.C.'   If I may again add an interpretation: Not a social misfit.   Therefore not a rebel.

In appearance Milne is extremely, extraordinarily fair.   He is of the middle height—perhaps a little above it—and to this day is as slim as he was when he first came down from Cambridge. His eyes are very blue, his face is thin but not pale, and I think it would be impossible to see him without realizing at once that he has an active and quickly—smoothly—working mind. There are authors who look stupid and angry; nobody could miss the intelligence of Milne's expression, and the ready but not especially effulgent kindness of his agreeable smile. An observer who knew nothing of his books and plays would probably discover that the face was notably keen and handsome, free from any sign of malice or cruelty, but lacking in what I may call the lines of boisterousness. He would not at first, I think, find it easy to understand what Milne said, owing to the inaudibility and little slurring quickness of his speech. He would notice that, like Barrie, Milne is devoted to the game of cricket. What else he would notice I do not know.

Milne dresses with marked taste and care (I mean no more than that); and he walks at a considerable speed without looking very much at those who pass him. I do not think he is at all interested in the casual. Certainly he is not interested in manufacturing conversation with strangers. An American visitor to England was once left sitting with Milne on a log while the rest of a cordial house-party went for a longish walk. Upon their return, the walkers found Milne and the American still sitting on the log, perfectly content, and still in the attitudes in which they had been last seen; and the American joined his hostess for the short journey back to the house. As they strolled, he said thoughtfully: 'You English are a wonderful people. You convey so much. And yet you don't say a word.'

Unlike the man whose mind is unoccupied, then, Milne does not tirelessly volunteer conversation. Nor, however, does he repress it in others, as do the haughty; a fact from which I draw an inference concerning Milne the writer as well as Milne the man. The inference is that while plentifully blessed (as Barrie has been) with fancy, and even more plentifully blessed than Barrie with verbal adroitness (as witness his versification), he does not command that gift of the great romancers and novelists, a profuse fecundity of invention. Although by no means unappreciative of these traits in other men, he is deficient in vulgarity, in energy, in largeness of thought, and in exuberance of action.

Milne's first books consisted of reprinted pieces from *Punch*, the slight sketches to which I have already referred. They were delightful nonsense. His children's verses are familiar, innocent, arch, and charmingly turned. His one detective story is high among the lighter examples of a popular craft. All these books have a polish and bubble iridescence that make them excellent in their own department of letters, and all have large numbers of admirers. But it is by his plays that Milne has made his most ambitious claim to attention, and, finally, it is upon his plays that the critic must concentrate.

The first of them, apparently, was *Wurzel-Flummery*, the story of a trick played upon two proud men by a dying eccentric who left each a fortune on condition that each changed his name to Wurzel-Flummery. A name, as those who have read Lamb's *Mr H.* well know, is not a strong theme for a play, and *Wurzel-Flummery*, which began in three acts, is now printed in one. *Belinda*, another trifle, remains in three acts, and is about an inconsequent woman, her daughter (newly returned from a convent school), a long-missing husband, and two absurd suitors —one of them a juvenile poet, the other a middle-aged statistician. Here again the theme is slight to tenuity. Here again the amusingness of the play lies almost entirely in the persiflage which passes between shallow and very pleasing persons until the curtain falls. Both plays were very much like *Punch* sketches written in dialogue form at greater length; both were extremely nonsensical; *Belinda* gave a delicious part to one of the most charming actresses the English stage has known; but neither play had what may be called an 'idea.' The story in each case was just sufficient to hold together the various nimble sayings of the actors, and no more. But *Belinda* held the first of those former or missing husbands who have figured so prominently in the Milne drama.

Mr Pim Passes By was about another of them; but this time the husband did not appear, and in fact he did not (at the moment of the play's action) exist. Another delicious part for the same actress, and a success for the author in the commercial theatre. From *Mr Pim* onwards, a Milne play has been a recognized type of theatrical entertainment. I shall not at the moment dwell upon the minor plays, except to notice that former and either desirable or undesirable husbands figure in at least two of them—*To Have the Honour* and *Michael and Mary* —but shall go straight to Milne's most considerable dramatic work.

The Truth about Blayds, an ambitious piece which had only a short run in London, is about an almost centenarian poet who has carried on a lifelong literary imposture. At the end of the first act he dies. And as he dies he whispers with his last breath to the daughter whose life he has spoilt the fact that he did not write the poetry upon which his tremendous reputation has been built. He has stolen the profuse work of a dead friend and passed it off as his own. The remaining acts turn upon the posthumous incredulity and dismay of his family, and their relief when they invent a formula with which to discredit the confession and when they discover a will by which they legally retain the fruits of the old man's shame.

The second play, *Success*, is about a prominent and careerist Cabinet Minister who has old memories stirred, meets again the only girl he ever loved, re-lives (visibly, in an interpolated dream scene) the days of his childhood, determines to relinquish career for love, and then, just when the crucial moment arrives, is pulled back to the baseness of politics by the offer of the chancellorship.

Both *Success* and *The Truth about Blayds* failed in the theatre; the latter not unexpectedly, the former through an error in popular judgment. *Blayds* begin with a serious and deeply interesting first act; but as soon as the situation had been grasped the play ceased to amuse, and was even a cause of some discomfort to those who saw it. *Success* was badly received by the dramatic critics, who thought that Milne had dared to presume upon their favourable verdict. It has more feeling in it than any other play of Milne's, is extremely skilful, both as to plan and character, and is full of good, quick, effective dialogue. It deserved quite another fate than failure.

But both plays have the weakness which it seems to me is apparent in Milne's work whenever he is most serious; that is, they suffer from a kind of punitive zeal against wrongdoing. Milne has such a contempt for backsliders and materialists and sycophants that he cannot withhold a moral foreclosure which affects the structure of his play. Barrie, after seeing *The Truth about Blayds* (the first play by Milne, I believe, of which he had not read the typescript), is said to have remarked, with a wise theatre man's laconism, 'I should have kept the old man alive'; and this comment, by whomsoever it was made, is really, as one thinks of it, devastating. It is much more than a technical criticism. It goes to the root of the whole question. For *Blayds*, which might have been a great comedy about an impostor, shifts its centre to the impostor's dependants, ignominious indeed, but of no significance. To castigate the meanness and hypocrisy of those who, after an earthquake, are trying to pretend that there has been a shower, is to bully the demoralized.

Similarly, in *Success*, although the reawakening of Mannock is made credible with extraordinary skill (this is quite Milne's best play), and his downfall before temptation is exciting and convincing, a moral judgment—not a doom—hangs over the entire play. It is not tragedy, but an arraignment. I suggest that owing to his knowledge that Mannock was going to collapse, and his bitter dislike of venality, Milne has been unable to allow Mannock as much character as he should have done. So the fall is not great enough, because Mannock has throughout flown too low; the failure of a bigger man would have been a greater loss to his true love, and would have moved us more.

I had in mind this criticism of Milne's work when I said that he was deficient in certain qualities of the great romancers. At times his invention is meagre; it is always hampered by a lack of boldness, an inability to shake off the author's strict moral standards. Thus, while in every play the dialogue is fresh and full of life, the content of the play, where it is not a jest, is too often conventional.

I do not mean only conventional in the theatrical sense, and yet it is true that on the whole these plays of Milne's deal with a life peculiar to the theatre. I say no more as to the husbands who turn up or who refrain from turning up; but what of the wives to whom these husbands have in the past belonged? They at least are principals in the action. If their husbands come and go in this wanton manner, do not the wives also lose something of acceptable reality? A husband who is mislaid as if he were an article of jewellery may serve as a pretext for drama; but the wife, charming chatterbox though she be, who merely resumes her life as if she said, 'Dear me, I don't seem to have a husband this morning; never mind, I expect he'll turn up again some time,' does put a slight strain upon our credulity. Of course these ladies are before us: we see them, we hear them, we relish their wit. But when they leave the stage, or when we leave the theatre, we cannot help feeling that they have been only make-believe wives, make-believe women, like the dolls which little girls ask to tea-parties and forget as soon as they have been put to bed.

That is the character of the Milne drama—make-believe. In a sense it is the character of the Barrie drama. Here are embodied whimsies, delicious fancies, nonsensical dreams, tender memories of play and young illusion, an enchanting aptness of phrase, sometimes a piercing revelation of unseen things, a charm that is not poetic but half real, half arbitrary, in the manner of a child's game. But neither Barrie nor Milne ever, it seems to me, goes quite the whole hog. Neither deals quite with the real world, or quite with the world of faery. The real world is too harsh, or at least too stubborn, for fanciful treatment; the world of faery too incredible. Once we listen to the coaxing, winning 'Let 's pretend,' we are at the mercy of both authors; but they know as well as we do that they are pretending. A time will come when they will put away the toys and return to reality as represented by the grown - up evening newspaper. They will not absolutely let go at any time of the pleasant normal circumstances of well-bred and easy-mannered society.

VI. JAMES STEPHENS

SHADBOLT. I am to lie?
POINT. Heartily. But thy lie must be a lie of circumstance.
The Yeomen of the Guard.

Once more taking advantage of the loose structure of this book for my own purposes, I proceed to illustrate the foregoing by reference to another writer who is not a Scotsman and who has no Scots blood. It could not be said that the inhibitions which check the Scots have any effect upon the Irish. Where the Scot bent upon a spree first counts his money, the Irishman never troubles. Where the Scot makes a point of catching his train, an Irishman will accept a shake-down for the night and may stay, regardless of any physical discomfort, for a week's fine talking. And where a Scotsman, who loves truth as a miser loves gold, will hesitate to tell any story which has not at least a substratum of truth and a somewhat strictly assessed degree of probability, an Irishman is unaware that his own truth has any limits whatever. In this way, Scottish writers have been economists, biographers, and historians, and when they have turned to fiction have been often *historical* novelists (using the national bent for the antiquarian); but Irish writers have been poets, dramatists, and fabulists of the most luxuriant order, and when they have essayed history or biography have never been able to command the assent of their fellow-countrymen in such measure as to es-tablish permanent reputations for themselves or their works.

The writer who illustrates my remarks on the caution with which Barrie and Milne leave the familiar is James Stephens; and James Stephens, accordingly, is like Milne brought forward among the older writers in spite of the fact that he, too, was born in the year 1882. The place of his birth was Dublin, and the place of his present residence is London. But if you look in the reference books you will find no more than the date of his birth (if that) and the titles of his works (or some of his works). I do not know what his father was, or what were the circumstances of his early life. I only know that when he was old enough to begin to earn money he worked for a time in the office of a Dublin attorney, and that later, through the intervention of Thomas Bodkin, now Director of the Birmingham Art Gallery, he was for a few years engaged in some occupation requiring his daily attendance at the Dublin Art Gallery.

But he was not so much absorbed in routine as to disregard the development of his own gifts; and I remember that in 1909 the London newspaper, *The Daily Chronicle*, then a literary power, reviewed at column-length a small book of what were considered very bold poems entitled *Insurrections*, the nature of which review (coupled with the support rendered by quotations from the book itself) was enough to send a friend and myself straight to the publishers for copies of *Insurrections* and to keep us for an hour busy in reading or quoting its more vigorous stanzas. When, shortly afterwards, I noticed that a story called *Mary Make-believe* was being serialized in some publication, and recognized the author's name as that of the insurrectionary poet, I subscribed to the publication and thus read the fairy tale subsequently published in book form as *The Charwoman's Daughter*. In Dublin, no doubt (for *Insurrections* was dedicated to A E), Stephens was already well known. In London he had still to make a reputation.

The Crock of Gold followed in 1912, and established that reputation. *Here are Ladies* came in 1913 and *The Demi-gods* in 1914. Having thus made innumerable readers his toys, Stephens visited America, lectured with something like triumph, making many Americans his slaves, wrote and published many more poems, and at last for the time being abandoned Dublin. He settled in a London suburb, and from this suburb he now regularly descends upon the West End for the sake of intellectual conversation with his peers.

In person Stephens is small and slight. His face is an old face —it has, I think, resemblances (but these may be solely those of brow and natural tonsure) to that of Oliver Goldsmith—and a droll face, the face of one who dwells for ever in a world mocked and twisted by fairies. It has been said to me by the Irish that he is exactly like a leprechaun; but I have never seen a leprechaun, and so I cannot say if the description is a just one. He is a talker. He talks more magnificently than any other person I ever met. He recites poetry better than anybody else I ever heard—better even than Desmond MacCarthy, who recites very beautifully—and will embark upon an evening's monologue without the smallest hesitation. His mind is quick, rich, unhesitating; his interests are so varied that he is never at a loss for illustration or metaphor. Across his droll face steals constantly a little dry, quiet, melancholy smile, as if the consuming laughter of his hearers, being long continued, at last, for an instant, had conquered his gravity. He does not monopolize conversation; but when he speaks it is from an original knowledge of art and life before which the accomplished wit of the sophisticate loses virtue.

His work now very slightly resembles the poems which were published in *Insurrections* (these, I admit, have in the passage of years lost something of their first pungency, but not all of it); and in narrative has all the whispered assurance of the folk tale. Indeed, it is of the character of the folk tale, reinforced by an intricacy of saying and allusion such as only a witty mind could invent and keep of a piece with the whole. First it is a tale, and then it is philosophy, and then it is nonsense; but all these qualities are so merged and, for the reader, confounded, that the effect is one of profound laughter. At no time is there a hiatus between what is thought and what is said; all is of the same relish.

This is a very rare quality. Stephens's imagining is unaffected by interruption from an outside and alien judgment. He never sniggers. For this reason he commands us entirely, as Lewis Carroll does, who for as long as a book lasts never interposes Kensington into Wonderland. Thus, where Chesterton's fairies are but figures of rhetoric, and Barrie's are little bells and flitting lights, Stephens's are as cunning as the elves in old tales, before cleverness came to quiz invention.

In the centre of the pine wood called Coilla Doraca there lived not long ago two Philosophers. . . . Their faces looked as though they were made of parchment, there was ink under their nails, and every difficulty that was submitted to them, even by women, they were able to instantly resolve. The Grey Woman of Dun Gortin and the Thin Woman of Inis Magrath asked them the three questions which nobody had ever been able to answer, and they were able to answer them. That was how they obtained the enmity of these two women which is more valuable than the friendship of angels.

The Grey Woman and the Thin Woman were so incensed at being answered that they married the two Philosophers in order to be able to pinch them in bed, but the skins of the Philosophers were so thick that they did not know they were being pinched. They repaid the fury of the women with such tender affection that these vicious creatures almost expired of chagrin, and once, in a very ecstasy of exasperation, after having been kissed by their husbands, they uttered the fourteen hundred maledictions which comprised their wisdom, and these were learned by the Philosophers who thus became even wiser than before.

That is the opening of *The Crock of Gold*, and it is typical both of Stephens and of the Irish invention. I do not pretend to be able to explain why no Scotsman would write in that way; but it seems to me to be a demonstration of what I said a few pages back. Certainly it explains for me why Stephens is one of the writers as to whose rank in the hierarchy there is no immediate question, and why Irishmen, who in general have no sense of humour whatever, must frequently laugh as they con lists of great English authors, to find in those lists the names of so many of their compatriots.

CHAPTER VI: TRAVELLERS

I

Where are the Spanish Main, the Guianas, and the Brazils? . . .
They are in Raleigh's *Golden City of Manoa*, in Burney's *Buccaneers
of America*, with Drake, Humboldt, Bates, and Wallace. . . . We
borrow the light of an observant and imaginative traveller, and see
the foreign land bright with his aura; and we think it is the country
which shines.

H. M. TOMLINSON, *The Sea and the Jungle.*

EVERY division of this book is arbitrary; and by 'travellers' I
mean, not men who go to some country to observe customs and
practices, flora and fauna, for the sake of writing scientifically
about them, but men to whom the life of cities is as disagreeable
as life in a cage must be to the wild bird. Also men who have
crystallized their experiences into tales and personal narratives
marked by style giving them interest as literature. The archetype of such men in modern letters is Herman Melville, traveller,
romantic, and superabundantly eloquent writer. In some instances those grouped in this chapter were born free; in others
they have escaped from conventional life and have wandered
far; all, whether free or bound, have brought to contemporary
literature the atmosphere of distant lands and what seems to
ordinary citizens the romance of violent and exceptional
adventure.

How have they been able to do this? For that re-creation of
the strange is something very different from the re-creation of
the recognizable which has proceeded simultaneously in the more
typical fiction of the period. Well, it is probable that in the first
twenty years of their lives the majority of men accumulate all
the fresh personal experience they are ever to enjoy. They are
young for just that period, and no more. The conventional age
early; the scholastically trained do not age, but they tend to
prefer books to adventure; those who are neither conventional
nor academic may nevertheless find a sufficient range in the
life of cities. When they are no longer young, all may learn

consciously, and with effort, and perhaps with greater intelligence; they can still suffer, and thereby create a flying illusion of renewed youth; but for the creative writer nothing whatever can take the place of that impulsive, unconsidered susceptibility to experience which is unreflective and almost wholly emotional. For the creative writer, that is, a prolonged youth is Fortune's greatest gift.

The men I have called travellers have been bent first of all upon adventure, 'seeing the world,' and embracing its opportunities. They have been non-academic in education. They have been able to keep young for longer than other men. But having seen the world, they have thought, in the manner of all men born to be writers, that they would like to tell the world what they thought of it. So they have taken to the pen with much of the enthusiasm they feel for life. They have not wanted to be 'just literary.' Most of them have thought of the literary world as a world of indoor dandies, none too wholesome, and of their own writing rather as a contribution to the good talk of travelled men of wit than as a contribution to the pleasure of fashionable readers. Here again they have shown a unique combination of youth and good sense, for most of them have had to wait many years before the general public took any notice of their work. If you ask me to explain this neglect, I can do it in a few words: travellers do not write much of women.

For one reason or another—sometimes for reasons of arrangement and sometimes through incapacity—I make no attempt to discuss here the character and work of several traveller-authors whose names will immediately occur to the experienced reader. Charles Doughty, for example, stands outside my period, a commanding figure of the pre-Georgian era. So, in a different category, does Sir Hugh Clifford. Nor shall I speak otherwise than briefly of some very good writers who ought to figure in a Georgian panorama; if I were to write of them at length, this book would be an encyclopaedia.

No; the first traveller-author who belongs by right to this chapter is Robert Bontine Cunninghame Graham, the aristocrat Socialist, the rebel against society who ornamented Society, the man who is said to have provided Shaw with at least an external model for the character of Captain Brassbound, and an author who has been privately and singularly 'discovered' for themselves by probably more people in different quarters of the globe than any other British writer of his period. It is of Cunninghame Graham, accordingly, that I shall now speak.

II. ROBERT BONTINE CUNNINGHAME GRAHAM

To my Friend
R. B. CUNNINGHAME GRAHAM
('Singularísimo escritor ingles')

Who has lived with and knows (even to the marrow as they would themselves say) the horsemen of the Pampas, and who alone of European writers has rendered something of the vanishing colour of that remote life.

W. H. HUDSON, Dedication of *El Ombú*.

R. B. Cunninghame Graham, of Ardoch, was born in 1852. Upon his mother's side he was of the Elphinstones, an old Scottish family of soldiers, sailors, and royalists. Having been at school at Harrow, he became a Socialist, a political candidate, and finally a member of Parliament from 1886 to 1892. He was the colleague of H. M. Hyndman and John Burns, and in 1887, when the Life Guards marched up Whitehall to drive unemployed demonstrators from Trafalgar Square upon 'Bloody Sunday,' he had his head cracked and was arrested as one of the ringleaders of the riot. For some years after that he continued to play an active part in the Labour struggle; but after 1892 he was unsuccessful at election times, and the first of his published writings appeared in 1895.

I do not know who first used the word 'hidalgo' to describe Cunninghame Graham. It may have been Morley Roberts. But there was a pride, an elegance, and a nobility in his carriage such as we associate with the grandees of Spain in other centuries than this. He was always a very handsome man, a magnificent horseman, and a picturesque figure altogether. Even in advanced age his vitality, the grandeur of his manner, and the intellectual command of his mind, were superlative. He was an aristocrat. And there can be no doubt that there is a great deal of the aristocrat in his writings. It is this quality, combined with the fact that they have what perhaps I may call a static rather than a serial interest, which has prevented them from becoming popular. One does not read them feverishly to see what happens; one cannot zestfully embrace the proud and critical view of life which they express; they are not for the soft-minded; their chief admirers, I judge, are men of a mental detachment akin to his own.

They have one extraordinary quality. Whatever scene they describe, whether it be laid in the desert, on the South American pampa, in Scotland, at sea, or upon the west coast of Africa, they catch the very atmosphere of the place and the very mind

of the people with whom they deal. The author is at home
everywhere. In a single ironic sentence he will communicate
all that a lesser man would tell at interminable length. When
we read what he has written we are for a dozen pages—the
extent of his sketch—in baking heat, in snow, in Yorkshire, in
Menteith, among the gauchos, or travelling to Mecca to find why
there are no old women in Paradise. The effect is not obtained
by a total immersion in memory; it is constantly heightened by
comparisons which suggest themselves to a mind richly endowed
with humour and imagination (those two requisites for true
irony). It is irresistible.

So quiet the garden was, that when the lizards chased each other
through the dead grass, the noise they made was as distinct (in its
degree) as if a troop of cavalry had passed. A scent of mint and of
decaying orange blossom filled the air; all was old-world and still;
and the bare-footed, white-clothed people passed about among the
trees, as they were shades of some old life, making one feel, in
looking at them, as one feels in looking at some pre-diluvian foot-
step, stamped in the rock, which once was river mud.
'Yes,' said the Angeri, 'once Allah let all animals both speak
and pray to him in Arabic, so that men, listening to them, could
understand their speech.' A dreadful time it must have been, if
with their speech they also enjoyed reason, and could accuse us to
our faces of all our crimes against their kind. Who that could
contemplate their speech and not go mad, with thinking upon all
that they might say? But as it happened, God having let them all
speak (once upon a time), and as the God the Angeri knew was
Allah, the merciful, compassionate, capricious, envious, the invisible,
and therefore unapproachable, except by prayer, that smoke the
human mind gives off under its fire of cares, the animals had all to
pray, or else to lose their speech.

That is the beginning of a tale in a volume called *Progress*,
which explains why a certain small kind of lizard is known as
'el Khattaia-es-salaa'—for the gift of speech was suddenly withdrawn from birds and animals, and this lizard, forgetful of the
passage of time, missed its last opportunity for prayer.

Running, back downwards, on the ceilings of the mosques, all day
it chased the flies, basked in the heat, flattening itself against the
white-washed walls, its feet expanding flat, like paddles, and its
slim tail acting upon the air to steer it as it whisked through horse-
shoe arches, and shot out upon the vine leaves which grew up outside the holy place. Chasing its fellows in the sun, and catching
flies, the sand ran through the glass and, at the mogréb, when the
last quavering 'Allah' died away, only the lizard, in its joy of life,
did not give thanks to God.
Despair fell on it, and its tiny grief shook its prismatic sides, whilst
little tears stood in its beady eyes. Its tail hung quivering, and its

head bowed miserably, as it stood silently and without power to glorify the Lord. Then, darting to the mosque, it flittered up the walls, its little feet showering down lime upon the worshippers. Just over the mihrâb it stopped, and, as the faithful in the mosque below looked up at it, scratched 'Allah Ackbar' with its claw upon the roof, and, scurrying back, was lost beneath the eaves.

'So,' said the Angeri, 'it saved itself from Allah's wrath, and showed its faith'; and from that time we know it as *Khattaia-es-salaa*, that is, the prayer-scratcher; praise to His Holy Name!

Readers of the above will have noted several peculiarities of style. They are to be found—they and their like—through Cunninghame Graham's work. His ear is sometimes faulty; he is not aware that 'old-world' is an estate agent's term; his grammar is his own (unless the printer has helped him); he is sometimes obscure and sometimes—it is his humour—slightly affected. Those are small blemishes. More interesting—and I should like to understand the cause of that omission—is the fact that he has nowhere essayed a longer fiction. What he has done instead—one of the things he has done, and the most notable of them—is to write a superbly rich and amusing account of a journey in southern Morocco, under the title *Mogreb-el-Acksa*. In this he is exultantly humorous, instructive, eloquent, and sardonic by turn, and altogether at his best as a writer. In this, also, he is at his most characteristic, doing with glorious gusto exactly what he set out to do. For him a city was a compound for slaves, and the world an open space for every adventure. For him the theorist and the miser, the stay-at-home and the preacher who does not practise his profession, were all ridiculous anomalies. He was for action; and for action with humour. And so, when he wrote, he thought only of setting down his account of an episode, or a scene, a reminiscence, a tale, with the grace and manner of a free man who, by the gift of the gods, was also an original artist. Diversely, he told with an air what befell him upon a journey; but it was not all or by any means all that befell him, only what amused him, or what it amused him to tell. When he had related what he liked, he passed on, indifferent to the reader's unsated curiosity, and greatly amused by his own private reflections. That is why he was always the grandee, and never the humble suppliant for public favour. It is also why he keeps his admirers.

For the rest, when this great man wrote at length it was the biography of some notable Spaniard otherwise little vaunted in English, or the tale of an exploration which he thought should be better understood and which it interested him to recall from the past. In these excellent books the same descriptive and ironic gifts to which I have referred are displayed; but they are not sensibly augmented. It is therefore in *Mogreb-el-Acksa* and in his original sketches and brief stories that he is best read. Here his work has an edge and colour, a salt, a noble ease, which makes it seem like the lesser performance of a master to whom even greater triumphs were denied only because he did not seek them.

III. WILLIAM HENRY HUDSON

A field-naturalist is an observer of everything he sees—from a man to an ant or a plant.

W. H. HUDSON, *A Hind in Richmond Park.*

There is all the difference in the world between Cunninghame Graham and W. H. Hudson. The one was born in Scotland and from a natural love of adventure travelled much, fearlessly, in other continents; the other was born in the neighbourhood of Buenos Aires, had his heart ruined by rheumatic fever when he was fifteen, and from the age of twenty-nine, when he came 'home,' as he called it (although his father and mother were both citizens of the United States), never again left the British Isles. In their writings, the one has an air of scattering odd fragments of his mind and genius as fancy prompts; and the other, the 'field-naturalist' of his own phrase, observes, re-members, records, but scatters nothing.

William Henry Hudson was born on 4th August 1841, and although he lived until 18th August 1924, he was never a strong man. His father, who was of English descent, was originally of Marblehead, Massachusetts, and his mother was a New England woman; but before any of their children were born these American parents, for reasons of health, settled in the Argentine. Hudson, accordingly, was born and reared among the pampas. From the age of six he was given to stealing away from his brothers to a little wood where he could watch the animals, snakes, birds, and insects common to the country; and after his great illness, which followed a terrible experience of driving cattle through a blizzard, he was more than ever a solitary. When doctors announced that he could not hope to live long, he was faced at the age of sixteen with despair so great that he made no effort to fit himself for adult life. He idled, he read; and his passion for nature remained in effect the one solace of his mind.

Time passed. He began to keep a journal of his observations. Then he became a corresponding member of the Zoological

Society, and sent overseas a few slight papers recording what he had seen. When his father died in 1868 he left South America and came to England, where he remained for more than fifty years, always a semi-invalid, always aloof, silent, and in some degree a stranger. His first years in Hampshire and in London remain mysterious; all that is known of them is that he managed somehow to subsist until 1876, when he married a boarding-house keeper fifteen years his senior.

From that time onward nothing but failure attended Hudson. Three boarding-houses proved unprofitable; Mrs Hudson earned but little money by giving singing lessons; Hudson wrote descriptions of South American birds and South American scenes which few editors would print. He had only his observations of nature to write about, and in the last decades of the nineteenth century nobody wanted them. When he tried to write a conventional novel, *Fan*, it was as great a failure as the more typical *Purple Land*, but more deservedly a failure. Only the bequest of a heavily mortgaged house in West London, which was let out into flats, saved the Hudsons from starvation.

This life continued for some years. At times the two would creep away to the country for fresh air, and Hudson had a few literary and other friends with whom he visited the coasts and southern counties of England. His books show that he was as closely interested in English beasts and birds as he had been earlier in those of his first home. Both *Idle Days in Patagonia* and *Birds in a Village* were published in 1893; *British Birds* followed in 1897, *Birds in London* in 1898, and *Nature in Downland* in 1900. In the latter year Hudson became a naturalized Englishman. Subsequently he received a Civil List pension of £150 a year; but by this time his fortunes were slowly improving, and with the aid of influential critics he was presently to have a valuable success with the long-prepared novel, *Green Mansions*. In the last twenty years of his life this success was translated into money.

I first saw Hudson some time before the publication of *Green Mansions*. He came into the office of J. M. Dent & Sons when I was reception clerk there, on some business connected with his two books, *A Naturalist in La Plata* and *Idle Days in Patagonia*. These books had been taken over by Dent's from another firm of publishers, and had so little sale that the bound copies still bore the old firm's imprint. The author of them, I found, was a very tall and thin man of middle age, in a very long overcoat which seemed to reach his heels. His head looked remark-

ably small at the top of this cylindrical enclosure, and his face
tanned and shrunken; but his ears stood out from under a black
hard felt hat.   He was already grey-bearded.   When I realized
who he was I no longer wondered at Hudson's power to stand
and watch unconscious animals and birds; for he was extraordinarily silent in all his movements, and he sat on the edge of
a table, glancing at a book, without ever shifting his position.
He had very bright eyes which my recollection makes as black
as black currants; the brows were thick to bushiness; the nose
hooked.   He resembled a bird.

Of his work I continue to think *A Naturalist in La Plata* and
Idle Days in Patagonia the best examples.   The former is a
collection of essays reprinted from magazines now of an obsolete
type; the latter a narrative presumably based upon journals
kept at the time.   The material is authentic, and the manner
plain, clear, and attractive.   And although the English books
are full of good observation, curious incidents, and excellent
quiet writing, the freshness of his early first-hand acquaintance
with nature is never quite recaptured.   His autobiographical
Far Away and Long Ago is informative, charmingly written, and
full of reserve; the work of a really old, sick man, looking back
to childhood through a mist.   It was influenced by Aksakov's
memoirs, for which Hudson felt great admiration.

The Purple Land, a rambling romance of a man's adventures
in South America, which I have only read in the revised version
of 1906, and which, in the earliest draft of all, was a wellnigh
endless 'History of the House of Lamb,' has many beauties and
vigours, and if Hudson had known better what he was intending
to do with it might have been very distinguished indeed.   Unfortunately he did not know what to do with it (except go on
writing), and the book remains what publishers and reviewers,
when they are forced to describe highly unsystematic inventions,
despairingly miscall 'picaresque.'   Cut and revised though it is,
The Purple Land remains a broken and spasmodic book.

The style in which it is written, however, is much less studied
than that drenching his other famous novel, *Green Mansions*,
which took him several years to write, and was a rage with the
reviewers of 1904.   Here again the scene, the strange and haunting scene, is South America; and here again forests, prairies,
birds, and the naturalist's observations provide the basis for a
romantic but ill-knit story of love and adventure.   *Green
Mansions* begins enchantingly, first with that little device by
which Conrad and others sought to heighten romance, or perhaps

only to disclaim autobiography, the encounter with a mysterious stranger, and then with the stranger's own narrative. Abel, elderly and sad, has had his hour of life. He has sought gold, and met sorrow: we hear his tale. Now as long as there is still a mystery in the tale, as long as the warbled notes which he hears in the fairy wood can be imagined as in some way supernatural, the book is odd and interesting. But from the moment when Rima is seen as a young girl, the magic declines. It might have been otherwise; it ought to have been otherwise; there is no reason, other than the poverty of imagination, why Rima should not captivate us as much as a woman as she does as a spirit. Unfortunately she can only chirp; the wonderful knowledge she possesses is incommunicable. Her talk is leaden stuff. True, when she discovers Abel's inability to understand her chirrup she enjoys our sympathy, although we feel that a few lessons might have been attempted, and thus suspect the whole affair. True, there is a shock of horror at her revolting end. But as soon as Abel finds her no spirit the movement of the book becomes mechanical; its invention grows feeble; it is contrived.

That is the penalty paid by a naturalist turned romancer. His ability to imagine character with continuous power is insufficient. While in the case of both Rima and Dolores (the deceived but amorous young woman in *The Purple Land*) the romantic note is pitched very high indeed it is not supported by any spontaneous play of emotion. Instead, there is a reaching up to literary beauty. Hudson knew painfully well the effect he wished to achieve—indeed, I suspect that both Dolores and Rima were dream heroines with whom he had long been preoccupied —but the very fact of knowing paralysed his talent. It is one of the misfortunes of self-conscious literary art that the creative gift cannot be forced to work for a master. Hudson was an observer, strongly susceptible to the moods of nature; but he was emotionally and imaginatively cold. Hence his failure as a novelist; for his coldness, which at first has charm, produces in the end an impression of labour. His best work outside the record of observed facts and inferences from those facts is to be found in the book of four short stories or sketches called *El Ombú*, the first of which, the title story, if mannered, is fine and full of suggestion.

What he was, in a high degree, was just that 'field naturalist' which he called himself. The close and absorbed observation of nature, begun in his earliest years, and continued even when he thought himself dying, runs through every page of his work. It is never sentimental, always humane and in a sense philosophic, and of rare excellence. He had but to leave the town and go fifty or sixty miles into the country to find almost all he needed for happiness. The sight of a moral struggle between a draggled blackbird and a relentless chaffinch, or even that of the sensitive movement of a hind, which he thought betokened an interest in the world about her not inferior to his own, would start him upon a train of reflection; thoughts upon eyes, on the curious friendship of pumas towards the human species, on his favourite flower, the evening primrose, on a pair of scarlet flycatchers in lands far away, give every book its thoughtful and thought-evoking quality. He is not a Gilbert White; he has hardly any kinship with White. Indeed he says:

One of the books I read then for the first time was White's *Selborne*, given to me by an old friend of our family. . . . I read and re-read it many times, for nothing so good of its kind had ever come to me, but it did not reveal to me the secret of my own feeling for Nature —the feeling of which I was becoming more and more conscious, which was a mystery to me, especially at certain moments, when it would come upon me with a sudden rush.

It may be asked what this feeling was; and Hudson answered the question himself in another book by calling it animism. He said:

It must be explained that *animism* is not used here in the sense that Tylor gives it in his *Primitive Culture*: in that work it signifies a theory of life, a philosophy of primitive man, which has been supplanted among civilized people by a more advanced philosophy. Animism here means not a doctrine of souls that survive the bodies and objects they inhabit, but the mind's projection of itself into nature, its attribution of its own sentient life and intelligence to all things—that primitive universal faculty on which the animistic philosophy of the savage is founded. When our philosophers tell us that this faculty is obsolete in us, that it is effectually killed by ratiocination, or that it only survives for a period in our children, I believe they are wrong, a fact which they could find out for themselves if, leaving their books and theories, they would take a solitary walk on a moonlit night in the 'Woods of Westermain' or any other woods, since all are enchanted.

But if Hudson has no kinship with White, he has neither the emotionalism of Jefferies nor the vanity of Thoreau. Like Borrow, whom he does not otherwise resemble, he has a power to encounter strange people and converse with them, so that his books teem with tantalizing episodes. But he never obtrudes his own figure; there is a striking impersonality in all that he relates. That is his virtue, a coldness which many might link in their minds with inhumanity; it is in his style, which is quiet and without warmth, and which by some is thought too careful, or, in the case of *Green Mansions,* too conscious; it is in his relations with other men, to whose natural ebullience he would oppose silence or at most a monosyllabic abruptness. At their moment of farewell in 1869 his younger brother, whom he loved deeply, was forced to say, in the warm candour of parting: 'Of all the people I have ever known you are the only one I don't know.'

IV. JOSEPH CONRAD

. . . But the Dwarf answered: 'No; something human is dearer to me than the wealth of all the world.'

Grimm's Tales.

When Hudson visited the English coast with Morley Roberts and other friends, it was his custom ritualistically to scoop up a handful of sea water and drink it as soon as he could reach the water's edge. Just why he did this was never explained, and it is not clear from any writing of his that the sea had any special claim upon his affections. But the case was different with Joseph Conrad, to whom the sea—at least in boyhood—was a passion.

Conrad's two passions were the sea and the human species; the sea in boyhood, and then, as he grew up and met them in the course of his voyages, men. To these two passions he added in time a third, that of language, which should express richly and eloquently the passion he felt for men and the sea. When he was a boy, Conrad would pore over maps, and, putting his finger upon every large open space he found, he would say: 'When I grow up I shall go there.' And as soon as he was old enough to do so he went to sea, where he stayed for twenty years, until he had written his first novel and until, in despair of getting another ship, he one day sat down to write a second. From that time, almost by accident, he devoted himself to novel-writing, and after some years — I make the distinction deliberately — he became a professional novelist.

Teodor Josef Konrad Korzeniowski was born at Berdiczew, in Poland, on 3rd December 1857. His mother was a woman of family, his father an energetic and enthusiastic revolutionary of literary gifts who was not shrewd enough to escape exile, hardship, and early death as the result of his sanguine love of freedom.

A man of great sensibilities [said his son]; of exalted and dreamy temperament; with a terrible gift of irony and of gloomy disposition. . . . His aspect was distinguished; his conversation fascinating; but his face, in repose sombre, lighted all over when he smiled.

Before Conrad was twelve years old he had lost both father and mother.

He first saw the sea at Venice in 1873. In the following year he went to Marseilles determined to become a sailor, and in 1875 he actually took a brief voyage. But it was not until 1878, after some of the strange doings recorded in *The Arrow of Gold*, that he went to sea and stayed at sea. In that year he sailed in three ships: first the *Mavis*, in which he visited the Sea of Azov and returned to Lowestoft, second the *Skimmer of the Seas*, in which he learned to speak English and plied between Lowestoft and Newcastle, and third the *Duke of Sutherland*, in which as a common sailor he made the voyage to Australia. In 1881 he was second mate of the bark *Palestine* (the *Judea* of *Youth*); and in 1887 went out to the East as first mate of the *Highland Forest*, left the ship at Samarang through illness, and joined the *Vidar*, in which as second mate he made a number of voyages between Singapore and Borneo. These voyages were crucial. In the course of them he met the originals of several of his most famous characters; and he also obtained that first-hand knowledge of Malaya which afterwards supplied so much material for his fiction.

In 1889 he was back in England, already with a pen in his hand; but before he could do more than begin a book he determined to go to the Congo, where he thought that through certain family influence he could obtain command of a Belgian river steamer. Some of the details of this exploit are to be found in *An Outpost of Progress*, most of them in *Heart of Darkness*; but he did not get his command and he soon returned to London ill and discouraged. It was not until two years later that he was offered the post of mate in the *Torrens*, 'one of the most successful ships ever built, one of the fastest and for many years the favourite passenger ship to Adelaide'; and it was during one of the trips made by the *Torrens* that he formed his first literary friendship—with John Galsworthy.

Galsworthy, at that time a sanguine young man, had been upon a pious pilgrimage to Samoa (which he did not reach); and when he joined the *Torrens* at Adelaide he very soon observed with interest one of the officers of the ship.

Very dark he looked in the burning sunlight, tanned, with a peaked brown beard, almost black hair, and dark brown eyes, over which the lids were deeply folded. He was thin, not tall, his arms very long, his shoulders broad, his head set rather forward. He spoke to me with a strong foreign accent.

The officer not only spoke to Galsworthy; he entertained him on the voyage home with yarns and expositions. He quite enchanted the young traveller, who recorded that

fascination was Conrad's great characteristic—the fascination of vivid expressiveness and zest, of his deeply affectionate heart, and his far-ranging, subtle mind. He was extraordinarily perceptive and receptive.

The strong foreign accent remained with him throughout life. Illness made him yet thinner, his hair grew grey, he aged early; but what he was then he continued to be until the end of his life. The subtlety, the perceptiveness, the receptiveness, and the love of yarning were all a part of the novelist's temperament. And when in 1893 Conrad left the *Torrens* (and also, although this was far from his intention, the sea) he gave himself entirely to the task of completing a written yarn which he had begun five years earlier. The book, *Almayer's Folly*, was finished by the end of May 1894, was then sent by messenger to the London publisher, Fisher Unwin, and by Unwin was immediately accepted for publication.

That was the beginning. It might have been the end; for Conrad still thought of himself as a sailor. But Edward Garnett, a young reader at Unwin's, who happened to be precociously the greatest discoverer and encourager of literary artists English publishers have ever known, took a hand. He said to Conrad: 'You have the style, you have the temperament. Why not write another?' Conrad, enchanted by this simple suggestion, proceeded to write *An Outcast of the Islands*. He then married (on 24th March 1896) an English girl, on his honeymoon began a third novel, and at the same time tentatively experimented with the kind of writing for which, without any question whatever, he had the greatest talent—the long short story, or narrative, sometimes of an episode or series of episodes occurring at sea, sometimes of a situation arising among men who live remote from civilization in the tropics, but always of a problem of character or conduct. To this period and type belong *An Outpost of Progress*, *The Nigger of the 'Narcissus,'* *Youth*, *Heart of Darkness*, *Lord Jim*, *Typhoon*, and *Falk*. All were written by 1903. He never afterwards wrote anything as fine.

Besides being much delayed by illness, Conrad was a desperately slow worker, for it was his ambition to be what he called 'an artist in words.' His literary aim was 'the just expression seizing upon the essential.' Almost all his stories were published serially, but they appeared in magazines with relatively small circulations; and in book form, despite the applause of reviewers, they had no popularity. Consequently Conrad remained poor. If it had not been for the help given him by his agent, J. B. Pinker, he might have starved. By his own admission, once he had re-created those seascapes and those pictures of the Congo and Malaya, he felt there was nothing left for him to write about. In vain, having exhausted his first strength of inspiration, did he try new styles. He was tempted, in this hour of difficulty, to the difficult and treacherous craft of collaboration; and at first in extravaganza and then in a joint rewriting of a sentimental romance, conceived and partly executed by his friend, he worked with Ford Madox Hueffer. Finally he settled to the composition of a long and elaborate novel about silver mines in a South American state. The result was *Nostromo*.

At the time of its publication and for long afterwards it was usual to say that this was Conrad's greatest book. In the infection of the moment (for I had discovered Conrad at the age of seventeen, and was then at the height of admiration) I too thought it was a masterpiece, and so it may be; but I should not now hold to that opinion. *Nostromo* was the first book of Conrad's to be built or manufactured. But the first time he departed from the imaginative reconstruction of lives and episodes drawn from the fibre of his own experience. He invented a whole *milieu*. From a single paragraph in a book of reminiscence he derived the hint for a tale involving many lives, and he planned this with the most profound seriousness and wrote it with scrupulous care. Unquestionably the result was a disappointment to him, for *Nostromo*, however highly praised, was a failure with the public and always remained a comparative failure. The book is very elaborate; it is as rich as can be in comprehensions and in diverse characters; but its movement is extremely slow, the detail of its intrigue is not always intelligible; and it does not quite escape dullness.

For ten years after this (1904), his fiction was the least interesting part of his writing, and only *The Mirror of the Sea* and a gradual absorption by the public of novels and tales written earlier maintained a position which had seemed to be assured upon the publication of *Lord Jim*. His health was poor, and that choice of subjects which in a couple of melodramatic tales brought complicated ingenuity to bear upon Terrorism was unfortunate. He had lost his way. His fortunes were at their lowest. In 1911 something like a sensation was caused among strangers by the news that Conrad had been granted a Civil List pension of one hundred pounds a year.

And then, quite unexpectedly, everything was changed. A book which was to have been published in the autumn of 1913 was held over until the spring. It appeared at the very beginning of 1914, and created a furore. The book was *Chance*, in which for the first time he romanticized the character of a woman; and from that moment he was a prosperous author. The reintroduction of Marlow, the imaginary self, the penetrating seer of life and character who narrated intricate tales to other men as he sat unseen in the darkness; the return to the yarn which was Conrad's happiest medium of expression; and above all the accidental use of a theme—the theme of what may be called deferred or doubtful consummation—which has led to so many fictional successes in the past, was irresistible. The book has charm, fluency, suspense, a few vividly drawn persons, and a great deal of that singular probing beauty which was a chief cause of Marlow's (and Conrad's) fascination. *Chance* was a tremendous success. If an author, for whatever reason, has been long neglected, there seems no end to the enthusiasm which accompanies the turning tide; and in this case the tide led on to fortune. And when for the theme of his next book Conrad went back to the East, a further fond blurring of the critical faculty and a further rejoicing among all who had long admired the work of a distinguished artist followed his journey. Though the old glory was diffused, success had warmed his memory, and *Victory* rounded off the tale.

Prosperity continued until Conrad's death. He did not write anything more which can be compared with his best work, and his health slowly declined until 1924, when he died, was saluted with dignity by his own generation, and in some slight measure was forgotten. But his best work is still better in its own way than the best work of his successors, and a re-reading of it is very reassuring to those who recall with misgiving an enthusiasm of the past. This I say notwithstanding the fact that *Lord Jim*, which is his most interesting novel, loses its authentic quality in the middle and drops to a quality not wholly beyond the range of a lesser writer. It is a book about a sailor whose nerve

failed in an hour of crisis, who was arraigned and punished for
his failure (while the greater criminals escaped), and whose
subsequent life, haunted by something more than his own
memory, was a series of misadventures. *Lord Jim's* quality
lies in the curious intricacy and subtlety of the method by which
we are made aware of all the circumstances of failure and
discovery, and the beautiful delicate sureness with which two
scenes, those of the inquiry and the failure of nerve, are so
pictured that our imaginations are quickened to the highest
pitch of understanding, to positive complicity in the scenes
themselves. By contrast with these scenes, the rest of the
book, although vivid, is of lesser importance. What stirs us is
the evocation of those crucial moments.

The evocation is attained by means of Conrad's oblique method
of narration. He does not tell the story himself: that would be
too simple. He does not tell it as a straightforward tale: that
would be too crude. He tells it in the form of a yarn in which
the subtle and omniscient narrator has power to hold hearers as
the Ancient Mariner held the wedding guest, diverging, doub-
ling, speculating, bringing to his elucidations all sorts of other
yarns, in one moment as near to his subject and in another as
far from it as he pleases, as exact or as vague at all times in any
detail as will best suit the dramatic emphasis he desires, as
colloquial or as eloquent as the author thinks fit for his purpose.
What an elastic method! How intimate and how pictorial!
How reflective and how dramatic! Its impact, when it has the
sea and seamen perfectly within grasp, is breath-taking.

It would be interesting to trace the history of this method,
and to know how Conrad came to make use of it. The yarn, of
course, was natural to him as to other travellers, and as a kind
of informal literary form it was used considerably during the
nineties by Kipling and Conan Doyle and several more. Henry
James, further, had in *The Spoils of Poynton, In the Cage*, etc.,
allowed one subtle mind to reconstruct and so dramatize a whole
series of significant circumstances. But Conrad took the method
farther. Where James was content with subtlety in itself, the
thing 'done,' Conrad wanted to explain the thing—whatever it
was—quite down to its ethical basis. While James hummed
and faltered over the small domestic object which in *The Ambassadors* could not be mentioned, Conrad very anxiously probed
to the occasion when Falk had eaten human flesh, and why he
had done this, and indeed must explain just how everything
came about. Yet he too had his irony, and *Falk* is brimming

with it; and there is no doubt in my mind that if it had been told in any other way but this *Falk* would have been either trivial or disgusting.

The simple explanation of this difference probably lies in the fact that Conrad was a traveller and James was 'just literary,' that Conrad had known Falk and James really could not be bothered to bring his mind to a definition of the object. 'So-ome small thing,' he said, waving a hand; 'it doesn't matter what.' But there is more in the contrast than that. James enjoyed the mystification. Towards the end of his life, rather than be definite he would take refuge in an ejaculation—'She's wonderful'—or a vagueness. But Marlow, who 'had sunken cheeks, a yellow complexion, a straight back, an ascetic aspect, and, with his arms dropped, the palms of hands outwards, resembled an idol,' was in despair at his failure to ascertain and reproduce every delicacy. When his host on one occasion murmured 'You are so subtle, Marlow,' Marlow answered in melancholy: 'Who? I? Oh, no! . . . Try as I may for the success of this yarn I am missing innumerable shades—they are so fine, so difficult to render in colourless words!' James was absorbed in the exquisite ingenuities of his craft; Conrad in his search for the very essence of truth. 'But do you notice how, three hundred miles beyond the end of telegraph cables and mail-boat lines, the haggard utilitarian lies of our civilization wither and die, to be replaced by pure exercises of imagination, that have the futility, often the charm, and sometimes the deep hidden truthfulness, of works of art?'

Conrad objected to the general belief that he was a writer of sea stories. He said: 'It seems to me that people imagine I sit here and brood over sea stuff. That is quite a mistake. I brood certainly, but . . .' He regarded himself as a psychologist. 'I insist not on the events but on their effect upon the persons in the tale.' And again: 'In everything I have written there is always one invariable intention, and that is to capture the reader's attention, by securing his interest and enlisting his sympathies for the matter in hand, whatever it may be, within the limits of the visible world and within the boundaries of human emotions.'

Norman Douglas, perhaps thinking of *Lord Jim*, ingeniously suggests that the worth of Conrad's psychologizing was nullified by very strict standards of conduct, and an irrelevant conception of 'honour.' Douglas knew Conrad, which I never did; but the novelist's concern is with what Conrad called 'the matter in hand,' and even Douglas, I presume, would not deny that it is legitimate to show standards of conduct, however conventional, operating in simple minds. On the larger question of whether there were heights and depths beyond Conrad's recognition, or beyond his sympathy, there may be room for debate. His positive performance remains. Using for the sake of its simultaneous intimacy and detachment the free form of the yarn, and sometimes, to the horror of purists, the quoted yarn within a yarn, Conrad brought sea and tropics more immediately home to the minds of men than any other writer has ever done. Captain Whalley in *The End of the Tether* and Captain McWhirr in *Typhoon*, Lord Jim as long as he is a sailor, are palpable. The scenes in which they move lend such stimulus to the imagination that we experience them as we read. To myself, this conjunction — some may call it stereoscopic — of intimacy and detachment represents the highest achievement of realistic art. It preserves the picture; it rouses the emotion; we see and understand all; and when the spell is withdrawn we are again, without shock and without disillusion, in the life we know.

V. H. M. TOMLINSON

Bates actually arrives at his destination in the first sentence. He steps across in thirty-eight words from England to the Amazon. . . . Well, I did not. I say it is a gross deception. . . . How Bates got over to his wonderful blue butterflies in those forest paths under a tropic sun in thirty-eight words I do not know.

H. M. TOMLINSON, *The Sea and the Jungle.*

I should have liked to dwell at some length, here or elsewhere, upon two writers who deserve celebration in the pages of any such book. They are Morley Roberts and David Bone. Roberts, the friend of Gissing and Hudson, and a novelist and short story writer of merit, claims mention in particular on account of *The Western Avernus*, one of the best records of a man's travel experience ever written; while Bone has written in *The Brassbounder* a glorious picture of life at sea in the days of sailing ships. But Roberts must be excluded because nearly all his non-scientific or non-medical work belongs to its time, which is long pre-Georgian; and Bone's total literary product is so small in bulk that when I have expressed admiration for it and the reader's complaint that Bone should have continued to be a practical and ageless traveller all his life there is little to add.

David Bone was born in Glasgow in 1874. He is one of three

famous brothers (there is a fourth, less famous, who has also published some account of his adventures), of whom one, Muirhead, is an artist and etcher, and the third, James, London editor of *The Manchester Guardian,* is a writer and character whose part in the Georgian literary scene is unseizable, though at the same time beyond question.   His is a humorous eye; he is a great yarner; and he has such a sense of phrase that there is not a spare word in *The Brassbounder* or in *Merchantmen-at-Arms,* but only a mastery by which scenes are brought to life and given their original colour and movement.   It is the same whether he speaks or writes; sense is so exact, voice so rich, pen so unfaltering.   I have never been to sea upon a ship commanded by Captain Bone, but if I were to do so I should expect to arrive punctually after an experience of all the beauties and braveries that the sea can offer, and with a memory fit to last for ever.

That must be a sufficient testimony to a fine sailor and a magnificent writer.   My business now is rather with a landsman, but a landsman who has been to sea a number of times, and into the jungle, too, taking with him a mildness of manner, a warmly coloured pen, a small voice, and an eye and sensitiveness rare among professional writers.   His Christian names I do not know —I doubt if he knows them himself, for nobody would dream of addressing him by one of them when an abbreviation of his surname is quite obviously all that is needed.   I have already identified this man at the head of the section.   He is H. M. Tomlinson; and his literary discoverer, round about 1911, was Ford Madox Hueffer, then, as I have previously told, editing *The English Review.*   Prior to that, Tomlinson, having escaped from an office job, had at the age of thirty or so (he was born in 1873) joined the staff of *The Morning Leader.*   He was later to work as war correspondent for Dickens's old paper, *The Daily News,* under A. G. Gardiner, and then for the weekly review, *The Nation,* under Henry Massingham; and like Massingham he could not write the smallest paragraph without stamping it with his own personality.   But his books began in 1912 with *The Sea and the Jungle,* and *The Sea and the Jungle,* which was not at the time a popular success, remains still his most characteristic production. You will find in its luminous pages all the various Tomlinsons who have since expressed themselves so picturesquely upon the subjects of the sea and the war and the politicians and other matters.

In that book he gives an account of his participation in an

exploratory journey from Wales to the Amazon and farther up the Amazon than any ship of such draught (23 feet) as the *Capella* had ever previously been. He had a friend who was chief engineer on this ship, and he was engaged nominally as purser for the voyage. There are no lies in *The Sea and the Jungle*. It begins at the beginning, with our author finding his way aboard in darkness and rain. It continues with an account of a storm, not as a sailor sees it, but as we ourselves (who are not sailors) would see it and feel afraid and very uncomfortable. And we then see and feel the atmosphere of Pará and other Amazonian features. It is an experience. We actually sail in the *Capella*. Although our vocabularies may be smaller than that of our guide and companion, we share all his sensations. Here is Tomlinson mildly ironic at the moment preceding the start of his journey:

I have a clear memory of the newspapers as they were that morning. I had a sheaf of them, for it is my melancholy business to know what each is saying. I learned there were dark and portentous matters, not actually with us, but looming, each already rather larger than a man's hand. If certain things happened, said one half the papers, ruin stared us in the face. If those things did not happen, said the other half, ruin stared us in the face. . . . You paid your halfpenny and were damned either way. If you paid a penny you got more for your money.

That is one mood. Here is another, describing the hour of storm:

I turned up the dull and stinking oil lamp, and tried to read; but that fuliginous glim haunted the pages. That black-edged light too much resembled my own thoughts made manifest. There were some bunches of my cabin-mate's clothes hanging from hooks, and I watched their erratic behaviour instead. The water in the carafe was also interesting, because quite mad, standing diagonally in the bottle, and then reversing. A lump of soap made a flying leap from the washstand, and then slithered about the floor like something hunted and panic-stricken. I listened to numerous little voices. There was no telling their origins. There was a chorus in the cabin, whispers, plaints, creaks, wails, and grunts; but they were foundered in the din when the spittoon, which was an empty meat tin, got its lashings loose, and began a rioting fandango on the concrete. Over the clothes chest, which was also our table and a cabin fixture, was a portrait of the mate's sweetheart, and on its frame was one of my busy little friends the cockroaches; for the mate and I do not sleep alone in this cabin, not by hundreds. The cockroach stood in thought, waving his hands interrogatively. . . .

Finally, as the ship reaches land:

The *Capella* continued to stand in, till America was more than a frail and tinted illusion which sometimes faded the more the eye sought it. Presently it cast reflections. The islands grew into cobalt layers, with vistas of silver water between them; they acquired body. . . . Curtains as black as bitumen draped to the waters from great heights. Two of these appalling curtains, trailing over America, were drawn a little apart. We could see beyond them to a diminishing array of glowing cloud summits; far through those parted black curtains of storm we saw an accidental revelation of a secret and wonderful region with a sun of its own. And all, gigantic clouds, the sea, the far and frail coast, were serene and still. The air had ceased to breathe. . . . We went slowly over a lower world obscurely lighted by phosphorescent waves.

Tomlinson's style is a natural product, and it results from his lifelong habit of mind and ear. The sentences form themselves in his head as he writes; they are not laboriously reshaped after they have been set down. Any reader who knows the author will recognize every cadence they contain, and every word, even where it seems conscious, as if it were uttered as part of the conversation in that hoarse little undertone. He will see Tomlinson's surprisingly tall, bony head, and a hand at the ear to catch whatever reply is made, the almost anxious gravity of Tomlinson's expression, the sad, dry smile preceding a story, never afterwards forgotten, which sets the party in a roar, the thoughtfulness, the honesty, the convulsed silent laughter, and above all the scepticism which runs through his mind like a whisper.

He began by taking to heart the ways of two meditative writers who are still among his favourites. His pen and his speech are alike the pen and speech of a lover of Henry David Thoreau and Ralph Waldo Emerson. For Thoreau, in particular, he has a feeling that approaches veneration. That is because he is by temperament half a philosopher—one who turns over and over in his mind the nature of man, his needs and his errant civilization—and half a journalist. Also, having seen the action of much humbug, he is socially indignant, so that when he writes (or when he speaks) of suffering or of what he believes to be injustice or villainy he is often moved, as cold-hearted people are not moved, to emotion. Cold-hearted people, accordingly, or those who fear the display of emotion lest it should break down altogether too many restraints, suppose Tomlinson to be sentimental; whereas he is in reality so simple that he still believes in the opposition of virtue and vice. He believes that the rich are unscrupulous, and that the very poor never have a chance. But unlike so many of our self-righteous *rentier*-communists of the latest literary movement he has experienced the life of the very poor, and knows what a slum is

like, so that some indignation, however unsophisticated, may
be permitted him.   Besides, the doctrine preached by Tomlinson
is old-fashioned Liberalism, and whatever he may call himself
(I do not know) he is an old-fashioned Liberal.

All his journalism has been done for periodicals appealing to
socially indignant Liberals of the reforming kind—*The Morning
Leader, The Daily News, The Nation*.   These papers are gone,
as Liberalism is gone.   The more sentimental Liberals of the
middle class, to whom they appealed, have taken a farther step
to the Left; those who wish to maintain the world as they knew
it have moved for safety to the Right.   Tomlinson's views are
anachronistic.   Very well, he has written four novels; and the
latest of them, *All Hands*, is in terms of novel-writing the best.
But Tomlinson is not a born novelist.   The books have been
written less as novels than as testimonies to the author's view
of life; and he has with difficulty mastered a craft that seems easy
and is very difficult.

I do not profess to be able to explain what the novelist's
special gift is; but I think that one prime need is an interest in
characters for their own sakes, irrespective of their political,
social, and moral significance.   That may be an old-fashioned
definition; but it would explain why many writers of considerable literary ability and much intelligence write works of fiction
which do not stir the imagination of their readers and which in
fact are without life.   It would explain why some of those who
cannot write novels nowadays declare that the novel is an exhausted form.   In Tomlinson's case there is a great experience
of life and scene, all of which has its value in making a book
readable or important to the reader.   But I doubt whether
Tomlinson has the detachment to be either a good critic or a
good novelist.   He has too many, or too strict, moral notions.
They get in the way.   He sees other people from the outside,
trusts them or distrusts them, likes them or dislikes them, but
never has amused himself by imagining them as enchanting
labyrinths, as fiery particles of flesh and spirit, as children, as
human beings.   To him, in a sense, they are all moral ideas.

That is not to say that he is a prig, or uncharitable, or humourless.   On the contrary, his literary enthusiasms of later date are
for writers of a mordant and sceptical cast, for Lucian, for
Anatole France, for Norman Douglas; and his own patient and
yet scornful humour has an acid bite that never contradicts
his astonishing charity.   But he does not relish character as
character; his gift is for writing.   He is reflective as Thoreau

and Emerson were reflective; and he is a natural descriptive writer. When he has something to describe which has deeply moved him his writing is genuine communication, and as such ranks high in our time.

VI. NORMAN DOUGLAS

A man who has tried to remain a mere citizen of the world and refused to squeeze himself into the narrow methods and aspirations of any epoch or country . . .

NORMAN DOUGLAS, *Alone.*

My last traveller is one who has been not only far and wide upon a part of the earth's surface but some way into the heart of the mystery as well. Rightly to appreciate Norman Douglas one should be a Scotsman, a student of antiquity, an epicure, a wit, a naturalist, and an amoral philosopher. He is all of these things, and more. He is not solely a Scot, for his mother was partly German. He was at school at Uppingham and in Germany. He has been in the diplomatic service, sub-editor of *The English Review*, a teacher of French to American soldiers in Paris, and many other things. He has written books on *The Herpetology of the Duchy of Baden, London Street Games, Old Calabria,* and the private lives of gods and other prehistoric persons. How old he is I could not say; I assume that he is now nearing seventy, for he announced some years ago that he had passed the grand climacteric (which is the age of sixty-three), and of his own Mr Keith, said by many to be a self-portrait, although Douglas did not so intend it, he says:

Mr Keith was older than he looked—incredibly old, in fact, though nobody could bring himself to believe it; he was well preserved by means of a complicated system of life, the details of which, he used to declare, were not fit for publication. That was only his way of talking. He exaggerated so dreadfully. His face was clean-shaven, rosy, and of cherubic fullness.

To this kindly description D. H. Lawrence adds the gloss:

D—— was decidedly shabby and a gentleman, with his wicked red face and tufted eyebrows.

But Mr Keith, who although 'a perfect host,' was at the same time 'an egoist, a solitary, in his pleasures,'

disliked funerals. For all his open mind and open bowels, Mr Keith displayed an unreasoning hatred of death and, what was still more remarkable, not the least shame in confessing it. . . Mr Keith was in love with life. It dealt fairly with him. It made him loth to bid farewell to this gracious earth and the blue sky overhead, to his cooks and his books, his gardeners and roses and flaming cannas; loth to exchange these things of love, these tangible delights, for a hideous and everlasting annihilation.

To which I shall add two quotations from Orioli's *Moving Along*, in which there are charming glimpses of Douglas. The first:

Norman said he felt quite at home here. He was really in Old Calabria now, and I could see he was enjoying it. We could sit round the brazier all night, he said, getting our clothes dry gradually, smoking our pipes and drinking wine. What more could anybody want? As to sleeping—damn it, if one cares to sleep, one need only rest one's elbows on one's knees and put one's head into one's hands, and there you are. Delicious!

And the second:

Norman ate more than the rest of us put together and then regretted that he could eat no more; he said a man could not expect to have a proper appetite at his time of life.

You have the impression from these quotations of one who is interested in good food—an epicure. By his own account, given in the autobiographical *Looking Back*, he has been much interested in other corporeal matters. He has loved life, women, boys, food, drink, and knowledge. And he quotes with approval the story of a Leontine philosopher who, when asked 'how he had managed to attain a hundred years with such glowing health and jollity,' 'was wont to shake his hoary locks and roar out "Because I never went a step out of my way to please anybody but myself."' Like so many Scotsmen he was born an antiquary, and like his own Mr Keith again he 'knew too much, and had travelled too far, to be anything but a hopeless unbeliever.' That is, he is not merely a sceptic, but is completely without the ordinary human need to justify himself to others. For this reason his work has been unpopular, and has sometimes inspired disgust in squeamish readers.

Not because the work itself has ever been pornographic: far from it. Merely because those who regard themselves as most emancipated from convention are usually most conventional. Rationalists comport themselves with a kind of glee in conscious blasphemy; and the very ironists of recent fashion do not care to endure the irony of others and in fact fear it. Douglas, they feel, might—so remote is his soul—laugh even at them. Horrible! Horrible! 'An egoist, a solitary,' said Douglas, speaking of Mr Keith. Yes, entirely selfish, no doubt, and a hedonist; an utterly irreverent mind beside which the incredulities of others are but the self-conscious waywardnesses of youth. And yet 'a perfect host,' and a man of whom Lawrence, never sanguine regarding the virtues of his friends, was forced by candour to say 'D—— has never left me in the lurch.'

Douglas, whose literary work has been fitful because he cares less for literary fame than for life, has written several books in a style to make all who care for right expression envious of such perfect skill. And these books are packed with original observation and research presented so allusively and with such a damping of irony that one must love wit for its own sake to appreciate all the learning out of which it flows. If Douglas, with his reading of saintly biographies and his curious enjoyment of human idiocy, had kept to the narrow path of scholarship, he would have received the rewards of dignity. Or if he had been less intent upon knowing the details of the past, and had given his time to verbal decoration, he would have had the shallower sort at his feet to hear a flow of ridicule and invention such as his conversation affords. But he is not ambitious. He has wanted to enjoy himself. He has wanted to learn, not for the sake of exhibiting his own splendours, but because the whole business of life has seemed to him to be very odd and interesting and worthy of exploration.

Having his own pleasure in view, he has not sought to teach others. That is the worst feature of the Scottish kind of humour; it is self-sufficing. Having no belief, he has not wished to breed disciples or scatter his faith abroad. And that, too, has been a mistake. The young and ardent, always looking for assurances of immortality, or at least of importance, have found him negative. Only to lovers of classic civilization and literature has he afforded the spectacle of a modern Ancient Greek, too wise for illusion, and not in the least bothered by his lack of credit.

It is to *South Wind* that most readers of Douglas turn for pleasure; they would do better to read and re-read *Old Calabria*, which is his masterpiece. By comparison, *South Wind* is a light record of the extraordinary life led by dwellers upon the island of Capri. We assume that it is a work of irony, and that no such fantastic creatures could ever be gathered together in a single spot (I am not sure, by the way, that *South Wind*, in this aspect, is not the begetting cause of many artificial gatherings lately popular with novelists of hotel life, liner life, tenement life, and so on); but Francis Brett Young, in his preface to the English translations from Cerio's *Aria di Capri*, says that it is but a transcript from life made in all simplicity. It embraces a little mock hagiology, some doubtful geology, a plot (Douglas is firm as to the plot, and also the moral, which many have missed), and some delicious writing. It is full of entertainment, and without doubt, in company with the equally delicious works of Thomas Love Peacock, has served as an inspiration to Aldous Huxley, among others. But it is, beside *Old Calabria*, a by-product, a holiday, a nonsense-version of many-sided truth. *Old Calabria* is the real thing, and a work of unique character. It is a travel book, a history book, a system of philosophy, and a self-portrait all in one. Too rich a diet for some minds? No; the difficulty is one of concentration. The sweep and toughness of Douglas's curiosity is greater than any we can summon, and we put the book aside for reflection. Sometimes we do not take it up again. That is true of all Douglas's work.

Old Calabria is the best of his books because Douglas has always felt at home in Calabria. For one thing, he can persuade himself that it must have looked, in ancient times, much as it looks now; for another it is full of news for the antiquary who is also of a scientific turn and a collector of legends. He has his own method of acquiring knowledge, and a simple one. Orioli says:

> Norman gave chocolates to the children. . . . He never travels in the less frequented parts without sweets in his pocket for the young ones, and without snuff for the old ones. He says that they are the only people worth talking to; all the middle generation in this country is useless for his purposes, too worldly and material, no legends, no poetry. How many hearts has he not conquered with sweets, and how many stories has he not collected with snuff! I have seen him giving snuff to old women of eighty, and then talking to them for hours and hours.

Well, the hours and hours are not wasted; and they were not wasted when he was gathering the material for *Old Calabria*, for he is well grounded in natural science, he already possessed much out-of-the-way knowledge, and he loves travelling and seeing and knowing so dearly that no discomfort or danger could possibly deter him from making every necessary investigation. Nor did he hesitate to buy and read masses of saintly biography with a solemnly mischievous attention that never becomes merely derisive. The book was a labour of love. Hills, villages, saints, critical asides, curious facts, and the author's personality all jostle each other in its pages. It is fit reading for sage and ribald, for ethnologist and the student of comparative hagiology.

The lesser books, such as *Siren Land*, which is similarly notable for what Douglas calls 'that (characteristic) veneer of erudition,' and *Fountains in the Sand*, have much virtue as monologues; and the queer autobiography, *Looking Back*, which is built upon an array of visiting cards used by the author as stimulus to memory, and which brings us closer than any other to his conscienceless temper, will be read as long as books are read at all. But only by the few. And when I say 'the few,' I am not using that term in the snobbish, or even the Stendhalian, sense, for I do not share the genteel notion that what other people like must be contemptible, but solely 'the few.' Douglas is, and must be, enjoyable only to those who share at least one of his many interests. When he writes such a prehistoric tale as *They Went*, for example, I can only feel faintly amused; and when he writes shorter works such as *In the Beginning* I find them quite without point. That is because these works are outside my sympathy. To classical students, on the other hand, *In the Beginning* is a marvel; and to those who know how much erudition is displayed in *They Went* that book evidently has peculiar value. I mention my own deficiency, not to exalt the deficiency (that is too often done), but to explain why certain works of Douglas may miss fire with certain readers, as these two do with me. The fault does not lie with Douglas, although perhaps a greater, and less self-sufficient, man could have brought his scholarship less desultorily and more universally to book.

CHAPTER III: BLACK AND WHITE

I

Every artist goes to real life for his matter, and from its chaos brings us an idea. . . . The specific difference of the realist is that, having extracted his idea, instead of further distilling it (as the Classicist does) or disguising it with mysterious essences (as the Romantic does), he endeavours to restore to it the flavour of reality. He endeavours to manifest the very texture and illusion of Life itself. Having unravelled a thread, he shows it us with a new artful tangle of his own.

GEORGE CALDERON, Preface to *Two Plays* by Tchekhov.

THE realist is inveterately plain, and not coloured; and the fact that the lives of wealthy people are so rarely treated with realism has led many to suppose that realism is pure squalor. But English realism is undoubtedly as old as Thomas Nashe, and while it has come to modern readers tinctured by French and Russian influence we have no more realistic writer than Neil Lyons, who is a humorist. I wonder whether George Calderon, in the extract I have quoted above, was quite right in his belief that realism is a technical matter: may it not, rather, be a personal matter? As a rough division of men, it may be said that there are some who, like Stevenson, think every action the better for a bit of purple, and some who shun colour. There are, it is true, the Quakers, but I am not thinking of them. Purple was used by Stevenson figuratively—as a synonym for bravery, or display; and his heroine, Catriona, who is rather like Stevenson, after saying that she ought to have been a man child, goes on:

In my own thoughts it is so I am always; and I go on telling myself about this thing that is to befall and that. Then it comes to the place of the fighting, and it comes over me that I am only a girl at all events; and then I have to twist my story round about, so that the fighting is to stop, and yet me have the best of it; . . . and I am the boy that makes the fine speeches all through, like Mr David Balfour.

Stevenson and Catriona were both romantics. They saw themselves, as Pyramus did, in heroic parts, triumphant parts, fine costumes, speaking grand words, doing glorious deeds. Steven-

son's books are the echo of romantic ambition, and his stage is
a toy stage.

And there are those others who, while they cannot deceive
themselves with the stuff of charades, are yet chiefly delighted
at the thought of appearing a little noble or brilliant, self-
sacrificing, brave, enduring, arch and sensitive; and they are
the sentimentalists, to whom we owe the bulk of our fiction.
Others again, and these are inverted sentimentalists, are never
satisfied with life, but must show it as something more bitter and
testing and less heroic than we had hoped, a terrible disillusion
for those who will not swim with the tide and run with the mob.
They cry 'Woe! Woe!' but in reality it is their object that we
should admire them for what they refuse to do and say; and it is
quite true that we are often impressed with their castigations
of society and human nature.

But if we all have our favourite roles in life, and wittingly or
unwittingly play them in our books, there are some who, for
one reason or another, do not wish to take the lead, and do not
wish to impress by the display of their own brilliance or courage
or disillusion. These are the realists or potential realists, for
whom the scene is complete if it be played by others, so long
as these others are human (and not dolls), and so long as *they*
can but watch and relish all that happens, and gratify vanity
(it may be), or compensate themselves otherwise, by setting it
down without adornment but with satisfying precision. Their
preferred role is that of spectator, recorder, critic, not protagonist
or participant; and their wear so sober that it will attract no
notice at all from their fellow-creatures.

You could say, if you liked, that these were men in whom
what used to be called the feminine element is very strong. Or
that they are without passion; or that their minds are too strict
to allow passion its rein. Or that there is some physical reason,
such as the stammer from which both Arnold Bennett and
Somerset Maugham have suffered, or Galsworthy's shyness, or
that curious accident of George Moore's childhood which he thus
describes:

It is difficult for me to believe any good of myself. Within the
oftentimes bombastic and truculent appearance that I present to
the world, trembles a heart shy as a wren in the hedgerow or a mouse
along the wainscotting. And the question has always interested
me, whether I brought this lack of belief in myself into the world
with me, or whether it was a gift from Nature, or whether I was
trained into it by my parents at so early an age that it became part

of myself. I lean to the theory of acquisition rather than to that of inheritance, for it seems to me that I can trace my inveterate distrust of myself back to the years when my father and mother used to tell me that I would certainly marry an old woman, Honor King, who used to come to the door begging. This joke did not wear out; it lasted through my childhood; and I remember still how I used to dread her appearance, or her name, for either was sufficient to incite somebody to remind me of the nuptials that awaited me in a few years. I understood very well that the joke rested on the assumption that I was such an ugly little boy that nobody else would marry me.

But whatever the cause it seems to me that there is more force in an argument for negative qualities in the realist than for any belief in a determined choice of realism as against any other ism whatever. 'This craving,' says Moore in another place,

this craving for observation of manners, this instinct for the rapid notation of gestures and words that epitomize a state of feeling, of attitudes that mirror forth the soul, declared itself a main passion. . . . With the patience of a cat at a mouse-hole I watched and listened; . . . and though I laughed and danced, and made merry with them, *I was not of them.*

II. GEORGE MOORE

I came into the world apparently with a nature like a smooth sheet of wax, bearing no impress, but capable of receiving any; of being moulded into all shapes. Nor am I exaggerating when I say I think that I might equally have been a Pharaoh, an ostler, a pimp, an archbishop, and that in the fulfilment of the duties of each a certain measure of success would have been mine.

GEORGE MOORE, *Confessions of a Young Man.*

George Moore was the son of a landed Irish gentleman who became a member of Parliament and who bred and raced horses. He was born in 1852. His childhood was spent partly upon the paternal estate in the west of Ireland and partly in London, and neither in Ireland nor in London was he able to learn anything at school. Although the son of Roman Catholic parents, he became very early, through his private reading, an agnostic; and although to please his father he agreed to be a soldier he really wanted to be a painter. Finding military training excessively disagreeable, he soon abandoned it for the companionship of not quite excellent artists, actors, and their free-living friends. He 'cultivated with care the acquaintance of a neighbour who had taken the Globe Theatre for the purpose of producing Offenbach's operas'; and when once he had done this he was in the true Paradise of all coldly sensual young men. 'Bouquets, stalls, rings, delighted me; and of all, the life of the theatre—that life of raw gaslight, whitewashed walls, of doggerel verse, slangy polkas and waltzes, interested me beyond legitimate measure. . . . My mother suffered, and expected ruin, for I took no trouble to conceal anything; I boasted of dissipation. But there was no need of fear, for I was naturally endowed with a very clear sense of self-preservation; I neither betted nor drank, nor contracted debts, nor a secret marriage; from a worldly point of view, I was a model young man indeed.'

Still, however, his mind had no positive direction; only a bent towards pleasure and the arts. As soon as he was of age (his father died when Moore was eighteen, and Moore inherited the estate), he set out for Paris. There, continuing his interest in painting and literature, stage and opera, he established himself among rather more excellent artists and writers than those whom he had known at home, and, while he soon gave up painting, lived for ten years the life of a dilettante, deep in the aesthetic fashions of an age already drawing to its close. Not until near the end of his stay in Paris did he awaken from a kind of strolling complacency of self-indulgence; and then a manifesto by Zola in praise of realism shocked him into new and positive literary faith. He knew at last what he must do with his talent, and the genre for which his temper had prepared him.

But in the middle of the dream and at the very moment of Moore's awakening to direction, news came that his estate was in difficulties, and he was forced to leave Paris. In London he lived twelve years in comparative poverty before wealth returned and he became again independent. During those years he wrote art criticism, and consorted, as he has amusingly told, with a group of men who gathered round Tinsley, the publisher; and he began to produce his earliest realistic novels.

The first of them, written when Moore was thirty, was *A Modern Lover*; the second that landmark in modern literature, *A Mummer's Wife*. Acquaintance with poor artists and actors, then and in the past (a fellow-lodger was an actress, and the wretched Alice in *A Mummer's Wife* began her downfall by an effort to be sprightly in the part of Serpolette), was invaluable to him. Boyhood memory of his father's racing stables and the social ways of the Irish gentry and the Irish peasants was always at his call. And, having embraced the realistic method, he pursued it unremittingly. Nothing was lost upon him. He used to talk with a hard-pressed and illiterate maid-of-all-work at his lodging-house, and later with his charwoman in the Temple; and he says that while the charwoman 'didn't inspire the subject of *Esther Waters*, she was the atmosphere I required for the book, and to talk to her at breakfast before beginning to write was an excellent preparation.' Excellent indeed; for Moore explained that he had used another model 'without shame or stint, as I have used all those with whom I have been brought into close contact.'

When the Boer War broke out at the end of the century, Moore found himself much opposed to the British Government in that matter, as many English people did; and he was inclined to shake the dust of the accursed oppressor from his foot. He therefore went to Ireland for two years, where he met Irish writers and had a good deal to do with the founding of the Irish Theatre, a scheme sponsored by his friend Edward Martyn and by W. B. Yeats. He was a severe critic of all that was done, and he did not find himself completely in accord with his countrymen, with the result that he left sore memories behind him in Dublin, and did not improve his relations with the Irish when he came to write, many years later, his memories of that period.

At last, however, early in the new century, he was back again in London; and by then matters had so much improved with Moore that he left his garret and took a flat in Victoria Street; and later he went to that house in Pimlico with which his name will always be associated. Ebury Street, where he lived until his death, is a long, rather featureless thoroughfare; but after the European War it became both inglorious and glorious in London history as the scene of the assassination of another Irishman and the pursuit and capture of the murderers by an unarmed mob. It is also immortalized in the title of one of Moore's works. I was going to say 'one of Moore's most characteristic works,' but they are all, either in themselves or in relation to his work as a whole, highly characteristic, for he was an original. He always wrote the kind of book he wanted to write, and it was a kind of book peculiar to himself. It is because he was an original, and not because of his realism or his later style, that he will survive in memory; and no writing about him could possibly equal his own writing about himself, which was marked with so much curious detail, so precise, so candid (where he wished to be candid), and at all times so illuminative of his personality.

There exist paintings of Moore at several ages, and the best portrait of him is the famous one by Manet. But for those who wish for a verbal picture it would be difficult to improve upon that given by Susan Mitchell. This she printed first in a little book about Moore which was published about twenty years ago, and of course it represents its subject as he was at the beginning of the century. I will only add that the Moore whom I saw in 1920 corresponded well to Susan Mitchell's account, except that his hair was white, or appeared so by artificial light, and that he stooped somewhat. Here is the picture:

Moore, who every one said was a very wicked man, had the rosy face and innocent yellow hair of young virtue, kindness was on his lips, though his eyes were not quite so kind, a little slow in following the lips. . . . George Moore seemed to me then to be a man of middle height with an egg-shaped face and head, light yellow hair in perpetual revolt against the brush, a stout nose with thick nostrils, grey-green eyes, lips thick in the middle as if a bee had stung them. He had champagne shoulders and a somewhat thick, ungainly figure, but he moved about a room with a grace which is not of Dublin drawing-rooms. . . . George Moore's is a face dear to the carica- turist and in itself at times a caricature; the yellow hair, the fat features, the sly smile, the malice, the vanity. But as has been said to me, let someone begin to discuss an idea and in a moment the contours change, the fat shapelessness falls away, the jaw lengthens, the bones become visible, the eyes darken, the brows straighten, a hawk-like keenness is in the look. One does not caricature this Moore.

'The sly smile, the malice, the vanity': one sees them all in Moore's more personal writings, *Confessions of a Young Man, Memoirs of My Dead Life, Hail and Farewell, Avowals, Con- versations in Ebury Street*. At first, until the attention is caught, they may seem the outstanding characteristics of his work; but no writing as limpid as his could escape insipidity if it were not that every sentence has been overseen by a mind both keen and clear. One thinks one is listening to Mr Woodhouse, Emma's father, whose conversational style might almost have been Moore's model. But in fact one is listening to a man in whom slyness is but the gentle handmaid of scarifying and tenacious judgment.

I said just now that Moore was candid when he wished to be candid; and I meant that in his printed discussions it is always he who chooses the ground, just as it was always Socrates, another deceptively simple casuist, who chose the ground upon which he could discomfit other spirits more generous in assertion. Moore's criticisms of Thomas Hardy, to take one instance, are based upon isolated passages or single poems, and they take no heed of Hardy's work as a whole or of Hardy's character as a writer. It is true that Hardy's poetic preoccupations are often with death and decay. It is true that Hardy's prose style is occasionally clotted. One could catalogue other faults. But if preoccupations and faults and single paragraphs were to settle a writer's calibre, some of Moore's own shortcomings could be made to damn him for ever. I also meant that his confessions sometimes swear with his professions. I cannot quite reconcile the wicked Moore of Susan Mitchell's phrase (I do not doubt that this was his reputation) with Moore's own 'I am as timid in life as in literature,' 'I was naturally endowed with a very clear sense of self-preservation,' 'Within the oftentimes bombastic and truculent appearance that I present to the world, trembles a heart as shy as a wren.' I think he was a greater lover on paper than in reality, and that the tales he told of himself were coloured to please, because if they had been quite plain they could never have gratified his own malice. It was an Irishwoman, Miss Sarah Purser, who said: 'Some men kiss and tell; Mr Moore tells but doesn't kiss.'

The truth is that there is a coldness in all of Moore's writing, and he was never more cold than he was in that tale of love, *Evelyn Innes*. His realistic novels set down a series of facts which one accepts or rejects according to one's own experience; and I am far from rating them as positively high as some other commentators would do. They seem to me to have a woodenness, an unleavened literalness, which takes no heed of surrounding colour and movement. They have no humour. Not only has the author no passion, but his dramatis personae kiss without conviction—one seducer enchants his love by dilating upon the qualities of Balzac as a writer, and, having had his offer of horses refused, is more successful with a set of the *Comédie Humaine*. By comparison with books written since in the same order, they are one-syllabled and one-toned. But when they are read in relation to the history of the novel, as pioneer works in a stage of fictive literature which otherwise was largely sentimental or decorative, they are outstanding. While other writers of the eighties and early nineties were being 'just literary,' or witty at the expense of others (few can be witty, of course, at their own expense; but still fewer make the attempt), or romantic, or ingenious, Moore and Gissing alone, or almost alone, were trying in the published novel to tell the world something about life at first hand. And in Moore's case it was quite extraordinary how the choice of detail and the continuous succession of plain incidents produced both an effect of nature

and a progressive interest. Where Gissing showed his personal
grievance and rebelliousness, Moore recorded. He was detached.
He did not explain or expound (as Gissing did), but refrained
from all personal comment, leaving to his characters any reflections which had properly to be made upon such situations as
seemed inevitably to arise in the course of the tale. To me these
books miss a thousand shades; but that is their strength, for
they are as firm as engravings. No wonder they impressed
themselves, and still impress themselves, upon candid minds as
very striking reproductions of reality. There is no question that
they gave rise, towards the end of the nineties, to a new school
of naturalistic writers, Edwin Pugh, Arthur Morrison, Somerset
Maugham, and others. We know that a reading of *A Mummer's
Wife* drew Arnold Bennett towards the re-creation of life in the
Five Towns upon which his lasting fame depends. Merely to
record the facts is to establish Moore's importance as an influence upon his age.

But he gradually moved away from tales of poor artists, maid-
servants, and travelling actors. Already, in 1886, he had passed
across the Irish Sea to his own land, when he painted in *A Drama
in Muslin* his picture of husband-hunting in rural Ireland, a book
which in spite of crudities has beauty and sympathy and a
quality of its own; and though he returned after this to the rigor-
ous simplicity of *Esther Waters* he dwelt in that book for the last
time upon the ways of very poor people. In *Evelyn Innes* and
Sister Teresa love and theology and the arts were his themes;
and in *The Lake* and *The Untilled Field* the consequences of his
long visit to Ireland were to be seen. These books were very
much better written than their predecessors. Those short paragraphs, as wearisome as couplets, in which *A Modern Lover* was
written gave way to a more sustained prose which has enchantment for the ear. The Irish books, in particular, showed his
advance in skill; for while they appeared literal they were
approaching the colloquial simplicity which he was later to
perfect. But *Evelyn Innes* and *Sister Teresa* betrayed a thin-
ning of direct inspiration from life. He was in truth at the
end of mundane experience; and had reached the condition of
sedentary debate and literary inspiration in which the remainder
of his life was spent.

From that time onward (that is to say from the comparative
affluence which came to him with the new century) he was less
a novelist than an editor, talker, and commentator. He began
to rewrite his earlier books. The mood revealed long before in

Confessions of a Young Man took complete control of him. He was ready to confess all and more than all about himself and his friends. Seeking for material upon which to exercise his gift, he found only the past, in men and in books. He was over fifty when he related the *Memoirs of My Dead Life*; the great trilogy *Hail and Farewell* followed; for the rest he re-presented what had been written before. His own novels, the story of two medieval lovers, the story of two lovers of antiquity, and at last the New Testament itself, were all rewritten with a most cunning mastery of language and a strong and artful, rather than a subtle, intelligence.

It is interesting to recall that when Moore was writing his early novels, they were the cause of fierce combats with the libraries and the moral censors of their day, when in reality no more rigidly moral novels have ever been composed; and that whenever he wrote of Ireland he was the centre of noise and argument inseparable from all discussion of Irish affairs; and that as he took up the life of Christ similar discord marred the acceptance of his work and averted its neglect. Like other Irishmen, he enjoyed exasperating his fellows; and in the future, when passions are concentrated upon more contemporary matters, he may lose some of the benefits of exasperation and fall into oblivion. As to the Irish scene, the fury it arouses has never been quite explicable to Englishmen, who are unconscious of their own power and always suppose that they are being kicked by cleverer people than themselves. And as to *The Brook Kerith*, it is a most discreet and polished work, the continuous interest and beauty of which testify to the author's genius. Its concentration upon Joseph of Arimathaea is very shrewd; the refusal of St Paul to abandon his faith is justified by experience. On those grounds, it seems to me, Moore is with difficulty assailable. His other rewritings are of very little permanent interest. I doubt if they will continue to be read. *Aphrodite in Aulis* and similar palimpsests have no more vitality than *The Well at the World's End* or *The Water of the Wondrous Isles*; and what will survive is the personality of Moore.

Not a creative personality; a critical, discomfiting personality, malicious, relentless, much-considering, cold, and with no capacity for self-surrender. Not without sympathy, for otherwise he could not have written novels such as *Esther Waters* and *A Mummer's Wife*, but as shrewd as he was vain, as teasing as he was unhumorous. When he was summoned to Ireland to his mother's deathbed. some peasants wailed that they had bad news for him. But Moore said to himself, 'Not altogether bad news; my mother is dead, but I have been saved the useless pain, the torture of spirit I should have endured if I had arrived in time.' And yet what an interesting personality it was! And is! How excellent a book he wrote about his young days, and how full of malicious quality is the trilogy which he wrote about his Irish friends and associates! When he describes a person—the young, black-coated Yeats as a rook, for example—the reader can see that person as if the few inevitable words held magic; not only the features, but the spirit, the tone, the movement of hands and eyes—all are portrayed. Our judgment of Moore is imperfect if we neglect two qualities in him, his observant quietness and his scrupulousness. Though his perceptions are tinged with cruelty, they are untinged with sentiment; they are referred always to his sense of truth, and what he sees he expresses with a fidelity as fine as it is beautiful. What he sees . . . It was not a generous mind, but though full of treacheries to friendship it was unwavering in strict loyalty to itself.

III. ENOCH ARNOLD BENNETT

I cannot conceive that any author should write, as the de Goncourts say they wrote, 'for posterity.' An artist works only to satisfy himself, and for the applause and appreciation neither of his fellows alive nor his fellows yet unborn. I would not care a bilberry for posterity. I should be my own justest judge, from whom there would be no appeal; and having satisfied him (whether he was right or wrong) I should be content—as an artist. As a *man*, I should be disgusted if I could not earn plenty of money and the praise of the discriminating.

ARNOLD BENNETT, *Journal*, 28th January 1897.

Arnold Bennett, the son of a solicitor, was born on 27th May 1867, thirty years before the words I have quoted were written. As a boy, he suffered a serious nervous shock when he crushed his hand in a mangle, and this led to a stammer which nothing ever cured. As soon as he was old enough to do so, he worked in his father's office, but in 1893 he left the Potteries and came to London. Like his own 'man from the north,' he felt himself to be 'a certain kind of youth of whom it is said that he is born to be a Londoner. The metropolis, and everything that appertains to it, has for him an imperious fascination.'

At first Bennett was in a solicitor's office; but while there he gave everybody the impression that he was potentially a literary light, and as, like his own Denry Machin, he was always sensitive and responsive to the expectations of others, he took heed of so complimentary a view. A parody of a sensational serial first brought some prize guineas; then he essayed brief articles and stories; and by the time he was twenty-five he had obtained by what he called the grossest kind of 'influence' a post as sub-editor of a paper for women. Later he was editor of this paper; and it was while he was editor that he recklessly engaged himself to write for a provincial syndicate a sensational serial better than anything else of its kind. That was Midland bounce; many people were deceived into thinking it Arnold Bennett. But it was not Arnold Bennett. In those early years he was incessantly studying the great French novelists, and he was also writing an entirely serious, unpretentious, and still readable novel about a young provincial in London, which he published under the title of *A Man from the North*. Out of this book, on its first appearance, he made a profit of one pound. The sensational serial paid better than that.

Bennett did not therefore embrace the career of sensational serial-writer. It is not without significance that *The Grand Babylon Hotel* and *Anna of the Five Towns*—the fantasia and the realistic study—both achieved book publication in the same year. He had found an enthusiastic admirer in Andrew Chatto, the publisher; and Andrew Chatto continued to publish for him (at a loss, it must be said) until 1905, when, having very unwillingly published *Sacred and Profane Love*, he suffered Bennett to go to another firm, and so lost *The Old Wives' Tale*.

In 1902, having established his ability to earn a living by means of fiction and journalism, Bennett did what George Moore had done thirty years earlier: he went to Paris. Either there or at Fontainebleau he busily wrote novels, short stories, plays, and many articles and reviews for London literary papers. And when he was forty he wrote a very long novel indeed, so long that the publishers who had contracted to publish it shivered at the prospect of a colossal printers' bill and—for at that time Bennett did not earn the seventy-five pounds advance which he was in the habit of receiving—a small sale insufficient to cover costs. The book was *The Old Wives' Tale*. It was at once hailed as a work of importance, and while its sales were not at first as large as everybody imagined (Bennett once told me that they did not in England pass six thousand), it established him as one of the leading novelists of the time. In America it gave the author, slowly but surely, a standing still unsurpassed (although it has declined) by any modern English writer.

Meanwhile Bennett had married a French wife, and under the pseudonym of Jacob Tonson he contributed to A. R. Orage's weekly political review, *The New Age*, a letter about books which was so much the best thing of its kind that it became the talk of bookish London. While Wells was publishing *Tono-Bungay* and *The New Machiavelli*, and Bennett *The Old Wives' Tale* and *Clayhanger*, these two men were the heavenly twins of literature, and wonders of the age. The young men of 1909 and 1910 felt that with Shaw and Barker and Galsworthy in the theatre, Bennett and Wells and in a lesser degree Galsworthy in the novel, and Chesterton and Belloc in the press, there was thrilling life in the intellectual world; and they were right. There never has been so much life since; but there will be later.

Presently, Bennett determined to leave Paris and live in England. He returned for a time in 1911, and presently he bought an elderly house in Essex, which was made habitable under the care of his closest friend of that day, E. A. Rickards, the architect, and to which from the first he invited not only his older English literary friends but those of the younger generation —J. C. Squire, Hugh Walpole, Robert Nichols, and others. He was established in this house early in 1914, and as he was able to keep the *Velsa*, his barge-built yacht, at Brightlingsea near by he seemed, in those peaceful days, to be assured of a long life of good work and literary eminence.

But in the summer of 1914 the War came. Bennett was swallowed up in it, as husband (for Mrs Bennett, being French, was at once tragically agitated by the fate of her country), as journalist, and finally as an active force in the Ministry of Information (or Propaganda), to the directorship of which he was in the end appointed. For Bennett the War years were years of intense pressure, literary, political, and social. From the first (and for the first time in his life) he was surrounded by military officers, politicians, and busy men of affairs generally. Strange and exciting as the emergency was, it completely changed the course of his life. He had been a novelist; he found himself an active publicist. He had been devoted to the arts; he found himself called upon to 'sustain the morale of civilian populations.' That seemed to him to be a wonderful experience. He flowered under it, never too busy for his friends and beneficiaries, but absorbed perpetually in the demands of the hour, like a banker or a Cabinet Minister, 'winning the War.' Cabinet Ministers, indeed, welcomed his company and his views. He had some power; he knew men who had more power and who would use it as his request.   At the Ministry of Information he was brought into close contact with Lord Beaverbrook, a Canadian financier and newspaper proprietor whose influence upon him was immediate and irresistible.   By Beaverbrook he was led more and more into the great world of affairs, until his novels looked to him, and became for others, smaller than life, instead of equal to it in size and worth.   His other acquaintances were innumerable; his days full; his importance once and for ever after less that of a creative writer than that of a public character and oracle.

All these excitements had their due effect upon a nature which, under an air of strength, was sensitive to excess.   The War was an overwhelming blow to Bennett.   His experience in meeting what must be called the fashionable society of that time shocked deeply all the fundamentally rigid and 'decent' notions of his bourgeois upbringing, from which he had been delivered only in his own imagination.   Those people who objected to *The Pretty Lady* as pornography did not recognize that it expressed a loathing on Bennett's part for what he had been seeing.   It was not a realistic book by a man of the world; it was a cry of horror by one whose standards of conduct had been outraged.   The levity and folly and recklessness portrayed in *The Pretty Lady* were seriously abhorrent to him.   True to his new character as man of the world, which had insensibly replaced that of the all-seeing and all-pondering artist, he pretended that these things were, and that they must be faced; but in my view he was never socially or politically an easy-going moralist, and I believe his will was then shaken, and his credence in a progressive world wrecked.

After the War, in 1919 and 1920, Bennett Was so tired that he was in danger of serious illness.   His closer friends noticed this, and several of them were greatly alarmed.   It has been suggested that the unquestioned decline of his work in fiction was due to the fact that he was spoiled by success; I think it was due to physical exhaustion and the strain of the War.   He continued to write steadily and regularly, because writing steadily and regularly was his habit, and he could not live without writing (I went with him in the early months of 1920 to Portugal, on the understanding that as a holiday was necessary to save his health he was to do no work at all; but on the third day following our arrival at Mont Estoril he confessed that he had written six hundred words before breakfast.   When I said 'Oh, no; *that*'s not what you 're here for,' he answered: 'I know.   I had to');

but nothing he wrote after the War was equal to what he had written earlier.

Let me try to present him as he appeared to those who saw him in the flesh. He was stoutly built, and about five feet nine inches in height. He held himself very erect and his shoulders very rigid, so that his body had no natural swing as he walked, but rather swayed stiffly from side to side. He always walked slowly and with great seriousness. His brow was square, and rose straight from eyes that looked tired, because of rather heavy eyelids, to the small flourish of hair which latterly replaced the famous coif made fun of by caricaturists. His cheeks were clear and showed a faint colour. His mouth was irregular, and his upper teeth were also irregular. The eyes, once the first impression of tiredness was passed, were a warm brown, and smiled. Bennett was a master of the wink. When some effusive stranger buttonholed him to express admiration, Bennett was at all times courteous; but, if he caught a friendly eye beyond his enthusiast, one of those heavy lids would irresistibly quiver.

In repose his expression, I should have said, represented calm melancholy. But his smile was very sweet, and the aura of kindness which surrounded him was such that he was extremely popular with children. Odd as it may seem to some, he could converse with children very effectively. But he was a shy and sensitive man, who normally talked little. He talked more towards the end of his life, from politeness, to 'make things go,' and he did this very well, though sometimes with exaggeration of his own mannerisms. His voice was rather harsh, and gave the impression of being high-pitched. As far as his writing was concerned, although to strangers he professed to be very well satisfied, he was excessively modest, and if some of his work received great praise he would naïvely repeat the praise to me, and add, 'It's . . . extraordinary.' That was because he was very simple-minded.

That simple-mindedness, that *naïveté*, was what made Bennett friends who still cannot think of him as dead. When he was alive they teased him and were teased by him. They contradicted him and were contradicted by him; and nobody a penny the worse. He kept a strict eye upon the grammar of his friends (my own, alas, ever the worst), and they in turn rebuked him for eccentricities of phrase or judgment. One day we all joined in protesting against the word 'motivated,' which he had used. He said: 'What else can you say?' Suggestions were made; he was assured by our senior classical scholar that the word was

shocking. Undaunted at the end of ten minutes, he said:
'Damned if I don't use it again next week.' If he had again
referred to the matter he would have said: 'A-and . . . I *did* so.'

It is the simple-mindedness of Bennett that causes those who
like to regard themselves as European to call him 'provincial.'
He was in many respects the young man from the midlands.
Whereas Gissing, also a provincial, had condemned the foul
ugliness of cities, and Moore had hardly seemed to know what
they looked like, so interested was he in clambering like an ant
over the lives of wretched people, Bennett was delighted to
embrace the beauties as well as the disfigurements of urban
civilization. He not only saw the town, but he could see what
it represented in the creative life of man. 'As squalid as you
like,' he said in effect; 'but none the less full of a grandeur, full
of the proper stuff of romance.' It is a view which may be called
bourgeois; but it is a view which the realistic novelist may quite
properly take. Nor was it anything but Bennett's natural
attitude; for while he was as sensitive to ugliness as any man I
have ever met he was quite definitely a townsman. The countryside was pleasant, lovely, stuff to paint, exquisite to see; but
there were not enough men and women, not enough houses, not
enough of the movements and conflicts of human beings, to
satisfy him. It was in people that he took all his interest;
people who set their wits against each other, people who set
their wits against the world, people who got on with their jobs,
people who came to London and conquered it.

He enjoyingly laughed at such people in some of his books,
of which *The Card* is the best and the best known, and lesser
examples, *A Great Man, The Regent, Mr Prohack.* He made
them grotesque in such books as *The Grand Babylon Hotel* and
Hugo and *The Gates of Wrath,* which are well-written shockers.
He made them horrible and piteous in *Riceyman Steps,* a study
of misers. In *The Old Wives' Tale* and *Clayhanger* he made
them real. *The Old Wives' Tale* and *Clayhanger* are by far the
best of his books. Into them he put without stint his humour,
his scrupulousness, and his old knowledge of midland life. In
them he was completely an artist. These books have not that
peculiar excitingness that Balzac alone can impart to the life
of the fictitious mundane; they seem to me to have everything
else that the naturalistic novel can compass. They are full of
character and truth to character; the scene is clearly set; one
reads with the sense of being taken not only into a tale of
individual human beings but into the homes and shops and

hearts of the midlands and the midland people; above all, the books and the people in them grow, not arbitrarily, but organically. If it is true that they remain small, as small as human beings are in real life, that must be set down as a deficiency in the realistic novel itself, for in that genre only Balzac's and Dostoevsky's people are larger than life, and Balzac's live in a world altogether fabulous, while Dostoevsky's are so large as to be fantastic (or it may be only Russian!) to the verge of the gigantesque. In Bennett's best books one is still among the normal. It was his object to deal with the normal. That was what absorbed him.

I have never agreed with those who set *Riceyman Steps* on a level with the author's major books. Beside them it is tired and meagre; two misers and a servant girl and a certain deliberately observed *milieu*. He went daily to Clerkenwell while he was writing it, to gain knowledge; but the district was not in his blood as were the Five Towns. Some others of his novels, however, have not yet had enough credit given to them. There is *Whom God Hath Joined*, which had a curious history, being published by a firm hitherto specializing in legend and folk-lore. Along with C. F. Keary's *Bloomsbury*, a long book in the Gissing tradition, it looked strange in such a list, and as it had been printed in a foreign country the first edition was disfigured with extraordinary misprints. It is with difficulty recovering its place in the canon. There is *The Price of Love*, to which at all times critics have been less than fair, so that it is supposed to be a twice-cooked pudding, when in fact it is, though minor, only just minor. There is the latter part of *Lord Raingo*, a book which suffered from some confusion of mind in the author and some confused criticism from eminent publicists. This book was supposed to deal with the life of a real person; but it is in reality an extraordinarily sincere portrait of Bennett himself, in late middle age, and in pain and fear of death. It should not be overlooked by the student of his work, although the political passages are incredibly bad.

Bad, too, are all the books in which Bennett tried to reproduce the artistic temperament, or the abnormal—for examples, *Sacred and Profane Love* and *The Glimpse*. The hardness of the former is due, perhaps, to the fact that he was trying to be French; the hardness of the latter lies in the fact that he was doing something in which he did not believe. He was never at his best unless he could be both humorous and humane, unless he could be amused by his people as well as devoted to their representation. That is the success of *The Old Wives' Tale*, that the two sisters and Mrs Baines and Mr Povey are within his heart as well as his head. He liked nice people; they need not be good, but they must be simple and they must be honest; they might lie or be grandiose (for that sin he had some kindness), but they must not be treacherous or cruel, or anything but the plain people who grow rich or keep poor, who do their best towards those whom they love, and who certainly do their best towards what they believe to be the truth. There are millions of such people in England, and all over the world. They continue the work of civilization; and Bennett is their historian. Only when he went away from them, and tried to picture what is vicious or vulgar in itself, did he give away the secret of his own innocence. He was not sophisticated.

But he was attracted to grandeur as a moth to a lamp. That is made a cause of complaint against him by some; to his friends, who loved him, it was ever a matter for amusement. His clothes, his knowingness, his gaping wonder at gilt restaurants, have all been over-emphasized: my own belief is that he unconsciously yielded in later days to what he found to be a general belief in his love of the baroque. I do not deny such a love; I merely say that it figures in his lesser works, at first, in fun, because it amused him; latterly, in blindness, because he felt it was expected of him. Being tired, he grew lazy, and caricatured himself. The caricature was never conscious or deliberate, but it represented what was almost a mechanical act on the part of one who desperately needed rest and who could not, and was not allowed to, enjoy that rest.

Now let us take a final look at Bennett's work as he left it. There are plays, as to which I have said nothing. *Milestones*, in which he collaborated with Edward Knoblock, had a great success, and was called by Bennett himself 'a neat enough trifle.' *The Great Adventure*, which he wrote alone, had similarly a great success, and owed much to two pieces of magnificent acting, on the part of Henry Ainley and Wish Wynne. *The Title* had some success. The rest were not successes; and it does not now seem to me that they were ever more than trifles. Of course, *What the Public Wants*, that skit upon the vagaries of great newspaper proprietors, was extremely amusing and full of cheek; but the others lacked form and growth. They were too easily written, for fun, to show that he *could*; . . . but he couldn't, or rather would not, take the trouble to do something that was well within his power.

In his best novels, *The Old Wives' Tale* and *Clayhanger* (I do not include the remaining books of that trilogy, because *Hilda Lessways* was never equal to its predecessor, and *These Twain*, which is powerfully sincere, had no relation to *Clayhanger* and *Hilda Lessways* but dealt with an unforeseen conflict) he brought urban England to life and gave it significance. In the lesser serious books he only failed to do as well because the themes failed in importance or the method in freshness. In the good humorous books—*The Card, A Great Man, Buried Alive*—he amused himself and others, consumedly, for these books, too, were authentic Bennett, escaping from seriousness and enjoying himself. In the lesser books, the so-called pot-boilers, he amused himself and some others, but with *The Ghost, The City of Pleasure, The Regent,* and *The Strange Vanguard* he hardly communicated the joke. In the thoroughly bad serious books—*Sacred and Profane Love* and *The Glimpse*—he paid the price for applying the realistic method to matters of which he had no real understanding. In the books which are called his 'pocket philosophies' he gave a helping hand to the self-improving, which is enough to damn them with the cultured; but they did in fact help many, and while they consist of truisms expressed with all the emphasis created in Bennett by his stammer, that is enough to show that they were not superfluous.

Henry James, in criticizing Wells and Bennett, objected that they regarded life as a gigantic orange, to be squeezed indefinitely for the purpose of their fiction. He thought that they did not select, compose, 'do' the job of art, concoct a situation or a picture and lavish all care, in the Jacobean way, upon its treatment. He found Wells so abounding in vitality and richness of experience that he winked often enough at what offended him and what he regarded as a squandering of wealth to no artistic end. Wells was a prodigal. Bennett he admired, but condemned. He said:

> We confound the author of *Tono-Bungay* and the author of *Clay-hanger* in this imputation for the simple reason that with the sharpest differences of character and range they yet come together under our so convenient measure of value by *saturation.* . . . Our argument is that each is ideally immersed in his own body of reference, and that immersion in any such degree is really among us a new feature of a novelist's range of resource.

However delicately expressed, that was a charge of 'No art'; for the objection raised by Henry James was to the seeming assumption of both writers that memory and experience could all be poured out upon the pages of a novel and make something significant in itself. Well, there is, certainly, this problem to be encountered in assessing the realistic or quasi-realistic novel; which is, the point at which virtue is its own reward and truth its own touchstone; and Bennett would have admitted that a literature entirely composed of *Clayhangers* would soon be an enormity. That book did give rise to a number of works of an autobiographical or semi-autobiographical character which in turn have resulted in further books of the same nature. But Bennett did not intend the sequel: his notion was that *he* would write in three volumes a history of a man and his wife from their childhood to their advanced age. He thought it worth while to show them in their environment, which chanced to be the environment with which he had been familiar. The artistic object may have been remote, in the sense that what he proposed was a highly detailed fresco, instead of a concentrated piece for the easel. But the object, in Bennett's case, was there. The surface was to be large, precisely because he wanted to 'do' the job thoroughly. Not grandiosity was his aim, and not detail for its own sake (an absurd assumption), but thoroughness. Therefore, to me, James's criticism loses validity. Having failed to appreciate a large design, executed or to be executed with some copiousness, he mistook the nature of the work. If the work as a whole is a failure, that is another matter altogether.

IV. JOHN GALSWORTHY

For that is, my dear Jack, what you are—a humanitarian moralist. . . . This fact which you cannot help and which may lead you yet to become the Idol of the Public—if I may so express myself—arises as the greatest danger in the way of your art. It may prevent the concentration of effort in one single direction—because your art will always be trying to assert itself against the impulse of your moral feelings. . . . A moralist must present us with a gospel—he must give counsel, not to our reason or sentiment, but to our very soul. Do you feel in yourself the stature for that task? That you must meditate over with great seriousness — because, my dear Jack, because it is in you to be a great novelist.

JOSEPH CONRAD (*to John Galsworthy, in a letter*).

I include John Galsworthy in this chapter, less because he was in any sense a realist than because he gives me an opportunity to draw a distinction. Whereas the two writers mentioned previously in this chapter owed much to French models, Galsworthy was I think the first English novelist to turn for what may be called technical inspiration to Russia. And whereas

French realism always directed its attention towards an objective presentation of life, Russian realism was always tinged with philosophy (that is to say, with ethics and metaphysics) and with politics. The same is true of Russian literary criticism. In Galsworthy's case it was never denied that his earliest books were written in direct imitation of the novels of Turgenev; and his whole work was coloured by that humanitarian moralizing to which Conrad—always an acute critic—refers in the letter quoted above. Galsworthy thought as much of the moral of everything as Alice's Ugly Duchess.

Another point to which I wish to refer is that Galsworthy was the first genteel novelist of the Georgian scene, and only the second genteel novelist in English literature. Unlike his predecessor, he was no snob, though he too was a critic of snobs. He was a man of independent means, and was educated at Harrow and Oxford. Born in the year after Wells and in the same year as Arnold Bennett (1867), he was prolonging his adolescence while his two contemporaries were already biting hard at life. Their culture was personal, original; his the culture of a class. To him, honour, justice, breeding, and self-sacrifice were first principles; he represented all the virtues of what is called in England the public school spirit. Nobody could ever have thought Wells or Bennett 'public school'; nobody could ever have imagined Galsworthy as anything else. He never quite caught up with his two great contemporaries in practical acquaintance with all classes except his own; and I think his fastidiousness in the matter of breeding, dress, and deportment prevented him from wholly enjoying either their company or their confidence. Bennett rather scoffingly liked him very much; I imagine that Bennett constantly set Galsworthy's teeth on edge. Wells must have missed in him that malicious *camaraderie* which sets all at ease. He was very fastidious, very shy, and probably very timid. It was a timid face.

It was also a very serious face, full of kindness, but ever thoughtful. He was very short-sighted, and the glasses he wore were thick. He was obviously a gentleman, not only in his modest speech and bearing, but in Hillcrist's sense of 'a man who keeps his form and doesn't let life scupper him out of his standards . . . I assume, of course, that he's honest and tolerant, gentle to the weak, and not self-seeking.' It was his aim to set all those who were in his company at ease. While Wells's quick blue eyes see everything at a single flying, mischievous glance, and while Bennett's brown ones wisely paused in scrutiny for perhaps two pulse-beats, Galsworthy looked patiently and gravely for quite a long time through his glasses, and behind the glasses the eyes were, I believe, a cold grey. You might have thought him a lawyer (as he had been); you certainly would have realized his kindness; but you would not—or I should not—have been very confident of his power to accept teasing. Nevertheless, he had great sympathy; and only a lack of humour and self-confidence, probably, prevented him from achieving an air of geniality.

Having been born, as it were, to plenty, he made a romantic marriage and lived happily ever after. He could not have passed Gissing's test of the good writer, for Gissing, upon hearing that a new light had appeared on the literary horizon, used always to ask: 'Has he starved?' Galsworthy had not starved. All his sympathy with poor people was the sympathy of a sensitive and highly strung humanitarian who tries to put himself in the place of those whom he does not understand; those between whom and himself there can be no intercommunication. Whether lambs or horses, dogs or guttersnipes, social outsiders or performing seals, all who did not belong to the English affluent middle class—the Forsytes—were in a sense dumb animals. He suffered their pains a thousand times over; but the last plumbing degrees of insight, of identification, were beyond him. As in the case of Gregory, in *The Country House,* it was to his 'reforming instinct a constant grief that he had been born refined. A natural delicacy *would* interfere. . . .' That is why, when one has been poor, one never quite accepts Galsworthy's poor people, who are poor before they are human.

He started, in the vein of Turgenev, with tales of lovers; and many of his books are tales of lovers, some of them better tales and some of them less good tales, but always sensitive, marked by a kind of trembling emotion, and always about well-bred idealists who do wrong with the best motives, or from instability, or who avert wrongdoing by reason of some strong call to duty or virtue. In these books he took from Turgenev's method what he needed—measure and delicate precision; and he shared with his master a thrilling sense of beauty, irony, and an extraordinary feeling for tragic young love. Galsworthy often returned to this theme, trying to pitch the note high but always decorously, to catch a pure ray of emotion and at the same time woo reality and escape the namby-pamby. He did not always escape, and he did not catch the pure ray, which comes unsought to genius but may not be laboured for; while as to reality it has evaporated in the passage of time and is no more to be found in the tender pages. *Jocelyn, Villa Rubein, The Country House, The Patrician,* and *The Dark Flower* all belong to the same order; and if these books now seem to us to be sentimental, while Turgenev's *On the Eve* and *A House of Gentlefolk* continue to shine in memory as things of beauty, the explanation may perhaps lie in the fact that while Turgenev was at bottom a poet Galsworthy was at heart a gentleman, 'born refined,' as he has said, and for ever constrained by his natural temper to make his characters 'nice.' If you are born refined, you cannot *allow* yourself to see everything or to write of everything; not only 'good form' inhibits you, but a terrible lack of moral courage.

Having begun to be a writer (he used the pseudonym 'John Sinjohn' for his first three books), Galsworthy very soon revealed his moralizing impulse. He had been born into a comfortable class, and he found members of that class intolerably less sensitive to the evils which he saw all about. Like every other English moralist, he cried out upon the English hypocrisy. He arraigned his class for using every advantage which wealth and the British legal system provided. When he first went into the theatre it was to draw a pointed contrast between the lot of a young man of good family and a working man, both of whom, when drunk, had committed theft. He went on to show how one-sided any strike or lock-out may be, owing to the innate power of Capitalism to live upon itself while the unemployed workers starve. But while he arraigned, he could not bring himself to portray the rich as deliberately evil, and so he was again forced into the use of types and symbols, all of whom stood for their own point of view, for pride, for obstinacy, for selfishness, and for suffering. He was too modest to be severe; and as he painted in low tones it was thought that he was a realist, pointing out to the world candidly and with moderation where it was wrong. That was not the case. He was uneasy, uncomfortable, unhappy; and the cause of his unhappiness was an imagining of the pain and injustice which the world held and to which the world paid no heed.

It must have been a knowledge of this preoccupation on the part of a friend which caused Conrad to write his words of warning; for that horror of pain and injustice runs through the whole of Galsworthy's work, and affects its ultimate importance. The artist may rightly see and protest against injustice; but if he does this too narrowly, if he is but a fabulist, he may well miss truth for the sake of his moral. Once again it would be my suggestion that Galsworthy suffered from the cramped movement of his imagination. He had constrained his lovers; he now constrained his sinners and strikers and class-conscious neighbours and clubmen. He could not forget the claims of niceness; he could not forget the fact that a man was poor or rich or stupid or dishonest or a Jew. Not a human being, but the embodiment of a state of mind or a state of body. Any writer who has such strict notions of what is good and what evil, and who dare not let his principals stray outside a rigid code of conduct or behaviour, keeps them very short of character. And so while Galsworthy's plays (for in this section of his work the plays form a large proportion) are excellent as moralities they are exceedingly narrow moralities. Suffering as he did from that emotional sympathy with the loser in any fight which is the mark of humanitarianism, he unconsciously distorts both sides of a wrangle in order to produce his plea for the unfortunate, the weak, the dumb. He was a pleader.

But he was not only a pleader. Quite apart from the fact that he had an altogether exceptional sense of the theatre, which makes his plays very effective pieces, and a sure and delicate hand in the presentation of a story, which makes even his inferior novels readable, he had in one instance a mastery of family history and family psychology too notable for oblivion. I do not think the later instalments of the Forsyte Saga show anything but a decline; but the first Forsyte book, *A Man of Property*, was and is an original and vital contribution to the modern novel. In that book is embalmed for all time a departed way of life. The characters in it, although not full of life, are full of type. The moral prejudice which hampers Galsworthy elsewhere is lifted, and a romance is unravelled. Probably some who have come to maturity in the past few years may not realize how new *A Man of Property* was at the time of its publication: the plan of that book has produced a thousand imitations. But it was new, original, deeply interesting as a period piece, deeply interesting as a sign that a modern novel could be as rich in three hundred pages as anybody pleased. I think *A Man of Property* will continue to be read when most of Galsworthy's other work has passed into dust; just as I think that some of his plays will continue to be performed as long as there are repertory theatres in the world. Their freshness may go—it has already gone from the lesser plays; their interest as comments upon social conditions will assuredly lessen; but they are such good theatre, and they still read with so much life, that they will survive fashion and enter history.

To sum up, then, Galsworthy was serious in both the commendatory and the depreciatory senses of that word. He had, I am sure, no humour at all. He was too sensitive to pain and to the susceptibilities of others to be a major artist; and as he was at the same time a moralist his restricted view cramped his plays and novels and made them into fables or 'instances.' He had the misfortune, in a creative writer, to be born to a life of comfort; and, while a poor man may suffer some social inconveniences after he has achieved success, a rich man, or one who spends his freshest years in a small circle, has the disadvantage of never being able to learn at first hand and with precision the life of any but that small circle. Galsworthy's poor people have been seen from without. His post-War young people have been seen from without. His business men, rich Liberals, and clerks have been seen from without. Owing to his temperament he was not an ebullient mixer, and with shyness, good breeding, kindness, and refinement as his handicaps he had a hard struggle to get any sort of authenticity into his work. But he had some essential qualities. He had sympathy, a great sensitiveness to beauty of scene and conduct, a clear style adequate for all the calls he made upon it, especially in earlier work, a sense of technique in both novel and play, great sincerity. That he had at the same time altogether exceptional talent is shown by the fact that in spite of a great dislike for publicity he made, by *The Silver Box* and *A Man of Property*, when he was thirty-nine (both play and novel belong to 1906), a reputation not inferior to any of that moment. For the rest of a long life he wrote plays and novels which had greater commercial success; but nobody ever thought of accusing him of any sin greater than that of being out of touch with post-War psychological assumptions.

V. WILLIAM SOMERSET MAUGHAM

Et ego in Arcadia vixi: I too have been a highbrow. . . . I could not help noticing that a play produced by the Stage Society did not lead to very much. After the two performances they gave it and the notices in the press it was as dead as mutton. I felt a trifle flat after the production of *A Man of Honour*. I looked reflectively at the Thames and was conscious that I had not set it on fire. I badly wanted to write plays that would be seen not only by a handful of people. I wanted money and I wanted fame.

W. S. MAUGHAM, Preface to *Plays*, vol. i.

Anybody less like John Galsworthy than Somerset Maugham it would be hard to imagine. Both have been novelists and dramatists with equal success; both have also written works which were neither novels nor plays (but Maugham, if he has attempted verse, has cautiously refrained from tempting the reviewers by publishing it); and there the likeness ends. Maugham was born in 1874, and after attending King's School, Canterbury, and the University of Heidelberg, he studied medicine in London, at St Thomas's Hospital. He is both a member of the Royal College of Surgeons and a licentiate of the Royal College of Physicians. But he began to write books when he was in his early twenties, and from 1897 onwards he has been a professional author. Like George Moore and Arnold Bennett he lived for some years in Paris, and first met Bennett there; the two men were friends until Bennett's death.

Many readers of Maugham's most famous novel, *Of Human Bondage*, must have assumed—for it usual to make all sorts of assumptions regarding authors, on the strength of what seems to be an autobiographical book—that Maugham, like Philip, suffers from a club foot. He does not. In fact, it is never safe to believe a word an author says, whether he speaks in the first person singular or writes about a young man's growing pains. Not a word of *Of Human Bondage* must be taken literally, for all its deceptive directness of statement. Maugham is not Philip; but I will not deny that he seems to me at times to resemble Ashenden. He is not a very tall man, is very dark, and has small, extremely dark brown eyes which one immediately notices. He is very slim, and one's first impression is of a small head, a gentle manner of great modesty, and a slight hesitation in speech. One then discovers that all his remarks are unusually brief. And that when he tells a story it is in so few words, and with such point, that there is time in his company for a considerable amount and range of conversation. Nor is the conversation merely brief; for Maugham is so quick-witted that he stimulates others to similar unself-conscious brevity, and, whether the effect is one of imagination or not I cannot say, one leaves him with the sense that everybody—including oneself—has been very amusing. This is a rare and highly complimentary talent, and it deserves mention in a period—among English writers of any pretensions to intellect—of meagre, highly superior, and discouraging verbal exchange.

Readers of Maugham's books will immediately appreciate the brevity which is part of his method. Not only is he a dramatist the speeches of whose characters are rarely longer than fifty words (he does not rival Noel Coward in snip-snap), but when he writes a novel his sentences would seem abrupt if it were not that they combine in an unusual degree quickness and continuity. He has the ruthlessness of perception which goes with clear thinking. As to his literary manner, he has said of himself that

in my strenuous youth, in order to learn English, I spent part of each day in copying out certain classical writers whose style pleased me, reading a little and then trying to write it from memory; and in this way I went through some of Dryden's essays, much of the *Holy Dying* of Jeremy Taylor, and the whole of Swift's *A Tale of a Tub*. It was tedious, but it enabled me to express my thoughts, such as they were, with facility. I hasten to add that there is no particular reason why the dramatist should have a literary training, and besides the ease it gives him in writing, an acquaintance with literature is perhaps chiefly useful in helping him to avoid the literary.

In those last words speaks the man who once gambolled upon the heights of Chelsea and Bloomsbury and who either slipped (as some would say) or found a path leading to reality. I think he found a path. But is it not a strange coincidence that George Moore used almost exactly the same tone in his *Conversations in Ebury Street*? What Moore, speaking also of plays, said was:

Literature is never literary. And the manager is duped by the highbrow, and the highbrow in turn is duped by the disagreeable: else I should drop, he says, into the commonplace.

Maugham was fortunate in that he had work to do which did not long allow him to be literary. He was a medical student; and 'he found the work of absorbing interest.' Of the hospital he says:

There was humanity there in the rough, the materials the artist worked on: . . . the directness of contact with men and women gave a thrill of power which he had never known. He found an endless excitement in looking at their faces and hearing them speak; they came in each with his peculiarity, some shuffling uncouthly, some with a little trip, others with heavy, slow tread, some shyly. Often you could guess their trades by the look of them. You learnt in what way to put your questions so that they should be understood, you discovered on what subjects nearly all lied, and by what inquiries you could extort the truth notwithstanding. You saw the different way people took the same things. . . .

To the others men and women were only cases, good if they were complicated, tiresome if obvious; they heard murmurs and were astonished at abnormal livers; an unexpected sound in the lungs gave them something to talk about. But to Philip there was much more. He found an interest in just looking at them, in the shape of their heads and their hands, in the look of their eyes and the length of their noses. You saw in that room human nature taken by surprise, and often the mask of custom was torn off rudely, showing you the soul all raw . . .

There was neither good nor bad there. There were just facts. It was life.

These words are taken from *Of Human Bondage,* and may be regarded with justification as expressing Maugham's own experience. Upon an earlier page of the same book is another significant paragraph, which I shall also quote because it throws light upon a manner of approach.

Philip hated Watson, and yet he would have given anything to change places with him. The old feeling that he had had at school came back to him, and he tried to throw himself into the other's skin, imagining what life would be if he were Watson.

And finally, this time from *Ashenden*:

Ashenden admired goodness, but was not outraged by wickedness. People sometimes thought him heartless because he was more often interested in others than attached to them, and even in the few to whom he was attached his eyes saw with equal clearness the merits and the defects. . . . He was able to pursue his study of the Caypors without prejudice and without passion.

Those remarks all refer to one who was and is a born novelist and dramatist of the non-heroic type; in fact, to a realist. One cannot imagine Maugham writing a romance. Melodrama is possible to him; the flippant is often upon the tongues of his characters. But besides being vulgar, as Maugham says it is, the life known to all except those who dwell in literary selectness is apt—once it leaves the humdrum—to be slightly sensational. Melodrama is quite proper, therefore, in the work of a realistic writer. But romance calls for a different temperament, a love of coloured raiment and display. It also calls for a little glad self-deception. Now Maugham could not possibly deceive himself with any kind of gladness.

It so happened, as I have previously explained, that when he began to write there was a vogue for tales of mean streets. Gissing and George Moore were established writers, Barrie had given fancy to desperate poverty in the early pages of *Sentimental Tommy*, Arthur Morrison, Israel Zangwill, Pett Ridge, and the Edwin Pugh of *Tony Drum* were in one way or another using the very poor as literary material. At work all day in St Thomas's Hospital, and living in the South of London, Maugham had learnt as much about the life and speech and thoughts of the poor as anybody not born among them could do; and he experimented, after he had sold some short stories, with a book in this vein called *Liza of Lambeth*. It took its place in the fashion, and was thought to be very stark; and although it is a rather lifeless book and not quite accurate in Cockney vocabulary and phrase its aim is truth and its seriousness perfect. However, Maugham did not intend to keep his talent in Lambeth, and he was not long in moving farther afield. He had his eyes upon the stage, and he was free to dramatize in fiction some aspects of the middle-class life in which he had been born. *Mrs Craddock*, for example, was the tale—it might first have been written in three acts—of an emotional woman of means who married a stupid farmer, cherished him, discovered his stupidity, and was in due time released from bondage by his exceedingly stupid death. Again the book was thought very bold (so that Maugham had difficulty in getting it published), and it really was interesting and original. But it helped to label its author, who was also, very shortly afterwards, the author of a gloomy play called *A Man of Honour*, as a pessimist, a cynic, and a teller of sordid tales. As such, though unpopular, he was admired by those who regard themselves as the select few. 'The highbrow in turn is duped by the disagreeable.'

Maugham was perfectly ready to deal with disagreeable subjects, and he has always dealt with them when it pleased him to do so. The disagreeable has slightly more tang than the agreeable. But his bent was, and is, for comedy. Having been serious because he wanted to be serious, he became a determined writer of comedies for the stage. Before he was thirty-five he had achieved his object. He had three plays running at the same time in London theatres, all of them flippant and amoral, all of them salted with witticisms which readily occurred to him as he wrote; and he had completely removed the stigma of seriousness, although not that of cynicism. 'Ashenden,' wrote Maugham, 'had no illusions about himself and such success in current letters as had come to him had left his head unturned. He distinguished acutely between fame and the notoriety that rewards the author of a successful novel or a popular play; and he was indifferent to this except in so far as it was attended with tangible benefits.' But the tangible benefits without doubt enabled Maugham to fulfil a great ambition; they enabled him to travel.

He travelled. He still travels. He must have been very nearly all over the world—to China, to Spain, to Burma, to the South Seas, to Canada, and the United States. And, true to his conceptions of the novelist's art, he has used his travels as material from which to draw new and ever-varied tales, and he has also enriched the literature of travel with at least one very delightful book entitled *The Gentlemen in the Parlour*. Wherever he has gone about the world, moreover, he has taken his neat figure, his neat mind, his quick tongue and pen; and if he had written nothing else but *The Painted Veil*, which is about China, or *The Moon and Sixpence* and *The Trembling of a Leaf*, which are about the South Seas (the former being about Gauguin and his life in Tahiti), we should have known him as a writer in a thousand who had seen curious and unforgettable things with his own eyes.

Nevertheless, his most ambitious book is that long account of a young man's life, from early childhood to marriage, which is called *Of Human Bondage*. Home life at Blackstable, school life at Tercanbury (both names so easily decipherable), university life at Heidelberg, art study in Paris, hospital training in the south of London, hardships, love affairs—all these in chronological order follow (with innumerable vignettes of character bearing all the marks of verisimilitude) what must have been the outline of Maugham's own experience. But it would not therefore be wise to regard the book as a literal transcript of the author's life. No author, not even the most realistic, copies exactly.

I think indeed that most novelists, and surely the best [says Maugham in his Preface to *First Person Singular*], have worked from life. But though they have had in mind a particular person this is not to say that they have copied him nor that the character they have devised is to be taken for a portrait. In the first place they have seen him through their own temperament and if they are writers of originality this means that what they have seen is somewhat different from the fact. They have taken what they wanted of him. . . . Nothing is so unsafe as to put into a novel a person drawn line by line from life. His values are all wrong.

That is sufficient. *Of Human Bondage* is to be read as fiction, but fiction with so clear an air of truth as to be as absorbing as candid autobiography. And *Of Human Bondage* differs from other chronicle novels in its peculiar simplicity and in the fact that Philip, its hero, is depicted without archness, defence, and unnecessary explanation. The temper of the book is neither busy nor benign nor romantic; it is as completely unsentimental, and as bold in its bare statements (I refer especially to the dialogue, which though that of a dramatist is courageously uncoloured) as a novel can be.

Further, a comparison of the manner in which *Of Human*

Bondage is written with the manner of George Moore's *A Modern Lover* is most interesting. In both books perfect simplicity of statement is aimed at. In both books a career is shown as crossed with love affairs. But whereas one reads *A Modern Lover* with reluctance, as if one were walking over a long stretch of sand with no goal in sight, one reads *Of Human Bondage* as if one ran effortlessly home upon a good road. Such lightness and sureness are excessively rare; few authors can leave well alone; they have not the nerve. In the two books the method is fundamentally the same — a narrative without comment, in which but for the most occasional contributory use of information outside the hero's knowledge all attention is concentrated upon the central figure—but Maugham had mastered the art of writing both explicitly and suggestively, which Moore had not done when he wrote *A Modern Lover*, and as Maugham has said: 'A natural effect can only be got by an artificial simplicity.' Those who suppose that *Of Human Bondage* is a good book by chance, or by reason of the intrinsic interest of its material (considerable though that is), underrate self-critical and self-assured literary talent of a high order. Of all modern authors, Maugham is the man who most nearly says, hardly as it were opening his mouth, precisely what he means to say.

As to what he says, which does of course matter a great deal, I think it would be true to suggest that he is at his best with the personal and the concrete. For the dissemination or even the discussion of general ideas he has little inclination; in a play or a novel he would believe it literary and in fact laboriously clumsy. Not does he as a rule wish to impress, as do those who parade learning and familiarity with current metaphysics. It is the object of the realist to decipher and record; never to display his own ingenuity.

Maugham's reading, which is wide, has been practical where it has been done for any purpose but that of pleasure. He is the least academic of men, and without iconoclasm the most independent in literary opinion. He regards it as the novelist's business, and the playwright's business, to present a situation and drop the curtain. He is not a moralist and not an apologist. He has coldness, wit, and malice. He at once sees what he looks for in a man or an affair (as a doctor might do), and abstracts it for his own purposes. And since he does not credit the perfectibility of the world or humankind, but finds life continuously interesting (if he is bored, he moves on), he is the nearest thing to a true realist among those named in this chapter.

While Moore was maliciously vain in his fundamental attitude, and Bennett magnanimous; while Galsworthy was full of pity, Maugham, who thinks that sympathy suggests condescension, seems to bring to his contemplation of the world the spirit in which Philip contemplated the out-patients' room at St Luke's Hospital: 'There was neither good nor bad there. There were just facts. It was life.'

To some, an inexplicable conclusion; but to the artist in black and white by no means displeasing.

CHAPTER VIII: THE CRITICAL THEATRE

I

The advocate for a National Theatre can plead its mere utility, can show that it will do what no other theatre is likely to. But he had better take yet higher ground. He must plead for the drama as something more than casual entertainment, as an art worthy to rank with other fine arts, and as having its spiritual functions too.

H. GRANVILLE-BARKER, *A National Theatre.*

IN writing earlier of Bernard Shaw, I gave a slight sketch of the rise of Scandinavian and Teutonic drama in England, and of the part played in that rise by Shaw, Archer, and others. And in speaking of George Moore's work I spoke of the journey he took to Dublin to lend a hand in the formation of what was called the Irish Literary Theatre. Those events occurred before the end of the nineteenth century. It was not until the early years of the twentieth century that the New Drama (as it was named) began to drift into common consciousness; and when it did so the chief organizer was Annie Elizabeth Fredericka Horniman.

Miss Horniman was the lady who supplied the money for the production of *Arms and the Man* at the Avenue Theatre in 1894. Nearly ten years later, she acquired the lease of the Abbey Theatre in Dublin, rebuilt the theatre, and gave the Irish National Theatre Society free use of it. From that time may be dated the true activity of Irish folk drama, to which W. B. Yeats, J. M. Synge, and Lady Gregory all contributed plays according to their gifts. It was the day of the great Irish literary revival, justly celebrated by Ernest Boyd, Moore, and many subsequent writers. It falls quite outside the scope of the present book.

In London in 1904 there was established at the Court Theatre that 'congregation,' as Shaw called it, which gave support to what was not so much a Repertory Season as a season of short runs, mostly of plays by Shaw. The business manager of the experiment was J. E. Vedrenne; the producer a young actor named Harley Granville-Barker. At first, the Court was engaged in Shakespearian production, and Barker's first effort was made with *The Two Gentlemen of Verona*; but there were some matinées of *Candida*, and from these developed the famous Vedrenne-Barker partnership. It gave nearly a thousand performances of Shaw, Barker, St John Hankin, John Masefield, Euripides, Galsworthy, and other at that time non-commercial dramatists. Then in 1907–8 Vedrenne and Barker took the Savoy Theatre, which was in the centre of London, and the partnership ceased.

In those same years of 1907–8 Annie Elizabeth Fredericka Horniman took it into her head to reform Manchester; and she did there what she had already done in Dublin. She acquired the Gaiety Theatre, rebuilt it, and established a second Repertory Theatre, thus giving a tremendous fillip to Lancashire dramatic writing, which accordingly produced a 'school' of its own. Manchester had previously been famed for its school of political economists (now, alas, quite outmoded); and with Miss Horniman's help it became the home of advanced or intellectual drama—the drama of ideas, as it was called—as that appeared to dwellers in the Edwardian and early Georgian period. The dramatists who made their mark at the Gaiety Theatre, Manchester, included Stanley Houghton, Allan Monkhouse, Charles McEvoy, J. Sackville Martin, and Basil Dean.

In 1910, a little less than three months before King George came to the throne, Charles Frohman opened at the Duke of York's Theatre in St Martin's Lane, London, a repertory season which lasted for seventeen weeks; and in the course of that season a play of Pinero's was revived, and new plays, either long or short, by George Meredith, Anthony Hope, Shaw, Galsworthy, Barrie, Barker, and a new dramatist of lower-middle class or suburban life named Elizabeth Baker, were performed. The producers for the season were Dion Boucicault, who ordinarily produced for Frohman, and Granville-Barker.

In these different seasons may be glimpsed something of the dramatic situation as it stood when King George came to the throne. Outside them, Hubert Henry Davies and Somerset Maugham both entertained lovers of comedy, and Rudolf Besier had already scored a success with *Don*; St John Hankin, a follower of Wilde in what is called artificial comedy (but in Hankin's case comedy of such slightness as to seem too pale for the commercial theatre), was dead in 1909. I have written of Shaw, Barrie, and Galsworthy; some of the others have not quite held their places in dramatic history; others I shall mention again later. Nearly all of them differed from such veterans as Pinero and Henry Arthur Jones by reason of the fact that they sought their inspiration in the moral and domestic problems of unremarkable parents and children, and tried to solve those problems, or at least to present them, without extravagance. Not the best, but the most typical, of such dramatists was Stanley Houghton, and the title of his first long play was significant. It was *The Younger Generation.* The new note in the novel was realism; in the play, it was an extremely natural treatment of social philosophy.

In a moment I shall speak a little of the Manchester school; but for the present I shall stay in London, where we all thought —those of us who were growing up in that time—that we discerned the first glory of a new great dramatist.

II. HARLEY GRANVILLE-BARKER

PHILIP. . . . Finery sits so well on children. And they strut and make love absurdly . . . even their quarrelling is in all good faith and innocence. But I don't see why we men and women should not find all happiness . . . and beauty, too . . . in soberer purposes. . . . And I want an art and a culture that shan't be just a veneer on savagery.

H. GRANVILLE-BARKER, *The Madras House.*

Barker was born in London in 1877; and at some very early age determined to be an actor. What he had done before he went to the Court Theatre I do not know (he acted as early as 1895 in a play by Alfred Robbins called *Mixed Marriage*); but he made a good Lance in *The Two Gentlemen of Verona* when he was twenty-six, and there is no doubt that in spite of possessing a voice which lacked resonance he would have become a leading actor if he had wished solely to act. However, he had too much versatility to care for playing only one part in life. He wanted to produce plays (for there was something new and good to be done in that direction); and he wanted to write plays; and he wanted most eagerly to discipline and instruct the world. He was an intellectual. He made one of his young spokesmen say that he (the spokesman) had married his wife because she preferred Bach to Offenbach. Nor did Barker see that this was the way to achieve a sterile union. He was too much in earnest, then, to laugh at himself. How that last act of *The Madras House* has worried him ever since!

His first play, written when he was only twenty-three, was *The Marrying of Ann Leete*, which was about a young lady who married a gardener. It was written, quite clearly, by one who adored the work of George Meredith. It has a charming preciosity; a touch of Pierrot and Pierrette; melancholy and tender smiles, exquisite speeches. But it moves rapidly; nobody who had not had feeling for the stage could have written it. His second, *The Voysey Inheritance*, was written four years later. It was not only in the new movement, but must be considered as having done much to stir the movement towards a natural drama. Fancy had gone; great sobriety had taken its place. An audience was asked to be, not amused, but deeply interested in a middle-class family faced with a crisis both moral and financial.

With the third play, *Waste*, Barker invited attention to the fact that by English social convention any man prominent in affairs who is guilty of a disclosed sexual offence must pay for indiscretion with disgrace. He had in mind, no doubt, the cases of Parnell and Sir Charles Dilke, both of whom were ruined as the result of divorce proceedings. Nor did he stop at the theme and at the comment indicated in his title, but supplied our rulers with advice, gratis, upon two or three other social questions. At this time, speaking in public, he demanded great range for the drama. Not only in the matter of morals, but in the matter of form and content. He said that he would like to see a play which was in effect the dramatization of a Blue Book. That shows how far the serious drama had progressed in England under his care.

Still engrossed in sociology, he wrote for the Frohman repertory season a fourth play, *The Madras House*, in which he presented many aspects of the woman question. He showed half a dozen melancholy spinsters in a family; he showed the young intellectual to whom I have referred and his lovely, intelligent, and possibly extravagant wife; he showed an elderly man whose view of women was oriental; a young woman who took an original and independent view of her own misbehaviour and its consequences; and the whole discussion (for the play was a discussion as well as a piece of dramatic entertainment) took place in relation to a colossal drapery stores known as the Madras House. This was the last of Barker's original and full-length plays to be produced. It was, socially, the most ambitious of them. It was for three-quarters of its length engrossing in the theatre; and it made one feel that when the author had grown to his full stature he would be fit to paint the whole of English life as no other modern dramatist could do.

He has caused disappointment. Later plays, although printed, have been obscure, with scenes of beautiful subtlety but considerable difficulty, and they have remained unperformed; he has preferred, so far as stage production is concerned, to collaborate with his wife in translations of Martinez Sierra, the Quinteros, Schnitzler, Guitry, and Jules Romains.

He has also retired from the production of other men's plays; and all the promise to which we attached so much importance in the early days of King George's reign has remained unfulfilled. We must take what we have and assess its value as a completed task. In doing so, we must not forget that, outside creative work, Barker has written much practical analysis of the working of a National Theatre (to the idea of which he has long been devoted) and some prefaces to the plays of Shakespeare as they are seen by a great dramatic producer which embody the wisdom of a subtle and ingenious mind. Without doubt, these prefaces have already affected the production of Shakespeare, and they will do so more than ever in the future.

But it is a mind bent upon expressing views. To Barker a fact is not so much a fact as an instance. He is more didactic than Galsworthy, because more hardly an intellectual. Where Galsworthy says 'Be good, be honourable, be just!' Barker says 'Be right!' Adversely, one could say he was a purist, which means 'a prig'; but adverseness is always an easy choice for the critic, and it is untrue that Barker is a prig. His plays could not be as rich as they are if he were a prig; and they are fuller of valuable and explicit human insights and knowledges than any other plays of their day. Nevertheless, they are also fuller of a determination to talk things out in the interests of civilization. As their author has said: 'Neither art nor literature, nor even religion, are always on the heights, nor need they be. But they need to have the heights in view.' That was and is his standpoint. And so while his characters do and say things which are of a natural and amusing and stimulating kind, the things they say are always related to an extremely high and dissatisfied view of life and culture commoner nowadays than it was when they were written and never wholly free from pragmatism.

The plays of Barker are at their best when they permit of free exchange between character and opinion, view and counterview; then they are astonishingly full and alert and courageous. But they are at their weakest when the persons of the play attempt to be idealistically constructive without altogether committing their creator to the line they take; because every

timidity of ridicule steps in and constrains the author to antici-
patory defence.   Impossible to say or let them say this or that,
for it is open to the same kind of destructive logic or laughter
(but from a different angle) which one has so effectively used
upon others.   Oh, dear!   One must not be *too* serious!   One
must guard oneself against absurdity by being rather depre-
cating. . . .   Then, indeed, the persons of the play begin to
mention their sense of humour; and—how terrible!—those who
become whimsical and speak of their sense of humour are much
in the position of Simple Simon when he was asked to show his
penny.   Seriousness of aim, and a view of the heights, interfere
very considerably with the creative act, which must be free,
unscrupulous, and unconstrained if it is to escape the paralysis
of the literary.

Barker's work does not quite escape that paralysis.   It is as
though he drank in Meredith with his mother's milk, turned
actor and learnt all that there is to be known about stagecraft,
and then discovered the Fabian Society, and was sterilized by it.
His genius was free when he wrote *The Voysey Inheritance*; but
in *Waste* and *The Madras House* it was struggling with two
powerful rivals—his intellect and his ethical sense.   The Fabian
Society had supervened.   Since *The Madras House* I think he
has swung back to Meredith, or perhaps to Shakespeare; and his
drama is again experimental.   But his talent remains as great
as ever; his personality as charming and as subtly dominating
(in his younger days he aroused the superstition of those who
came under his spell, and some of them thought him inspired by
God); and if he has not done what was expected of him in the
regeneration of the English drama, it is because he has preferred
to do something that interested him more.

III. ALLAN MONKHOUSE

I want to make it intimate and searching; I want to get at the
truth.   Prologue to *Men and Ghosts*.

Barker did not create a school of dramatists.   The Abbey
Theatre did, and the Gaiety Theatre, Manchester, did.   The
great dramatist of the Dublin stage was Synge; but there have
been many others since Synge who have pictured the life of the
Irish peasant, from Lady Gregory to Lennox Robinson and Sean
O'Casey; and the object of the Irish dramatists has been to create
folk drama.   With Manchester the object was to persuade
theatre audiences first that the ordinary, the commonplace, the

hitherto negligible had its dramatic aspects and second that a decided change was in progress in both manners and morals, for which something interesting and thoughtful might be said. The first play to be given by Miss Horniman in Manchester was about just such a clerk and his family, and it was called *David Ballard*.

The author of *David Ballard* was Charles McEvoy, who never repeated the success he had with this play. *David Ballard*, imperfect though it is, was an excellent example of what could be done with plain material. The central character was a young man whose family scorned him because he was a poet; but he won a prize of one hundred pounds for a poem in praise of Sunlight Soap, and this brought about his emancipation, incidentally also enabling Percy, a more admired brother, to repay money which he had borrowed from the till of his employers. It was the first realistic play of the lower middle class to be performed on the English stage. Its theme was over-simple, but the play had life of its own and its dialogue was written by a man who had listened well and with both amusement and indignation to the talk of stupid people. If its scene was London, and not Manchester, that was because it was written before the Manchester school came into being. Its influence upon that school was considerable.

Another influence, and a notable one, was that of *The Manchester Guardian*, the newspaper which has unrivalled prestige wherever the English language is read. The *Guardian* was owned and edited by C. P. Scott; and its chief leader-writer, C. E. Montague, was at the same time its chief dramatic critic.

When Lindsay wanted a new man on the staff he wrote to some bigwig at Oxford and asked for a list of the best young men about. Brilliant young double-firsts tumbled over one another to get on the *Herald*, but they had to be something better than double-firsts to stay there. Yes, the pace was hot. . . . It was one of the jocular traditions of the office—and not without some foundation—that George Meredith had been refused a job there. He wasn't quite good enough. So the young intellectuals would put it to heavy outsiders. They played at being prigs. Never was such a set of boys. They were boys even when they verged on middle age and they would write like boys. It came of the inspiration of the great Secretan, who was an article of religion in the office, and of a religion unstaled.

For the *Herald* in that quotation from a book by Allan Monkhouse called *True Love*, read the *Guardian*; for 'Lindsay' read 'C. P. Scott,' and for 'Secretan' read 'C. E. Montague.'

The entire staff of the *Guardian* was literary; that is to say, all those who wrote for the paper represented what may be described as a state of polished intellectual culture. They wrote with conscious grace; they read with assiduity; their intellectual and aesthetic aims were high and rarefied. And they supported the Gaiety Theatre. They all, or nearly all, wrote plays to fill its repertory; and when they did not write such plays they made a point of going to see what their comrades had written, and of criticizing it as they would have done if they had been still in the literary set at Oxford. They made a family, and a happy one. And the family had the feeling that its affairs were of supreme importance to modern literature. Such confidence, which alone allows a group to tolerate the work of other groups, is uncommon, and to-day in a distracted literary England is non-existent.

I have said that Stanley Houghton was the most typical of the Manchester dramatists; and there can be no doubt that his play, *Hindle Wakes*, made more stir in the theatre than any other play originating in Manchester. Houghton had been a dramatic critic on the *Guardian*, though he was not an Oxonian; and if he had lived (he died in 1913 at the age of thirty-two) he might greatly have influenced the course of the modern drama. On the other hand there was in his work an element of triteness which causes me to doubt whether he was capable of great expansion. I prefer to say only that *Hindle Wakes*, marking a decided advance upon *The Younger Generation*, set an interesting example to dramatists of the new school.

Another dramatist whose work continued into our own day deserves to be noted on account of his plays and of his admirable and too little read novels. His name was Allan Noble Monkhouse and he was born in 1858. He was a Durham man, but he emigrated early to Manchester, where he entered the cotton trade and presently joined the staff of the *Manchester Guardian*. That was inevitable; for from the first he was a book-lover and an enthusiast of the right kind for the *Guardian* office. And his greatest enthusiasm—again very proper in a member of the *Guardian* staff at that time—was for George Meredith. The hero of *Men and Ghosts* (Monkhouse was fond of the first person singular, and used it with ease), in describing his boyhood, remarks:

I remember how we chanced on Meredith long before he was the fashion. We read all that we could find, we tried to get books that were out of print and even wrote reproachful, insulting letters to publishers for not reprinting them. For years, while we disputed among ourselves whether he was the greatest of novelists or only one among the greatest, we never met anybody who had heard of him. Later, his poetry was to become a big influence and his *Joy of Earth* became a notable qualification of such fragmentary philosophy as I picked up. It is still one of the great books of the world to me.

Enthusiasm for Meredith, whom he regarded as second to Dickens among the great English novelists, persisted in Monkhouse to the end; as did an absorbing love of Shakespeare. And as he knew nothing of London, but lived for nearly eighty years in Disley, in Cheshire (the Darley of his novels), Monkhouse's world was comparatively a small one, as it was certainly and unashamedly a provincial one. Manchester and Disley between them provided backgrounds enough: these he knew intimately. And there can be no question that the offices of *The Manchester Guardian* in Cross Street have been a fairly constant scene of his intellectual interchange with men of his time. Further, in *True Love* as in *Men and Ghosts*, *My Daughter Helen*, and *Farewell, Manchester*, the note of autobiography, restrained and ironic, gives intimate, almost conversational character to reflective treatment of a small assembly. How else should a man of restricted experience relate literature to life?

Having written one novel, *A Deliverance*, before the end of the nineteenth century, and a couple more—*Love in a Life* and *Dying Fires*—before the accession of King George, Monkhouse was soon drawn into the Gaiety Theatre. He contributed to its repertory, indeed, the best known of all his plays, *Mary Broome* (1911), which was at once recognized as an outstanding addition to the new drama. He was not, thereafter, solely a dramatist, but his novels were brief and superficially slight in theme (whatever their implications), and at all times it was the talk of people, their communication by words of mood and temper, which held his attention.

Mary Broome was a play about a maidservant who had been seduced by the son of her employers, an improvident and paradoxical young literary man, and who, following a forced marriage to the futility of which the young man drew attention, and the birth and death of her baby, resolved to go to Canada in company with another lover, a milkman. In the first act news of Mary's indecorum reached Leonard's father through her misappropriation of a photograph of Leonard; in the last act she announced to her father- and mother-in-law with calm and dignity that she had decided to forsake her gasbag of a husband for another. Calmness and dignity, in fact, were the chief characteristics of Mary Broome; and it is a little difficult to imagine so discreet a young woman yielding to passion or the importunities of an egoist. No doubt a parlourmaid's training is apt to produce at least a semblance of dual personality; but here the author was more concerned with the effect upon others of Mary's conduct than with the consistency of Mary herself. However, that is comment upon execution, which is no part of my immediate object. At the moment the point of *Mary Broome* to which I direct attention is that the young and talkative seducer addressed his parents in these terms:

> LEONARD. You parents are in a middle stage. Once you'd just have been brutal to the girl. I don't mean you, but parents generally. Presently we may have more sense. I'm a selfish brute, but I've got some sense. But I'm powerless. [*To his father.*] Haven't you any imagination? It's all very fine to make a scene here and put down your foot and coerce me into your beastly righteousness, but think of the years to come. Do you see us married? Do you see our married life?

That was the voice of self-conscious thought in 1911. That was the critical theatre. 'You parents . . . I don't mean you, but parents generally . . . I'm a selfish brute but I'm powerless . . . Your beastly righteousness.' Monkhouse, it is true, gave the moral an ironic twist highly personal to himself by allowing Mary to take the initiative in parting; but the argument was against Puritanism and against responsibility, and it revealed the fact that the post-Shavian stage in England, however quietly, was at last moving towards living commentary upon current morals and manners.

It was a pity, I think, that in so moving the Manchester dramatists, schooled by the *Guardian*, paid such fastidious heed to the literary tone of their work. Nobody cares less than I do for raw gobbets of life or for the noisy violences of those who aim at 'strength.' But there is more truth than the ironic author realizes in this wry report upon Manchester's reception of Geoffrey Arden's play *Alice Dean* (which can be taken to represent *Mary Broome*):

> People went to see *Alice Dean*, and it had a certain vogue; as a local attempt it was not so bad, though it was understood that these *Herald* people take themselves too seriously, and constitute a sort of mutual admiration society. Besides, such plays as *Alice Dean*, clever as they are, miss the broad, human touch.

If the broad human touch as conceived by sentimentalists is legitimately matter for ridicule, an absence of breadth decidedly leaves plays a little thin. Max Beerbohm, who is no gobbeteer, mentions in his essay on Ouida that 'Art, in a writer, is not everything. Indeed, it implies a certain limitation. If a list of consciously artistic writers were drawn up, one would find that most of them were lacking in great force of intellect or emotion.' In the case of *Mary Broome* there is a constant self-destructive quizzicalness and under-emphasis which, if the dialogue were not so delicately poised, would stultify the dramatic idea.

It might be true to say that Monkhouse's chief inspiration has been literary. There is not a book of his which is not rich in references to the Shakespearian tragedies and in quotations from the poetry of Meredith. When the people talk to one another, their talk mounts quickly to the quasi-Meredithian. It was all very quick; thought is always quick in Monkhouse's characters, and they speak briefly and in phrase—not brokenly and as if they groped for words. All have a flair for language. Either they are speaking, or the author himself is browsing among implications, turning them gravely and ironically, sometimes analysing, as in this:

> Men like me, who are modest enough on the surface and quiet and introspective, have our secrecies of insolence and elation. We are too wary to brag and strut—and, indeed, we scorn such crudities—but we can realize attitude and spectator in ourselves; we can indulge secretly an aptitude for showing off.

Elsewhere, Monkhouse causes a hero to recall a friend's saying that 'when you want a thing the best plan is to take the simplest means of getting it'; and he adds: 'Obvious as this is, it is not realized by those who conduct their lives on a complicated system of denials.' 'A complicated system of denials': is not that a most illuminating phrase? Does it not conjure up a temperament? Applying it to the author, does not one flashingly comprehend his restraint? Is it not a complicated system of denials, rather than of affirmations, that gives his plays and novels their air of fineness, of withdrawal from rough and tumble, of reflective treatment of the supposititious? Both books and plays are full of fully delicate feeling; but if one once loses the sense of quality they become curiously abstract, as if they dealt with posed situations, and as if the various misconducts of the errant characters had no greater reality than hearsay. Have these girls really been seduced? Is not their seduction merely a necessary preliminary to discussion?

Queer fish enchanted him; but only as abnormalities flung disconcertingly into a small, intelligent, less unconventional group of persons, old or young, to do the things which a local code of honour condemns. They have no scruples — from Leonard in *Mary Broome* to Marmaduke in *My Daughter Helen* and Paul Felice in the play to which he gives his name. They parade their lack of moral sense. They enlist the author's sympathy without quite conquering ourselves. Are we at fault? But always they are presented as masters of that quick literary talk of which I have given examples, with relish, with success. Granted the author's 'case,' whether it be that of the young writer who goes against his will to the war and returns sick with horror to dodge the village band and a reception which he regards as indecent, or the parlourmaid who is so innocently refined though she is going to have a baby by the young master, the treatment is at all times full of charm, wit, wisdom, and a sense of those heights which Granville-Barker thinks the dramatist should never forget. Where they have failed to arouse popular enthusiasm it has been because, in my view, they were too 'literary,' and because the small, the fine, the delicate, while they have their delicious joys for those of like mind, do lack robustness, power, and the colour and movement of irresistible life.

IV. ST JOHN GREER ERVINE

Too much attention is devoted to these squawkers in contemporary literature. They may be the victims of their environment, although I suspect them of plain self-indulgence, but a man is a poor creature who is victimized by any environment, and I am not prepared to make a hero of him. . . . I am, as my readers will have observed, a very humble-minded man, and am always willing to learn from my betters.

ST JOHN ERVINE, in *The Observer*, 22nd July 1934.

Nobody could accuse my last typical dramatic writer of being too 'literary,' for if St John Ervine has a fault it is that he is, in his journalistic writing, too bluff and manly to be endured by the fastidious. I doubt whether there is any other writer who arouses such repulsion in the delicate-minded. In the same way I doubt whether there is any other writer whose real gifts have been so much blanketed by that specious breeziness which is his version of what Keats might have called the Shavian or egotistical sublime. I should have difficulty in convincing quite a number of people that Ervine is a serious and extraordinarily

able novelist. And yet I am persuaded that this is what he is.
I would give all his plays (and of course all his dramatic criticism
and comment upon current affairs) for his two novels, *Mrs
Martin's Man* and *A Wayward Man*. I take pleasure in saying
that if these two books had been translated from the Icelandic
they would have given pleasure to all who now regard Ervine
as a noisy and offensive blasphemer against elegance and the
recherché.

But Ervine is a Belfast Irishman, born in 1883, who for some
good reason was in 1915 made manager of the Abbey Theatre,
Dublin. Prior to that, he had been a clerk in the London office
of an insurance company and a member of the Fabian Nursery,
and a riotous reviewer for A. R. Orage's weekly review, *The New
Age*. He went to the War in 1916, and lost a leg; he has been for
years the chief dramatic writer on the London weekly newspaper,
The Observer; an untiring lecturer, a jocular commentator, who
trails his coat and bangs heads as soon as look at them, and—as
if incidentally—the author of several plays (two of them celebrated and successful in the United States, a third one of
the most popular ever performed at the Haymarket Theatre,
London), and of six novels so casually produced over a period
of twenty years that they have hardly at all impressed the general
critical mind.

In person, Ervine is of the middle height, very fair, with a
round, babyish face and fresh colour, a smile that holds both
benignity and sarcasm, an extremely friendly manner, and a
decidedly Irish accent. He is persistently jocular in speech, and
he has a fund of highly disconcerting information regarding men
and affairs which he freely imparts. His chief characteristic is
shrewdness (I do not mean financial shrewdness); and considerably more intellectual activity occurs in his head than the simple
face would lead a casual beholder to expect. If he had been
content to stick to Ulster and the novel, he would have been
recognized everywhere as 'the Ulster novelist.' Instead, he has
created turmoil and ferocity in two countries by his outspoken
theatrical criticisms, and as an original writer is grievously
underrated.

I must not be thought to belittle Ervine's critical writing,
which at its least extravagant is full of sagacity; but I think it
true that he sometimes impersonates himself when he jovially
deals out his rights and lefts, his kicks and cuffs, and his charges
of sloppiness, mawkishness, and 'refanement.' Such an impersonation is inevitable in a privileged writer with large tracts

of Sunday space to fill. If one boiled down all that Ervine had written when the mood was on him, one would find the result a strong broth of good sense, and good sense about the theatre is so uncommon that this is quite remarkable enough to excuse the brawl of noise which rises from Ervine's typewriter whenever he is at work upon the truth. All the same, Ervine's shouting and clouting do make harder than it would be the demonstration of his value as a serious artist.

Further his two highly successful plays in England, *The First Mrs Fraser* and *Anthony and Anna*, are by no means the best of his dramatic works. His best play is *John Ferguson*, which has an Ulster scene; and this tells the not uncommon story of a mortgaged farm, the brutality of the mortgagor, his rape of the mortgagee's daughter, and his murder by the mortgagee's son, followed by an inevitable sad parting between the amiable characters as one of them goes to render himself to justice. The influence of Synge upon Ervine in this play was as great as (and no greater than) the influence of Synge upon all other contributors to the Irish drama. There is a half-wit who spins the plot, and there are some poetical phrases, local idioms, and a general air of enduring poverty. But the play has its own life, it moves clearly, and it is written with power.

Some of the other plays, while they show skill and accomplishment, do not rise sufficiently above those qualities to impress themselves upon a reader. *The Ship*, sincere though it is in an attempt to make tragedy of a young man's death in the sinking of a ship in which he had no mind to sail, lacks resilience; *Mary, Mary, Quite Contrary*, which aims at lightness, misses brilliance and is a little heavy; *Jane Clegg*, produced at the Gaiety Theatre, Manchester, in 1913, belongs to what I have called the Manchester school, deals with poor people, a humbugging commercial traveller who embezzles to get his mistress out of the country, and his wife who parts with a legacy to save him from disgrace and then parts from him to save herself from further contamination; and despite slick character sketches does not escape obviousness and repetition.

It is in two novels, *Mrs Martin's Man* and *The Wayward Man*, that Ervine reaches the most natural expression of his great talent. Both are narratives, the former the simple tale of a long-suffering woman shopkeeper in what I understand is Donaghadee, the latter the tale of a wandering son of just such another woman. Mrs Martin, marrying a sailor, has two children by him, guesses that he is unfaithful to her with her own sister, and at last, when she is deserted (for her husband clears out for America with the least humane of motives), she opens a shop and deals successfully in hardware. When her husband returns home again, his children are grown up, and the situation as it then stands between all the members of the family provides material for the tale. It is original, beautiful, and deeply interesting. *The Wayward Man*, also highly original, has something of the same quality. In that book, however, interest settles upon a boy who runs away to sea and spends some time in America before he turns to Ireland and marries. Here, as in *Mrs Martin's Man*, there is nothing of the conventional novel, but a clear narrative of which the impression throughout is complete authenticity. I do not regard Ervine's other novels as equal to these two books; but these two books seem to me to be so excellent that I am prepared to rank their author very high indeed, on the strength of them, among modern writers.

It may be said that I have strayed from 'the critical theatre,' and that is quite true. So have Granville-Barker, Allan Monkhouse, and St John Ervine. The critical theatre, to be quite truthful, had not and has not the seeds of eternal literary life in it. A critical attitude, and a self-conscious attitude, does not and cannot develop creative literature. We need criticism; but we need it as a corrective, not as an inspiration. That is why, bad and vulgar as popular literature may be, it has a vitality denied to the writings of those who know only too well the weakness of the instrument. Shaw could criticize and create; but Shaw is Shaw, an exuberant force who will always risk folly for the sake of fun. There is no other contributor to the critical theatre who has not paralysed himself or petered out through fear of his own judgment.

CHAPTER IX: LITERARY MEN

I

THE author of a recently published manual for young writers states that 'there is scarcely any necessity to read as models any writer farther back than Stevenson and Gissing'; and a young friend of mine who told the English Literature master of a large school for boys that he had with pleasure been reading *Tom Jones* received the reply: 'Who or what is Tom Jones?' These two comments are both highly significant of the critical change occurring in the last twenty-five years; for when King George came to the throne nothing written after 1850 was in any sense 'literature,' and in 1910 progressive authors raged in vain against some academic veterans whom they styled 'mandarins.' It was the mandarins, one understood, who then fixed the limits of 'literature,' and dropped a curtain between the great and good and the merely current.

If I am asked to name the mandarins, I cannot do so. I assume that they were the more stuffy professors of English literature throughout the British Isles. Generations familiar with Arthur Quiller-Couch as a professor will hardly believe that his Cambridge appointment caused at the time profound academic disquiet. He had written novels. He was suspect. Fortunately he had read widely, and he had a way with undergraduates. Hence his success. But I doubt whether even Quiller-Couch ventured to advance the canon by many years. Shall we say as far as 1894? Nowadays everything is altered. The mandarins are all 'modn.'

There were one or two mandarinic personages at whom no brickbats were aimed by original writers. They were growing elderly, and of course they grew more elderly and in the fullness of time died; but while they lived they were tolerated. The men I have in mind were George Saintsbury, Edmund Gosse, and William Robertson Nicoll. To them might be added Thomas Seccombe, genial lecturer and journalist and historian. All four were practising men of letters. Saintsbury was generally understood to have read everything ever written; and when he wrote a *History of the French Novel* he gave a great deal of space to Paul de Kock, a fact which in any less professorial writer would have been censured but which, in the case of Saintsbury, who was much loved, aroused delighted murmurs. He also contributed prefaces which are the best things of their kind to forty translated volumes of Balzac's novels. He was a slovenly and eccentric writer, but an interesting and humanely learned man.

Gosse—pilloried at the beginning of the twentieth century by Churton Collins for writing about eighteenth-century literature without taking the trouble to read the whole of it, and by Duncan Tovey for reprinting a corrupt text of Gray's letters while boasting that he had collated every word with the originals, still in 1934 being pilloried by Carter and Pollard for accepting as genuine several glaring modern literary forgeries, and in fact ridiculed or lambasted by almost all who have seriously tilled the ground he lightly scratched—contributed much to English knowledge of French and Scandinavian literature and wrote a book about his father which, when it was published in 1907, caused every scholarly sin to be forgiven him by the non-pedantic. To the end of his life he gossiped in print about books, and hobnobbed with writers, old and young. He had in his temperament both malice and vanity, and perhaps was a snob (which means that he preferred the literary *ton*, and liked to stand well with the fashion); but he had taste, a pen, and a tender feeling for letters.

Robertson Nicoll was a very different man from either of these. He edited the great English nonconformist newspaper, *The British Weekly*, for which he wrote under more than one pseudonym, and his activities were without end. He was a little Scotsman with a sighing voice, weary eyes, and a straggling moustache, and he would often muse, stroking his chin with a wavery hand, preparing gentle retorts which stung more the longer they were recollected. He figures in Wells's *Boon* as Dr Tomlinson Keyhole, from which name one may gather that he also was something of a gossip. In fact, he knew all the literary gossip ever told (or not told), and forgot nothing. Nor did Nicoll deal exclusively in gossip; for his interest in gossip was but a section of his interest in all human affairs. He had a keen eye for authors. It was he who sighted Barrie from afar and arranged the book publication of *Auld Licht Idylls*; it was he who persuaded Heinemann to reconsider and eventually to publish Maugham's *Mrs Craddock*, hitherto rejected; it was he who knew at once which young novelist would move towards fame and fortune (although he was keen to detect a fault, and of one who has since become famous he quietly said after a first meeting: 'How *coooold* he be ainy goood? He knows naaaathing about saix!'); and it was he whose first editorial mistake—the commissioning of a series of highly critical articles on Lloyd George which he could not have published without alienating a powerful friend—killed him.

Since I have mentioned Nicoll, who among other professional activities was a publisher's reader on a very large, indeed colossal, scale, I think I should name here two men whose chief activity in the panorama of Georgian literature has been of great but anonymous importance. They are E. V. Lucas and Edward Garnett. Everybody of course knows Lucas for his own writing —his humorously sentimental novels, his essays short or long, his anthologies, and his editorship of the works of Lamb, for these are enough to give him unique celebrity; not so many are familiar with the plays of Garnett, or his book of satires, *Papa's War*, or his Conrad-prefaced study of Turgenev. And yet Lucas and Garnett, as publishers' readers, have done more to encourage the growth of modern literature than any other men of their day.

II. EDWARD VERRALL LUCAS

On the surface he might be mistaken for a mere cricket enthusiast. Dig down, and you will come, with not too much difficulty, to the simple man of letters. Dig further, and, with somewhat more difficulty, you will come to an agreeably ironic critic of human foibles. Try to dig still further, and you will probably encounter rock.
                                ARNOLD BENNETT, *Books and Persons*.

Well, if you were to study the subject of anthologies, you would without any doubt at all find that the best known of all modern anthologies is one called *The Open Road*, published in 1899, and edited by E. V. Lucas. Lucas was born about seventy years ago, by 1899 he had mastered the greater part of English light literature. He loved walking, and he loved dogs; he had urbanity, ruthlessness of observation (as witness his unsurpassed account of a visit to Swinburne and Watts-Dunton towards the end of Swinburne's life), and taste. These qualities he preserves. In a deep voice, hardly moving his lips, and certainly using little gesticulation, he quietly and not expansively talks with the grim wit of a rich and implacable mind. What he says is worth hearing.

That is equally true of his essays, which are among the most agreeable of our age, and of his historical and topographical works; for he is a traveller in cities and picture galleries as well as among books and men, and he records his every journey with the same slightly bitter benignity, and a charm which is never merely honeyed. It is true of his novels, with this reservation, that while they are based upon ingenious ideas, and are full of whimsy and information, they are deficient in the continuity arising from persistent imaginative travail. Lucas has a great appetite for the curious, the human, and the ridiculous. Offer him a story, an incident, or an absurdity, and his mind will instantly shape it with wit and form. He can read a character with wisdom, and gravely turn it to fun. He will versify a fancy, or concentrate in an anecdote or instance all that a vaguer mind might stagger for an hour to express. But his is the mind of a critic and a commentator; and the hideous sustained labour of the ambitious novelist would be abhorrent to him.

It would involve digging below that rock to which Arnold Bennett referred; it would involve for Lucas the excavation of harshness and passion. This is so because he is not a writer to whom the levels are final depths, and if once he were determined to go deep he would go deep. In his thoughts he has no superficiality; but his essays and fictions are written with his fancy and his playful mind, and it is only at times, as in the Swinburne sketch, that one glimpses a judgment to which the facile enthusiasms of his fellow-creatures are as the idle howlings of tomcats on urban rooftops.

He is recognized as the pre-eminent editor of Charles Lamb's works and biographer of Lamb. No edition approaches his in completeness and fullness of annotation. It is a monument, rendered doubly a monument by the complete series of Lamb's letters, to lifelong sympathy and devoted research. As for his work as a publisher's reader, that is more difficult to describe; for it has been personally unobtrusive and I shall not attempt to analyse it. I do, however, assert that he has been so much abreast of the literature of the twentieth century, as well as so exceptionally familiar with that of a hundred years ago, and so well read in that of all periods, as to make his encouragement and understanding invaluable in former days to many who now enjoy general appreciation. This good work should be added to those works for which Lucas already receives appropriate credit.

III. EDWARD GARNETT

'Come and dine with me, Truth,' begged Justice, and his stern eyes shone with the undying passion he ever cherished to make her his own. . . . 'Come with me, Truth! Your eyes are the loveliest thing to me in the wide universe.'

EDWARD GARNETT, *Papa's War.*

Edward Garnett was much less well known to the public as a bookman than Lucas. His plays, one of which deals with Joan of Arc, were published in book form, and single performances may have been given of them; but the chief bulk of his published writing was in the form of criticism, and in the way of reports to publishers he was among the most prolific of men. He used, long ago, to write for an old weekly called *The Speaker*, which was merged in *The Nation* (now in turn merged in *The New Statesman*); and his articles for ever drew attention to new work by English and continental novelists who otherwise might have whistled for praise. As a very young reader for Fisher Unwin (he was born in 1868) he was the first to discern Conrad's future greatness in the book submitted in 1894. He was the friend and encourager of W. H. Hudson and John Galsworthy. To him we owe the abridgment of Doughty's *Arabia Deserta* and a valuable selection from Cunninghame Graham's work. His encouraging connection with struggling younger writers, Lawrence and others, is well known. But there is hardly a man or woman writing novels of serious intention who did not at one time receive from Garnett that praise and support which to the artistically scrupulous mean so much more than financial rewards.

Nor is this all, for his widow, Constance Garnett, is the translator of Turgenev, Dostoevsky, Tchekhov, and some of Tolstoy; and in conjunction these two devoted workers introduced to English readers four novelists (to name no others) of immense importance for those ready to appreciate the significance of Russian art. It would be hard to exaggerate the impression made upon young readers in 1912 by the appearance of *The Brothers Karamazov*. It would be equally hard to exaggerate the influence of that translation of the Tales of Tchekhov by Constance Garnett which by the active effort of her husband was begun in 1916. The Turgenev is an older debt owed to the Garnetts, and for Edward Garnett Turgenev was always the ideal novelist.

Opinions as to the positive merits of Constance Garnett's

translations differ. I have been told by those who write and speak Russian that they are deficient in exactitude; having at one time made a careful comparison between Ralston's *Lisa*, Constance Garnett's *A House of Gentlefolk*, and Davis's *A Nest of Hereditary Legislators* (all of them versions of the same book by Turgenev), I believe the Garnett translations to be, so far as the general character of the work is concerned, as accurate and as fine as translations from so difficult a language as Russian can be, but slightly lacking—more particularly in the dialogue— in what I shall call exquisiteness of rendering. I have not compared her translations of Tolstoy with those of Aylmer Maude; and I think that Long's two volumes of Tchekhov, published before Constance Garnett began her work, have occasional superiorities. Nobody, however, has conferred so substantial a benefit, and one of such consistent faithfulness, upon English readers of Russian fiction as she; and she may be considered in this respect beyond reach of cavil.

IV. FORD MADOX HUEFFER

I call him Ford Madox Hueffer because that is the name he bore in the days of *The English Review*. He has now changed his name to Ford Madox Ford; and under that name has for years continued to publish his oddly uneven work in considerable quantity and to give rise in the literary world to innumerable rumours. Hueffer is to me one of the enigmas of current literature. He has great talent, and much taste, to which he adds considerable coarseness of spirit and a carelessness of statement which constantly spoil a reader's enjoyment of his work. He has written remarkable poetry, some historical romances which just miss being excellent, many novels on modern themes and situations which with much skill and passages beyond the reach of most living authors combine the coldness of the mortuary, criticism which for a paragraph here and there seems very like revealed truth and then drifts off into perversity, and memoirs of his own life and the lives of others which seem all the time to be boasting of his own unpleasantness.

He was editor of what was without doubt the most interesting periodical of our time, *The English Review*, in which were published (besides that bizarre relic, a poem by Arnold Bennett) specimens of the work of almost all the established and arriving writers to 1908-11 (*The English Review* continued its work under another editor after the first glad Huefferian dawn), and in which living literature for the first time in English history was treated as quite important and quite exciting—much more important and much more exciting than students of English literature could imagine, and even more exciting than the contests of politicians or sportsmen. Books such as *The Fifth Queen* and *The Good Soldier* should be familiar to every investigator of what has been written in this century. *The Critical Attitude* as to about one-third is a stimulating and valuable work. And yet the total effect created by Hueffer is less than the total effect created by men of insignificant talent.

In person, Hueffer is a large, rather unwieldly fair man whose mouth, like Coleridge's, is always open, and whose speech recalls Carlyle's description of Coleridge's speech. He tells lengthy and delightful stories with absorption and skill; he is a good talker, with a considerable sense of his audience; he improvises to admiration, and is lyrical at a moment's notice. But for me he remains both in himself and in his writings an unsolved puzzle. I must not forget to mention that when he wishes to do so he writes with eloquence and beauty.

V. CHARLES EDWARD MONTAGUE

But Dick had fads. One was for a kind of writing; not the right kind; not saying what he had to say, and that 's the end of it, but a plaguey, itchy fussing over some phrase, planing it down or bevelling it off, inlaying it with picked words of a queer far-fetched aptness, making it clang with whole pomps of proper names, that boomed into their places, like drums and cymbals in symphonies, or twinkle and tingle, shot with ironies, or rise and fall like a voice that means more by the tune than the words.

C. E. MONTAGUE, *A Hind Let Loose.*

One of the men who were introduced to the notice of a different —not a wider—audience by *The English Review* was Charles Edward Montague, who wrote for it an essay upon 'the wholesome theatre.' But Montague was by no means new to the world in 1910, for he was born in 1867, and for some years had been the perpetual boy on the staff of *The Manchester Guardian* as to whom I used earlier a reference of Monkhouse's. He was chief leader-writer to the paper; and as long as he wrote leading articles leading articles were dishes for literary epicures. Such epicures, I think, had to savour Latin feasts rather than those of a purer classicism; but they had a daily edification. They still receive similar feasts from other hands, especially when they read of cricket and music; but it was Montague who set the example and created the style. His delight being in the theatre, he also attended many a Manchester first night in the spirit in which genial spinsters attend weddings—from a love of a good institution, and the sight of happiness in others. 'A man,' says Tennyson, '"imputes himself." If he be decent he readily thinks other people are decent.' That was an article of the Montague faith. He loved the stage, and especially the stage of the Elizabethans, in which he was word-perfect.

In 1910 he wrote his first novel; and that, curiously enough, was about a leader-writer. But Fay, in *A Hind Let Loose*, was no Montague; he was a comic character, a man who wrote one leading article for the Liberal newspaper in a city called Halland (which in its pride much resembles Manchester), and another for the Conservative rival newspaper in the same city. In his double role, he scourged and counter-scourged himself nightly. However, he was found out; and both his employers discharged him, only to find that their own substitutional efforts were thought as dull as tracts by every reader. So both surreptitiously returned to the rascal, and pleaded for his sole service in future, which (to both for consideration) he promised; while a third employer, another rival and a new one, was added to the first two, and Fay's earnings much increased by the entire transaction. Great fun, literary fun, but fun of richness and spirit throughout, and the author's fluency never at a loss.

Montague followed this with another—*The Morning's War*— perhaps a rewriting of something said earlier, and certainly less striking than *A Hind Let Loose*; and what he would normally have done next I do not know. But the War came, and in spite of the fact that he was forty-seven (he was said to be white-haired, but that sounds like a story), he boldly and enthusi- astically enlisted as a private soldier. 'The early volunteer in his blindness imagined that there was between all Englishmen then that oneness of faith, love, and courage.'

Montague, still enthusiastic, was duly sent to the front, and after a time it dawned upon those under whose command he was that this was no common soldier, and perhaps that he was less of a youth than he pretended. So they gave him some sort of rank, and he had then the task of showing distinguished literary visitors here and there about the battle zone. As he did this, he would say: 'I think we can just cut across here; it saves a mile; the Germans have all got their heads down; it will be all right.' And with that he would lead the way across the open, while the visitor scampered after with his heart in his boots.

But the mood of ecstasy in which Montague went to the War did not survive his experience of the War. As soon as the fighting was done, and he was home again, he began to write fragmentary articles for *The Manchester Guardian* about his experiences and his views of war; and these were so much his own that he was urged to make a book of such material, which he did. And it was called *Disenchantment*, a proper title for such a work; the work itself expressing the feelings of all that part of a generation whose thought could expand to comprehensiveness.

In their vices as well as their virtues the English preserve a distinguished moderation. They do not utterly shrink from jobbery, for example; they do from a job that is flagrant or gross. They give judgeships as prizes for party support, but not to the utterly briefless, the dullard who knows no more law than necessity. Building contractors, when in the course of their rise they become town councillors, do not give bribes right and left: their businesses thrive without that. An Irishman running a Tammany in the States cannot thus hold himself in: the humorous side of corruption charms him too much; he wants to let the grand farce of roguery rip for all it is worth. But the English private's pet dictum, 'There's reason in everything,' rules the jobber, the profiteer, the shirker and placeman of Albion as firmly as it controls the imagination of her Wordsworths and the political idealism of her Cromwells and Pitts. Like her native cockroaches and bugs, whose moderate stature excites the admiration and envy of human dwellers among the corresponding fauna of the tropics, the caterpillars of her commonwealth preserve the golden mean.

That is bitter, as well as true and amusing and eloquent; but Montague's was the first pen to tell England what returning idealists thought of the land for whose continued freedom they had struggled with the horrors of war. As they did, he saw and felt and thought so deeply that his mind at last was sunk in a mood of restless melancholy. He was not disillusioned with life, but with the post-War world. And so when Montague had written this book, and eased his mind of the thoughts which buzzed there, he settled down to do the work he had always wished to do. He left the *Guardian*; he went to live at Oxford, near his old university; he began another novel; he published a volume of short stories called *Fiery Particles*. And then, unexpectedly, he died. The greater works he had planned remained unwritten. We are to content ourselves with what is already in print.

VI. MAX BEERBOHM

Well! For my own part, I am a dilettante, a *petit maître*. I love best in literature delicate and elaborate ingenuities of form and style. But my preference does not keep me from paying due homage to Titanic force, and delighting, now and again, in its manifestation.

MAX BEERBOHM, *More*.

From this early confession it would be easy to conceive Max Beerbohm as a literary dandy; and so, in a sense, he is. He was always elegant. Born in 1872, he was just old enough to contribute to *The Yellow Book*. But he was still up at Oxford in 1893, and even yet he is by no means an old man. Also, in spite of elegance, he has not the mental characteristics of a dilettante. He is very sincere. He is very wise. He has both wit and humour (a rare conjunction). He has style, taste, the power to sympathize while laughing, a penetrating critical gift; and in verbal interchange his attention is so quick that he will take any reference (however remote) and respond to it as soon as it is made. But he will not sacrifice the topic to the *mot*. He could do so; he does not do so. That means that he is a conversationalist, and not a talker. These traits are so rare in one person as to confer distinction. The man who is as witty as Max Beerbohm usually wishes to shine alone; the man who is as kind often has no elegance; the man who is as critical has no enjoyment. I wonder nobody has ever thought Max Beerbohm dull.

All are familiar with his later portraits, those of the polished nobleman with heavy-lidded eyes and a moustache acute as a wren's tail, demure lips and an expression of debonair calm. The portraits do not lie; the man is superficially recognizable from them. He is as quiet and as sad as they make him appear. But no portrait quite suggests the natural sweetness of his manner, for which we must go to his printed writings, and especially to *Enoch Soames*.

In that story Beerbohm describes his entry to London and the glories of the aesthetic nineties; and in that story does he describe the association with *The Saturday Review* which led to his regular weekly appearances in that paper as successor to Bernard Shaw in the criticism of plays. You would not gather from what he says that he ever contributed more than a few 'middles' to *The Saturday Review*: in fact, he was dramatic critic for twelve years; and it was with a feeling of consternation that readers learned of his abandonment of this appalling task just

at the beginning of the Georgian era. He had always been a
critic; he has always been a literary man. Now, from afar, he
surveys the English literary scene with possibly less pleasure
than he had of old; for English literature has passed into a
different mood from his own. But he surveys it still, as his
later caricatures (which depict a paunchy Shaw and thereby
lose realism) proclaim. The elegant have grown malicious and
factious; he distils them for amusement. His old loves are dead
or dreary; he dwells courteously upon their past grandeurs. He
is in fact a little out of touch with the Georgian era.

If he had been less modest, he could have affected this
era profoundly, for some aspects of our own day strongly
resemble typical aspects of the day in which Max Beerbohm
found life at the Café Royal. But he is so far a dilettante, that
he has written only what it amused him to write, and solemner
talents than his strut their little hour upon a stage he might have
occupied. It is to his elegance that all refer, as if he were no
more than a survival from a gracious period; and not to that
deep laughter which is the source of his quality as a writer. How
unjust that is to Beerbohm! From the early nonsensical essays
(which are so wise, as well as so fastidiously written) to the in-
comparable parodies brought together in *A Christmas Garland*,
the extravagance of *Zuleika Dobson* (that delicious supplement
to the novels of his adored Ouida), and the fantastic literary
anecdotes to which he gives the title *Seven Men*, he had been
laughing pointedly and without cruelty at the foibles of men.
According to the analyses of humour prepared by the humourless, Max Beerbohm is impossible. He could not exist. He
laughs where he loves; and loves where he laughs; but he neither
beams nor sniggers. By the annotated laws of laughter, no
man could behave so anomalously. The question arises whether
Max Beerbohm is a man or a fairy.

VII. KATHERINE MANSFIELD AND JOHN MIDDLETON MURRY

Oh God! Suddenly it sweeps over me again. We are writers!
You are a poet and I write stories. But how this knowledge makes
me *ache* for us to be together.

Katherine Mansfield to J. M. M., 3rd June 1918.

I should not attempt to excuse the abrupt transition from so
bland a writer of belles-lettres as Max Beerbohm to a couple of

such serious literati as Katherine Mansfield and Middleton Murry
if it were not that, as Stevenson says,

> The world is so full of a number of things,
> I'm sure we should all be as happy as kings.

I therefore draw attention to the fact that the world of 1910
onwards (the world, in truth, of King George) was quite as full
of other people as it was of Max Beerbohm. One cannot explain such heterogeneousness; one can only record and marvel
at the busy activity of men and women with pens in their hands.

It was towards the end of 1912 that I received one day an unexpected letter from a complete stranger. The writer said she
had just reviewed a novel of mine for *The Westminster Gazette*
(of which Naomi Royde-Smith was then, I think, literary editor),
and that she thought the book so good that she wished to meet
me. The letter was signed 'Katherine Mansfield.' It came from
an address in Chancery Lane, London; and I remember going
one day to tea to a not very cheerful flat in a block of buildings
there. At that time Katherine Mansfield must have been very
young (about twenty-four); a small, very slim, very dark girl
who spoke in a carefully modulated murmur, hardly parting her
lips, as if she hummed or intoned her words. She sat very still,
smiling faintly, and explained in this low voice, with much sweetness, that she did not know quite what she would do in the future
—with her life, she meant, for the alternatives of children,
literature, and a career seemed all to be possible; while she and
Murry, who was as gently ingratiating as he has always been,
otherwise spoke a good deal of French and Russian authors,
particularly of Stendhal, for whom we all felt intense admiration.
The beautiful idol-like quietness of Katherine Mansfield made
her absolutely enchanting; and it was clear, from the fact that
two or three other young writers were also present, that something like a young group was in process of formation. The
Murrys were conducting a periodical called *Rhythm*—that word
was less common in 1912 than it has since become, and I think
they must have been early among English users of it as an
aesthetic term—and they were looking for allies who would
diversify *Rhythm* with stories and essays of a non-commercial
character.

Within a short time *Rhythm* was merged in a new and—in
its conception—much grander journal called *The Blue Review*;
which was described as a serious attempt to give a lead to modern
literature. But *The Blue Review* did not last; there was a

collapse in the Murrys' financial situation; and until after the War, in 1919, the world did not again hear of them. Murry was appointed to the editorship of *The Athenaeum*, a very important event indeed; for under his editorship *The Athenaeum* (which had ceased during the War to be a paper dealing with the arts, and had become a miscellany) was restored to its place in letters, and published a truly astonishing number of articles and reviews and letters written by men and women who have since taken leading places in the literary world. Not only older men such as Santayana; but those of a younger generation than my own—Aldous Huxley, T. S. Eliot, Herbert Read, the entire force of Bloomsbury, from Bertrand Russell and Lytton and James Strachey to Clive Bell and Virginia Woolf. I am not sure that Murry found himself absolutely at ease in this gallimaufry; but he certainly coped with it until further financial considerations led to the discontinuance of *The Athenaeum* as a separate paper.

Katherine Mansfield wrote for *The Athenaeum* until she was too ill to write any more, a weekly review of some outstanding novel (these reviews have been collected into a book); but she also began to publish her books of short sketches in the manner of Tchekhov, which decidedly established her as an original writer of distinction. Murry, meanwhile, wrote a book on Dostoevsky and a novel entitled *Still Life*, and had other literary activities. In January 1923, Katherine Mansfield died. She had always been delicate, had suffered much from rheumatism, and in 1917 she caught a chill which led to tuberculosis. Many different residences and treatments were experimented with, unavailingly; and the two constant features of her pilgrimages were increasing illness and unfailing bravery. Many of her letters were subsequently published, some more volumes of tales, her journals; all with Murry's approval and under his supervision.

Having been long associated in the public mind with Katherine Mansfield and her work (as well, of course, as with his own writing), Murry has in the last few years taken the eye as an old friend and biographer of D. H. Lawrence, and as the subject of attacks from more than one of those whose loyalty to Lawrence takes the form of indignant malice towards everybody who can be supposed to have wronged him. Murry has been lampooned in novels, has turned first Christian and then Christian Communist, and has been one of the chief exponents of what is called psychological criticism, writing of Shakespeare, Keats, and Blake rather as Frank Harris wrote of Shakespeare in 1909, but with something less than Harris's fire.   To myself, this kind of criticism is completely exasperating; it seems to me verbose, full of desperate assumptions, completely unreliable, the application of a false principle to the study of art.   But it has had a vogue, and it impresses all who in earlier days would have enjoyed bathing with God and Truth and the Categorical Imperative in metaphysics, mysticism, and other searches for the Absolute; and to debate it would take more time and space than I can afford.   My present object is merely to show some of the stages in Murry's progress, and, as I believe, his influence upon the literary concentrations of the Georgian era.   I dwell upon his work with *The Blue Review* and *The Athenaeum* for historical reasons; because both these periodicals successfully assembled in common effort other writers more *creatively* important than Murry.   With his curiously emotional relationship with Lawrence I have no concern; his taste in the matter of Katherine Mansfield's literary remains and the biography of Lawrence is not mine, but it is a detail in the record of the time; with his critical writings about classic authors it is not my duty to deal at length.

There is naturally no question of comparing the respective talents of Murry and Katherine Mansfield.   They were husband and wife, and good friends to the last; their ideas were not recognizably similar, and with the later developments of Murry's mind it is possible that Katherine Mansfield would not have sympathized.   Katherine Mansfield was a very fastidious person, a literary person, enamoured of art.   She was herself a simple person.   But she tried hard, at one time or another, to be something a little more grandiose.   Any reader of her letters will be struck by occasional notes of exclamatory and italicized sentiment, and by her flutterings after fundamental critical conclusions; at times I think she was a little too literary and perhaps even a little insincere—both accidents inevitable in one who was quickly moved by her own writings and by kindness from others, and one who was still, as far as I can see, seeking some aesthetic touchstone.   She was a good critic for a paragraph or two, with excellent darts of insight; when she became vague she possibly was inclined to guess.   In her tales, which are her most important work, there are very many delicacies of touch and suggestion, and considerable felicity of style.   She had a great eye for little things, for simplicities and tendernesses which touch and please the reader.   It was not a robust talent, however; and it was overweighted by an impulsive admiration for the tales of

Tchekhov. When these tales were first translated into English (Katherine Mansfield probably had met some of them in German before English translations began to appear), their effect upon nearly all readers who were also writers was very strong. Such writers either felt that Tchekhov was an author to be imitated or that he left them no justification for their own continued literary activity. Katherine Mansfield belonged to the first type, and she imitated Tchekhov disinterestedly and devotedly. He was her author. She found in him, as others have found, a really perfect artistic satisfaction. I say Katherine Mansfield imitated Tchekhov; but I wish not to be misunderstood. By 'imitation' I do not mean plagiarism, but a kind of aspiring, exulting study and comparison which led the writer—sometimes—in the search for similar perfection to expunge every sign of life and sinew from work in hand. Katherine Mansfield's tales, like Tchekhov's, were records of mood and sensitiveness; smaller moods, less generalized sensitiveness than Tchekhov's, but authentic enough. At times they had a trembling beauty very pleasing to taste and perception. At other times they were fragilities. Occasionally they were sentimental. But she was a charming, pathetic figure; and this she remains in her work and in her letters.

CHAPTER X: PRE-WAR POETS

I

I AM aware that any attempt on my part to discuss with an appearance of seriousness the progress of poetry in the Georgian era would be ridiculous. I have not the necessary knowledge; and the plan of this book causes me to divert into other chapters the discussion of at least two of the most important of modern poets—D. H. Lawrence and T. S. Eliot. But having given this fair warning, I feel constrained to sketch something of the poetical history of the time, and to dwell upon several outstanding figures whose most notable contributions to modern literature have been in the form of poetry.

At the accession of King George I suppose that the living writer who held highest place as a poet was unquestionably Hardy. *The Dynasts* had been completed only two years earlier, and it was almost unanimously considered to be the most majestic poetic creation of the age. Hardy's lyrics, too, brimming with the sense of mortality and decay, had their temporary glories, now very much assailed by modern poet-critics and as stoutly defended by poets and critics to whom the modernity is not absolutely the *dernier cri*. At a distance stood Rudyard Kipling, then at the ebb of poetic reputation but, by virtue of his genius, supporting the efforts of his attackers and continuing to exist as a major figure in literature. From Ireland W. B. Yeats shed the misty splendours of fairyland and legend upon the people of this country. In England Robert Bridges, physician, grammarian, and poet, had in late middle age his profound admirers, although these were fewer in number than they are to-day. And, enjoying wide respect but a slightly suspect eminence, were Alice Meynell, William Watson, Sturge Moore, Laurence Binyon, and Gordon Bottomley. John Masefield and Walter de la Mare were recognized as exceptional talents (the former very widely, the latter by a number of people); W. H. Davies had established himself by his earliest poems and by his *Autobiography of a Super-Tramp*. Otherwise, though new poets were springing up in little books which they published for themselves or in the ordinary way, without hope of gain (and it is quite a mistake to suppose that the writing of poetry was a War-time innovation), interest was concentrated upon the novel and the play. Poetry—always excepting the thrilling doggerel of *The Everlasting Mercy* and *The Widow in the Bye-Street*—was not in fashion.

But poetry was being written by a number of men who were not at all interested at that time in writing plays or novels; and these men were drawn together by a common interest, as well as by the existence in Georgian England of a truly remarkable character. This remarkable character was apparently destined by Nature to be Private Secretary to innumerable Cabinet Ministers, and in his spare time to be one of the greatest encouragers of young poets that the world had seen. His name, Edward Marsh, though familiar to poets, to those who read poetry, to those who visit first performances of plays in the West End of London, and indeed to the whole of London Society, is less well known out of town. He would delight Americans, because he is one of the few Englishmen to wear a monocle; his tall and easy form is an adornment to any row of stalls; and his sweet, fragile voice is like the cooing of doves. He has translated to perfection—it is a terribly difficult task, only to be accomplished by one who has a mastery of ingenious English and can do more than piece together the words of a foreign tongue—the *Fables* of La Fontaine; but it is as a patron of poets, rather than as a poet in right of his own performance, that he would wish to be known, and will with gratitude be remembered, by posterity. He did more, from 1911 to 1922, to further the cause of modern poetry than any other man. He organized its reception. He was not only Private Secretary to Winston Churchill and J. H. Thomas; he was Private Secretary, nay, Accoucheur and Wet-Nurse, to Euterpe in her most respectable modern rebirth.

It was Edward Marsh who, one day in 1911 or 1912, as the result of a talk with Rupert Brooke in which their enthusiasm had mounted as high as action, gathered together in his chambers Wilfrid Wilson Gibson, John Drinkwater, Harold Monro, and Arundel del Re (the two last respectively editor and sub-editor of *The Poetry Review*); and planned with these men to publish a new kind of anthology—an anthology of poems drawn entirely from publications of 1911 and 1912. Not all poets were to be included in the anthology; some, in fact, in later volumes, were almost harshly excluded from it, so that they fled into the pages of *Wheels*; but only those who came within the scope of a clear plan. As the editor of *Georgian Poetry, 1911–1912*, remarked in his prefatory note:

It has no pretension to cover the field. Every reader will notice the absence of poets whose work would be a necessary ornament of any anthology not limited by a definite aim. Two years ago some of the writers represented had published nothing; and only a very few of the others were known except to the eagerest 'watchers of the skies.' Those few are here because within the chosen period their work seemed to have gained some accession of power.

We need not take the words of this preface with absolute literalness (for in the making of anthologies a great variety of considerations enters upon which it would be tactless to dwell); but at least the editor's aim was unmistakable. It was to strike a blow for young and eager poets who felt that in the solid publicity accorded to the novel and play their own art was treated as of too little account. The poets who were included in the first volume of *Georgian Poetry* are worth noting here. In alphabetical order, they were Lascelles Abercrombie, Gordon Bottomley, Rupert Brooke, Gilbert Chesterton, W. H. Davies, Walter de la Mare, John Drinkwater, James Elroy Flecker, W. W. Gibson, D. H. Lawrence, John Masefield, Harold Monro, T. Sturge Moore, Ronald Ross, Edmund Beale Sargant, James Stephens, and R. C. Trevelyan.

Such was the official birth of Georgian poetry. But it would be unjust to ignore the claims of the two most eminent poets who fell outside the range of the anthology projected by Edward Marsh and his friends; and I must therefore speak briefly of both Robert Bridges and W. B. Yeats. Having done that, I shall pause for a moment with Walter de la Mare and John Masefield, whose talents one may consider individual rather than Georgian; and then I shall return to Marsh's 'Georgians,' to find them augmented in numbers with the passing of years, and at the same time subtly changed. As early as the fourth volume, of 1918–19, Masefield has disappeared, and the editor is replying to criticism.

II. ROBERT BRIDGES

> I will be what God made me, nor protest
> Against the bent of genius in my time,
> That science of my friends robs all the best,
> While I love beauty, and was born to rhyme.
>
> ROBERT BRIDGES.

In his lifetime, Robert Bridges was described by a friend as being 'somewhat shy, somewhat austere, fastidious, difficult.'

* G 943

He was also a man of fortune and culture, educated at Eton and
Oxford, at one time a physician, a scholar and experimentalist
in technique, a grammarian and exponent of something called
'Pure English' (as to which an exasperated friend used to send
me pamphlets written by Bridges, in the vain hope that I should
learn something from them), and finally a poet.   I mentioned all
his other qualifications because I believe them to be handicaps
to the poet.   I think they were handicaps to Bridges.   There
was in him an extraordinarily beautiful vein of pure poetry, the
poetry of restrained love (which he called 'dignified passion')
and of natural description.   But while this vein was a clear one
it was not powerful; it was even rather restricted.   And while
one may take exquisite pleasure in reading the shorter poems of
Bridges, and may be conscious that they are full packed with
thought and sensitiveness, the impression left upon myself (I
speak for no other) is that of a rational and well-bred man of
fine culture, who never used a word without comprehending
its niceties of meaning, sitting upon the head of a true poet.
One's relishing delight in Bridges's poetry is less in something
spontaneously created than in something beautifully and carefully wrought.   This is the case in his natural descriptions as in
his experiemnts in classical prosody:

> Nor more of heavy hyacinth now may drink,
> Nor spicy pink,
> Nor summer's rose, nor garnered lavender,
> But the few lingering scents
> Of streakèd pea, and gillyflower, and stocks
> Of courtly purple, and aromatic phlox,

where one notices every word as an illustration of the poet's art,
but cannot receive—as one can in Shakespeare's lovely assem-
blies of flowers — the sense of an impulsive communication.
Bridges is a poet for students, not for those who read poetry
alone for its music and its evocations; he is a poet for students,
not for those who read poetry for its rapture or its metaphysical
refinements.

As far as rapture is concerned, Bridges would have none of it.
The word 'joy' was much upon his pen; but as the name of an
abstraction.   It was his word, perhaps, for some temporary
escape of his genius from tutelage; one feels, at least, no joy as
one reads, no light-hearted and light-headed nonsensical delight
in playfulness.   An ethical joy, perhaps.   Bridges refers to
Keats's remark that he was ill at ease in the society of women
because they did not answer to his preconception, and adds:

'Certainly what appears to be the delineation of his conception often offends taste without raising the imagination, and it reveals a plainly impossible foundation for dignified passion, in the representation of which Keats failed.' Now one sees perfectly well what Bridges means in this curious piece of prose; but I am bound to say that dignified passion seems to me, after some thought, to be a rather priggish ideal. Bridges is after what Colvin used to call Keats's 'under-breeding'; and I am myself conscious of a slightly disagreeable exhalation from some of Keats's raptures. But whether such fastidiousness is not a mark of over-civilization I cannot be sure. One can be passionate, and one can be dignified; but is not dignified passion a little gentlemanly? A more humorous Bridges would not have used such a phrase; a Bridges who was all poet could not have supposed it a serious criticism of Keats. He was not free.

Bridges was extremely well read in the poets, and he could imitate old models with remarkable fidelity. He was also, given much leisure, engrossed in the study of the craft of poetry. Here lies his chief influence upon the newer generation of poets, who owe him a great deal (I forget whether they admit the debt). The old models did not satisfy him, and he sought for new. He wanted to experiment in prosody, and to this end he not only practised incessantly, but conned the practice of others and wrote down in book and pamphlet the results of his observations. Invaluable work. devoted and often illuminating, possible only to one who was both poet and scholar. His conclusion was that

when English poets will write verse governed honestly by natural speech stress, they will discover the laws [of prosody] for themselves, and will find open to them an infinite field of rhythm as yet untouched. There is nothing which may not be done in it, and it is perhaps not the least of its advantages that it makes excellence difficult.

You observe the disdain, almost the arrogance, of that last remark? It is the scholar who speaks.

As a mentor, therefore, as one who can be studied with advantage, both in his theory and his slightly differing practice, by the most modern of poets, Bridges occupies a unique position. He is both student and executant—of a difficult excellence. I am not seeking in any way to minimize his standing as an original genius; although I think the genius is less than is sometimes assumed by those always impressed by hauteur. Since Bridges was born in 1844, and published *The Testament of Beauty* when he was eighty-four years of age, it is unquestioned that he

provides an invaluable link between the old and the new poetry.
I only suggest that his importance is greater as a link than as
an individual master.   As for his own work, the imitations are
admittedly so expert that in some cases they might deceive those
who began by assuming their antiquity.   His original work is
always distinguished, and often full of fervour expressed with
great dignity and beauty; when it deals with very simple things
it is usually exquisite.   But it is never unrestrained: it is always,
in my wicked view, middle class, the product of genius overlaid
by breeding, or rather by those conventions by which the
exclusive separate themselves from the world.   If Keats was
'under-bred,' as they say, is there not a possibility that the
contrary may be true of themselves?   'Somewhat shy, somewhat
austere, fastidious,' said Bridges's friend.   He added 'difficult,'
which means, not that Bridges was hard to understand, but that
he was hard to please.   Hence the character of his work.   Hence
the extent and peculiar effects of his influence, the whole of
which we have still to realize.

III. WILLIAM BUTLER YEATS

>   . . . to him, who ponders well,
> My rhymes more than their rhyming tell
> Of things discovered in the deep,
> Where only body 's laid asleep.
>   W. B. Yeats, *To Ireland in the Coming Times.*

By contrast to Bridges, in spite of all his more recent activities,
Yeats is not so much austere as pure, and not so much difficult
as lost in a dream.   He is a singer.   He was born twenty-one
years later than Bridges, in 1865, and the place of his birth was
Sandymount, near Dublin.   He comes from two families of the
Anglo-Irish, and his father was a Protestant who supported the
cause of the Irish patriots.   He himself is a patriot, a mystic,
and a mythologist.   He is also a teller of lovely tales.   But
above all he is a singer, and it is no surprise to us that he was
writing verses when he was a boy at school.   He was publishing
them by the time he was twenty; and at twenty-one had his
first book printed in Dublin, a dramatic poem called *Mosada*
which has disappeared from his collected works and is never
mentioned by anybody except biographers.

Later on, in the eighteen-nineties, Yeats was in London, the
friend of Ernest Dowson, Lionel Johnson, and Arthur Symons;

and then, as I have mentioned in an earlier chapter, he was associated with the founding of the Irish literary movement in Dublin. He wrote plays for the Irish theatre; he supported Synge when Synge was attacked by the Irish who resented *The Playboy of the Western World*; he took his part in political controversy; and all the time he gave his heart to the study of the folk-lore of his native land, and wrote ballads and lyrics about the past and present and future of Ireland which were meant, not to be printed and read, but to be spoken, to be sung. That last is the reason why one never quite reads Yeats's poetry in solemn silence, with a finger to the brow, watching his metrical ingenuities. Metrical ingenuities may be there—Yeats, too, is a theorist, and must have his say when poetry is the topic—but for the reader unversed in technical complexities they might as well be absent. All he knows is that the words have been written to be said or chanted, and he instinctively sings them to himself.

Some of these words appear to me not to mean very much; but the poet expressly warns us that if we ponder well they will reveal—but that was his earlier version, and the later one, which I have quoted at the head of the section, is less plain—

> . . . more than their rhyming tell
> Of the dim wisdoms old and deep
> That God gives unto man in sleep.

Some of them are no more than a sigh; some tell a simple tale, and others of a pious resolve; some recall the men Yeats has known—

> We were the last romantics—chose for theme
> Traditional sanctity and loveliness:
> Whatever's written in what poets name
> The book of the people; whatever most can bless
> The mind of man or elevate a rhyme—

and some go deeper yet into self-communion, upon the subject of emblems and souls, enemies, life, and the secrets of understanding. But though the subjects vary, the voice is ever the same, a singing voice, the voice of one who listens for faery horns and sometimes thinks that he hears them, or that if they are not the horns of faery they may almost equally well be the voice of the spirit or a message from the stars, so long as it is agreed that they come from another world than ours. To all these possibilities he would offer his mind, at once credulous and sceptical; for he is a man of logical imagination, and not of illogical dogma, and will submit his intellect to anything finer than intellect, so long as he may after investigation of its properties turn away to something else.

He has changed often, from this attention—it is hardly more than that—to Magic, to Mysticism, to esoteric Buddhism, to Symbolism, to a view that the hope of Irish literature lay in the discovery of a new ballad style that should be 'musical and full of colour,' to a belief that there are only two ways before literature,

upward into ever-growing subtlety, with Verhaeren, with Mallarmé, with Maeterlinck, until at last, it may be, a new agreement among refined and studious men gives birth to a new passion, and what seems literature becomes religion; or downward, taking the soul with us until all is simplified and solidified again.

He has, like George Moore, rewritten his earlier work (sometimes not to its improvement) in a sort of impatience with it, and in defence of his rewriting he has said:

> The friends that have it I do wrong
> Whenever I remake a song,
> Should know what issue is at stake:
> It is myself that I remake.

But in one sense he has changed nothing, either in his work or in himself; for all these attentions and remakings have been but the turnings of a mind powerful enough and confident enough in its own power to go freely upon its own business, disregarding the flutter of other minds less cold or less curious. Such a mind as Yeats's, with its complete aversion from the material, has already had its influence, and it will be at the service of future poets when (if ever) Yeats's old dream comes true, of a time when

the renewal of belief, which is the great movement of our time, will more and more liberate the arts from 'their age' and from life, and leave them more and more free to lose themselves in beauty.

IV. WALTER DE LA MARE

> The bitter past
> And the untasted future I mix up,
> Making the present a dream-figured bowl.
>
> T. L. BEDDOES, *Meditation.*

W. H. Davies says it is impossible to ask Walter de la Mare any questions about himself, because he is all the time asking questions of his own. I do not remember that he ever asked me any questions (perhaps he knew all the answers already); but there is no doubt that de la Mare's mind is full of inquiringness, and ill content with either egotism or inactivity. It will go upon long journeys by itself, journeys that carry it far from land and into the borders of horror and death as well as into the sunnier paths of make-believe; and if one travels with it awhile one may pass from a smart dinner party into dankness and ghastly fear as readily as into the mind of a child. Even the mind of a child may prove to be occupied with perplexity at a funeral. The thought of disease and mortality, indeed, is one to which de la Mare's muse constantly returns; he may be playing with airy fancy, mockingly engaged with butterfly or Jenny Wren, and suddenly at the turn of a page this will vanish and he will be running madly through some terror-haunted wood with unseen and uncanny monsters panting at his heels or corpse or coffin before his eyes. To people such as myself, who do not dream, these mysteries are disconcerting; but nothing disconcerts an author whose imagination launches itself into space and eternity as the merry spider chances all upon the waywardness of a gossamer strand.

Walter de la Mare was born at Charlton, in Kent, in 1873. When he began to write he first of all used the pseudonym of 'Walter Ramal,' but when there was no longer any object in disguise he threw aside this pseudonym, and has ever since been widely known and admired under his own name. It was by his *Songs of Childhood*, published in 1902, that he attracted attention, and by a collection of *Poems*, in 1906, that he established himself as a poet; but when he cared to do so he could enchant more than children with his tale of monkeys, *The Three Mulla-Mulgars*, and frighten adults, as well, with his prose romances, *Henry Brocken* and *The Return*. *The Return* is still placed high by lovers of the occult; higher yet, upon all hands, rests *Memoirs of a Midget*, which was published in 1921, and which details the experiences of a lady Hop-o'-my-Thumb among men and women who almost all give me the impression of having been raised from the dead.

> Once died—and lived—a corse named Lazarus:
> Remember, then, to all men else than they
> Who will not blab, you have been three days dead—
> And, that far gone, even princes are forgot.

His poetry and his prose alike are the writing of a man who lives upon familiar terms with trolls and gnomes, toads and owls, as well as with fairies, ghosts, smart society women, and others of the creatures who used to be described by a former employer of mine as 'bizair and outray.' Such acquaintance is bound to influence a poet's inventions; and sure enough through much of de la Mare's work there passes the air of deserted houses, forgotten ghosts, and the chilling melancholy of tombs and dread. When he essays prose fiction, as in the celebrated *Memoirs of a Midget*, he fills his pages with lovely descriptions such as this:

And he told me, whether in time or space I know not, of a country whose people were of my stature and slenderness. This was a land, he said, walled in by enormous, ice-capped mountains couching the furnace of the rising sun, and yet set at the ocean's edge. Its sand-dunes ring like dulcimers in the heat. Its valleys of swift rivers were of a green so pale and vivid and so flower-encrusted that an English —even a Kentish—spring is but a coarse and rustic prettiness by comparison. Vine and orange and trees of outlandish names gave their fruits there; yet there also willows swept the winds, and palms spiked the blue with their fans, and the cactus flourished with the tamarisk. Geese, of dark green and snow, were on its inland waters, and a bird clocked the hours of the night, and the conformation of its stars would be strange to my eyes. And such was the lowliness and simplicity of this people's habitations that the most powerful sea-glass, turned upon and searching their secret haunts from a ship becalmed on the ocean, would spy out nothing—nothing there, only world wilderness of snow-dazzling mountain-top and green valley, ravine, and condor, and what might just be Nature's small ingenuities—mounds and traceries. Yet within all was quiet loveliness, feet light as goldfinch's, silks fine as gossamer, voices as of a watery beading of silence. And their life being all happiness they have no name for their God.

But, having captured our imagination for this land, and for a thousand other beauties, he has no story better to tell than that of ugliness, suicide, and deformity. It is strange to me that one who treads with such charm every kind of pleasant land should be thus mocked by the charnel house and post-mortem decay. But since it is so, I must say that I would as soon have de la Mare's guidance through a graveyard as anybody's. He sees every beauty there—the long grass, the flowers, the memory of dead loveliness and sorrow—and he has so strong a power of conjuration that spirits do indeed arise from behind the broken tombs and speak authentic tales of life beyond reach of our eyes. It may be that my objection to the themes of de la Mare is based upon a feeling that he does not quite explain the journeyings of his mind from this world to the next, and that his characters are like Strephon, in *Iolanthe*, fairy only as far down as the waist, and for the same reason; but if that is so it still remains to be said that he is unsurpassed among living writers in the delicate expression of what he has to tell, whether it be of the contrasted songs of birds or the murder of a prince or of terror by night. His poetic imagination is strong, his lyric gift delightful.

V. JOHN MASEFIELD

John Masefield was born in Herefordshire and educated on the training ship *Conway*. He is said to have sailed before the mast and to have worked in a New York saloon. How long he spent in this kind of life, I do not know; but it cannot have been a great while, for he was back in England, and working for *The Manchester Guardian*, early in the new century. When he was twenty-seven he published a book of *Salt-Water Ballads* (containing two of the poems by which he is known to every English person who ever attended performances of a choral society or that party of entertainers known as the Co-optimists). In 1905 and 1907 he published books of short stories called *A Mainsail Haul* and *A Tarpaulin Muster*; in 1908 his first novel, *Captain Margaret*; and in 1909 (but it was produced a year earlier by Granville-Barker) his play *The Tragedy of Nan*. When, in 1911, he wrote the long ballad, *The Everlasting Mercy*, he became generally famous. Although attacked and parodied, he was the first Georgian Poet; for he did something which at that time no other young poet could do—he made the general public read what he had written.

Time has led to certain changes of taste; and it is probable that Masefield is not the idol of really 'modn' people. He has become Poet Laureate, which fact in itself (despite his predecessor) is enough to alienate opinion. He has written successful novels; his book about the Gallipoli campaign was extremely popular; he has been tempted to repeat the kind of ballad which first brought him attention; he has written rather more copiously than a great poet should do; and so on. But from a historical point of view it is necessary that the importance of Masefield in the Georgian panorama should be emphasized. He, among the Georgians, first made new poetry a rage. Whatever the cause, and whatever one may think of the poetry, he did this before Edward Marsh schemed with his fellow-enthusiasts to produce an anthology; and *The Everlasting Mercy* was the work that started all the excitement.

It started excitement because upon its publication nobody

could positively decide for all whether it was good or not. It was vehement, the language used by some of the persons depicted in it had all the air of being obscene (e.g. 'you closhy put,' which proved to be disappointingly mild), the revivalist fervour of the later pages was to some very moving, and in fact those who prided themselves upon their fastidiousness were compelled to read it in order the better to ridicule it. As to whether *The Everlasting Mercy* deserved the praise or the condemnation given to it, I can only say that it always seemed to me to be unworthy of either.   Probably Masefield had long admired A. E. Housman's *A Shropshire Lad*, which is partly written in what I suppose to be a sort of Salopian vernacular, and almost certainly he was influenced by it.   Though himself, clearly, a most serious and delicate-minded man, he was familiar with the doings and sayings of a number of rough customers.   His feelings and his pen were both facile; verse came easily and naturally to him; he wrote *The Everlasting Mercy*, as my old employer used to say, *con amore*.   And it was read and discussed with a sort of inflamed fever of controversy such as, in a case of poetry, I cannot in memory match.

There was room for one other experiment in the same type of writing; and *The Widow in the Bye-Street* followed very quickly upon *The Everlasting Mercy*.   Some thought it better than its predecessor, and some thought it worse; but again all read it. When Masefield did not stop, but went on to *Dauber* and *The Daffodil Fields*, he lost critical esteem, and for some years he published no more ballads.   When he returned to the ballad with *Reynard the Fox*, he once more caused excitement, this time almost universally pleasurable, and of his longer poems I presume this to be the favourite.   In my opinion it is, although over-long, the best.

Earlier than *The Everlasting Mercy* in chronological order come the first two plays in which Masefield told simple and either horrible or pathetic tales of a kind long absent from the English stage.   They were, as it seems to me, attempts to do for England what the Irish dramatists were doing in Dublin.   Although *The Campden Wonder* and *Nan* are both written in prose, it is (always allowing for the difference of tongue) poetic prose of the kind to which readers of Synge were accustomed.   Here again one is aware of Masefield's facility of emotion, always provoked by the suffering of others.   He feels very quickly indeed—in some respects as Galsworthy felt, and with the same delicacy— and he records his feeling with considerable earnestness.   It was at first thought that his feeling was deep, and that *The Tragedy of Nan* was indeed a great work; now opinion among moderate-minded critics seems to have veered, and he is described even by those who are not bent upon discrediting the established as a sentimentalist. Well, I think *The Tragedy of Nan* has a slightly portentous title, and that the author does mistake seriousness for something else; but the emotion he feels, though rapid and superficial, is a genuine emotion, and his expression of it (in the plays) embarrasses us rather because Masefield lapses into bathos through lack of warning humour than because he is less than earnestly intent upon his theme. If to this it is retorted that he is in some sense deceiving himself by his own emotion I have no answer to make. The plays do not affect me as tragedies; but I think they affect Masefield as tragedies. He yields in them to the impulse of pity.

In his novels, apart from *The Street of To-day*, which is tedious, and a part of *Multitude and Solitude*, which is conventional, he is upon a high uniform level of performance. He began in this genre a little elaborately with *Captain Margaret*, and it has taken him a good many years to conquer a too staccato and highly self-conscious brevity of sentence (the first *Captain Margaret* I ever had in my hand was a library copy, in which some previous reader had written upon the first page: 'This reads like the attempt of a child of five to write a book'); but in the long list from *Lost Endeavour* onward he has at all times written well, with beauty and feeling, and as he has matured he has gained in narrative ease. He can still, as in *The Hawbucks*, abruptly hand the rest of his story to the reader's imagination with the words, 'She was the woman whom he married; but it had cost him some pain to find her.' On the other hand, he does not in the novels fall into pity and solemnity, because he is engrossed either in telling a tale or in painting a countryside or some vivid scene upon or across the sea. His power of fluent, rapid description is one of the greatest of his gifts, for that swift movement of feeling which I have mentioned carries him tumultuously into fight or fall, and only the ensuing mood is a danger to his integrity as an artist. He is a painter, and extremely sensitive to sounds, sights, and suffering; these lead to a kind of inebriation of the imaginative faculty, so that he paints with a full brush. In sober mood he is a little pedestrian, and possibly a little lachrymose.

Masefield was the first Georgian poet to arouse excitement in more than a clique. Since that time, which was in 1911, he has been subjected to so much condemnation on the part of successive schools of poets that he is rather in the position of Nanki-Poo, in *The Mikado*, when Ko-Ko explains that he is 'as good as dead —practically he *is* dead.' Nanki-Poo, of course, is not at all dead, and in fact is upon the stage at the time. I mention this parallel, not in order to be offensive to Masefield, but because he so plainly illustrates a curious fact regarding literary reputation. A man, because his talent is exceptional, rises above his fellows. No merely advertised person can do this for more than a season. But the moment a genuine talent has established itself in any certainty of reputation, the fashion changes; a new crowd comes in (much as a new South American government comes in) and sweeps out, as far as it can do, all trace of the older fashion. Nothing is so bad as the older fashion has been.

But for some inscrutable reason, fashion never quite succeeds in impressing itself upon that strange general taste which really consolidates reputation. Perhaps it is too partisan or perhaps it is too centralized—I cannot tell. I only know that certain unfashionable writers, writers who have never been celebrated by a clique or a spontaneous movement, do in course of time attain to a place in the firmament higher and more respectable than that claimed by faction for its own particular stars. And, in another and more immediately apposite degree, a writer condemned is a writer mysteriously beyond condemnation. The condemners themselves feel respect for him; they would not, indeed, in England, have attacked him if they had not respected him, or if they had not feared his predominance. They say he is dead; but they know he is very much alive, or they would not be speaking of him at all. This happened to Shaw, during the War; and we know what has happened to Shaw since the War. I do not say that Masefield, who of course, although critically decried, has at the present time a distinguished public reputation, will equal Shaw in literary survival; but having of late re-read his ballads (with much regret for some parts of them) I am inclined to think they have a vitality which the critics of an age more generous than ours will acknowledge with enthusiasm. Their faults of excess in such a case will be set down, rightly as I believe, to the contrast between Masefield's shrinking delicacy of temperament and the roughness and squalor or brutality of scene which his experience or some motive of enforced courage leads him to depict. From the fact that he has never moved freely and relishingly in that scene arises his tendency to italicize it. But the effort, however febrile it may sometimes appear to us, to portray something of the life and manners of men (and not the chewings of a bookish mind) is commendable, and it has its place in the literary history of our time.

VI. JAMES ELROY FLECKER

He preferred the exact word to the vague; he was always on his guard against the 'pot-shot' and the complaisant epithet which will fit in anywhere. With passionate deliberation he clarified and crystallized his thoughts and intensified his pictures.

J. C. SQUIRE, Preface to Flecker's *Poems*.

I shall permit myself the invidiousness of separating Flecker from the Georgians because, like others of whom I have spoken or shall speak, he had a distinctive and not a group talent. How great that talent was, I am unable to judge; I know only that to me he has always seemed to be following his own will, his own theory of the place and purpose of poetry, and not a theory generally applicable to the work of his day or accepted by his fellow-poets. This he did as an original; and not for the sake of being different from others. He claimed to be a Parnassian, that is to say, a Classicist; but his vision was a romantic vision, and it was the Orient, even before he went to the East, which coloured every imagining from which the verse-making inspiration sprang.

He was born in London in 1884, the son of a schoolmaster; and he fulfilled the dream of many a London begger by attending the universities of both Oxford and Cambridge. He then entered the consular service, and went as a representative of Great Britain to Constantinople, Smyrna, and Beyrout. Unfortunately he contracted tuberculosis, and the last years of his life (full of ferocious work as they were) had to be spent in what proved to be fruitless journeys to different Swiss resorts in pursuit of a cure. He was at all times, from youth onwards, a joyous and indefatigable talker, was no dreamer but one who had a thousand opinions upon the proper government of the world and the education best suited to the production of wise men, and from excessive readiness as a boy to versify upon every subject he gradually developed into a poet who united great self-discipline with a well-considered exoticism.

This exoticism was instinctive, but it was greatly enriched by his stay in the East, where he saw and tasted all those marvels of colour and strangeness which had been his mental feast from boyhood. From the East came his poetic drama, *Hassan*, which was produced in London after his death, with great success; from the East, too, came his most mature work, such as *The Golden Journey to Samarkand*, in which the zest and freedom of his personality were in full play:

> What shall we tell you? Tales, marvellous tales
> Of ships and stars and isles where good men rest,
> Where nevermore the rose of sunset pales,
> And winds and shadows fall towards the West.

It was not in his power to use his poetry as an instrument of criticism or for the portrayal of English urban life, for his aim was beauty alone; but he could and did make what he wrote both shapely and thrillingly full of himself. The brilliance of his skill with words does not always cover the limitations of his interest; the poetry is never excessive in its ambition; but what Flecker knew and felt he could tell in such a way that he sang it separately to every reader.

Such a combination of passion and coldness as he displays is very rare indeed in English poetry; less rare, perhaps, in those very Parnassians to whom he gave his praise, but rare in any language. And in the same way such a union of colour and directness is so uncommon that if there were no other gift it would distinguish Flecker's work from that of his contemporaries. They had their virtues, of greater passion than his or of greater coldness, but they had not Flecker's magic. Furthermore, the older he grew the more he became a master of his mind and his poetic instrument; so that in his case regret for the untimely loss of a talent is heightened by a sense of what he might have done if he had lived. He could either have contributed to our day an untroubled beauty which it lacks, or have lent strengthening aid to those 'modns' who in reaction from sentiment and copiousness are threatened with drouth. For himself, addressing *A Poet a Thousand Years Hence*, he begged modestly only to be read:

> O friend unseen, unborn, unknown,
> Student of our sweet English tongue,
> Read out my words at night, alone:
> I was a poet, I was young.

VII. J. C. SQUIRE AND THE GEORGIANS

There was a general feeling among the younger poets that modern English poetry was very good, and sadly neglected by readers.

EDWARD MARSH, *Memoir of Rupert Brooke*.

Five volumes altogether of *Georgian Poetry* appeared, the last of them covering the years 1920–2, and in them one can trace (with a little help from the imagination and by sundry glances between the lines) what was the progress of poetry between 1911 and 1922 in England. First of all, the book arose from the common enthusiasm of Edward Marsh and Rupert Brooke. They took into their counsels other poets or enthusiasts. And so bold and ingenious a plan to make poetry readable and—that was more important and no doubt was fully recognized—*discussable* as a literary phenomenon had its immediate success. You could take the title in several ways, for it was a stroke of genius. 'Georgian'—with King George barely, you might say, upon his throne, a whole literature was announced: What! is the age as active as all that? 'Poetry'—what! have we, then, some poetry apart from Masefield and the old ones? 'Georgian Poetry'—what a claim! It suggested that the poetry of the age differed from the poetry of all other ages. The claim was more modest than the title; the claim was merely to present in a single volume examples of work done by a few proper writers in the preceding two years. These writers were poets admired by Edward Marsh and his collaborators. But 'Georgian'! Did not that indicate something rather more than the preferences of a group?

As long as the group could deal with the numbers of poets who had published books within recent memory the difficulty, although great, was not overwhelming. But Marsh and his friends had not imagined that the War was coming to stir every undergraduate who took a commission into publishing his verses. They had not foreseen that their bold title would be turned against them. They had planned a peace-time rallying point for an unfashionable art; in time of War they found themselves bombarded with every kind of poetic artillery. The alternatives were an obstinate restriction of entries to those writers for whose work the editor felt some personal sympathy, or such an enlargement of scope as would turn the two hundred pages of the first volume into an omnibus book in which everything was printed *en masse*. Quite obviously, the latter alternative was unacceptable.

But by this time the title, *Georgian Poetry,* had a prestige, and similarly there had arisen some poets who did not quite conform to Edward Marsh's extremely gentle but extremely firm notion of what poetry was and what it should be. The attitude of these poets was: 'You call this book *Georgian Poetry*; I am a Georgian; therefore my poetry ought to be included in your book.' When told that his poetry could not be printed in our book, every such rebel replied with heat that the title *Georgian Poetry* was a lie. Every malcontent either started a rival show or rallied to slay all who were sealed of the tribe of Marsh.

Several of the chief contributors to *Georgian Poetry* have been or will be dealt with in other chapters; but of the rest I must not fail to mention here Lascelles Abercrombie, Rupert Brooke, W. H. Davies, John Drinkwater, W. W. Gibson, Harold Monro, Ralph Hodgson, Francis Ledwidge, W. J. Turner, John Freeman, and J. C. Squire. Rupert Brooke had more to do, by accident, with the renaissance of poetry in War-time than any of the others. He had started, with Abercrombie, Gibson, and Drinkwater, a quarterly anthology of verse (to which only the four were contributors) named *New Numbers*; and when war broke out the fourth and last issue of *New Numbers* contained sonnets written by Brooke which moved to ecstasy all who read them. Brooke was personally very popular. He was a handsome, gay boy, who was loved by all who knew him. He had been born in 1887, and had been educated at Rugby and Cambridge University. He had all the talent of a happy and charming boy, and that talent sang in his verses. It was not a powerful talent, and it is not likely to survive in the memory of later generations; but when Brooke died the shock to numbers of people who knew him was shared by thousands who had never seen him. The thought that poets were dying for their country caused many to wish to read what these and other young poets, also soldiers, had to say of the great sacrifice; and there was a tremendous consumption of new poetry, published at the time in quite innumerable little books. That it was partly a sentimental consumption I think is true; but the production and consumption were great enough to create the legend that poetry had been reborn in the War. At that time, it must be remembered, all pathetically bellicose men of letters were prophesying a grand and glorious revival of splendour in our literature as the result of the purification of war.

Of Brooke's collaborators (who were also contributors to *Georgian Poetry*), the one best known to the general public was John Drinkwater, whose play, *Abraham Lincoln*, impressed two nations, and whose other works kept him prominently in the news for a considerable period. Drinkwater was born in 1882, for some time was associated with the Birmingham Repertory Theatre, where he acted, lectured a great deal and read his poetry to large audiences, and besides writing this poetry followed *Abraham Lincoln* with a number of chronicle plays upon the same lines and a number of bucolic comedies and other dramatic works. His poetry was always polished and musical, but unmarked by any force of thought or feeling; his plays were the work of one whose sense of the stage was invaluable to him, and *Abraham Lincoln* at least of the chronicle plays is a remarkable piece of construction which set a fashion and a high standard for such pieces.

Lascelles Abercrombie, born a year earlier than Drinkwater, in 1881, was by far the most distinguished of the quartette which founded *New Numbers*. In 1910, with *Mary of the Bramble*, he began publishing his own poems from a cottage in the country; and afterwards he gathered them into larger volumes until at last he was honoured, as only one other author has been in his lifetime, by having a collected edition included in the Oxford series of English Poets. I do not personally find Abercrombie's poetry very interesting, although it has great dignity and beauty of phrase; and it is for this reason, and not from any hesitation as to his talent, that I refrain from commenting upon it. I have great admiration for his contributions to the study of aesthetics.

Finally, W. W. Gibson, a poet devoted to simple narrative, telling quiet stories without number, always with feeling and reticence, gave his sober naturalism to the publication. If Abercrombie was stately and measured, Brooke like a jet of flame, and Drinkwater a contented murmur, Gibson had ever the homeliness of peat and heather. All brought these same qualities into *Georgian Poetry*, and helped to give its earliest volumes their character.

W. H. Davies was there, too, with his sweet songs; and Ralph Hodgson contributed his famous poem, *The Bull*; while W. J. Turner, an Australian whose imagination had a strangeness which has often since then startled the reading world as much as his musical criticism has done, gave variety to the third volume, in which he occupied first place. But the name which is of most significance in the present survey is that of John Collings Squire, to whom I have already referred; and it is of Squire that I shall now, in conclusion, speak.

J. C. Squire was born in Plymouth in 1884. He was educated at Blundell's School and Cambridge University, and towards the end of 1912, when *The New Statesman* was first projected as a weekly political and literary journal expounding Fabian ideas under the editorship of Clifford Sharp, Squire was its literary editor. He had at that time written a biography of William the Silent which has disappeared from the lists of his published works, and if one may accept the testimony of Arnold Bennett's *Journal* for 1913 it is to this effect: 'Long hair. Jaegerishly dressed. But sound, competent, honest in argument.' Those were early days for Squire.

He contributed to *The New Statesman* a causerie which he wrote over the pseudonym 'Solomon Eagle,' and thus established himself as a literary critic. His first reputation as a writer came from his excellent parodies, *Imaginary Speeches* and *Steps to Parnassus*; but in the same year that he published *Steps to Parnassus* (1913), he published also his book of serious poems, *The Three Hills*, and thus challenged the world upon higher ground. Whether these books, and his work for *The New Statesman*, would in themselves have been enough to make his reputation I cannot say, but Squire had and has a drive and assertiveness which distinguish him from other men, and his personal influence in the War years was so strong that by the end of the War he had great power in London critical journalism. During the War he acted as literary editor of *The New Statesman* (part of the time he was in charge of the paper) and literary editor of *Land and Water*, and after the War he founded *The London Mercury*, in which he continued his work as an active force in the literary world. He also was for a number of years book critic-in-chief to *The Observer*.

Poets of all kinds (excepting the revolutionaries) gathered about Squire during the War and when *Georgian Poetry* had ended its series. He generously befriended them, and gave them work and encouragement. To them, especially in their capacity as reviewers, Edward Shanks gave the name of 'the Squirearchy,' and it was thought that they represented a rather too solid phalanx of critical opinion, so that they became unpopular with other scribes. The assumption of solidarity, however ill-founded, increased that tendency towards factionism which had been created by annoyance with *Georgian Poetry*. Squire, accordingly, was a centre for attack. He was never the spearhead of a retaliatory movement. Although exceedingly outspoken, to the point of brusqueness, he is not quarrelsome; and in fact is a very kind man who is merely tenacious of his ideas and satisfied with his own judgment.

I have already told how Middleton Murry returned to editorial work on *The Athenaeum* after the War; and it will be seen that with Squire leading a devoted band of poet-critics, and Murry leading a somewhat disunited band of aesthetes, intellectuals, and novelists, there was at this time great variety of critical judgment. Some people would say that criticism was in the melting-pot. It certainly was in a state of uncertainty. On Squire's part, all criticism was moderate in tone; for Squire is in literature a conservative. He was thus a typical contributor to *Georgian Poetry*, and his influence was all in favour of traditional forms of verse. Though he was personally acquainted with all the young War poets he did not share their views upon war or versification. Nor, in spite of original experiment, has he shown himself over-sympathetic to newer aesthetic theory. He stands, in chief, for the old: for that reason he fittingly concludes this chapter, as the War hastened changes in taste and it is with a changed taste that the later chapters of the present book will deal.

CHAPTER XI: YOUNGER NOVELISTS

The business of trying to present one's contemporaries in a fair light is embarrassing. Writers like Hugh Walpole, J. D. Beresford, Gilbert Cannan, Francis Brett Young, Frank Swinnerton, W. L. George, myself, and several others had the same general idea of our direction, but our approaches were so different that each was inclined to fancy that his own road was the best road to our destination.

COMPTON MACKENZIE, *Literature in My Time*.

I

BEFORE a deluge, there are usually a few preliminary warning drops of rain, the edge of the coming storm; and this is true in the matter of books as well as in the matter of weather. Somewhere about the year 1870 those forces which are productive of literary depressions gave a glance into the future. They said, in effect, that in a dozen years or so a storm of young novelists would arise; and as such a storm without presage would be disconcerting a few large spots of literary talent must immediately be released. Within the next ten years, accordingly, several novelists were born who had their own non-sentimental way of looking at life. I dare not guess at the ages of the women; but among the men Charles Marriott, J. D. Beresford, and Oliver Onions were born before 1880. The deluge began in 1883, and reached its height in 1884, and its climax in 1885.

That does not mean, of course, that each previous decade had not seen the due arrival of a sufficiency of individual talents; for at all times, according to Dean Inge, this is a world where every one is wanted, but no one is wanted very much, which means that there are always enough of each kind of people to go round. If I were merely to name the excellent novelists who have entertained the reading public since the beginning of the century, I should arouse disquiet in the minds of those who think the novel a useless form of letters. Violet Hunt, for example, was writing *The Maiden's Progress* in 1894, and still impressed critical readers with her subtle and powerful *Tales of the Uneasy* in 1911; the Countess von Arnim published *Elizabeth and Her German Garden* in 1898, and, as the Countess Russell, wrote her best book, *Vera*, in 1921; Ethel Colburn Mayne contributed to *The Yellow Book*, wrote her life of Byron in 1912, and in fiction within comparatively recent memory surpassed her best with *Gold Lace*. Maurice Baring's tales and explorations of character range from the incredibly long to the minimum of brevity, and exhibit a fine intelligence, style, humour, and distinction. And Charles Marriott produced between 1901 and 1915 a series of critical tales in which moral and intellectual tendencies of the day were presented and examined scrupulously and in an original manner. To these and others I make my apologies for seeming cavalier; but a book of this kind has inevitable limits and omissions.

All the immediately pre-Georgian writers whom I have named, and those whom I cannot even mention, differed from their major rivals in the respect that, whereas these majors sought to build or rebuild a complete material universe, they were psychological novelists, penetrating inward towards subtleties of mind and character, and holding the world, as Antonio did,

> . . . but as the world;
> A stage where every man must play a part.

None of them, I believe, had any acquaintance with the German and Austrian pathologists who have since effected such a change in the ideas of exploratory novelists. Violet Hunt and Ethel Colburn Mayne almost certainly learnt a great deal from the Jacobean method and were more or less content to feminize it; Charles Marriott, cautious, thoughtful, and curiously sympathetic to the misfits of polite intercourse, was chiefly interested in the individual as he affected society and was affected by society; Maurice Baring, highly familiar with Russian literature and Russian discursive concern with the psyche, amused himself, with people from his own witty and teasing standpoint, and to this moment remains an unplaced and mockingly unplaceable personality of whose fertility, versatility, and distinction there is no doubt. All were men and women of talent and intelligence; for some reason, which might be coldness or shyness or reserve, they did not and do not shock critical and popular minds into a state of chronic attention.

And as I have mentioned the Russians, let me here emphasize the fact that in the early years of King George's reign Russian art and Russian literature were the rage with all those sensitive people who may be expected to produce the more cultured varieties of fiction, painting, music, and formative criticism. Arnold Bennett, at the height of his influence with such people, had committed himself to the statement that all the great novelists of the world were Russian; one heard for the first time —or at any rate for the first time with appreciation—of Goncharov, Schedrine, Leskov, even of Tchekhov (but members of the Stage Society in 1911 walked out in large numbers at the first performance of *The Cherry Orchard*), and others; the novels of Dostoevsky, of which, previously, only *Crime and Punishment* and *Poor Folk* had been familiarly known in England, were translated complete from 1912 onwards.

They were not the only Russian novels to be brought to the notice of the literate, for every London publisher by this time was aware of the demand for such necessaries of life; and by 1916 a complete translation of Tchekhov's tales was begun.   Nor were novels the sole influences upon our younger pens, for Anna Pavlova, of the Russian ballet, reached England in 1910, at once created a furore, and was the forerunner of the Diaghilev ballet with Nijinsky as the sensation of the period.   What the coming of the ballet did by infection for letters in England I cannot explicitly say.   It created an entirely new state of mind.   Its rich *décor*, so bold and at times so bizarre; the triumph of its strangeness and its beauty (upon artists its beauty, upon aesthetes its strangeness—for I take aesthetes to be the apes of art); the unfamiliar rhythms of its musical contributions—all had, for noncosmopolitan stay-at-homes, the glory of a new world.   To an English public weary of English things and already longing for whatever was savage and untamed, the wildnesses of *Scheherazade* and *Tamar* were like firewater to the innocent native; to a less jaded English public which prided itself upon its refinement, the sentimental delicacies of *Carnaval* were as exquisite as Turkish delight.   Lovers of the romantic had *Le Pavillon d'Armide*; and lovers of the modern, *L'Oiseau de Feu*.   Diaghilev, with his contempt for Gounod and Delibes as composers of ballet, appealed infallibly to all classes of rich, patronizing, and intelligent English people.   No wonder the snobs at this time, adopting a Russian word, began to call themselves the 'intelligentsia.'

As for Dostoevsky's novels, they had power and subtlety, emotion and picturesqueness, altogether outside the range of any English novelists whatsoever.   They were overwhelmingly long and communicative; the characters in them, diseased, mad, and vehement, were like nothing ever seriously created in English. They were like the nightmares of an epileptic to whom Dicken-

sian grotesques were as serious as an empty stomach. Amid
cries of dismay from the apostles of the fine, the delicate, the
sought, and the confined, Dostoevsky became the rage. He
seemed then (he now seems less) to pour all the terrors of emotion
into print and all the truth; he drew away veils from souls in
conflict and agony and showed them as struggling with the very
devil; his readers had all a sense that when they read about
the Karamazovs and the Versilovs they indulged in spiritual
debauch; if these readers were humanitarians with a leaning
towards mystical Christianity they embraced Prince Myshkin
with passionate yearning for just such humility as his; we heard
upon all sides, from our own voices as well as from the voices of
others, roars of ecstatic discovery. How pale Turgenev seemed!
How material and common in grain our own realistic writers!
How drab our life of restrained feelings! From Russia came
release. Possibly a little incoherence? Come, come, come!
'Life is real, and life is earnest!' To the serious, every continental master is or should be sacred.

However, the enthusiasm for Dostoevsky and the ballet succeeded at least two other influences. I say nothing of Bergson,
who was intellectually a power at this time, or of Eucken; my
business is with the younger novelists. There was the influence
of Samuel Butler, the publication of whose *Notebooks* in 1912
intensified growing interest in his one novel, *The Way of All
Flesh*; and there was, in my view unquestionably, the practical
influence upon such novelists of Wells and Bennett. And while
it may be suggested that Wells and Bennett were totally different
writers, there was, as James discovered, this likeness between
the two, that both were profoundly interested in the physical
life about them—the active social and sociological life of their
time. Wells was interested as a participant; Bennett as an
observer. Both used, in their different ways, the autobiographical method which James so decried. Wells in *Tono-
Bungay* spread the whole of his zest for the movement of life
before the reader; Bennett slowly narrated in *Clayhanger* the
growth and progress of one man through the environment which
had been his own. Young novelists, coming to books (for of
course they read them) which appealed so strongly to their
natural self-interest, saw that autobiography, disguised or un-
disguised, held decided possibilities. They did not, as a rule,
want to copy. They wanted only a convenient looseness of
form; and as they too were as interested as could be in life, and
wished to speak the truth about it as they saw it, the invitation

offered by the method was irresistible. Dostoevsky was the king of all novelists; but Wells and Bennett were more English and less vehemently abject in disclosure, and therefore were simpler models.

The statements I have made above are general; not particular. But these things were in the air. They were a part of the spirit of the time. Other influences, the influence of Hardy, the temporary influence of Romain Rolland (also, by the way, lengthily autobiographical), the influence upon those who knew them of German thought and German pathological research, were all effective. Everything was heading, perhaps, for change; but to the casual eye it seemed only to be moving in a steady channel towards—I must take this opportunity of saying—an extension of the realistic method to the middle class. It is to be noted that whereas, of all the novelists and playwrights of the older generation, Galsworthy was the only one to have had a public school and Oxford or Cambridge University education, several of the newer novelists belonged to families in which intensive culture was familiar; and for this reason, when they came to write of familiar life, they no longer dealt with poor boys and girls as Wells and Bennett, Moore and Gissing and Maugham, Pett Ridge and Arthur Morrison, had done. The novel had taken a step upward in the social grade; it was still to be realistic, but it had become what my gardener calls 'more classical.'

II. ROSE MACAULAY

I must except Rose Macaulay at once from any general statement as to the influence of the Wellsian or Bennettian novel. I must, in fact, except all the young women writers of that day; for their interest in the doings of cits and groundlings was small and unfriendly. Either they wrote of the cultured and financially independent, or they embraced the rural, the raggle-taggle gipsy, the home farm, the Fells, and the old family. How conservative of them!

Possibly the fact that Rose Macaulay is the daughter of a professor (her father was G. C. Macaulay, a good scholar, and Lecturer in English Literature at Cambridge University) is accountable for her detached attitude towards the human species; but as I see it, the real trouble is that she feels herself, and always has felt herself, to be fully adult in a world of children. Not her own children, and not altogether nasty little brats, but children in whom, for their own good, she takes an auntly interest and to whom she finds it necessary, in print, to administer slightly repressive words of reason. She has a strong moral sense, much scepticism, a great dislike of those who are cruel, thoughtless, stupid, and selfish, and a feeling between pity and contempt for those who are innocently silly. And she cannot restrain her wish to demonstrate the undesirability in a civilized community of the stupid and the silly. At the beginning of her life she thought she could lecture these faults of mankind out of existence. Now she hopes to ridicule them to death.

Rose Macaulay published several novels before the War—one of them, *The Lee Shore*, winning a thousand-pound prize competition—upon themes suggested by the trend of current thought (for she is a commentator upon what she reads in the weekly reviews, and not an originator of ideas); and for several years her books were intelligent, serious, critical, and illuminative of the minds of middle-class people of culture. But the War changed many things for this writer, and life, from being a *pis aller*, became something of a futility. Had she preserved the solemnity of her first youthful tales, she no doubt would have become a sort of Mrs Humphry Ward (cultured, current, and for those of goodwill and breeding highly instructive); but she had a faculty denied to Mrs Humphry Ward. It was the faculty of derision; and derision became tremendously the fashion among intelligent people immediately after the War. It was a way of shrugging one's shoulders and washing one's hands of the politicians and admitting wryly that life was 'a poor business,' while at the same time indicating that one knew of much better ways of managing mankind than any that had been tried. Accordingly, after the War (and she now seems to ignore her pre-War novels), Rose Macaulay definitely gave herself to the composition of topical comedies. These faintly extravagant and ridiculing novels follow a formula. They collect a number of cranks and sillies and puzzled people, twist and turn them for our laughter, burlesque common vulgarities by quotation (as Henry Mencken burlesques them in *Americana*) or by merciless ridicule, and are uniformly crushing towards sentimentalists. One pictures these unfortunate characters—who of course are primed with every contemporary cliché—as dashing, full of enthusiasm, like dirty little boys, into the clean, well-aired, slightly under-heated house of a female connection. They are too excited with their fancies to wipe their shoes or their noses; and they run up to Rose Macaulay (in the silly way of thoughtless children) to pour

out their fatal nonsense. 'And the bull . . . the aeroplane
. . . Positivism . . . advertisement . . . amazing . . . Youth . . .'
—these are their excitements, the things they have just found.
Rose Macaulay listens with a quiet smile, a little remote. Finally
she says, crisply: 'Yes, very interesting.   Now, don't you think
you'd better wash your hands and come to luncheon?'   Or
'Yes, I know; but that was said quite a hundred years ago by
William Godwin.'   Or 'You shouldn't say "mephitic," darling;
you mean "dense," don't you?   Like yourself.'   I wonder she
is not at times haunted by the poor wretches whom she has so
unsparingly made amusing in her books.   Perhaps that fate is
in store for her.   She has sympathy for none but the critically
alert, those who stand aside from the follies of man and laugh
(not jeer) lest they should weep with exasperation and shame.
As her first heroine said—I can hear Rose Macaulay using the
words herself: 'It always rather riles me . . . to see people
behaving in what strikes me—well, as a foolish manner of behaving, you know.'   She is not really angry, not hot with the
passion of a zealot; only impatient with the noisy and self-
deceiving and easily fooled.   She cannot endure their idiocy.
But for the bystanders who virtuously never make fools of
themselves she has a fellow-feeling, because (she says it of Rome,
the heroine of *Told by an Idiot*):

without opposition and without heat, she had refused to be made
an active participant in the business, but had watched it from her
seat in the stalls as a curious and entertaining show.

Curious and entertaining.   You might have thought she would
be a realist?   Not at all; for the duffers and cranks and cowards,
taken as a matter of course by realists, and as a matter for
reverent treatment by defenders of all emasculates from the
pressure of machinery and convention, move her but to laughter.

III. SHEILA KAYE-SMITH

Closely following upon Rose Macaulay in this new movement
of novelists came Sheila Kaye-Smith, whose first novel, *The
Tramping Methodist*, was published in 1908.   She was born at
St Leonards, a Sussex seaside resort, and her father was a doctor.
She has an entirely different opinion of mankind from Rose
Macaulay.   She is more humane, or more pitiful, than her sister-
novelist.   She is not amused by follies, or exasperated by them,
but seriously traces their rise and influence.   On the whole, her

vision of life is tragic. Let her but see a dull woman looking
over a hedge, and where Rose Macaulay would picture a
sentimental gossip who might amusingly take her newspaper-
fed mind on to a desert island in company with a dozen other
absurd creatures, Sheila Kaye-Smith at once quietly pictures
that woman in her home, a little dumb, and possibly doomed
(as she would be in a novel by Hardy or Eden Phillpotts) to
frustrated passion or contented matrimony with a poacher. She
is not sceptical, but devout, a Catholic. She cares less for the
town than for the countryside, which she knows by heart. Set
her down in a village, and she will at once weave a story about it
which brings in several generations of squires, the doctor, perhaps a gipsy, some animals, the ploughing of the land, both love
and silent pain, lush grass, starry nights, a convincing picture of
rural England. But I do not think anybody in the story will
make a joke, or be the subject of a joke.

Taking the county of Sussex for her own ground (and in spite
of Kipling, Belloc, and E. V. Lucas Sussex had no official
novelist), Sheila Kaye-Smith has made Sussex, which to many of
us is a holiday home and the name of an adored cricket team, as
much as a place of simple passion and pride as Devon or Dorset.
She has perhaps been influenced in theme and conception by the
novels of Thomas Hardy and by Galsworthy's chronicle of the
Forsyte family; but when she began writing novels a love of
writing, and no literary influence, was the spur. The early
books were slight, a young girl's dreams of romance in dingles
and upon the Downs; but the later ones, as the author's touch
grew more sure, show an increase in confidence and power, as
well as in bulk and solidity. *Little England* and *Joanna Godden*,
the more ambitious *Tamarisk Town* and *The End of the House of
Alard*, and their companions, have brought Sheila Kaye-Smith
in the quarter-century of her literary activity to a high place
among her male and female professional contemporaries; and in
one respect she is, I believe, superior to all the other equally
industrious traditional novelists of about her own age.

That respect is an important one in the craft of fiction,
although it is often undervalued by amateurs. Sheila Kaye-
Smith's novels, which at first took a rather conventionally unconventional view of love, grew steadily in that substance which
comes of care in building. They told sober and progressive
stories, into which one was slowly inducted and in which one
never—the point is two-edged, and yet I must make it—wholly
lost oneself. And above all they were models of construction,

with the quiet beginning, the natural development of interest, the clean drawing of character, the attainment of a serious warmth of emotion, and sometimes—for she has courage—the climax of death or disaster. Conscience was in them, and comment was absent from them. They were dramatic narratives, which stood of their own accord as excellent, honourable work. They do not, in my opinion, claim higher praise than that, although the American critic, Mencken, sets them above all other English novels of their day and seems to believe that they have been underrated in England. I regard them as sound work, with, however, no such quality as would justify Mencken's view; and while they have neither brilliance nor humour they have great sincerity, and I think they will always command respect from those to whom honesty is not necessarily synonymous with dullness.

IV. HENRY HANDEL RICHARDSON

In that same year of 1908 which saw the publication of Sheila Kaye-Smith's *The Tramping Methodist*, another first novel appeared of which the history has been one of the strange records of our time. The book was called *Maurice Guest*, and the author was described as Henry Handel Richardson. Nobody knew anything of Henry Handel Richardson, and *Maurice Guest*, being published, was praised in the newspapers, sold out its first edition, was reprinted seven months later, and thereafter seemed to be at the end of its active life. Never was such an assumption more false. The book remained out of print; but its life continued very extraordinarily, for writers of all kinds passed the word to each other that this was something of a masterpiece, and *Maurice Guest* was a legend in the professional world. The author published another novel, *The Getting of Wisdom*, in 1910, and this novel failed to repeat the mysterious success of *Maurice Guest*, so that just as the public ignored Henry Handel Richardson the writers knew him only as the unidentified author of a single book. Between 1910 and 1914 it was a favourite sport of literary journalists to write articles naming outstanding young novelists, and to paw the young reputations by asking whether this one was better than that, or whether this one had increased his reputation by his latest book or slipped back a point in the busy race for distinction and the like. But Henry Handel Richardson was never, as far as I recall, included in the field; and it was only because, like Falkner's *The Nebuly Coat* and *The Lost Stradivarius, Maurice Guest* quietly passed from hand to hand, that its fame grew with the passage of time.

Seven years elapsed before Henry Handel Richardson began to publish a three-volume history of the life of an Australian doctor named Richard Mahony; and at length a new edition of *Maurice Guest* made its appearance. It was politely greeted (in 1922), and thereafter its admirers had less difficulty in obtaining copies for their friends; but even yet its great qualities have been insufficiently recognized. *Maurice Guest* is a very good novel indeed. It combines apparent literalness with subtlety, and passion with wisdom, in an altogether exceptional manner. For those interested in the technique of the novel, it shows as few other books do the possibility of combining narrative with Henry James's 'blessed law of successive aspects,' and the un-romantic treatment of a romantic theme which yet leaves no tenderness and no conflict of mood and personality unrevealed. It is a book full of subtlety, as rich as living memory, as detached as a philosopher's mind. Although it moves slowly, it is never tedious; although, towards its end, the scenes turn upon a single note, it is never repetitive. Every scene takes us deeper and deeper into heart and nature. It might, we feel, be transcript; but no transcript could so surely keep to the essential.

The story, if I state it baldly, will seem obvious enough. It is that of a young Englishman who, against the wish of his mother, abandons schoolmastering in England for a period of pianoforte study in Leipsic. There, besides meeting other men, he makes the acquaintance of a kind and very shrewd young Englishwoman; and he falls in love with an Australian girl who is already the mistress of a young composer and amorist. The stages by which Maurice moves, first to acquaintance, then to friendship, and finally to tragic, torturing emotional relationship with this girl are described in detail, for they form the substance of the narrative, and they culminate in his suicide. But the book is no simple study of frustrate love; it has a profundity and searching analysis which deeply excites the reader who cares at all to understand ways of thought and feeling.

The Fortunes of Richard Mahony, a trilogy which occupies over a thousand pages and covers two-thirds of a man's life in Australia, back in England, and again in Australia, has many of the same qualities which make *Maurice Guest* so remarkable. It has not the poignancy of the shorter book, for the reason that its action is diffused; and most of the book is less immediate, less urgent in mood than the concentrated interest of *Maurice Guest*

compels.   But this very fact allows one to see what is the outstanding virtue of Henry Handel Richardson as a novelist—
steadiness of vision and sobriety of judgment allied to very
exceptional imaginative power.   The method is so quiet that its
merit, and in fact the essential imaginativeness of the work, may
be missed by those eager for display; a little formal as to style, it
has not the pace and brilliance of the best very modern exhibitions of life.   But the touch is unerring.

Critics of *Maurice Guest* all assumed that the book was the
work of a man.   Whether men or women are the actors they are
portrayed with equal assurance; and some of the scenes between
the male characters are among the most memorable.   But Henry
Handel Richardson is a woman, the daughter of an Australian
doctor, and the widow of Professor J. G. Robertson, who for many
years was professor of German language and literature at
London University.   During all these years of authorship,
she has been hardly at all known to the world as a novelist;
and this without doubt has retarded general acclaim.   Other
writers, her inferiors, have enjoyed greater celebrity.

V. OLIVER ONIONS AND J. D. BERESFORD

But to-day writers and painters no longer speak from Sinai-clouds.
Rather, from the pavement-edge, packed closer than the vendors of
penny-toys.

OLIVER ONIONS, *Little Devil Doubt.*

I turn now to two men who belong more directly than any of
the women I have named to the school which was modern in
1910.   The major works of both are in the key of Wells and
Bennett.   *Little Devil Doubt*, by Onions, and the Jacob Stahl
trilogy of Beresford are alike in the sense that both skim the lives
of young men who, with artistic impulses, have their misadventures in business, and especially in the business of advertising.
Drawing was Onions's first love; and architecture Beresford's.
Both know what the insides of business offices are like.   Both
are rueful as to what happens in business offices; and as to
what happens to young men whose ambition surpasses performance.   There is in the work of both this air of ruefulness; but
with Onions it has an accompaniment of joyless jocularity and
with Beresford a melancholy smile takes the place of jocularity.
Onions is harsh, Beresford sad.

It is somewhat the same with the two men as with their work; for Onions has a grimness of demeanour which throws out a suggestion of force and resentment, whereas Beresford, who was crippled long ago as the result of an unfortunate accident, regards the world with thoughtful sweetness but without vivacity. Both are realists, in the sense that if they contemplate any scene or circumstance they do it without sentimentality: their reactions to it, though not identical, would be in accord. They have seen the world of pushing and unscrupulous men, and are unwillingly aware of it; but they do not hide it from themselves by any curtain of false emotion. There it is, they say: what are you going to do about it? Neither would fake an attitude. Both are stronger in associative memory than in imagination.

Onions, a Yorkshireman, was once for a period in control of an art department in the Amalgamated Press (publishers of many magazines and weekly periodicals founded by Alfred Harmsworth, Lord Northcliffe), and his first book was published at the beginning of the century. It was a collection of chats in the manner of *The Dolly Dialogues*, but it did not achieve the lightness of the original. He then wrote a number of short stories, many of them powerful and some of them dealing with uncanny themes, which he has collected into volume form as *Tales of a Far Riding*, *Widdershins*, and *Draw in Your Stool*. But his chief books were the two semi-autobiographical studies of ambitious young men, *Little Devil Doubt* and *Good Boy Seldom*, and the brief masterpiece of grimness, *In Accordance with the Evidence*. This last, which he injudiciously followed with sequels called *The Debit Account* and *The Story of Louie*, remains in its own genre unsurpassed.

It was begun as a short story; and it grew by the demands of its material to the length of a brief novel. It arose from the notion that a young student of shorthand, bent upon murdering a rival, might obtain from that rival, under pretence of speed-exercise and subsequent transcription, a confession of suicide. He would thus clear his own path, and escape detection. The ruse succeeds; the tale, being told in the first person singular, is an exercise in that harsh vigour for which Onions's character yields all the stuff. *In Accordance with the Evidence* is not a pretty book; the manner of it is even common and gritty, as such a theme demands that it should be; but it is like no other book, and it bears re-reading after its denouement has lost all surprise. It has, that is to say, a permanent quality.

The remaining works of Onions curiously lack momentum;

one reads them with respect for their veracity, but one is conscious that the author is not a natural creator of illusion. He has no magic. And in the case of *Little Devil Doubt* and *Good Boy Seldom*, both of which are very sincere books based upon experience, the biographical method has a serious defect. It has always, in the work of every writer who has essayed it, had this defect. A novelist using, with however much skill and finesse, the skeleton of his own life and memory, tends to leave his central figure a colourless nonentity, a something to which experiences occur. For himself, that central figure is filled in by substantial memory—by egotism; but for the reader the central figure, a name only, represents vacuum. He has traits, but no character. He may suffer; but he is not objectively present. That is a cause of loss of interest in the progress of the book; for unless every detail has importance of its own (which it has for the writer) the book ceases to hold attention. It is the same whether the book is a narrative or an introspective study of personality; for unless the author deliberately creates for his chief actor a personality larger than life, there is nothing upon which the reader can fix his eye or his imagination. *Little Devil Doubt* and *Good Boy Seldom* are iridescent to the author, because they are charged with the colours of living memory: to the reader, who unfortunately, however eager, has no comparable self-identification, they are dead because recognition of truth is an insufficient challenge to sympathy.

This criticism, in effect, could be levelled with almost as much force at the Jacob Stahl trilogy of Beresford, which has the advantage, however, that Beresford does make recognizable persons of those with whom Stahl is brought into contact. Whether these are men or women, they are seen—shall we say? —with greater malice than any of Onions's characters; with clearer incisiveness. Moreover, there is an attempt to create the personality of Jacob Stahl: the other people in the tales do react to such a man, and criticize him as if he were there. We come to believe that however lacking he may be in the positives of human nature, at least he is rich in negatives. But if you take away from *The Early History of Jacob Stahl*, *A Candidate for Truth*, and *The Invisible Event* their plainly veracious account of what has happened to Jacob Stahl from his cradle, I wonder how much is left for the imagination to dwell upon?

As if in response to that criticism, for he would give a truthful answer to any question one put to him, Beresford has only once since the publication of *The Invisible Event* returned to the personal memoir. He probably sees its weakness as clearly as anybody can do. He has experimented with other technical methods, and has gone so far as to tell a couple of mystery stories; but while his most vigorous novel is probably *The House in Demetrius Road* (which was also his greatest success, ruined as it was by the outbreak of the War), his most characteristic books have been those in which he has sought to express in the form of fiction some of the philosophical conceptions of the modern world. He has always been a reader of philosophy, has always been interested in current ideas. His books have tended more and more to present these ideas, and his reflections upon intellectual tendencies, in the form of stories. What Rose Macaulay does with mirth and ridicule, Beresford does meditatively and with greater respect for the thoughts of others. Where Rose Macaulay dismisses what her rather old-fashioned mind does not much relish, Beresford absorbs it all without for a moment changing his expression of resigned calm. 'What is happening in the world?' he says; and by the world he means the universal mind. And instead of answering, as Rose Macaulay might briskly do, 'A lot of nonsense,' he inclines his ear for an answer.

He wants to know whatever men have thought. His thirst for such knowledge is unquenchable. That early book of his, *The Hampdenshire Wonder*, which some suppose to be the tale of a monster, is in reality a dream fantasy, the tale of a child who fulfils Beresford's own ambition, to be as full of knowledge as the *Encyclopaedia Britannica*. Health and temperament and circumstance have been against him in the personal quest for omniscience. A delicate boyhood, with its lasting effect upon his constitution, greatly delayed his maturity. Even now, failure in muscular energy accounts for the absence of all boisterousness from his work. Because of such delicacy, Beresford's early reading was desultory, and it was only after other ways of life had been tried that he became at last a writer and systematic reader. As one gathers from *Jacob Stahl*, he planned to be an architect; but since architecture was not to hold him he entered the advertising world, and there practised his pen with none too great a success in artificial persuasion. Novel-writing seems to have been, if not an after-thought, a slowly developed aim, and it was not until he was nearly forty that he joined the ranks of those who were known as 'the younger generation of novelists.'

Even then, in 1911, when he was influenced by the vogue for which *The Way of All Flesh*, *Tono-Bungay*, and *Clayhanger* had been original models, he was far from being one of the joyous amateurs. On the contrary, he had less profusion than mastery. His hand was firm; he was not adventurous; it was his own story that he candidly related. And the story? The man? Not without significance are the facts that he was at one time an expert chess player (to myself quite devastating), and that his chief hobby has been that of joinery. Architecture; chess; joinery; all of them crafts of form and adjustment and rule. Beresford has written books to the number of forty and more in the last twenty-three years; and not one of those books is casual or untidy or tumultuous. All are written with precision and scrupulousness; all are reflective and without colour. If it is difficult to read them with excitement, it is impossible to read them without respect and (if one is oneself a novelist) without deep admiration of the skill, the practised and finished craft of their opening, development, and resolution.

VI. COMPTON MACKENZIE, HUGH WALPOLE, GILBERT CANNAN

Whether he was stirred by the coming of a new king, or not, I cannot say: I have never asked him. But a young man decided in 1910 to change his employment. He thought that instead of reading books for another publisher he would start a publishing business of his own. For the purpose, he would use the very large sum of one thousand pounds which happened to be in his possession at the time. Within a few months he had acquired offices in the Adelphi, had arranged to publish one or two books by writers known to him, and had cast his eye expertly among the young authors of the day for those whom it would interest him to publish. He was resolved to confine his list to those whose work he personally admired. And first of all he wrote to a novelist whose book he had formerly recommended to his employer, only to be overruled by a higher power. He mentioned his earlier recommendation. The author responded that the admired book had since been declined by several other publishers, and that he would be delighted to accept the offer now made to him. His name was Compton Mackenzie; the book was *The Passsionate Elopement*; and the publisher was Martin Secker.

Another young writer of novels happened also to be ready to consider a new publisher; and he too brought his work to the Adelphi, with the result that Gilbert Cannan's *Round the Corner* was added to Secker's list. And as Hugh Walpole at the same time published (with the same publisher) his fourth and, to date, longest novel, *Fortitude*, and Mackenzie followed *The Passionate Elopement* with *Carnival*, the new firm made so definite an impression upon general attention that most people supposed a new school of novelists to have been founded. Mackenzie, Cannan, Walpole; they were not in the least like the three musketeers; but they stood together in the bold advertisements as if they were inseparable.

In Henry James's famous article on the novelists of his day, to the seniors Wells, Bennett, and Conrad, were added four juniors. They were Mackenzie, Cannan, Walpole, and ('toiling in the dusty rear') D. H. Lawrence. James did not mention Beresford, W. L. George, Sheila Kaye-Smith, E. M. Forster, or Oliver Onions. He highly praised Mackenzie, whom he had known as a child, was a little shy of Cannan, and while hedging on the books spoke of Walpole personally with warm affection and hope. Once again these three novelists were linked together and, simultaneously, singled out as typical of their generation. Henry James had then great power to influence the minds of the fashionable minority.

Mackenzie was off to the best start. His first book had been very highly praised, and his second book, *Carnival*, took readers behind the scenes of the theatre, into young men's love affairs, and into the west country, which for some time previously had been a recognized venue for passion and tragedy. It had other qualities, which are those of the author; but these were the features which assured it of popular success. *Carnival* ran away with the English public; just as Walpole's *Fortitude* did with the American public. Of the three, Cannan was the least generally read, but his work, too, was considered to have special distinction; and all the world knew that successors to Wells, Bennett, and Galsworthy had been found. It became a favourite pastime for critics to compile lists of young novelists destined to greatness. Gradually it was established that Mackenzie, Cannan, Walpole, Forster, Lawrence, and Beresford were the coming boys. Brett Young was heard of later (his first single-handed novel was not published until 1914); and W. L. George, although he wrote at least one interesting book, *The Making of an Englishman*, did not quite fit into the galley. Of the Big Six four had been to either Oxford or Cambridge, and Beresford was a public schoolboy. Only Lawrence continued the tradition of Shaw, Wells, and Bennett in coming to literature by the direct route.

Now Mackenzie is related to half the theatrical families in England. The theatre is thus in his blood, a fact which should not be forgotten in any consideration of his work. His father was Edward Compton, a very celebrated player in old comedy and in costume drama; his mother was Virginia Bateman, member of an equally distinguished family of actors and actresses. It is no wonder that his first literary work should have been a play, and when he attempted the novel he made it a romantic tale of Bath in the days of its glory, when manners were manners and petticoats petticoats. He was born in West Hartlepool at the beginning of 1883, went to St Paul's School, in London, and subsequently to Oxford. It was his ambition to be a poet, an ambition encouraged (it must be observed) by the atmosphere of Oxford, which developed in its undergraduates a taste for verse; and when he left the university Mackenzie retired to the west of England to cultivate a garden and the Muse.

Following the success of *The Passionate Elopement*, he returned to London, and there, amid all the excitements of the Russian ballet, some work for the theatre, and much talk, for which he has a great gift, he wrote his second novel, *Carnival*, a book about contemporary life. *Carnival* showed that Mackenzie was one of the few writers able to dramatize the Cockney scene. The Cockney passages in the book are among the best things of their kind in modern writing; for Mackenzie's strong humour and power of improvisation are at their freest. But the book also showed that when inspiration (and the Cockney scene) failed him he was inclined to relapse into romance, Cornishness, and a rather *fin-de-siècle* emotionalism. The end of *Carnival*, accordingly, was in a different genre from the rest of the book.

It is upon the successor to *Carnival*, which was called *Sinister Street*, and a greatly admired appendage called *Guy and Pauline*, that Mackenzie's fame now largely rests. *Sinister Street*, perhaps unread by the very young of to-day, is among the few novels of its period which continue to have a large and unfluctuating sale every year. It is the picture of the development of a very precocious boy into a sophisticated young man of the nineteen-tens, and the picture is painted with a detail and wealth of reference unattempted by other authors of Mackenzie's experience. It illustrates most of its author's gifts, and all his faults. It is lavish, it contains rodomontade, it is literary, sentimental, and florid. But it has no timidities; it is large and confident; it is a picture of something more than a single life.

It is the record of a departed generation. That it contains many passages in false taste I believe: it is so much the more true for that.

Mackenzie followed *Sinister Street* with *Guy and Pauline*, always considered to be his best novel by those who are not troubled by its sentiment; and there seemed to be before him a long and unbroken career of romantic writing, fluent, beautiful, and picturesque. Of all the young writers of the time, he had the widest range—from fashion to the theatre, from common life among the London poor to life among the rural middle class, from poets to comedians, from highways to byways of human nature. Assuming the continuance of tradition, he could do anything he liked. But at this point the European War broke out; and he was immediately involved in it. None of the writers of his generation so eagerly welcomed the path of glory.

He was attached to Ian Hamilton's staff, and went to the Dardanelles, as to which he has given a picture in *Gallipoli Memories* of his own natural courage and enjoyment of danger; later, he was Military Control Officer in Athens and Director of Intelligence elsewhere in Greece. At once he became legendary; tales were told of his exploits with spies and uniforms; he was in his element as a romantic leader and counter-plotter, fearless, adventurous, and extraordinarily receptive to all the delights of so romantic a life. The quickness of his mind, the power he has of establishing what is not so much friendship as a ruthless intimacy of understanding, his sense of the picturesque—all made him enjoy his work as a boy enjoys playing at pirates. For the duration of the War he had a whole international situation at his finger-tips.

But this ended, and he resumed his writing of novels. In 1918 and 1919 he published the two halves of *The Adventures of Sylvia Scarlett*, which he personally considers his best book. He followed this with a trilogy dealing with the life of a parson; and he also wrote very rapidly a number of less serious books which were widely read but which disappointed those who had expected from Mackenzie many additions to the serious literature of his country. He could still begin a book—as, for example, *The Seven Ages of Woman*—in a way to capture imagination and set it roving into adventurous distance; but he was for a time victimized by his own fluency, and the books were less good than one had hoped from their beginnings that they were going to be. Farce was always possible to him; no man alive has a greater readiness of comic invention, comic dialogue, general absurdity. *Poor Relations, Rich Relatives, The Old Men of the Sea* (an adventure book full of Stevensonian enjoyment of treasure, barratry, and combat) followed each other with rapidity. Charming evocations of the past, such as *Our Street* and *The Darkening Green,* have since revived general knowledge of his great gifts. But it was not until he began to write in the vein of reminiscence that he achieved fully once again the status of the pre-War years. Here for the first time that delightful side of his talent, the gift of anecdote, mimicry, and narration which makes him so admirable a conversationalist, was offered to the public in literary form.

The vividness of mimicry, of course, is absent from his printed novels. One there has the inventiveness and the fun, but not the tone. Furthermore, Mackenzie gives so much of his talent first of all to sportive conversation and then to a recital of the plans he has made for future books that the novels themselves, when written, invariably seem to be less brilliant than the first sketches of them which one has heard rendered with such verve. This explains, I think, in part the discrepancy between different estimates of the importance of Mackenzie's work. To his friends, that work will always be charged with a thousand tones and expressions which strangers may miss. But Mackenzie is not the only writer whose work is colder than his talk; and, since critics of books are to speak of them as books, it must I think be granted that Mackenzie's books suffer from two things. One of these things is a changed fashion; for Mackenzie belongs quite distinctly to his generation at Oxford, which adored the poeticized phrase and a romanticized decadence. The other thing is his own conception of the novelist's obligation to entertain the reader.

Nobody who can take his nose out of aesthetics and ethics will doubt the right of the novelist to entertain readers. Indeed, the only pertinent question which one would be likely to hear from sagacious persons in response to such a claim is, 'What readers?' We all try to entertain; but the person we try most eagerly to entertain is ourself. It is to ourself that we present each sentence we write; and if ourself is not pleased with it, we either push him upon one side or we rewrite the sentence. In Mackenzie's case, the self is at times indulgent. He has a very strong awareness of himself; he amuses himself. At his best, he is a good critic, because the range of his mind and sympathy is wide; but there are times when his taste betrays him, when an early tolerance of what he calls the *faux bon* supervenes. Then a flicker of what I should call false romanticism casts purple upon his writing and rose upon his picture. That is his chief fault as a serious writer. When he is in spirits, he has no superiors as a farcical raconteur; but farce has still to be reckoned among the highest forms of literary art. If I were to add that his sense of the comic is too great to allow him passion or the depths of tragic imagination, I should go beyond knowledge: I therefore add only that Mackenzie has still not plumbed his talent to the depths.

There were some who thought in 1913 that a greater gift than Mackenzie's was in process of getting itself expressed. They found in Gilbert Cannan's *Round the Corner* the product of a less romantic mind more apt to give us in fiction something of the form and pressure of the time. Cannan was a young man from Manchester, who had been at Cambridge University, and who besides writing novel reviews for *The Manchester Guardian* had acted as dramatic critic for *The Star*. His dramatic criticism was scathing—as scathing, I believe, as anything written nowadays in criticism by our youngest intellectual bigots—and his mind melancholy with regretful disdain of all elders whatsoever. He was a very tall and handsome young man, of whom one thought as Hamlet because he was so often lost in moody meditation, and because his expression, even when he smiled, was a sad one; but if statuesque he was not unfriendly, and he was a man of both talents and parts.

His first book, *Peter Homunculus*, published in 1909, was by way of being a self-study; his second was a less interesting account of a disagreeable episode. The third, *Round the Corner* (that was where life was), had as its motto—or rather, as the first of its many mottoes, for it was studded with aphorisms—the words:

On veut essayer de peindre à la postérité, non les actions d'un seul homme, mais l'esprit des hommes dans le siècle le plus éclairé qui fut jamais.   *Siècle de Louis XIV.*

And, true to his motto, Cannan proceeded to describe with much detail the lives and opinions of a father (he has unwillingly become a clergyman in his youth, because although promised a commission in the army he has had the commission filched from him by a younger brother), his children, and all those affiliated persons who go to make up a domestic and extra-domestic circle. *Round the Corner* was a good and opinionated novel; for it was not enough for Cannan that he should tell what happened to members of the family, and so he had many sententious things to say of life, marriage, freedom, and such-like matters. The book had vitality and humour, and it is as readable to-day as it was when it was published. But it was to be the best book Cannan ever wrote.

He wrote much after it, *Old Mole*, *Young Earnest*, *The Stucco House*, *Pink Roses*, and others (a good dozen of them) before his lamentable illness; but of these only the novel called *Mendel*, which told the story, or was Cannan's version of the story, of a young painter who was also Cannan's friend, was in any serious degree outstanding. Although opinions multiplied and verbosity increased, the talent remained stationary, and was covered over at last with a kind of rank growth of words. He made no progress; while his rivals went their different ways to the War, he stayed in London or in a cottage in the country, and at last became so ill that his work had to be abandoned. But the talent had been real enough, as those who will read *Round the Corner* and *Mendel* can determine to this day.

Nor was its exercise confined to the novel; and at least one dramatic trifle—it is only a trifle in a single act—called *Everybody's Husband* is still played and is still charming to read. He had an ear for talk, although he was rather gravely monosyllabic himself, and it is one of the pleasures to be derived from *Round the Corner* that the talk is full-bodied; it is better than the disquisitions, and yet the disquisitions, until they became intolerable, were well enough in a grandiose way.

As for the third of this oddly joined triumvirate, Hugh Walpole like Cannan was born in 1884, and like Cannan he published his first novel (which was called *The Wooden Horse*) in 1909. Walpole was born in New Zealand, the son of an English clergyman who ultimately became Bishop of Edinburgh; and, again like Cannan, he went to Cambridge University. I do not know if the two were friends there; but I am sure that they had nothing at all in common. Where Cannan was unrelentingly severe towards his seniors, Walpole had no contempts. He was impulsive, generous, and immature. He had dallied with the idea of following his father's example and entering the Church, and the earnestness which is one of his traits, as well as his love of public speaking, testifies to a natural bent for exhortation. If he had not been a writer, he would have been a successful preacher; his lectures are always delivered with a spontaneity and energy of the most persuasive kind. But he did not feel, after some trial of his abilities, that he could properly remain in the Church; and after a brief experience of schoolmastering he determined that he wanted—as Henry James, nearly fifty years earlier, had wanted—to be 'just literary.'

When Walpole began to write novels he was deeply impressed by the work of Hawthorne and Henry James. He still owes more to those two writers than to any others. Henry James was his friend, and to some extent his tutor; and there can be no doubt that for Walpole James's (and Hawthorne's) sense of the supernatural had a constant fascination. Although, as I have said, he was impulsive and generous and earnest, he was also very emotional. You can detect this, if you look for it, in his early work; for instance in *Mr Perrin and Mr Traill*, where the writing has all the time a quiver of excitement. It is in such a book as the *Portrait of a Man with Red Hair*. It occurs from time to time in other books, such as *The Green Mirror*. Walpole is not a simple character.

He is less simple than any other writer I know. His cheerfulness and good nature, which are perfectly natural to him, his impulsive friendliness, his wish to establish sincere relationships with those whom he likes, are enmeshed with many reserves and distrusts, with shrewdness and good sense and another trait which I vaguely decipher as a power to shut his mind to unacceptable aspects of life. He is capable of great loyalty, ardent championship, candour; and at the same time bottomless suspicion, evasiveness, and deep trouble of spirit. The cheerfulness is warrantably genuine; the morbidness is just as genuine; it is an essential characteristic of his work, in which there is a strain of terror as well as much jovial power to interest and amuse. He looks happy, his manner is always full of *bonhomie*; he can be teased—and is, although perhaps he now relishes it less than he did; he laughs readily and plunges into a room with massive energy; he talks well and with humour as well as good humour; he is extremely likeable; if one did not know him, and did not know his work, one would suppose him the most ingenuous soul in the world. The strange thing is that one would be right, as well as profoundly wrong.

When he was young, Walpole thought the society of other writers the most delightful society of all. He wanted to write well, and he wanted to be liked. Accordingly, when his third novel, *Mr Perrin and Mr Traill*, brought him to the notice of those watching for new talent, he was as happy as a young man could be. The book, that highly charged tale of schoolmasters who hate one another, was for a number of years Walpole's most admired novel. It remains, although plainly immature, one of his most interesting. When, subsequently, he wrote *Fortitude*, with its emphasis upon the need for courage in life, he had an even wider popularity than before; and while *The Duchess of Wrexe* had a less hearty welcome from some of his admirers it was well enough received to show that he had established his reputation.

Then the War came, and of course the literary life could not stand against such a storm of violence. Military service being impossible to him owing to shortness of sight, Walpole went to Russia on diplomatic business, and saw some service with a Red Cross unit on the Eastern Front. It was a wonderful experience for him, and, coupled with discovery of the Russian novelists, it powerfully affected his work. His next book, *The Dark Forest*, was not only very much more generally successful than any of its predecessors (for all readers were then curious about Russia), but it was in every way more mature and more interesting than anything he had written. Parts of it were so good that they converted readers who had hitherto been sceptical of the author's talent, and it was with *The Dark Forest* that Walpole really took unquestioned place as a leader of the then younger generation. His work was still in a literary sense derivative, but he had seen and felt strange, thrilling things, and a literary tea-party was no longer his ideal form of entertainment.

He remained in Russia, and was there all through the Revolution, writing *The Captives* while the whole bloody business was going on in Petrograd; and after that he lectured throughout the United States, where he is among the most popular of visiting Englishmen, and settled down to his literary task again with an enthusiasm as rare as it is magnificent.

Now it is possible that since the end of the War Walpole has not again so favourably impressed connoisseurs of the novel as he did with *The Dark Forest*. Apart from all question of post-War fashion, he has suffered in critical reputation by the popular success of his books. That was inevitable. The chillingly fastidious section of the critical public is so constituted that it cannot endure to see an admired author taken to the arms of the mob. At the slightest hint of success it averts its head. Walpole has suffered in England from the averted head. Not all the acclaim of his admirers can win back the purists.

Are the purists right? I think in any case Walpole must have been affected in literary reputation by the conflict between his desire to write well and his desire to be liked; but I think it is also true that his most famous book, *The Cathedral*, suffers from

mechanical invention. I shall not dwell upon the obvious fact
that Anthony Trollope had already created a complete church
society in the Barsetshire novels, and that one of his leading
characters was a powerful churchman named Dr Grantly. What
I have chiefly in mind is the fact that when a novelist conceives
the idea of a book about any dominant personality who is
brought low he is faced at once with certain plain possibilities
of invention. That is, the personality, if he is in a profession,
must suffer defeat in that profession; and he must also suffer
defeat in his home. Otherwise the defeat is but partial; since
many a man may be wounded in pride out of doors, and yet
escape from complete destruction if, domestically, he is un-
harmed. If he is to be crushed in the home as well, he can only
be affected by the loss of wife and children. Very well: the
powerful Archdeacon of Polchester is given a wife and two
children, one a girl, the other a boy (just as it happens in *Poor
Jenny is a-weeping*). The girl falls in love with a young man
disapproved by the archdeacon; the boy is sent down from his
university, and runs away—you have guessed it—with a bar-
maid; the wife—have you not guessed that, too?—commits
adultery. These events, singly, might have given the archdeacon pause: all together, they have such an air of artificial
contrivance that the reader is made uncomfortable. It is as
though Walpole had naïvely taken the first suggestions offered
by a mind too familiar with novelistic ruses for the domestic
discomfiture of the archdeacon. Greater worldly experience
would have started back from such an aggregation of simplicities.
For the rest, scenic effects are splashed into the book; the drama
is forced; the total impression of the tale is one, not of inevitability (which would have made it a tragedy), but of mechanism.
The more sophisticated one is, the more one recoils from so little
subtle a treatment of what might have been a suggestive and
very powerful theme. *The Cathedral* is not one of Walpole's
best books: it is one from which he will never escape.

And yet it is full of a quality which gives Walpole distinction
among his fellow-novelists. It has a vivid and rapidly communicated scene; it is immediately readable; it attempts an ambitious subject and it carries that subject through with great
address. The writing is full of liveliness. The author goes
straight to the dramatic and the informative. It would be easy
to see from this one book—though it does his talent less than
justice—that he was a natural novelist, and not one who had
turned novelist in despair of doing something better. Moreover,

such a book as *The Old Ladies*, where the scene is the same, but the plan less mechanical, is decidedly among his best books. Against the background of a cathedral city he occupies himself with the simple doings of pleasant people in that city, the good and the kind, the old and timid and gropingly superstitious; and these are his proper concern. They bring out his sympathy for what is pleasant and true; they allow his native ingenuousness full scope; and that delightful conversational style in which he tells fairy stories for grown-ups does not swear with the grim or gruesome, the savage or the sublime.

In the last few years, Walpole has essayed his most ambitious task, the picture of a family through several generations and through several historical ages. None but an enthusiast could have ventured upon so tremendous a task. None but a tale-teller could have filled four large volumes with such a wealth of narrative, talk, life and death. To say that the Herries books fall short of complete success is not to arraign the design; for no novelist has ever been more ambitious, and a glorious failure upon this large scale is in any event to be preferred to a dozen safe little ventures in subtlety. The books show a really gargantuan design. They attempt the business of heredity, the business of contemporary history (for portraits of historic persons are interpolated in the books, just as they were in Thackeray's *Esmond*), the business of entertainment, and a gigantic continuity. If the Herries books had been as good as only genius could have made them, they would have been monumental. If they are less than monumental, the heroism of the attempt remains. I shall say only this in adverse comment upon them, that magnitude of proportion is in fact a testimony to industry rather than to imaginative force; and that calls in question the value of copiousness for its own sake.

There are, and can be, no absolute standards for the judgment of a novel. Those who suppose otherwise are working from restricted experience and a slavish adoration of certain Aristotelian principles which concern an entirely different kind of writing. They are also confusing art with technique, as is not uncommon nowadays. The assumption that a small thing neatly done, a mere technical stunt, is superior to something sprawly but largely attempted, is comparable to a preference for the trained box over oak and elm. It is a sign of rigid and timid love of rule. The only objection to the large and sprawly is that it may be an excuse for lax work; and of course it is true that it cannot be as readily grasped and estimated. I also perceive that the horizontally ambitious is inferior to the perpendicularly ambitious, and personally prefer *King Lear* to *Le Grand Cyrus*.

It seems to me, then, that in a period when the small and very select is unduly admired, Walpole has shown courage in embracing the immense. Furthermore, if his work be compared in quality with work in its own genre, which I take to be the romantic or quasi-romantic tale written after Scott, it will be found to bear the test extremely well. Walpole is a professional novelist. So were many of the greatest novelists of the past. Shakespeare was a professional dramatist (unless one supposes that he was but Bacon's pseudonym). Dostoevsky, Balzac, Dickens, Henry Fielding, and others of the tale-tellers of the past all accepted the earnings of their books without feeling that they were prostitutes. But since the War—the arts in that respect having aligned themselves with sport—there has been much horrified shrinking from professionalism in literature, it being thought that the antithesis of professionalism is quality. The antithesis of professionalism in literature, on the contrary, is dilettantism. No word is more damning in any art or craft than the word amateurish.

VII. FRANCIS BRETT YOUNG

The green trees, when I saw them first through one of the gates, transported and ravished me; their sweetness and unusual beauty made my heart to leap and almost mad with ecstasy—they were such strange and wonderful things. The skies were mine, and so were the sun and moon and stars—and all the world was mine— and I the only spectator and enjoyer of it.

THOMAS TRAHERNE.

Francis Brett Young came too late to be included in the first onset of the 'younger generation'; but he quickly joined the band, and by 1914 had published not only a novel (written in collaboration with his brother Eric) called *Undergrowth*, but a critical study of Robert Bridges. From the beginning of his literary career, therefore, Brett Young's name was associated with an intelligent interest in poetry; and if we remind ourselves of the history of Edwin Ingleby, written in 1919 as *The Young Physician*, we shall remember how the little boy, Edwin, used to read Shenstone and Akenside and Prior and 'nearly every volume of poetry that he could smuggle' from the school library.

Edwin, without a doubt, in that respect was of the same temper as his creator; and his creator has been a reader and writer of poetry for as long as he has directed a pen.

Like Edwin, Francis Brett Young was born in the English midlands, and while several of his novels, such as *Deep Sea* and *The Crescent Moon, The Red Knight* and *Pilgrim's Rest*, have a different setting (some of them foreign and romantic settings), those upon which his fame rests have been markedly inspired by his love of the heart of England, Worcestershire and its neighbouring counties. It may in fact be true that Brett Young did not wholly find himself outside the midland scene. His earliest works, though they included admirable studies of midland life such as *The Iron Age*, and though they were almost uniformly interesting work, suffered from a variousness of character which disturbed those who like to know what to expect of any author before they open his book. But he was known for ever as soon as he wrote:

They crossed the drive and entered a grass alley within tall black hedges. The harsh odour of yews dropped, like a curtain, between them and the rose-garden on either side. Sometimes it seemed as if the curtains swayed and a ravishing gust blew through, so that Clare was conscious, without seeing, of masses of June roses breathing out sweetness under the heavy night. They passed quickly down the dark alley, Ralph with his long, free strides, Clare fluttering silently at his side. Where the yews ended stood a fountain of grey stone and a circular Palladian belvedere. The spray of the fountain rose in a starlit mist; its watery jets cracked in the air like whips; and when they reached it, every one, of a common impulse, paused for a moment and turned to look backward down the long yew vista to the fantastic bulk and blazing windows of the castle.

Having been at school at Epsom, and at Birmingham University, Brett Young became a doctor, and for some years he practised in a small and very famous town in Devonshire. Travellers from the United States, after losing the Lizard light and a dim shadow upon the horizon which passes as soon as it has tantalized the eye, have often enough excitedly in the early morning darkness found their ship amid a fleet of small vessels; and it was at Brixham, from which these trawlers set out, that Brett Young acted as a doctor. A glimpse of the place may be found in *Deep Sea*. But his heart was never captured by that strange corner of England; he loved best his own richly inland scene. A great scene, by the way; the scene from which Shakespeare himself came three and a half centuries ago. And sure enough, although they will not find Shakespeare's greatness there, those who read the tales of Brett Young will find in them a peculiar Englishness born of the author's deep feeling for English poetry and an English countryside far from the sea.

He has a third love, not always to be found with the first of those I have named; and this is a love of music. That, too, is evidenced in his work. And, having lived for some years in Brixham, and then (as Mackenzie did, and both Norman Douglas and Lawrence) having spent some time in Capri, Brett Young has now settled for the rest of his life in the countryside from which he sprang. If one may judge from his dedications he is already an idol in county society; and from his home in Worcester he is sending those long, slow, intimate studies of rural middle-class life which readers bereft of Galsworthy are finding so much to their taste. To him, rather than to any other writer, we owe the recent revival in amplitude in the novel; for *The Portrait of Clare*, which was published in 1927, contains very nearly a thousand pages of polished, tender, and humane writing.

As compared with his immediate contemporaries, Brett Young has less humour and invention than Mackenzie and less sense of the dramatic macabre than Walpole. He is a more considered stylist than either. His writing is unfailingly mellow, graceful, and delicate. If he does not at any time give an air of sharp actuality to the life he describes, that is probably intentional, for strict realism is not his object. His object is rather to present in tranquillity, and with beauty, the life of his imagined lovers, his country squires, his schoolboys and nail-traders, his doctors and soldiers, so that they compose into a country painting, a long, leisurely panorama of England. Not for him the picture novel of Henry James, the novel of situation and the gropings of half-mystified brains after symbolic truth. Not for him the rapidities of Mackenzie or the vehemences of Lawrence or the winning zest of Walpole. His pace is slower; he passes along the lanes and through the fields, and so, eventually, reaches home in good order. At times he summons a little violence to his aid, and he is not afraid to marry his lovers and tell what happened afterwards; but when he does either of these things he does it with so much measure and charm that we hardly know that our happiness has been threatened, and especially in the later books, which are full of the country, we rest content.

In war-time, Brett Young went to East Africa with British troops, and his book *Marching on Tanga* was the first thing he wrote which took him beyond enthusiastic reviews into the consciousness of the reading public. He was a contributor to

Georgian Poetry, that series of anthologies which first intimated to the world that a new generation of poets (as well as novelists) had come into being.   And it was *The Portrait of Clare* which brought him finally to his present position among those who have ceased to be the 'younger generation' and have become individuals known to all, and duly assailed as out of date.

CHAPTER XII: THE WAR-TIME AFFLATUS

I

FOR the most part this chapter will deal with the soldier-poets; but as I shall speak of Osbert Sitwell and his brother, and as it is usual for all writers (including members of the family) to speak of the Sitwells as though they were inseparable, I am going to conclude with Edith Sitwell. And as there was one woman poet whose work, first published in 1916, belongs to the War period (and to the future), I shall first speak of Charlotte Mew.

Before doing this, however, I wish to explain why I have grouped the other writers here. Robert Nichols comes first because his war experience was brief and quickly expressed; Wilfred Owen next because I believe him to have been the most striking of all the poets who were killed in the War; Blunden, Robert Graves, and Sassoon as if they were three musketeers because all three have written of their war experience in prose as well as in verse; the Sitwells last because while only Osbert had any practical contact with the War (he was in the Grenadier Guards from 1913 until 1919) they are a significant link between old and new poets. It was they who established the counterblast to *Georgian Poetry* called *Wheels*, and while they have lately turned to prose all three members of the family have so contributed to what is called 'this modernist stuff' as to be included in the list of poets pilloried in recent attacks.

There was at the outbreak of war a very rapid rush on the part of all sorts of young men to enlist in the Territorial Army, and as many of these young men had had their education interrupted just at the time when they were naturally engaged in writing verses, the heightened emotion of those times led to a good deal of what was known as War verse. Most of this was of no value at all. Some of it was as eager and burning as young hearts could make it. All found a ready market, because parents and friends wished for some record of their endangered boys, and—by some extension of sentiment—of the endangered boys of others. Several names detached themselves quite early from the rest—Julian Grenfell, Charles Sorley, Robert Nichols, Gilbert Frankau were among the earliest to tell in print what they felt or what they had seen and suffered—and they were duly read and celebrated. But then, after a time, the heroic note or the note of Kiplingesque onomatopoeia favoured by Gilbert Frankau (Frankau, nevertheless, had something to describe, and he had great gifts of versification, as readers of *One of Us* did not need to be told) gave way to a note of quite another kind. War was not the splendour it was imagined by fever-struck home-stayers; it was an ugly dirty business. The poets began to tell us that. Later still, they let us farther yet into their hearts, to the bitter contempt for stupidity and incompetence which their war experience had awakened. Then we had, for the first time, a new personal poetry of the War; then was first sounded the cry of disillusion, of disenchantment, which in prose, more lengthily, less poignantly, we read in the pages of C. E. Montague.

Disenchantment has been the cry of poets ever since that day; it is the cry of the youngest poets of all, although theirs, I some-times think, is a factitious bitterness, arising less from individual than common inclination to declare the world not all that sensitive hearts can desire. But the disenchantment of those earlier poets who fought in the War and who had gone into the fighting services with enthusiasm was by no means a convention: it was something true and original, the protest of some men who, coming from peace and hope into a shambles, had had their beautiful dreams of life broken.

II. CHARLOTTE MEW

Lend me, a little while, the key
That locks your heavy heart.
CHARLOTTE MEW, *The Pedlar.*

At least one of the women poets of the War years had some-thing more than casual emotion to express; and she, a born poet, did not live long enough to bring her gift to its highest level. She was not well known outside a circle of poets, and I think she has still to be recognized as fully as she deserves. Thomas Hardy knew of her, and felt admiration for what she had written; there may have been others of whom I have no awareness. To

the best of my belief she published only two collections of
what she had written, and since she died as obscurely (I speak
in terms of public acquaintance) as she had lived she was not
very celebrated.

Nevertheless, the volume called *The Farmer's Bride* contains
much that is of quite personal and unmistakable beauty. It
has, of course, some callow verses which are timidly inquiring
or in the fashionable mode of impersonation, but the effect of it
as a whole is deeply moving. I should like to quote here, for
example, in full, two long poems called *The Quiet House* and
The Forest Road, both of which achieve intense communication
of feeling and reverie. I cannot do so, because of their length.
The former, with its apparently inconclusive thoughts, by which
a history is made plain to us, is the perplexity of a girl made
manifest; the latter, a lover's dramatic apostrophe to a sleeping
woman, I can only suggest by the use of a few lines:

> The forest road,
> The infinite straight road stretching away
> World without end: the breathless road between the walls
> Of the black listening trees: the hushed, grey road
> Beyond the window that you shut to-night
> Crying that you would look at it by day—
> There is a shadow there that sings and calls
> But not for you. Oh! hidden eyes that plead in sleep
> Against the lonely dark, if I could touch the fear
> And leave it kissed away on quiet lids—
> If I could hush these hands that are half awake,
> Groping for me in sleep I could go free.
> I wish that God would take them out of mine
> And fold them . . .

Madeleine in Church, another and at times acutely successful
impersonation; the title poem, *The Farmer's Bride*; several
pictures of children; and *Arracombe Wood*, in dialect, all have
their individual effect; but all are raised by their surroundings
and the associations with what has been read before. In whatever she wrote, she was always guiltless of calculated gesture,
which to me is in itself a mark of quality. Her aim was to
communicate with scrupulous truth that vision which had come
with strong feeling as the result of a personal impression of life.
Her use of language is admirable; its suppleness constantly
enchants the ear; but what gives the poems perfection is a
sincerity which finds fit words because the impulse to write, to
tell, has been so intense.

III. ROBERT NICHOLS

> . . . despite these wars,
> My ship—though blindly blown,
> Long lost to sun or moon or stars—
> Still stands up alone.
>
> R. NICHOLS, *Thanksgiving.*

The first of the poets to attempt onomatopoeic renderings of the noises of battle were Gilbert Frankau and Robert Nichols. Both, in the first instance, were artillery officers, and both heard the guns in action with an enthusiastic sense of sound as well as the courage and splendour of those who took part in the warfare. Neither rendered, or sought to render, what to other and later soldier-poets was the dreary monotony of hopeless routine or the shocking waste of young life and young enthusiasm. For them the words of an Owen or a Sassoon lay in the distance: the immediate shock of conflict absorbed ears and minds. That was for the reason that they wrote in early days, and in heroic mood. Their vision of the War was still a vision of assault and counter-assault. Frankau, an extraordinarily skilled versifier, translated Kipling into modern terms; Nichols, all verve and excitement, pictured an attack as:

> Something meets us.
> Head down into the storm that greets us.
> A wail.
> Lights. Blurr.
> Gone.
> On, on. Lead. Lead. Hail.
> Spatter. Whirr! Whirr!
> *'Toward that patch of brown ;*
> *Direction left.'* Bullets a stream.
> Devouring thought crying in a dream.
> Men, crumpled, going down. . . .

He knew, and celebrated, the sense of loss of friends; the horror of carnage. But he did not reach the stage of protest; perhaps he would never have reached it, so sanguine and thrilling is his temper. He was thus a War poet of the second stage, the first being the purely patriotic or 'this is for ever England' stage, and the third a stage signified by Sassoon's 'But he did for them both by his plan of attack.'

Like Wilfred Owen, Robert Malise Bowyer Nichols was born in 1893, and was educated at Winchester and Oxford. He had been a poet from boyhood, a poet in the vein of the immature Keats or the never quite continuously excellent Darley, familiar with fauns and dryads, and as ready as either Keats or Darley to write rapid mellifluous verse about their pipings and sayings. I picture him in pre-university days as an eager youth whose imagination leapt high at a summer's day or a bosky grove, moods of joy and melancholy alternating, and his eye in a fine frenzy rolling. It was at Oxford that he wrote fragments of a dozen ambitious poetic dramas or poetic romances, and, but for the War, he might have finished them at leisure and made his name as a romantic poet. He was not, I mean, a poet created by the excitement of the War: he had enough natural fire to warm his Muse without external aid. But he was a poet diverted by cataclysm from his impulsive vein.

Since the War, his experience in which undermined health never robust, Nichols has made eloquent excursions into platform propaganda, the short story, the prose play, and lengthy poetic satire. Whatever he does, he does with such gusto that he seems aflame with emotion; no man was ever more clearly a poet. Tall, eager, always in movement, talkative, exuberant, he flies at truth as if he would tear out its heart. But he would not harm a beetle, and for all his vehement assault the truth escapes again in the way it has done for as many centuries as scientists allow the world to have been peopled (I forget the latest number). Nichols is not discouraged.

He is a poet; not an intellectual. He says of English poetry that it is

a thing governed from within by its own necessities, and not by rules of aesthetics imposed on it from without;

and this I take to be the true (as well as the romantic) definition of the unimportance of aesthetic theory in letters. But aesthetes will have nothing to do with such a definition, and Nichols cannot now be said to be in the van of poetic thought. He has not abandoned poetry, but he concentrates upon work of the heroic or mock-heroic character. In his plays, he is a poet still; one who deals forcibly with great themes as did the minor Elizabethans—or as they might do, in prose, if they lived nowadays. I like to see these plays as manifestations of a more recent Thomas Kyd (if that is the name of the man who wrote the better parts of *The Spanish Tragedy*); and none among living writers could more exultingly relish the glorious retort of Hieronimo when he says:

> In troth, my lord, it is a thing of nothing:
> The murder of a son, or so—
> A thing of nothing, my lord!

The dramatic, the tremendous, the odd impress of guilty knowledge upon the souls of men, appeal strongly to Nichols's imagination. He would be capable of any grandeur if something did not always inflate the grandeur; he could write plays, in prose or poetry, in which spiritual problems were seriously tackled if only he could discipline his own effervescence. His ambition is boundless. He has the temperament for bold and lofty works, and perpetually promises a triumph of music and passion over the commonplace. But he has not yet fulfilled his promise; and whether that relative failure is due to fluency in excess of intellect or to some other cause such as unfixity of purpose I am unable to say, so much does Nichols in the profusion of his talent seem able to perform.

IV. WILFRED OWEN

I do not for a moment call myself a musician, nor do I suspect I ever shall be, but there! I love Music, with such *strength* that I have to conceal the passion, for fear it be thought weakness.

From a personal paper by Wilfred Owen.

With Wilfred Owen, we reach the height of what may be termed strictly War Poetry. In his work, which was first published posthumously under the editorship of Siegfried Sassoon, and which has now been finally collected and introduced by Edmund Blunden, there is no effort to render the delights of war, or the noises of guns and other instruments of death. We have, instead of impressionism, a peculiar reflective hatred of war from which hysteria is entirely absent; an attempt to give in poetry, not the 'wukka-wukka' (as Hueffer) or 'toc-toc-toc' (as Nichols) of the machine-guns, but the silent thoughts of men, the deadliness of trench warfare, the deep indignation of the soldier at civilian barbarism. Owen, who was posted to a unit of the regular army, saw the whole War through; he was killed within a week of the Armistice. He was given the Military Cross for great bravery, and as an officer he represented the best type of unprofessional soldier.

He was born in 1893, and in 1910 he matriculated at London University. He went in 1913 to France, where for two years he acted as a tutor, returning to England in order to enlist as soon as his contract expired; and from that time onward he was almost constantly in physical danger and discomfort. His letters, frank and truthful, as well as humorous, show what horrors he had to endure; but they are full of courage. There was not in them, and there is not in any one of his poems, a slackening of courage. The horror of warfare which he expresses is reinforced by that fact.

He had, of course, written poetry before the War—some of it ingeniously experimental, as an example printed among his other poems clearly shows—but it was the War which produced his rapid maturity. And even then it was during his stay in a war hospital near Edinburgh, when Siegfried Sassoon was a fellow-patient, that he made the greatest progress. Sassoon was one of his poetic idols (for *The Old Huntsman* had been published, and Owen declared that nothing so good as the pictures of trench life in that book had ever been written), and Sassoon is a born mentor. He will watch over the talents of others, firm in criticism but ever kind in understanding, as no other man of his years could do. From Sassoon, therefore, Owen at once derived the best possible form of encouragement.

Encouragement was all he needed. His poetic instinct was so sure that he would sooner or later have discovered for himself all that could be taught. Since, however, time proved so brief, it is to Sassoon that we must give thanks for a friendship and influence which aided the production of Owen's best poems. If Owen had lived, he might have carried into the post-War period an even stronger power, as one infers from the magnificent fragment, *Strange Meeting*. As it is, the poems that we have deal chiefly with war conditions and war reflections; and of all the men active at that time he is the one most accurately described as a poet of the War. How far we are from former picturesque renderings of sight and sound in the terrible stanzas of *Exposure*, which begin:

Our brains ache, in the merciless iced east winds that knive us . . .
Wearied we keep awake because the night is silent . . .
Low, drooping flares confuse our memory of the salient . . .
Worried by silence, sentries whisper, curious, nervous,
      But nothing happens.

Watching, we hear the mad gusts tugging on the wire
Like twitching agonies of men among its brambles.
Northward, incessantly, the flickering gunnery rumbles,
Far off, like a dull rumour of some other war.
      What are we doing here?

I have quoted this poem in order to show what is, as it seems to me, a point of progress between the mellifluous lyricism of pre-War days (and first consequent impressionisms of the War) and the righteous anger passionately felt and expressed in other moods by Owen or with characteristic irony by Sassoon. Such points hint only at a development which somebody more competent than myself should trace simply for the understanding of common people; for the disillusion of the War poets has been appropriated by a later generation as if that later generation, too, had suffered; whereas it has merely not been able to climb out of a bitter convention and remains self-righteous. Owen could not have remained a pessimist: he must have constituted himself a positive voice in a day of negations. He had very exceptional talent, unusual skill and intelligence and enterprise in versification, the imaginative power to identify himself with other men and yet retain his own character unimpaired, and a breadth of sympathy unsurpassed by any of his contemporaries.

V. SIEGFRIED SASSOON, EDMUND BLUNDEN, ROBERT GRAVES

I group these three because they have been friends, because, having been poets in time of war, they live still and occupy prominent places in the lists of those who make current literature, and (a slender link, but not uninteresting) because all three of them have written in prose some account of personal experience in the War. Sassoon is the eldest of them (he was born in 1886), and for myself the most outstanding. His war poetry first heroically expressed something other than patriotism and nervous excitement, and his own autobiographical volumes, *Memoirs of a Fox-Hunting Man* and *Memoirs of an Infantry Officer*, are as excellent a record of character and feeling in pre-War and War years as any man of genius could have written. Since the War Sassoon has rigorously applied to himself the Malthusian doctrine which he untiringly presses upon other creators, with the result that only a small quantity of poetry, tentative and reflective, has been printed; and even this he has in some degree reserved for his friends by means of private publication.

Sassoon, if asked to describe himself briefly, would hesitatingly say: 'I'm ... er ... ordinary sort of chap.' He believes this. You could not persuade him that he was anything but a very simple fellow. Yet he has great pride—perhaps a pride in his simplicity, for of course he thinks (as I do) that simplicity is better than sophistication. On the other hand Sassoon exaggerates his own simplicity; it is somehow confused in his head with austerity, and not wholly so, either. He is no metaphysician, and no debater. He has tried to present himself in the *Memoirs* as an ordinary, shy, occasionally absent-minded cricketer and horse-lover who went to the War; who so hated it that he made up his mind to be killed—but was never hit; who after years of service was sent home ill; who resolved to make a public protest (which he did) against the continuance of so senseless a slaughter and horror; and, for the army authorities were disconcerted by such behaviour on the part of one who had been rightly decorated for gallantry in the field, and hardly knew what to do with him, who outstripped his escort on the way to some institution which was a cross between prison and a sanatorium and arrived there first. His escort, by the way, was Robert Graves.

Well, whether you accept Sassoon's account of himself as a fair one or not (it is very sincere), there is one point upon which you must be clear. It is that nobody but Sassoon would take him for an ordinary sort of chap. I doubt if anybody could take him for anything but a poet. He has, for one thing, a handsome and noble head. He has, in his diffident speech, a faculty for expressing wisdoms, fine taste, and eccentric ideas with considerable precision. I should say that he is not entirely incapable of enjoying other people's malice; but his own comments upon contemporaries are usually as kind as they are brief. He has a true passion for music; a scrupulous honesty of mind which will not allow him to deceive himself—except about his ordinariness; a great capacity for emotion. On the whole, he might be considered moody; he certainly is not lavish in displays of sociability. But he is one of the most attractive men I know.

Sassoon, who on his mother's side is a Thornycroft, was educated at Marlborough and Cambridge. As the first volume of his autobiography shows, he lived much in the country as a boy, played at cricket for the Sussex Martlets, rode to hounds, and read a good deal. Always solitary, he might not have made as many friends as he has done if the War had not turned the current of his life; but since he was at Cambridge, and knew Robert Ross (a great friend to young poets and their like, and a charming man of letters), he was not completely a stranger in literary London when he began to publish his poetry. And here, for it was poetry of the War, we had that new note in which joyous sacrifice and amazed sense of noise and movement gave way to insistence upon, not only death and loss, which have long been commonplaces in poetry, but the less inspiring aspects of modern warfare:

> . . . drizzling daybreak that reveals
> Disconsolate men who stamp their sodden boots
> And turn dulled, sunken faces to the sky
> Haggard and hopeless.

And again:

> I see them in foul dug-outs, gnawed by rats,
>   And in the ruined trenches, lashed with rain,
> Dreaming of things they did with balls and bats.

And finally:

> The boys came back. Bands played and flags were flying,
>   And Yellow-Pressmen thronged the sunlit street
> To cheer the soldiers who'd refrained from dying,
>   And hear the music of returning feet.
> 'Of all the thrills and ardours War has brought,
> This moment is the finest.' (So they thought.)
>
> Snapping their bayonets on to charge the mob,
>   Grim Fusiliers broke ranks with glint of steel.
> At last the boys had found a cushy job.
>
> .   .   .   .
>
> I heard the Yellow-Pressmen grunt and squeal;
> And with my trusty bombers turned and went
> To clear those Junkers out of Parliament.

It was no wonder that when he resumed civilian life Sassoon found himself a Liberal no longer, but a Socialist. He could not forget the War. If he had not harped upon the War he must have been false to his faith. And, by so harping, he continued to attack everybody who had been comfortably ready to sacrifice the young in a late encounter, and by degrees (with the aid of others, similarly minded) he consolidated a general impression in the minds of youth that anybody over forty years of age was inescapably a hypocrite and a profiteer. I do not remember when the country first read the words 'My generation' as applied to a new and better race; but the germ of that hostility to former generations can be found in the Sassoon poem quoted above.

Of the three books of *Memoirs* I shall have nothing to say. They are entirely free from affectation; they conjure up the countryside of old peaceful days and the calms as well as the storms and disgusts of war. They picture the author's days in saddle and cricketing pads. They subtly communicate his affection, his modesty, and that vagueness which all sensitive men feel within them while the impression they make upon others is objectively concrete. They are documents of our time. I see them as likely to be so regarded a century hence.

Edmund Blunden's *Undertones of War* is similarly remarkable as a sensitive man's description of encounter with a world altogether strange, for immersion in which every hour of his previous life had unfitted him. Blunden's war poems have less pungency than those of either Owen or Sassoon; the feeling in them is diffused; he was not a warrior, and war inspired his prose but not his best poetry. The truth is that he is by nature a pastoral poet and a bookman. He loves old books. If he had his way, he would dwell in a countryside peopled (besides the hinds and Hodges and birds and beasts) with Lamb, Hazlitt, Leigh Hunt, and the men of their hour.

Imagine this reader and lover of nature being called from his books and cottage to deliver death to those whom he had no wish to harm! He no doubt wore his khaki with a difference. But while *Undertones of War*, which is written in fine prose without ornament, is plainly the work of one who was not born for soldiering, it is equable in spirit. Blunden is no indignant philosopher, no rebel, but a sweet-tempered poet reading a book by the roadside and noticing the hues and the tendernesses of the landscape. He gives us none of the bitterness of some of his peers. We read in his pages:

It was the weather when leaves begin to turn, and sing a little dryly in the wind; when spiders apparently spend the night in making webs on fences; and when the distances dare assume the purple as the sunset dislimns. As far as battalion headquarters, one might notice these nocturnal effects. Beyond that point, the facts and probabilities of war obscured them. . . . Recollection paints these autumn weeks in the Beaumont Hamel sector as a tranquil time, etc.

I do not say that disagreeables are ignored in Blunden's limpid pages; but they assuredly are not enforced with a curative purpose in view. They are used as contributory detail to a picture painted in sober and candid colours. That is because Blunden is capable of savagery only to blasphemers against his literary gods.

As soon as we come to Robert Graves, we are conscious of a difference of approach to the world. Sassoon, in his prose books, is the quiet, meditative sort of chap with a love of a horse and a bat; Blunden, dreaming of old authors and present contemplation, is similarly at peace with a tranquil world, and the enemy of none. But Graves—it is clear from his own account—is of a more active and aggressive mental cast. He quarrels, not, as Sassoon, with a gloom and reluctance, but with zest. His verses are crisp. He says:

> I forced this quarrel; it was not
>   So much disgust with all you did
> As sudden doubt of whom and what
>   My easy friendship hid;
>   I carefully offended.
> It would be best if you too broke
> Acquaintance with a monstrous look,
>   Rather than stay to temporize
>   Or steal away with brimming eyes.

That is still another stage towards the modern temper, which is impatient, imperious, little tolerant of other methods and other sorrows. But Graves is far from being permanently angry; he has a great singing gift. His poems have often the simplicity of old ballads—they are not mimicries:

MOTHER: Soft and thick the snow lay,
              Stars danced in the sky.
         Not all the lambs of May-day
              Skip so bold and high.

         Your feet were dancing, Alice,
              Seemed to dance on air,
         You looked like a ghost or angel
              In the starlight there.

         Your eyes were frosted starlight,
              Your heart, fire and snow.
         Who was it said 'I love you'?
ALICE: Mother, let me go!

Sassoon and Blunden are English, Graves Irish. The Irish clearness of sight, impatience with what seems to be a soft slowness in the Anglo-Saxon (which slow softness, without doubt, is accompanied by inexplicable poetic riches) is again exemplified. Nor is this all; for Graves is not content, as Sassoon has latterly been, with what he calls 'lingual exercises' (some poems containing lovely lines and evocative pictures), but must carry experiment in verse to a pitch of almost obstinate obscurity as he searches for satisfying forms. He cannot endure the long pages of Dickens, but must arduously rewrite and condense *David Copperfield* until the echoes ring with Dickensian wails. He now rewrites Roman history, tells the tale of his own life from early years and rouses conflict among all who remember what he remembers in a different mood and different sense, and battles long and unsparingly with his critics. Upon him the War has left, apparently, if he had it not before, a perfect fury for change and charge. Through the smoke of literary battle we must insist upon seeing the beauties of those earlier simplicities of diction; and must .insist also upon the fact that Graves's original talent is greater than his controversial prowess. He was a friend; he remains a poet.

VI. THE SITWELLS

> Let us prune the tree of language
> Of its dead fruit.
> Let us melt up the clichés
> Into molten metal;
> Fashion weapons that will scald and flay;
> Let us curb this eternal humour
> And become witty.

OSBERT SITWELL, *How Shall We Rise to Greet the Dawn?*

It is unfair to each member of the Sitwell family to treat them as a trinity, for while when they began they might be confused one with another, all that is now changed. Edith retells fairy stories in glittering coloured rhyme and revives the eccentricities of old Bath in demure prose; Osbert has taken to the essay; and Sacheverell has turned his attention to the Gothick in both architecture and music. But there has been in all these years something deliberate in that insistence upon being not three, but one; and now they are inseparable in the public mind. I am not sure, either, that there is not something which may be regarded as a common Sitwellian base, and since I must try to define what that is I shall ask readers to look again at the short quotation from Osbert's poem, *How Shall We Rise to Greet the Dawn?* They are all wits.

In the beginning, they were three *enfants terribles*. Being excluded, either by their own act or by the repulsion of the editorial canon, from *Georgian Poetry*, they established a counterblast to which they gave the name *Wheels*; and to this all three contributed greatly, adding jovial and insulting annotations with which they lambasted uncomplimentary reviewers. They indulged in japes, such as their successive entries in *Who's Who*, advertisements in the personal columns of *The Times*, and so on. They satirized their rivals, their so-called 'enemies,' in ribald poems, and sometimes did the same for social ladies whose fault was only that they were over-zealous in entertaining the latest lion in any art or craft. In this way they drew attention to themselves, and caused warier folk to shake heads at such mountebankery. The tactics obscured the talent.

But the Sitwells did not mind. They were not poor young men, struggling to find a public, but were very much in the fashionable world. They were more in the fashionable world than any other writers. Osbert, with the profile of a Roman emperor or a Hanoverian sovereign, with his cold eyes and merciless tongue; Sacheverell, tall, more patently a young poet, haughtier yet, and in early days unable to laugh without apparent physical pain; Edith like a sibyl, beautiful and highly mysterious; all three oddly kind and generous despite their diabolical skill in ridicule, they held upon their resolute way. The talent was theirs. It must be acknowledged. It must be acclaimed. Those who did not acclaim it were traitors, who must die the death.

Now the talent of all three is admitted, but is not in all quarters wholly approved. Osbert, who was always in such haste that he could not give satire the final polish which made Pope a master of his art, has found a fitter, more generous, less cabined medium in fiction which ranges from topography to irreverence. His writing, in prose, has a most admirable firmness and character; and if his characters are less real than fantastically recognizable, that makes them only the more amusing to all who are in the know (or wish they were). He amuses himself in amusing others. Sacheverell, whose talent as a poet was always more delicious than his brother's, ruminates (with wit) upon architecture and the nature of man, turning from lovely fancies about cowslips and other wild and garden flowers to speculation which may be endless upon an endless theme. Edith, who has collected and selected her own poems with impressive effect, anthologises upon principles so original that hatred for Matthew Arnold seems the only constant, and lends her wit to resuscitation of old and deadly figures of fun. And, between them, the three stand as one man for their chosen cause—the suppression of pulpy humour, and the exaltation of ruthlessness of thought and speech.

CHAPTER XIII: BLOOMSBURY

They, the few,
The chosen, the peculiar.
                                    M. R. MITFORD, *Rienzi.*

I

BEFORE saying another word about books, I must explain to
those who know no better that central London is mapped for
some forgotten reason into different quarters. Thus, Soho,
which lies between Shaftesbury Avenue on the south and some
not quite clearly defined point to the north of Oxford Street, is
the home of a part of London's foreign population and is a centre
for French and Italian restaurants; Belgravia is the old highly
fashionable district west of the Green Park, Mayfair the extraordinarily aristocratic section north of Piccadilly and east of
Hyde Park, and so on. And Bloomsbury, which I have made
the title of this chapter, lies to the north of New Oxford Street,
between Tottenham Court Road upon the one side and Gray's
Inn Road upon the other. It is the great quarter for squares
and private hotels, straight plain Georgian houses (but Georgian
in its eighteenth-century sense), publishers, a few prostitutes,
and, residentially, a kind of bourgeois or aesthetic - bourgeois
selectness. In it lie the British Museum and the great Found-
ling Hospital of Thomas Coram; and it is the spiritual home of
exiles from Cambridge University. It is an actual home for
some of them.

Other members of this fraternity, the so-called intelligentsia,
live upon the farther side of Tottenham Court Road, and these
are the artists and rebels; more still live in Chelsea, down by
the river Thames, where artists, poets, and mere frequenters of
studios have given rise to more self-expository novels than any
other class of people living at the present day. Such younger
aesthetes are not the real thing; they see themselves as characters
in a 'modn' tale by Murger or a satirical novel by Aldous
Huxley, and are of no account. The seat of intellectual *ton* lies
in Bloomsbury. There, in the shadow of learning's home from
home, Bloomsbury (as the embodiment of an assumption) feels

strongly its intellectual superiority to the rest of British man-kind. It represents culture. It is full of what Desmond MacCarthy (to whom Bloomsbury is a shrine, and even its parents sacrosanct) calls 'alert, original men and women' and what I call ill-mannered and pretentious dilettanti.

I must make two things clear. First that I write harshly of Bloomsbury from sheer malice. I have suffered no ill from Bloomsbury: whenever I have had any relation with its chief figures that relation has been mutually kind. My dislike of it (which I avow, although in writing of its leaders I shall try as usual to explain their incontestable excellences) is due entirely to what seems to me to be a conflict between its performance and its presumption. The second thing to be made clear is that —in consequence of my inability to share it—I believe the love of Bloomsbury on MacCarthy's part to be an aberration. I by no means include MacCarthy among my dilettanti. He is a critic with whom I seldom agree (that can't be helped); but he is an intelligent man, an excellent and informative talker (given, perhaps, to monologue, but ever courteous to interrupters), and he reads poetry very well indeed. His essays are always urbane, and his knowledge of books and people far greater than my own. And he does not live in Bloomsbury. He is only dazzled by its glory.

Whether that glory is genuine or not, I cannot say; it is not a modest glory, and for me modesty is the only true glory. It has no love for others; and for me a love of others, which was good enough for Shakespeare, is essential to the production of great literature. I call it pretentious, because it seems to me to claim aristocracy. Criticism it regards as *lèse-majesté*, and meets it, or anticipates it, with personal insult—but that, perhaps, is a consequence of not being quite sure of its own superiority to criticism? I think it bad manners.

I presume that there is another side to the picture; and that Bloomsbury really does imagine itself as suffering from the assaults of Philistia. I do not know why it should do so. If the complaint is that ordinary people are too stupid to read the books of Bloomsbury, that seems to me a paradox, and Mahomet, you remember, went to the mountain. If nobody read my books, I should be sorry; but I should think it was because they were not interesting. Bloomsbury, as to its own books, takes a different view. It wants to boss and impress people into reading what it has written, whether they like it or not; that is, it wants to be read from snobbery—a snobbery of culture—and by writing above the heads of Tom, Dick, and Harry, to lead Tom, Dick and Harry to higher things. In the same way, very stupid Englishmen shout in English at foreigners, and then say: 'They 're fools; they don't understand English.' It is a kind of insularity—insulatedness—of mind, and arises from lack of familiar contact with other modes of thought and feeling than its own.

The odd thing about that is that Bloomsbury is politically Left, and only intellectually Royalist—royalist, you understand, to itself. It has a powerful wish to dominate the Labour Party, but it will not do this in the end because it wants to form an aristocratic caucus, a kind of group dictatorship of brains, after I suppose, the Russian model, in ignorance of the fact that the English as a nation (apart from the unemployed) are practically a petty bourgeoisie. Further, it alienates the very people it would impress by its determined patronage of the arts (and artists) and a tremendous parade of refinement. Ostentatious refinement, indeed, is a part of its assertion of superiority; and I have so long believed all ostentation to be vulgar that I am sure Bloomsbury, at heart, is vulgar. It loves the eighteenth century—the wits, you know—and is fashionably coarse in its conversation. That you would expect, if you had read Hazlitt's book of talks with Northcote; for Northcote said (I have telescoped two passages):

As the common people sought for refinement as a *treat*, people in high life were fond of grossness as a relief to their overstrained affectation of gentility. . . . Fashion is gentility running away from vulgarity, and afraid of being overtaken by it. It is a sign the two things are not very far asunder.

It dresses distinctively and—in the female part of it—does its hair as Mrs Gaskell used to do hers a hundred years ago, wearing long earrings and in some way managing always to look sickly. When it laughs, it grimaces desperately; for its laughter is painfully self-conscious. It speaks with great affectation, introducing all the vowels into so simple a word as 'no.' It is conversationally insincere, what one would call 'strained'; but although its tones are the tones of wit I constantly hear far wittier talk at my club, where men think less of showing off than of contributing to the general gaiety. It is very sensitive and sarcastic ('ahrony'); is full of jealous contempts; is spiteful and resents being ignored, although it goes in a good deal for the wilful ignoring of others. And it has the impudence to accuse all who do not support its pretensions to superiority of being either fatuous or of selling the pass to the enemy. The enemy is Democracy.

II

Cambridge is a world of subdued tones, of excessively subtle humours, of prim conduct and free thinking; it fears the parent, but it has no fear of God; it offers amidst surroundings that vary between dinginess and antiquarian charm the inflammation of literature's purple draught.

H. G. WELLS, *The New Machiavelli.*

So much for Bloomsbury of the present day. It will have been noted that I spoke of it as the home of exiles from Cambridge University; and I should like to try and show, very briefly, how I think Bloomsbury came into being, and how in War-time and immediately after the War it found its opportunity for taking the town. If the account I have given of the progress of young warriors from idealistic patriotism to hatred of all civilians and old men is superficial, this will be equally superficial. The whole subject calls for much closer investigation than I can give it, and a more scholarly experience than mine. Nevertheless, if one could succeed in providing only a glimpse of groupings and directions it would be better than nothing at all.

Earlier in the book, I have drawn attention to the rise of what is not so much a convention of classicism as a convention of 'classiness' in our modern authors. Until we reached the novelists of the 'younger generation' very few of our subjects had been men and women educated at the older universities. They had been boys and girls who pushed themselves into notice as the result of character and talent, and not boys and girls whose education had lasted continuously from childhood until the twenty-third or twenty-fourth year of life, so that they reached London ignorant of practical experience of life but primed with omniscience. This convention has been much increased of late years, and while the younger critics are miniature pedagogues, the typical novelists are men of encyclopaedic display.

I shall timidly venture a guess at the reason for this change. It is that authorship, and particularly the writing of novels, has become a recognized career for highly educated men. In the past, novelists were first of all printers or hack-journalists, spinster ladies or writers to the signet; it was not until the Victorian day that they lived openly and creditably upon their royalties and could afford to be known socially as entertainers of the people. For a time then they glittered in the public eye, and were beloved. But when the Victorian heyday of novel-writing passed, and when other professions could absorb all the rising ambition, it was not smart to be a novelist. Sales were less remunerative; circulating libraries called the tune; competition with women was more intense than it had been. Young men of good birth or middle-class family went to the universities, and if a career was to be followed they entered politics or the Law. There was a great opening in medicine; or in the banking or shipping worlds; there was the Civil Service, Home and Indian, in which with constant expansion many plums could be gathered. And so on. Such university graduates as became novelists in those days slipped into novel-writing while they were briefless, or during holidays from banks, or because they found time hang heavy on their hands in some other respectable career. They never said in youth, as they do nowadays, that they were entering, not the Church or the Army, not Parliament or the Law, but the Novel.

But with the development of competitive examinations, the great growth of the scholarship system, and the overcrowding of the professions generally, it has been increasingly difficult to find openings for young men of good birth and ordinary talent. Until the British Broadcasting Corporation and the new Police Force came along, there offered to such men only the alternatives of Politics, the Bar, Schoolmastering, or Business. Now there is Literature as well. Hence the Pedagogishness. Talent and taste cannot be taught; but aesthetic rules can be taught, and if you call any aesthetic dogma a 'principle' it can be used ever after as something indubitable and made a foundation for artistic practice.

Around and since the War, Cambridge University has supplied England with all the intelligentsia it can do with. Among philosophers and scientific teachers, McTaggart, G. E. Moore, A. N. Whitehead, Lowes Dickinson, and Bertrand Russell make a formidable group. Roger Fry and Clive Bell had from 1913 onward a glorious aesthetic day (am I wrong in thinking it now in twilight?); and in the recent dazzling success of popularized astronomy Jeans and Eddington have taken every prize. There have been novelists and poets innumerable, from Rupert Brooke to *les jeunes*. From the—to me, first-class—biographical works of F. A. Simpson and the charming caricatures of Lytton Strachey, we have all drawn our sense of the prowess of the age in this department of letters. And if I were to continue in detail

I am sure everybody would suppose Cambridge the fount from which all learning and literary facility flow. Fortunately I shall be able to stop at this point; for I have said enough to show that Cambridge is a very much larger place than Bloomsbury, and yet a place to which Bloomsbury owes both its best names and a certain devastatingness of mind little touched by the curious gift of imagination. Imagination I take to be the faculty by means of which one enters into the minds of others and is not surprised to find them full of good things. That is not the only power of imagination; but it is the one most interesting to myself. If he has any intellect at all, a Cambridge man can bring his intellect to bear upon a subject, and in so far as the subject can be put into mathematical or philosophical form he is capable of understanding it and possibly of illuminating it. But until he has brought out all his critical apparatus he is at a disadvantage and is highly suspicious of the subject, his interlocutor's knowledge of the subject, and of the importance of the subject. Even then, he is impervious to outside suggestion. He knows best. It was a Cambridge don, I feel sure, who figured in Stanley Baldwin's story of the undergraduate and the don. The don said: 'I met your sister last night'; the undergraduate said: 'That was my mother; I have no sister.' The don said: 'I think, on reconsideration, you will find it was your sister.' For the reasons I have given, when they are not striking untrained persons such as myself as pedants, Cambridge intellectuals strike him as bigots.

III

L'inconvénient du règne de l'opinion, qui d'ailleurs procure *la liberté*, c'est qu'elle se mêle de ce dont elle n'a que faire; par exemple: la vie privée. De là la tristesse de l'Amérique et de l'Angleterre.

STENDHAL, *Le Rouge et le Noir*.

I must now return to the moment of the outbreak of war, because I wish to indicate what effect this outbreak had upon some sections of the civilian population, and particularly upon such writers as remained in civilian life. But before coming to the writers I want to speak of one or two things which seem pertinent to the assumption of the young poets that all civilians were morally responsible to the continuance and the horribleness of the War.

Never before in the history of modern England had the entire population been engaged in warfare. The Boer War, it is true, had produced a call for recruits; but it had been a very distant humiliation and it had been fought with the small British standing army against an enemy calculable in thousands. This European War was an immediate terror. The conditions were all new, frightful, and exceedingly disconcerting. The English are not a warlike people (their great generals, for the most part, have been Irishmen and Scotsmen); and they did not at first realize how much the War was going to interfere with the life of nearly everybody in the land. Taken aback by unexpected calamity, they looked about them—it was instinctive in a peace-loving people—for reassuring catchwords; and while some of the youngest and most ardent, and the least thoughtful of all, shouted in the way of mobs, the elders hung upon the words of statesmen—who solemnly declared that 'we shall not sheathe the sword,' and thereby I am sure created unconsciously a new test of sobriety—or prophet-journalists such as Horatio Bottomley, or any other speakers or writers who could give them a verbal straw to clutch. Some genius at that moment seized upon a crucial aspect of the civilian problem. He said: 'Business as usual.'

That phrase was afterwards greatly condemned; but at the moment of utterance it was as excellent as the 'Keep calm, ladies and gentlemen,' of any theatre manager who soothes an audience in terror of fire. In effect, it said: 'Don't rush madly to the exits; you'll only be in the way. Wait until you are told what to do.' Casuists distorted it in a thousand ways, pretending that it was the cry of the profiteer, a smugness, an effort to ignore the War, and so on. They were wrong in doing this. The War brought many base things to the surface, horrible things; but I should include among these an intense and revolting self-righteousness upon the part of those who prided themselves upon being in a minority. 'Business as usual' was only a phrase; but it was a phrase calculated to calm a population better employed then in going about its daily work than in yielding to hysteria. Misuse of the phrase grew; but by that time the country had settled down to the War, had forgotten some of its idealism, and was dealing in cliché.

This brings me to another point. It was made a cause of accusation against the elders that they said: 'This is a young man's war.' That, too, became a cliché. But then, contrary to E. M. Forster's view that Dickens's characters were unreal because they were embodied repetitions, the majority of English people express themselves by means of stereotyped phrases.

They are not ready with eloquence. However deeply they feel, the words which issue from their lips are often enough stale old maxims which fastidious modern writers take elaborate pains to avoid. 'This is a young man's war' meant, not, as the indignant have tried to prove, 'we old men have made a war; thank God we haven't got to fight in it,' but 'I am ashamed of my own uselessness.' It was an apology; that it became perfunctory, and was soon perverted by pacificists into 'this is an old man's war,' is true; but the first impulse was genuine.

However, opponents of the participation of Great Britain in any war whatever must fasten as they can upon phrase and bogy. It is thought that they are dishonest, that they are prigs, that they hate their native land, that they are such physical cowards that (taking advantage of personal immunity) they shout affronts from safe places. All these things are untrue. Some of them are prigs, some are physical cowards, some are dishonest; but most pacificists are either moral or intellectual pedants, and in most of them a love of England and belief in her superiority to all other lands whatever has attained a fantastic height. They really do believe that England leads the world; and that if England would but hang herself in olive branches and go forth unarmed all other peoples would be so impressed that they would follow suit and the millennium be attained. But they are not markedly courteous to opponents in their advocacy of this course, and might be not inaptly called militant pacificists.

When the War broke out, while poets and common men rushed at least to offer themselves as sacrifices to truth (or what they believed to be truth), many intellectuals who were fixed in their ways refused to recognize it as a fact. They had supposed war to be an anachronism; they had proved conclusively that it would not pay; and they said they would by no means endorse the action of any Government which allowed the country to be dragged into any conflict. To heated (but stereotyped) inquiries as to what they would do if their houses were on fire, and did they want to be ruled by Germans, etc., they returned various answers. They thought they were guided by principles; but perhaps they were only incapable of departing from theory.

Moreover, there were other elements in their argument. Nearly all intellectuals of that day were or had been old-fashioned Liberals, and to old-fashioned Liberals Tsarist Russia had long been the Great Peril to Peace. They considered France as militarist and intransigent. They had German educational memories, or German social connections; and one at least of them, Arthur Ponsonby, had written and published a pamphlet called *Democracy and the Control of Foreign Affairs* (1912) in which the definitely anti-German trend of British foreign policy was arraigned and condemned. In so far, therefore, as there was any political leaning on the part of these Liberals it was in the direction of Germany. But they were not 'pro-German,' as was hastily said by the idiotic; their real interest was not in Germany but in the rectitude of their own country.

Now a zeal for rectitude can be very obstinate. It can be humourless. It can be a bigotry. For as you remember Macaulay says:

> The doctrine which from the very first origin of religious dissensions, has been held by all bigots of all sects, when condensed into a few words, and stripped of rhetorical disguise is simply this: I am in the right, and you are in the wrong. When you are the stronger you ought to tolerate me; for it is your duty to tolerate truth. But when I am the stronger, I shall persecute you; for it is my duty to persecute error.

These men, being in a minority, felt themselves wronged. Some of them insisted, in the spirit of martyrdom or the spirit of obstinate consistency, upon saying things on behalf of truth which to the Government of the day, heavy with responsibility for winning the War, seemed unhelpful. One or two of them were sent to prison.

Their disciples, who also refused to acknowledge the War, and who were of military age, suffered a good deal—I am not denying that the stupidest and most unimaginative people in the country, being narrow patriots in a funk, were terribly active in persecution—and, when conscription was introduced into England, were forced into the ranks of what were called 'conscientious objectors.' Conscientious objectors were supposed to be men who had a religious aversion from the idea of taking life; these more intellectual objectors were opposed to participation in any war because they thought war a stupid barbarism and because they saw no reason why they should be compelled to fight against their wills. Some of them were merely opinionated young men; others were men of such high principles that they would have died rather than sacrifice them. All, by their comfortably 'indispensable' critics in the Jingo press, were labelled 'pasty-faces.'

Among those who went to prison for his opinions was Bertrand

Russell, who on the outbreak of the War was a lecturer at Trinity College, Cambridge (of which college he was a scholar); and possibly the most distinguished of all the intellectual objectors was Lytton Strachey. There were many others who similarly objected, and where they were men known in good society they were sometimes lucky enough to be found what was called 'alternative' service, which left them at large and with time to follow normal pursuits. Others were less fortunate. Most of those whose names were known in the literary world, and who did not serve in France or the East, remained alive, and augmented the number of their publications. But they, too, like the young officers represented by Owen and Sassoon, were displeased with the turn things had taken. They had come into conflict with authority, with patriotism at its crassest; and, having by their action in resisting military service revealed obstinacy and some moral courage, they decidedly had moved in opinion towards something like political anarchy. A kind of moral anarchy had already been brought into existence by other circumstances; and this was quickly rationalized. The way was being opened for that post-War world of fruitless intolerance which is finding literary expression in the highly theorized work of the intelligentsia of all countries.

IV. BERTRAND RUSSELL

Even if the open windows of science at first make us shiver after the cosy indoor warmth of traditional humanizing myths, in the end the fresh air brings vigour, and the great spaces have a splendour of their own.

B. RUSSELL, *What I Believe.*

I have no business to write about Bertrand Russell—even as a writer: I am quite incompetent to discuss mathematics—while I ignore his greater mathematical collaborator, Whitehead; and yet I shall do so for the reason that Russell is known to me and Whitehead is not (I speak in two senses), and for the further reason that Russell has far more directly influenced young England than Whitehead has done.

Bertrand Russell belongs to one of the oldest aristocratic families in England, which I learn has been traced back as far as the god Thor. His grandfather, the first Earl Russell, was third son of the sixth Duke of Bedford, and Bertrand Russell himself, although it would be unbecoming in him, as a Communist, to use his title, is the third Earl. He was born in 1872.

In person he is not very tall, is thin, has a good deal of grey hair, a long clean-shaven upper lip and receding chin, and in conversation wears at all times a pleasant smile which is neither dry nor indulgent but which has in it the elements of both dryness and indulgence. His eyes, which one immediately notices, are luminous and amused. They are very intelligent eyes, bright and clear: I think they may be blue, but if not blue they are a particularly lively grey. His voice has no volume; it is slightly donnish, a buzzing tone vocalized chiefly between the tip of the tongue and the front teeth (I seem to hear him saying 'Yiss, yiss' without opening his mouth at all). He lectures well and interestingly but without zest; I presume in the way that men lecture at our older universities, rather conversationally. Several of his books consist of reprinted lectures. In talk he is considerate and friendly, does not laugh much (according to my recollection), but pays heed to what is said and is amused by it. He makes no attempt to shine; but is witty enough when need arises.

Russell is a mathematician, a sceptic, and a Communist. He believes in the utmost freedom for every human being (and for some years ran a school for children who were supposed to do whatever they pleased); and at the same time he demands that the will of the individual should be subordinated to the good of the community. His belief is that 'the good life is one inspired by love and guided by knowledge,' but when he defines love he is constrained to do so by means of the chilly word 'benevolence,' which in turn he defines as 'an indissoluble combination of the two elements, delight and well-wishing.' Ecstasy is rather outside his sympathy. In the same way, his definition of knowledge is 'scientific knowledge and knowledge of particular facts.' Wisdom, which lies less in a knowledge of facts than in a true interpretation of them, is unprovable, and therefore interests him little. Art, which is a mystery, is for him but a department of metaphysics. His universe is a material universe; his ideal world represents for me a tyranny of the reason.

But when he is presented with a moral question, Russell judges it, as far as I can tell, with as much prejudice as you or I would show. He has a great dislike of parents, schoolmasters, policemen, and judges—all of whom represent for him embodiments of authority. He hates the English public-school system, on the ground (among others, perhaps) that it encourages public schoolboys to imagine themselves better than other boys. I feel bound here to say that the men in England who now attack the public-school system show no sign of humility; their line seems rather to be that they are as much superior to ordinary public schoolboys as ordinary public schoolboys are superior to the rest of mankind.   Perhaps this arrogance does not strike themselves: it is evident to others.   In Russell's case there is a contempt for the herd.   Whether he knows that the herd is made up of individuals, I cannot say: I suspect that, being a logician and mathematician, he regards the herd as a dehumanized extension of the individual, and represents it in his mind by an algebraical sign.

His importance to the present age, and incidentally to this portion of my book, lies in the fact that he has given a lead to the 'modns.'   He resisted the War upon intellectual grounds; he wanted to try the method of non-resistance to aggression, which he thought would disorganize the Germans.   That showed that he was no realist; and that he was less psychologist than logician. But he was courageous, and those who thought him a crank and a danger to his country respected his courage.   They put him in prison—a sure sign of respect.   But his opinions could not be put in prison; and those men whom he had taught shared them. They, too, as I have related, opposed themselves to the Government in an emergency; they, too, made their claim to be above the State's command.   Several of them put into excellent literary form a protest against compulsion of any kind.   In so doing, they were conscious of going against the spirit of their countrymen; and became in a sense philosophic rebels, justifying rebellion upon logical grounds.   They began more and more eagerly to consider the different forms of ideal government which had been suggested in the course of history by Plato, More, Hobbes, Morris, and Wells.   They looked abroad, to the continent of Europe; where, since the War, many forms of government have been tried.   Democracy as England knew it, which was in effect government by the illiterate herd, would no longer answer.   It gave no scope to superior brains.

What alternatives were there to Democracy?   The Russian Revolution gave one answer; but Bertrand Russell did not feel satisfied with what he saw in Russia in 1920, and he said so. Bolshevism was too much like government by the herd to suit what I must repeat is essentially an aristocratic temper.   The common good was still his aim; but it was a common good reached through such liberty for the individual that every individual was an aristocrat.   No authority ought to impose an arbitrary will upon men; all men should work for the good life by following their own untrammelled desires. Somehow their desires, fulfilled, would provide happiness for all. The lines, limitlessly extended, never cross, because they are all straight, and all aspiring. Not England, where freedom is destroyed by the Christian doctrine of rewards and punishments; not Russia, where things, although different, are hardly any better; China, possibly (for he has visited China, and like other visiting English philosophers has been much impressed by the atmosphere of pure philosophy reigning there); not America — but Utopia is the ideal. In Utopia alone, where men are automata, things will be better, more logical, freer from the horrors of man-made authority.

There speaks the thoroughly dissatisfied man; the man who, in common with so many of the intellectual Left, is out of harmony with his fellow-creatures and curiously distorts their good nature, their selfishness, their absorbingly interesting manifestations of virtue and cruelty, and their unruliness, into a malignant system by which Bertrand Russell is oppressed and to which he opposes an uncompromising resistance. Russell can give you his analysis of social ills and his plan for a new and better world with the utmost clearness. His extensions are all accurately calculated, his arguments all well expressed. He is entirely convincing. If you want proof, he offers proof. If you are prejudiced, he confirms prejudice. He seems to win you not by heady eloquence, but by sober facts, facts, facts. If those facts are your type of facts, he is incontrovertible; for his argument from the facts is the argument of a considerable logician.

But for some people, such as myself, to whom logic is the enemy of truth, Russell is an unconvincing pleader. I think I know why it is so in my own case. It is because, sympathizing with so many of his views and assumptions, I find him entirely unreal in his pictures of life. They do not correspond to anything familar in my own experience. He speaks, it is true, of men and women; but not of men and women as I have ever known them—as strange persecuting brutes, judges, policemen, schoolmasters, parents; all oppressors. These people, I say to myself, have never been anything but kind to me; the men and women—and then suddenly I realize that when Bertrand Russell says 'men and women' he is not in fact talking about men and women at all. He is thinking of them, not as souls, or as Brown, Jones, Swinnerton, or Horatio Bottomley, but as x and y, j and k. He does not know them, and cannot think of them, as anything else. He is incapable of knowing men and women. They are no more to him than tables and chairs; much less—until they put him in prison for what they regard as irrelevance—than the quantum theory.

When once you have realized that about Bertrand Russell, you have encountered his paralysing limitation as a social philosopher. His training in logic and mathematics has given him a wonderful intellectual instrument, but he can only think upon straight lines. For him, knowledge is knowledge of demonstrable facts. In a world full of unreason he can only deal with phenomena by treating them as forces. To him the word 'magistrate' is the power to punish; 'good' the fulfilment of a positive desire; 'love' a combination of delight and well-wishing; of the abstract or the mystic he has no conception, for the impulsive and irrational no formula and no patience. The suggestion that a man may know everything and understand nothing would be meaningless to him. In that respect he is typical of the modern temper, dominated by a sense of the laws of science and economics, proud of its intellect and its formulae, but out of touch with men and women. Men and women, indeed, unless they are represented, for statistical purposes, as figures or letters, mean as much as that 'Man Power' upon which strategists used to lecture during the War, which is as much as to say that they are counters. To such counters, hypothetical as they are, hypothetically ideal freedom may be easily granted. One can picture a world of counters and rules, highly satisfying to scientists. But it is not the world as it exists to-day; and when the desires of real men conflict with Bertrand Russell's desires these men become in his view a mob, and their common view a tyranny to which anarchy is the only possible response. This is the aristocratic attitude; and can be held to-day only by those who favour dictatorship and those who are doctrinaires. Russell, politically, is a doctrinaire. The fact that he is also a very brilliant writer and philosopher has helped him to spread doctrinaire views throughout that small section of 'alert, original men and women' to whom imagination is a lost faculty.

V. ROGER FRY AND CLIVE BELL

Every company is differently circumstanced and has its peculiar cant and jargon; which may give occasion to wit and mirth within that circle, but would seem flat and insipid in any other.

CHESTERFIELD, *Letters to His Son.*

When we take a step forward to the aesthetic views of Bloomsbury we are in a different country from that inhabited by

Bertrand Russell. We are not concerned with facts, but emotions, and not concerned with general emotions, but with something which Fry and Bell seem both inclined to specify as a particular emotion, the aesthetic. The history of aesthetics must remain outside our purview; but it is necessary to remark upon the fact that a little more than sixty years ago certain artists revolted against what had previously been considered unbreakable rules in representational art. Whistler and his colleagues, who became known as Impressionists, claimed to be 'pure' artists, in the sense that they wanted not to go on painting in accordance with common knowledge of the nature of objects, but to present something else, the artists' unspoilt and unsophisticated vision of appearance. Put crudely, this claim was to the effect 'I *know* a table has four legs; but to me it looks like a shiny pool in the midst of shadow, and that is how I shall represent it. Stand away, close your eyes, peer, and see if you don't find something new—eh?' They were in revolt against literalism. The fact that their revolt was but a stage in the progress of art need not concern us here.

What concerns us is that when once Whistler and his fellow-workers had established Impressionism those who followed them carried the ideas of Impressionism farther and farther until they managed altogether to substitute design for representation, and to paint pictures which were not so much accomplished portraits of recognizable objects as (superficially) blobs of colour communicating inexplicable emotion to the beholder. The English public knew nothing, or very little, about the new movement among painters; for it occurred in France. But in 1911, a year after King George came to the throne, there was a sensation in London. An exhibition was held of paintings by some men who were called 'Post-Impressionists.' Screams and catcalls filled the air; one hastened to observe the newest horrors and decry them; or—either with sincerity or in the pursuit of taste—one reverently prostrated oneself before a tremendous innovation in the aesthetic ideas of the age.

But instead of passing away, Post-Impressionism stayed; and the man who by chance had been responsible for the gathering of those pictures which had made the fuss was Roger Fry. Now Fry was all his life a painter and a critic of art. He was more than that: he was a truly creative intelligence. Born in 1866, he had taken a science degree at Cambridge and had then turned his mind to the study of painting, which he followed in Paris after leaving King's College. Being, as I presume, of independent means, he was always free to follow his own bent; and being, unquestionably, a man of altogether exceptional taste and sincerity, he never collated his writings in order to make quite sure that each was strictly consistent with all the others. The consequence is that he really progressed with the years. He was one of the few men who learnt wisdom by experience: that is a sure sign of greatness. Not an absolutely first-class painter, he during the whole of his life interested himself in, and was never obsessed by, aesthetic theory, and his influence in that department of speculation upon men born in the eighties has been of great and ever-increasing virtue.

He himself dated some part of his development from a reading of Tolstoy's *What is Art?*, that powerful, sometimes profound, and absurd and self-confuting book, in which a moralist, after pointing out that art is a means of communicating the emotions, then establishes to his own satisfaction that the only proper purpose of art is the promotion of good deeds. Tolstoy's theory would set a lively tract above the greatest paintings, symphonies, and plays and novels ever written. Naturally Fry was much too subtle a person to be deceived by any such assumption; and so he took what was valuable in Tolstoy's essay and proceeded to the creation of his own aesthetic.

He was not the only man to be doing this round about the turn of the century. Croce, the Italian philosopher, who was born in the same year as Fry, elaborately divides the mind of man into two faculties, the imaginative and the rational, the first taking the form of aesthetic activity, the second of philosophy, and builds upon this a tremendous structure. Less ambitious than Croce, whom he much admired, Arthur Clutton-Brock, who must have been almost contemporary, and a friend of Fry's, did not as far as I know systematize his aesthetic theory, but applied exceptional sensitiveness to the study of individual paintings and individual books. All three were active at the same time; and of the three Fry published least. When he said anything he said it modestly and briefly and with great persuasiveness. You can find most of his opinions charmingly and beautifully expressed in a single volume of essays called *Vision and Design*.

Fry did not write a sustained defence of Post-Impressionism; but a friend of his, Clive Bell, did; and Clive Bell's *Art* provided a rallying point for all who in 1914 were for the new as against the old. It was a tremendously amusing book for anybody; really witty, really brilliant; quite different in tone and lack of charity from Fry's writings. Fry quietly and gravely sets out his idea, first that 'Morality appreciates emotion by the standard of resultant action. Art appreciates emotion in and for itself,' and second that:

I think we are all agreed that we mean by significant form something other than agreeable arrangements of form, harmonious patterns, and the like. We feel that a work which possesses it is the outcome of an endeavour to express an idea rather than to create a pleasing object. Personally, at least, I always feel that it implies the effort on the part of the artist to bend to our emotional understanding by means of his passionate conviction some intractable material which is alien to our spirit.

But Bell, using that same term, 'significant form,' is by no means as tentative. He has not only the business of defending an idea, but the enjoyable task of demolishing a million popular pictures. He leaps to it (as Mrs Benson said Robert Hugh Benson leapt towards the Roman Catholic faith) 'as a lover to his mistress.' Not content with demolishing pictures, he scatters through his pages a little general literary knowledge, vivacious statements about himself as a student of music and archaeology, about the Gothic, about Renaissance millionaires (they 'could be vulgar and brutal, but they were great gentlemen'), and many other things. The effect now is less positively impressive than it was in 1914, but Bell was younger then, and the critical world was less nobly aloof from poor mortals than its present demand for 'the best only' would allow.

He was born in 1881, so that he must have been thirty-three when *Art* was published. In the book he first discussed the nature of art, then its relations with religion, history, and ethics, then its history, and finally Post-Impressionism as theory, practice, and influence. But the important part of his work was precisely his attempt to define what it is in any work of art which establishes its claim to be art. He said:

Either all works of visual art have some common quality, or when we speak of 'works of art' we gibber. Every one speaks of 'art,' making a mental classification by which he distinguishes the class 'works of art' from all other classes. What is the quality common and peculiar to all members of this class? Whatever it be, no doubt it is often found in company with other qualities; but they are adventitious—it is essential. There must be some one quality without which a work of art cannot exist; possessing which, in the least degree, no work is altogether worthless. What is this quality? What quality is shared by all objects that provoke our aesthetic emotions? What quality is common to Sta. Sophia and the windows at Chartres, Mexican sculpture, a Persian bowl, Chinese carpets, Giotto's frescoes at Padua, and the masterpieces of Poussin, Piero della Francesca, and Cézanne? Only one answer is possible

—significant form.   In each, lines and colours combined in a particular way, certain forms and relations of forms stir our aesthetic emotions.   These relations and combinations of lines and colours, these aesthetically moving forms, I call 'Significant Form'; and 'Significant Form' is the one quality common to all works of visual art.

The quality, the assertiveness, and the seriousness of Clive Bell are all indicated in that extract.   You see the admirable and urgent talker who has hit upon a hypothesis completely satisfying to himself, and who has but to look about the world for illustrations of a theory to find them.   Bell is much more of a dogmatist than Fry.   He is compelled for the sake of his theory to restrict significant form to works of visual art; although it might be competent to a sceptic to say: 'If this one quality is shared by buildings and pictures and carpets, surely it ought to be found in works of literature?'   Bell would agree at once to that.   But when he leaves pictures he is forced to change the terms of his theory and to allow dissentients to substitute 'reality' or 'rhythm' as explanatory words.   Now I am not an aesthete; but I cannot help thinking that all these words are a substitute for what the Admirable Crichton called a 'Je ne sais quoi.'   We know that we receive some positive and delightful impression from what we style a work of art, and that a book which draws easy tears is a bad book; but while something in us demands that whatever we respond to emotionally (aesthetically) shall not be inane the word 'form' has so often to change its significance that it threatens to be meaningless.   That is, it is only an x, an unknown quantity; and whether we call it significant form or rhythm or reality we are meaning the same thing but have not yet found a completely satisfying definition.   For this reason 'Significant Form' has passed into limbo.   We have to-day other and equally marvellous aesthetic theories, which will also, in good time, join 'Significant Form.'

Clive Bell himself I should describe as a bubbler.   He bubbles with high spirits and laughter.   He is very pale, and his hair has been rather tawny.   He has great vivacity of manner, and that very nervous laugh which I have already mentioned is always trying to run away with him.   He is extremely pleasant in conversation; but in written controversy has some of the traits of a Bloomsbury retaliator.   His riposts to critics, for example, in The Athenaeum for which he wrote under Murry's editorship, make painful reading, especially when he is in the wrong.   But he is a man of lively mind, genuinely sensitive to the beautiful; and Art is both a milestone in aesthetic theory

and a work of entertainment deserving well of all shrinkers from
the dreary.

VI. GILES LYTTON STRACHEY

What then is the charm, the irresistible charm, of Walpole's
writings? It consists, we think, in the art of amusing without
exciting. He never convinces the reason or fills the imagination, or
touches the heart; but he keeps the mind of the reader constantly
attentive and constantly entertained. . . . If we were to adopt the
classification, not a very accurate classification, which Akenside
has given of the pleasures of the imagination, we should say that
with the Sublime and Beautiful Walpole had nothing to do, but
that the third province, the Odd, was his peculiar domain.

Macaulay on Horace Walpole.

Lytton Strachey was fairly tall, but his excessive thinness,
almost emaciation, caused him to appear endless. He had a
rather bulbous nose, the spectacles of a British Museum bookworm, a large and straggly dark brown beard (with a curious
rufous tinge); no voice at all. He drooped if he stood upright,
and sagged if he sat down. He seemed entirely without vitality;
and most people would have mistaken him for an elderly professor of languages who was trying to remember some grammatical rule which he had forgotten all about. Sad merriment
was in his eye, and about him a perpetual air of sickness and
debility.

But he had a sportive mind. If one could have seen behind
that disguising beard, one might possibly have found that he
was smiling. Certainly he was amused by anybody dead; he
may have been amused by one yet alive. He had the power
to read an official biography (that was what he had done in the
case of his first four subjects), think about it, and produce what
was not so much a portrait as a likeness. He knew how to
exaggerate a trait and give it an air of nature, how to contrast
one man with another, how to select that slightly ridiculous
aspect which is in each one of us, and, by pressing gently upon
our elbows, to draw attention to a comic stranger just as that
stranger was about to pass. He was always in time to snap the
ridiculous.

But he did not confine himself to the ridiculous. It was said,
when he began to collect material for his book on Queen Victoria,
that he had an unsurpassed comic character for extended lam-
poon; but as the months passed, and Strachey found out more
and more about the queen who was to be his subject, he found

laughter fade before a growing respect, admiration, affection.
Well, that is the note of his *Queen Victoria*, amused and respect-
ful malice. He found her a queen after all, a real person sur-
rounded by Teutonic artists, governesses, husbands, and uncles.
At the others he laughed very continuously; but for Queen
Victoria he developed something of a love.

And when Strachey had finished writing about Queen Victoria
he could not make up his mind what he would write about next.
His favourite reading (easy reading, I think) was among the
memoirs of the eighteenth century, Horace Walpole's chief
among them, and the first half of the nineteenth century; and
here he found material for admirable brief sketches. But a
large subject, one fit to follow that of a queen, did not suggest
itself. He played for some time with the notion that he could
write a new biography of Charles Darwin; but that notion came
to nothing. At last — I know not upon what impulse — he
carried his mind back to another queen, and one who had been
as great in her own day as Victoria, perhaps yet greater than
Victoria. Why he should have chosen Elizabeth, queen of a
time of which his knowledge was—by comparison with the
eighteenth century—so small, can only be told by somebody who
knew him. But the book he wrote, successful though it was in
the matter of popular reception, was in the larger sense a failure.
It has few friends.

It was the last long book he was to attempt, and for the rest
of his life he dwelt again upon familiar themes, such as Voltaire,
of whom he made such a hero in his *Landmarks in French
Literature*. I presume that his strength was ebbing, and that
he could no longer venture upon ambitious work; if, indeed, it
was not apparent to him that the short sketch was peculiarly
his *métier*.

It was his *métier* because he had an admirable gift for the
picturesque, a quick rather than a powerful mind, and a habit,
which is not unlike the romantic novelist's habit, of dramatizing
every scene he described. He could browse through a book of
memoirs and then sketch the writer of those memoirs; a lightning sketch such as one used to see executed in music-halls by
clever artists with charcoal and colossal sheets of paper. Instantly recognizable, nose, hat, strut, haw-haw, and baggy
trousers or sharp-pointed collar. When Strachey's first drawings
were made in *Eminent Victorians*, the contrast between Manning
and Newman was just such as a dexterous artist would choose—
light and dark, the world and the spirit, vigour and weakness.

When his last elaborate drawing, of the Elizabethan era, was attempted, the contrasts in a rapid narrative were necessarily so numerous that they had to be more and more heightened, and in the end *Elizabeth and Essex* is more like costume drama than history.   No wonder Virginia Woolf, in a list of half a dozen approved Georgian novelists, included Strachey.   Though he had not the power to invent stories, he loved effects, and he could get them.

Some of the best of his effects were obtained in the short and excellent *Landmarks in French Literature*.   There he was completely master of the material he wished to use.   He could explain and defend Racine against English distaste for the neo-classic, could rejoice in the badinage of Marivaux and the brilliance of Diderot, and could to perfection picture dramatically the life and person of Voltaire, for whom he had great laughing admiration.   Indeed, the eighteenth-century world of wits and poets and letter-writers was his natural element.   He knew it, so to speak, at first hand, in all those letters of Walpole and Madame de Sévigné, the Marquise du Deffand, Madame de Grafigny, Madame d'Épinay, and the rest; in the *Memoirs* of Saint-Simon, the *Conefssions* of Rousseau, and a hundred more. He knew it at second hand in the *Causeries du Lundi* of Sainte-Beuve and that string of French inquirers to whom we owe such curious and interesting glimpses into the manners of a past age. To a man of education and some leisure, a taste for wit and a love of oddity, this whole literature of the personal is an inexhaustible store of delight; and that was what it proved to Strachey. Though he wrote more ambitiously, he never, I think, wrote so much from his own enthusiasm as he did in *Landmarks in French Literature*.

Sainte-Beuve, I shall continue to believe, was the prime literary inspiration of Strachey's life.   That does not mean that he copied Sainte-Beuve.   He brought to such memoirs as he wrote his own characteristic manner of approach.   But his inspiration was from the French.   The inspiration of Bloomsbury has always been from the French.   Roger Fry and Clive Bell owe much to their study in Paris; Strachey to his reading in French memoirs; Virginia Woolf to encouraging acquaintance, at least, with Proust's endless masterpiece of psychologizing and memory; T. S. Eliot to his reading in French poets who for the most part are unintelligible to English readers.   And in Strachey's case, particularly, the brevity and illuminatingness of Sainte-Beuve's portraits was a clear call to similar work.   He had wit and malice enough to point every likeness; he had a clear, if not profound, sense of character; a pen free and vivid. To these obvious literary gifts he brought the temperament of a physically feeble person who could not endure the boisterousness of aggressive men and therefore sat aside and ridiculed it.

He was on the side of the weak, those who could not fight for themselves. He had a real shrinking from the loud and efficient, the smug and successful. He did not like them, and could not crush them; but he could think of all sorts of amusing things to say about them. He disliked the force of Cardinal Manning and Arnold of Rugby; he felt that Florence Nightingale was something of a busybody, one of these go-getters; he resented the industry of the Prince Consort, the solemnity of those Germans who came to the English Court and held their sway. They were all serious, and although he did not mean to misrepresent them he saw them as butts. His reaction from them was nervous; the result of his own inability to cope with a world apparently (I mean, in his eyes) given over to the strong and vulgar. He had not the ecstasies of the eremite; but he had something of the spirit that drives a man to sit alone in a cave for the sake of spiritual peace. Unlike the eremite, he had a very curious, rather donnish, interest in the human species, and if men were dead he could laugh at them with a good deal of satisfaction. Quite half the pleasure we obtain from Strachey is due to the fact that he amuses us at the expense of others.

His deficiencies arise, possibly, from a lack of intellectual intercourse with men of different breeding and culture from himself. He did not care for such men. He may have thought them, as Dr Johnson thought the girls, 'wretched' and 'un-ideaed'; but more probably he was paralysed in their company, as bookish people often are, and unable to shine. All his work was taken from books, and not from men. He was a bookworm and a talker with bookworms, a male bluestocking. That he was personally very kind I am sure; but in his writings his kindness is only for the weak, or for weakness in the strong. Owing to a shortage of emotional power (perhaps to self-consciousness), he becomes slightly sentimental when he leaves off laughing and tries seriously to sympathize, and this causes him to fall into a falsity indicated either by tremendously careful, cat-stepping use of language or into a kind of writing sacred to romantic novelists of the days when Strachey was a boy. But for the most part he prefers to keep his subjects at arm's length, in case he should pity them, or they should hurt him; and so by holding them up—how small they grow when so held!—he is able to exhibit them very prettily to our eyes. Homunculi to a man!

He does this with such skill that we are greatly diverted. He does not pretend that he has created his characters out of nothing, or out of a deep research into archives, but honestly gives us the material from which he has drawn information and from which we, too, could draw that same information, though without being able to emulate his delicate caricature of the real men. He is not a scholar, but a reader and lover of memoirs. His idol was Horace Walpole, and his ideal life was that led by eighteenth-century ladies and gentlemen who had little to do but —it seems—gather together and produce their well-rehearsed wit or write long and engaging letters to and fro describing what had happened in the polite society to which they belonged. He was not equally at home with the English life of a century earlier, as *Elizabeth and Essex*, in spite of its gallantry, shows. He could picture the Regency, for that was a sophisticated era in some respects not unlike our own, and almost voluptuously documented with authentic letters and diaries. But he shrank a little from the multitude and splendour of the Elizabethan age, which he found inexplicable by any rules learnt at Cambridge. Its combination of savagery and poetry, sweetness and lust, had little enough of the refined humdrum of Strachey's own life, and yet, since its living works could not be gainsaid, it was beyond reach of the shuddering hand with which he drew a curtain between himself and current vulgarity. Of whatever happens in the everyday homes of modern England he knew, and wished to know, nothing at all.

VII

The Stracheyan method had its imitators. Clever writers observed his success in puppetry and his use of the discovery that all sorts of things happened at the same moment in time; and having noticed both these facts they jumped into Stracheyan biography as wasps jump into jars of beer. Their sense of chronology was poor, and there came a time when they said recklessly that certain things had happened simultaneously which in fact had been separated by many years, and were rightly exposed as quacks. That whole simultaneous action business was a trick, and Strachey had used it as much as it could be used. It was a facile way of stippling in background or chiaroscuro. Furthermore, the de-bunking biography became a craze. Writers set out, with none of Strachey's skill, to make game of famous men. They took their man, called him throughout 'Mr' or by some Christian name which struck them as ludicrous, and in showing off their own cleverness took all the character out of him. Great men were butchered to make a smart suburban holiday. The proceedings became scandalous, and at last, fortunately, boring to all, so that any examples of the method which are now offered to the public are felt to have been more than three days dead. It is a great injustice to Strachey to associate him with such deplorable guying. His success, however, was so great that it was an encouragement to others.

It was an encouragement, possibly, to Philip Guedalla, who lives no nearer Bloomsbury than Bayswater and who had taken history at Oxford with satisfactory results. In the intervals of standing for Parliament in the interests of a moribund party, Guedalla—who began publishing books of poetry and parody in very early days—was writing portraits of great men. He was at first content with quite brief essays; but he grew bolder, and with an able, laborious, and over-jewelled gift for portraiture carried on the method of slightly ribald biography until he reached the Duke of Wellington. Now the Duke of Wellington was, without doubt, a great character. The memoirs of Greville, Croker, and Creevey, to name only three of the most famous men who make their day gossip again for our benefit, constantly provide delicious examples of the Duke's speech; his dealings with a lady who tried to frighten him are celebrated. One might have expected Guedalla to take the easy course of making him a figure of fun. To his credit, he preferred to write a serious book; and that book is far better than anything else he has written. It is both a portrait of a great man, and an historical account of a great soldier's campaigns abroad and at home. It is serious, ambitious, and sincere. Would that Guedalla did not consider himself a wit! I do not mean, by this, that he is without wit; I mean merely that, as Selden said, 'wit is upon the sudden turn,' and that there is never absent from Guedalla's pages an elaborateness of turning. Any reader who loves spontaneity will regret this fact; for Guedalla is an honest worker, and does not depend upon gems of style to dazzle us into recognition of the trouble he has taken to learn the truth about a period.

By comparison with Guedalla, the other exponents of the Stracheyan method are slight practitioners (when they come from Germany, they are heavy enough, although I have surprisedly heard fashionable ladies praise Ludwig's style for its 'economy of words'); and no doubt these writers have done good by bringing conciseness, if not irreverence, into biographical writing. Some interruption of the great tome or tomb habit among biographers was necessary. And in future we may hope that biographies will be both fresh and true in small space. But it would be a mistake to suppose that any of these biographers have done strict justice to their subjects; they have merely, in Stevenson's childish phrase, 'drawn a man,' and in trying, as Stevenson only offered to do, to 'draw his soul,' they have exposed their own souls to other eyes, with certain results.

An honourable exception to the fancy biographical school is F. A. Simpson, whose two volumes dealing with the life of Napoleon III are among the best books of historical biography to be published in our day. The first of them, written when the author was only five-and-twenty, is *The Rise of Louis Napoleon*; the second *Louis Napoleon and the Recovery of France*. Although a fellow and lecturer of Trinity College, Cambridge, F. A. Simpson does not appear to belong to Bloomsbury or Bayswater, and I can do no more than mention his books in this place.

VIII. WOMEN

The women are splendid.

War-time Saying.

Now in my earlier remarks on the subject of War-time influences, I said nothing about one of these, and this one among the most important of all. It was not because I had forgotten it, but because I thought I would leave mention of it until I reached this part of the chapter. And the influence is that of the so-called emancipation of women. Prior to the War, while women had for nearly a hundred years been making a steady advance (with the aid of the more just-minded men) towards something approaching political equality with men, they had not absolutely succeeded in attaining their object. In the election years of 1906 and 1910, and of course in the years between those years and after them, the Suffrage movement had gained ground and had been making itself a nuisance in a number of ways to the more obstinate among males. It had the support, I think I may say, of at least two kinds of men—those who care for justice, and those who hope, as Bernard Shaw hoped, that if women were given the vote, and allowed to do some reasonable work, they would cease to be obsessed by the notion of love, and would

become sensible.   But it had no support from all who believed
that women were a mystical cross between angels and drudges.

At last, in or around 1910, women really did take the most
violent steps to attract notice to what they believed to be their
importance in the world of men.   They began to break windows,
and burn letter-boxes, and cause other rumpuses.   They were
told that they did themselves no good by these violences, since
men could always be more violent than women; and many
women were also greatly distressed by the violences and dis-
owned them as unwise and harmful exhibitions.   But what
always happens in England is that when men are sufficiently
worried they yield; this is because they have a passion for peace,
which is sometimes called a love of justice and sometimes the
British Genius for Compromise, but which, as many women
know, is nothing but a hatred of fuss.   'Anything for a quiet
life' is the English motto; that is why there are so many Scots
and Irish leaders in our land.   And I think that probably the
Suffragettes would in any case have won the day.   They did
not succeed in winning the day, because the War came, and the
whole surface of life was convulsed.

I shall no doubt be contradicted for saying it, but I have always believed that the majority of women enjoy war.   That
is, they have an insatiable relish for sensation.   Not the finest
women, not the most intelligent women, but women in mass.   I
think, whether that is true or not, that the European War gave
all English women occupation.   It brought them out of their
homes as nothing else could have done.   The most loathsome
offered white feathers to young men who were not in uniform
(but they were only a fervid few): one woman went up to a friend
of my own who was in uniform and angrily demanded: 'How is
it you 're not *at the front*?'   We all know the stories about
women who 'sent' their menfolk to the War, and about camp-
followers and War babies: most of them were exaggerated, and
I am not going to repeat all the rubbish of that hysterical time.
What is true is that as men went to serve with the colours, women
took their places, worked at the making of munitions, at conducting tramcars, at driving lorries, and so on.   They showed
that with equal opportunities they could usually do as good a
job as the man they had replaced; and it was customary for
every newspaper in England at least once a day to print upon
its own account or as a quotation from some political leader
the words: 'The women are splendid.'   They earned, and were
given, the vote for which they had long been agitating.

But the vote was only a symbol: what women wanted was much more than a say in the election of Parliamentary candidates. At first they wanted a new standard of chastity for men; they wanted equality in the matter of divorce (that a husband should be divorceable on grounds of misconduct alone, whereas previously a wife had had to prove either desertion or cruelty); they wanted equality of pay; and many other things. What had happened was that over a long term of years more and more women had been receiving a scholastic education in advance of anything they had known in the greater part of the nineteenth century, and all these educated women were in conflict with what seemed to them to be the vested interests of men in the professions. The women who demanded rights, for the most part, were educated women. The others, the lorry-drivers and the tram-conductors, were happy-go-lucky enough, and only took the chances that offered; but the educated women were in this position, that without a change in the status of women they were doomed to waste their education upon domestic life or futile drudgery as subordinates. Something could be said, they thought, for Oriental notions of the harem; but nothing could be said for the incessant humiliation of the educated women who had nothing to do.

In the War period, women naturally brought their education to a better market. In the literary world, with which I am concerned (for these remarks have been but a brief explanation), the War-time gave a great opportunity to educated women. The writers left to function in England were those who were too old for military service, those who were physically unfit, the intellectual objectors, and women. Most of the men between twenty and fifty were very busy in the services or in work connected with the prosecution of the War; many of the educated women were likewise occupied with the War. But there were more women than men who could and did, as the weary months went by, present the country with books of one sort and another, and their influence upon the kind of books written may have been very important. They were intensively educated women, one must remember; and the intellectual objectors were usually intensively educated men. Not what our grocers mean when they advertise 'Well-educated youth wanted as errand boy,' or 'Well-educated young lady for cash desk: wages 10s.' Real wranglers, students of philosophy, and the like; very 'classical.' Poets have commonly belonged to the middle class, and the War poets were no exception to this rule. Scholars can hardly be other than men of education. In England, despite the great post-War increase in scholarships, which carry young working-class men to the universities, nearly all public schoolboys and university graduates are the offspring of well-to-do parents. Literature in this country since the War has been largely produced by the educated class; and this means that more and more even the novelists have been less concerned with portraying the simplicities of young love than with exhibiting their own erudition. The poets are all mathematicians and economists. Only the economists, when they write fiction, give us detective mystery stories. The number of women who have emerged as writers since the War has been very great, and nearly all of them are women of advanced education, as opposed to women of what a friend of mine used to call mother-wit. Chief among these women, and, since every class must have a rallying point much vaunted by enthusiastic cheer - leaders, idol of them all, is Virginia Woolf. It is with Virginia Woolf that I now end my chapter on Bloomsbury.

IX. VIRGINIA WOOLF

It always happened that when I awoke like this, and my mind struggled in an unsuccessful attempt to discover where I was, everything would be moving round me through the darkness: things, places, years. My body . . . would make an effort to construe the form which its tiredness took as an orientation of its various members, so as to induce from that where the wall lay and the furniture stood, to piece together and to give a name to the house in which it must be living. Its memory, the composite memory of its ribs, knees, and shoulder-blades offered it a whole series of rooms in which it had at one time or another slept; while the unseen walls kept changing, adapting themselves to the shape of each successive room that it remembered, whirling madly through the darkness.

PROUST, *Swann's Way*
(translated by C. K. Scott Moncrieff).

It was Clive Bell who said 'great writers, like Dostoevsky, Joseph Conrad, and Virginia Woolf'; and I now wonder whether Bell would entirely hold by his words. I doubt if he would do so; and have no wish to chain any man to his old opinions. Dostoevsky and Conrad, although they are still as good as ever they were, are both *démodés*, and few men in Bloomsbury would like to link their names again with that of a newer idol. But I quote the phrase because as far as I know it was the first public claim ever aggressively made on behalf of Virginia Woolf. The

fact that Clive Bell is Virginia Woolf's brother-in-law gives it a
fine domestic loyalty, but is not to be taken as indicating bias.
Bell was courageous. Where many men are timid as to making
claims on behalf of their friends or on behalf of any writers at
all, he braved ridicule as he braved challenge. The time had
come, he felt, to speak up. 'Great writers, like Dostoevsky,
Joseph Conrad, and Virginia Woolf,' he said. Virginia Woolf
then had published only one novel, *The Voyage Out*.

She continued, apart from her immediate circle, to be nothing
more than a faintly recognized name until *Jacob's Room* in 1922
and *Mrs Dalloway* in 1925 attracted more general attention;
but it was in 1929, when she published her feminist tract, *A
Room of One's Own*, that she enjoyed real celebrity for the first
time. Having long had the support of Bloomsbury, which is
very propagandist, she now had the support of all educated
women, to whom she had given a bible.

Virginia Woolf is the daughter of Sir Leslie Stephen, who
edited the *Dictionary of National Biography* and wrote many
essays of varying interest and accuracy upon the writers and
philosophers of his country, especially those of the eighteenth
century, in whom he took great interest. Stephen was a
mountaineer, and the friend of George Meredith and others of
the literary men of his day; and his daughter was thus from her
earliest years familiar with a bookish atmosphere. She married
in 1912 Leonard Woolf, a Cambridge man who had for some
years previously been in the Ceylon Civil Service, and in 1915
she published her novel first.

It was a novel unremarkable for incident, but was full of conversation, and—for this way of writing continued to grow upon
the author—it was full of a sense that when speaking or when
thinking people were not exclusively occupied with a single
subject. They said and thought one thing; but they also
thought, and did not say, another. Their thoughts were
apparently inconsecutive: it has never been quite possible for
any person to identify that liaison between thought and thought
which is too rapid to be caught in action. Still, however, both
The Voyage Out and *Night and Day*, which in 1919 followed
it, were recognizably attempts to spin from the author's preoccupations coherent and continuous narratives. With *Jacob's
Room* there was a change, and with two later books, *Mrs Dalloway* and *To the Lighthouse*, narrative had given place to what
must be considered Virginia Woolf's distinctive contributions
to the modern English novel. These were curious weavings of

impression and memory, the comings and goings of whimsical thoughts and fancies, sometimes from the moment, sometimes from yesterday, sometimes from long ago. Distastes for other individuals arose as if they were blown suddenly by a gust of wind; associations spread and narrowed, speculations jumped from nowhere, phrases came and went. A constant twitter of words and notions dominates these books. They specialize in disconnectedness.

To minds used to the solid four-square of traditional English fiction, the building up of a practicable *milieu*, the history of a family or a pair of families, the plain long formal description of faces, clothes, and circumstances, these novels by Virginia Woolf had one of two appearances. Either they were eccentric and wrong-headed, or they were wonderful novelties, works of genius. Virginia Woolf herself tried to assist readers by publishing, first of all as an article in *The Nation* and then as a pamphlet, an essay challenging something said previously as to the nature of the novel by Arnold Bennett. Bennett had described as a fault in (I think unspecified) Georgian novelists, excessive interest in details at the expense of characterization; and in his downright way had said 'the foundation of good fiction is character-creating, and nothing more.' Virginia Woolf, in the factious manner of Bloomsbury, could not answer Bennett without charging his work, and that of Wells and Galsworthy, with being 'already a little chill.' She maintained that the Georgians were pursuing essential character, a will-o'-the-wisp, simply, for truth's sake, showing the reaction of a human being to its surroundings. Thereby, it appeared, they were doing something really exciting, which distinguished them from their forerunners. Her list of Georgians, published later, contained the names of James Joyce, E. M. Forster, Lytton Strachey, D. H. Lawrence, and T. S. Eliot; that is to say, three novelists, one biographer, and a poet. These men (to whom must be added herself) were re-creating the English novel.

This is a most ingenious claim. As to Lytton Strachey I think it is unproven and unprovable, for his characters are made up, not of essentials, but of seizable lineaments; as to the other writers I have still to speak, and shall do so in the next chapter. But the claim is very important in considering the work of Virginia Woolf herself, because in that work more than in the work of any of the writers she has named, except T. S. Eliot, the tottering pursuit of the will-o'-the-wisp continues to this day. Objective reality has little importance to Virginia Woolf;

her interest is almost solely in the subjective. But not in what
Aldous Huxley says is the only thing he cares about, the *psyche*;
rather in the flutterings of mood and fancy. She will take a
person and show us the jumping of thought that goes on all
the time in that person's consciousness. Having done that, she
passes to another person. And since she introduces us to
several persons, who all jump in the same way, it is fair to
assume that she has in her own mind some clear conception of
these persons as separate individualities and believes herself to
be successfully rendering those persons as individuals; but that
is not my impression of them. Nor has the quiver and shake of
their thoughts, for me, any deeper revelation than that of a kind
of mental sickness, the sort of jumble that people have in their
heads when they are going under or emerging from an anaesthetic. At such times, I agree, they are not very distinctly
themselves. I should make this assertion of vagueness regarding *Mrs Dalloway*, *To the Lighthouse*, and *The Waves*. Of these
books I should say, also, that they are extremely well written,
and full of ingenuities, the last-named full of beauty. *Orlando*,
also, which is similarly very ingenious, is exceedingly interesting
as narrative, and is easily comprehensible, but as far as I know
does not pretend to be a novel. It is a calculatedly original work
(but calculated originality is for me a contradiction in terms).

What Arnold Bennett meant, I feel sure, in charging Georgian
writers with ignoring the first essential of novel-writing, the
creation of character, was that in the novels he had in mind
there was no person seen and presented, as they say, in the
round. In a book about Mrs Brown, there was, for the reader,
no Mrs Brown. Virginia Woolf replied that in life itself there
never was a Mrs Brown, only a 'Mrs Brownness,' the essential
something which to Mrs Brown is all that Mrs Brown knows when
she goes about her day's life. She claimed to be presenting not
Mrs Brown, but Mrs Brownness. That sounds splendid. But
in order to discover the Mrs Brownness Virginia Woolf is forced
to write solely of ruminative or introspective persons, and when
she had carried her exploration to the four minds in *The Waves*
she had reached as far as that particular method would take her.
There were four poetic somethings; but they all thought alike.
The reason for this, in my opinion, is that Virginia Woolf is
essentially an impressionist, a catcher at memory of her own
mental vagaries, and not a creator. She is aware, too, of many
of the latest scientific facts and theories about human beings,
but she is unable to imagine, to create, a human being who is

not exactly like herself. Such a person as Arnold Bennett or Frank Swinnerton she could not—would not wish to—imagine. Nor Mrs Brown either, I believe; for her Mrs Brown is but a dream-jumble of odds and ends. She thinks she is pursuing the essential, but in fact she is too sensitive, highly intelligent, and playful in mind, to have the emotional depth of an imaginative person. Psychologically she is as much at fault as the so-called realist, in thinking that if she chases every detail she will find truth. That is not the way to write great novels. Jane Austen was wiser and less anxiously exploratory; but Jane Austen had more creative imagination than cultivated brains. How odd that Virginia Woolf cannot see this.

And since I have mentioned Jane Austen, I must again refer to the charming book, *A Room of One's Own*, which is a mingling of feminism with reverie and invention. In this book Virginia Woolf traces, as well as the available material will allow her to do, the history of the education of women. Saying nothing of the Pastons, she looks through English literature and letters for news of the way in which through the centuries women learned to write and then, in time, came to write books and plays. She says nothing of several people who would possibly have been unhelpful to her examination, such as Maria Edgeworth, Mrs Inchbald, Mrs Gaskell, and Mrs Trollope; but comes to the conclusion that until a woman has a private income of five hundred pounds a year and a room of her own of which she can lock the door she cannot hope to be free to write good books—or do anything else. For the writing of good books, says Virginia Woolf, needs leisure, and no woman in the past has had any life of her own, neither liberty nor opportunity to do what she would best do.

With the argument of this piece I have no concern, for I am not here discussing feminism (I only object specifically to the statement that no genius ever came from the working class, because even if genius is confined by Virginia Woolf to literature there is always D. H. Lawrence, who never had a room of his own); but with the assumption that fiction is only to be written by educated women I must deal because it has a larger application. It is the view of Virginia Woolf, and those who think as she does, that no literary work done by any but highly educated persons of their own kind of culture can or should be interesting. This I must point out to be educational snobbery, which in Bloomsbury has succeeded the social snobbery of pre-Gerogian days.

CHAPTER XIV: POST-FREUD

I

In our modern mythology, Custom, Circumstance, and Heredity are the three Fates that weave the web of human life.

MAY SINCLAIR, *Audrey Craven* (1897).

A WORD as to the title of this chapter. It is a convenient term by which I indicate certain novelists who have interested themselves inquiringly or with the vehemence of genius in abnormal psychology, in psycho-pathology. I do not mean that they are all necessarily Freudians; but all have been aware of a certain progress in medical theory and have been affected by this knowledge in writing about their fellow-creatures. They no longer grope by the light of their own incandescence, but have the aid of handbooks, experts, and considerable quantities of statistics. I do not know what Henry James would have thought of Havelock Ellis's *Studies in the Psychology of Sex*; but to all modern psychological novelists Havelock Ellis's books are familiar. They were the first extensive studies of phenomena which when George V became King were not freely discussed. In those days the perfect limit of comprehensive psychological knowledge was contained in an extraordinary book by a young German suicide named Otto Weininger. This book was called *Sex and Character*.

The Germans and Austrians long led the field in the study of mental processes. They may still lead the field. While American students, and in a lesser degree French students, made considerable investigations in psychology, the English did not do so. Only in or around the year of the king's accession did innocents of the kind known to myself—young men able to read the weekly reviews of that time—first learn, still through Havelock Ellis, of the existence of Sigmund Freud; and only in 1913 did we discover that his great book, *The Interpretation of Dreams*, translated by Brill, was available for consumption. Brill's translation was of the third German edition. We had hitherto passed very little beyond those three Fates which May Sinclair declared in 1897 were the dominating myths of modernity—

Custom, Circumstance, and Heredity. We now learned of the Conscious, the Preconscious, and the Unconscious. We learned of Psychic Censorship and Repressions; the Ego, the Super-Ego, and the Id. We learned, in effect, the language of psycho-analysis, now a jargon.

Really to understand what Freud and his fellow-analysts teach, one should be an unremitting student of psycho-analysis. I am not such a student, and I cannot pretend to give a reliable account of this very fascinating and suggestive branch of investigation. I am still in the simple stages, where the picture of our normal conscious life as but a small part of our full mental life is a sufficiently delightful concept to provoke meditation. But psycho-analysis as taught by Freud and Jung is very much more than that. It is a great system of pessimistic philosophy. From Freud's first definition of a dominating human urge, which he calls the 'libido,' as the sexual instinct, through a point at which it became a general principle of 'pleasure,' to later definition by Jung which gave it kinship with our old friends the Life Force and the *Élan vital*, psycho-analysis has grown into a very intricate affair which no amateur can criticize. All the average person learns—when he does not see red, and with wild cries of 'Filth! Obscenity!' fall into a fever of denunciation—is that the child is a sensual being who gratifies simple impulses until, as the result of discipline or awareness that certain acts are unpopular, he forcibly represses them. The average person learns that these repressions seriously influence the after-life of each child, and sometimes produce mental disease. He is told how the conscious life of an individual is affected by these early influences (and even by ante-natal influences and racial influences), and how there is a constant activity of mind and instinct of which we become aware for the most part in dreams or with the aid of the psycho-analyst.

What more the average person learns depends upon himself. The divisions and definitions of psycho-analysis are almost innumerable. Whether we hear of the child's response to its parents or its own Ego, Super-Ego, or Id, or whether we plunge into symbolism or a species of fatalism, we shall discover unlimited possibilities in this extraordinary revelation of the mind. No wonder Freud has influenced modern thought to an incalculable extent. Merely to have given us that highly imaginative picture of the Unconscious perpetually struggling and intriguing—particularly by the agency of dreams—to get through the jealous guard of the Preconscious into the Conscious would have assured him of a place among the magicians. Though he leaves physiological causes almost entirely out of account, and though he is for that reason much criticized by physiologists, he has built up an entire system to explain human behaviour. He is an artist who is at the same time an unshockable scientist, and whatever may be the defects of his system it has a fundamental simplicity which has violently impressed the world.

Of his fellow-analysts, Jung and Adler, who have had a lesser but considerable influence, something must be said. I know nothing of Adler, except that he is a practical physician who has added more than one suggestive theory to the body of psycho-analysis, including one which he calls the 'impulse of aggression' or compensatory fortification of the weakest aspect in ourselves; but by Jung I must confess that I am quite confounded. Whether that is because the matter is difficult, or the original writing turgid and confused, or the translation not a model of clearness, I cannot tell. All I know is that after reading Jung I am less sure than I was that Freud is completely master his own theories, and inclined to suspect that the whole business of psycho-analysis has got a little out of hand. That, however, is by the way.

It would be too severe upon my subjects—for I must now return to the Georgian Literary Scene—excellent though they are in their respective ways, to confront them with the whole theory and practice of psycho-analysis. Though they must have been affected, as all modern writers have been, by some knowledge of Freudian theory, they are none of them avowed experts in that theory, and I would rather deal with them as novelists. May Sinclair, for example, wrote in 1922 a book called *The Life and Death of Harriet Frean* which was a genuine advance in a particular form of impressionistic realism then first attracting notice. This short novel, which told the story of a woman from childhood until her death under anaesthetic, was significant. It skimmed the cream, as it were, of a life; there were no redundancies, no comments, only such selected details as contributed to our calm knowledge of the way things happened to one ordinary woman. And Dorothy Richardson invented in *Pilgrimage* a new kind of impressionism in literature. She did not dodge, as Virginia Woolf does, among the past and present moods and memories of her heroine, but with extremely dexterous selectiveness managed to tell a continuous life-story as if it were in progress under our eyes. But so exact and indeed endless is her recollection that instead of compressing the life of Miriam into 184 pages, as May Sinclair compresses that of Harriet Frean, she makes every few weeks or months of it fill three hundred pages and could seemingly go on for ever.

II. EDWARD MORGAN FORSTER

And a third man he says in a sort of drooping regretful voice, 'Yes—oh dear yes—the novel tells a story.' . . . And the third is myself. Yes—oh dear yes—the novel tells a story.

E. M. FORSTER, *Aspects of the Novel.*

One of my earliest recollections is of my Scottish grandfather, whom I have described earlier as vocally indefatigable, singing:

'My name 's Edward Morgan; I live in Llanelly:
Of a truth I was born in the sweetest of vales.'

I do not know whether E. M. Forster is descended from this Edward Morgan (his father was Edward Morgan Llewellyn Forster); but it seems clear that he is of Welsh blood, and in that case some explanation is supplied of his subtle and complex nature. A Welshman, a lover of classics, an intellectual, a fellow of King's College, Cambridge, a novelist, a critic. But above all a moralist. Perhaps he does not himself realize that he is a moralist; but this I shall explain.

In person, Forster is of good middle height, very pale (he reminds me in several respects of André Gide; for both have a similar ivorine pallor, a similar grave sincerity of manner, a similar rather implacable courtesy), and with a peculiarly modest bearing. He is one of the very few men by whom I am consciously affected; by which I mean that something in him moves me to slightly exaggerated boisterousness of behaviour. I should not mention this if I had not found that he causes others also to feel coltish. But the fault is not in him: one has the sense of perfect integrity, calm, sympathy; however, a little remoteness, too. He is extremely intelligent; the most intelligent of all the novelists of the 1880–90 generation.

This is a great advantage to him, for he is enabled to play with all his themes, and interpenetrate them with a kind of piercing light of the spirit. But it is at the same time a disadvantage, for his books, however incandescent, hold little warmth. They do not embrace the whole of life; they are more like luminous demonstrations of cause and effect. They arise from deliberately realized ideas, and not from imaginative conceptions. But nevertheless they are full of fluctuating imagination which comes and goes from scene to scene, from paragraph to paragraph. He can be exquisitely malicious in sketching the spinster of foreign boarding houses; he can be very scathing at the expense of a male busybody; he rejoices in strange discomfitures; those are the things which amuse us in his work. They are not his chief concern. His chief concern is with something which he values above all else—Nature, Honesty, the need for mutual comprehension, the Good Life. He perpetually tries to personify this; never, I think, with complete success, but always thoughtfully and with a range of reference beyond the understanding of very simple readers.

At the risk of having it thought that Cambridge is an obsession of mine (whereas I regard it only as a curiously insistent and very important phenomenon in modern letters), I should wish to make an observation. It is this. At its lowest, the esteem in which Cambridge is held may be a snobbish esteem: 'Charlie's up at Cambridge'—oh, *Cambridge*; that means money, position, a career, such friends for after-life, etc. Oxford would be just as impressive: none of the other universities has such social *cachet*. That is the least interesting aspect. At its most persistent in the modern literary world, the pride of the Cambridge man is in a form of intellectual culture. I do not question the culture, and pride in it—with its contempt for all who have not shared its influence—is almost equalled by the comparable pride of the Oxford man who speaks of 'the best thought.' All I dislike is the irrelevant ostentation. But there is a third pride, a much higher pride, that in spiritual culture; and it is this pride in Cambridge that Forster has. It is illustrated at intervals in all his work; it perfectly shouts in his comment on an aspiring Cockney clerk in *Howard's End*, of whom Forster says: 'Perhaps the keenest happiness he had ever known was during a railway journey to Cambridge, where a decent-mannered undergraduate had spoken to him.'

That remark indicates that to Forster his experience at Cambridge is the most wonderful thing that ever happened to him. At Cambridge he came greatly under the influence of a man of exceptionally fine temper and gift for teaching—Goldsworthy Lowes Dickinson. Dickinson, the ideal don, whose biography Forster has written, is to ordinary readers known chiefly by his little manual, *The Greek View of Life*, which, though less than his best book, illustrates particularly his humane attitude of helpfulness towards unscholarly people. In this book he summarizes, very persuasively, the Greek attitudes to Religion, Art, the State, the Individual; and while it may be true that to scholars the work contains some jejune material and perhaps some sentimentality, its appeal to the uneducated is very strong. Dickinson is known otherwise to students as the author of certain dialogues on the nature of Good and the varieties of political philosophy, in which a love of discussion for its own sake is joined to a very earnest wish to ascertain by means of contrasts and definitions whether there is any common basis upon which thoughtful minds can build a more helpful philosophy of life. These dialogues, for those who relish points of view, are easy and delightful. They show a sense of character, and a willingness to preserve not only differences of opinion but the natural origins in personality of such differences. Though interested in abstract ideas, Dickinson was not therefore debarred from completely humane sympathy with men of many types. It was a beautiful mind, and a beautiful character, as these dialogues demonstrate. But his best work is contained in two books, one a fantasy suggested by Mozart's opera, *The Magic Flute*, the other a survey of European pre-War diplomacy entitled *The European Anarchy*. In these books the same beauty of mind and character is revealed; fastidious yet sympathetic, anxious yet tolerant; earnest yet playful. In the dialogues, no traps, such as we find in Plato; in the very simple *Greek View of Life* a loving wish to explain without condescension; in *The Magic Flute* a charming venture into the empyrean; and in *The European Anarchy* clear sight and honourable adoration of truth brought to the most controversial branch of history and analysis.

The power of such a man, who was Forster's friend as well as his teacher, is unquestionable. It is supported by much testimony, including Forster's own. And it must have helped, with those actual debates at Cambridge which Dickinson loved and in which, at the beginning of the century, Forster joined, to give clarity to his mind already possessed of unusual resource. Forster owes much to Cambridge, and this he acknowledges by his assurance that a Cockney clerk had his happiest moments as the result of being spoken to by a decent-mannered undergraduate. In himself he manages, it seems to me, to be more intelligent than his contemporaries without sinking to their fatal aridity.

His novels, excluding shorter works, are five in number. Two of them brilliant exercises in comedy, two lengthy and to me not altogether intelligible or admirable serious studies of middle-class people in various moral pickles, and one a subtle, very patient, brilliant analysis of the Anglo-Indian problem. I use the word 'brilliant' with a sense of responsibility; for I can think of no term which better describes the peculiar quality of radiant intelligence which the three books share. All five books are written in a style, at first markedly formal and later still decidedly cool, distinguished by wit and new-minted phrase. All five, in the matter of invention, are fantastic.

The fantasticality is an advantage in the extravagant *Where Angels Fear to Tread* and *A Room with a View*, a disadvantage in *The Longest Journey* and *Howard's End*, and a bewilderment in *A Passage to India*. This I shall hope to show. *Where Angels Fear to Tread* is about a shiftless widow of means who marries a cheap Italian, has a baby, and dies. Her brother-in-law, an amusing prig, is sent with his sister to a small Italian town to demand the baby for its English relations, and there is great comedy in the ambassadorial interviews with the baby's father. Finally the baby is stolen, is accidentally jolted from the thief's arms in the darkness to death in a ditch; there is a shocking night fight between the prig and the father; and the expedition, routed, comes to an end with, on the part of a contributory young woman, the confession of her hidden and horrified love for the cheap Italian. In some respects this is the most successful of all Forster's books; for the protagonists are vividly rendered, the talk full of verve, the zestful invention upon a uniform plane, and the total effect unmarred by contradiction or obscurity. It is brimming with laughter.

The book which followed *Where Angels Fear to Tread* has no such relishable zest. It is a long tale about a cripple of some private means who becomes under-master at a country school. He marries a girl bereaved by death of her first, instinctive lover. This girl at first mothers the cripple and encourages his literary experiments in paganism; and at last, because she is conventional, malignantly binds and seeks to crush him into a conventional shape. Her character changes, always for the worse, as the book proceeds, and for every malignance she shows to her husband Forster repays her tenfold by what becomes quite persecutionary arraignment. Now the cripple has an irresponsible half-brother (illegitimate); and this brother, an incalculable and savage bore for whom the author has a mystical veneration, is always breaking into the book as a curious symbolic figure. He upsets the conventionals; he arouses in the cripple an emotional sense of duty and distaste; he and his case both evoke from an obstinate young philosopher harangues of the utmost severity; but while one feels that he represents for Forster some truth, some reality of importance, he never succeeds in being for the reader anything but a tiresome oaf who would be better dead. Because of him, the story is involved with argument and symbolism, and the fantastic invention which has been in place in brilliant farce such as *Where Angels Fear to Tread* is in *The Longest Journey*, where it is perfectly sober, a cause of tedium and unconvincingness. The author, it seems, has at this period become attached to some 'Back to Nature' concept whereby his cripple is saddled with terrible responsibilities for the sins of the mothers; and he has also developed what might nowadays be called a Conventionality Complex. Conventionality is a horror to him. It is the enemy of Truth, Purity, and Romance. It is the unforgivable sin. It is to him what the Church was to Voltaire. In face of it he loses all command of his judgment. Instead of seeking truth below conventionality, and trying to understand why convention has such power, he can do nothing but vehemently expose it, caricature it, exaggerate it altogether beyond its natural proportions, punish it, and exalt its opposite, which he calls Honesty.

That same passion for the irrational—which seems odd and never entirely clear-headed in a man as civilized as Forster—is the driving force in *A Room with a View*. In this third novel, with something of the farcical brilliance of *Where Angels Fear to Tread*, we are introduced to a party at a Florentine *pension*, whose manners and timidities and snobbishnesses are all mimicked without mercy. But, to our horror, we find in the *pension* a truth-telling eccentric who, if he had been in a novel by Galsworthy, would long ago have been ridiculed to death by the intelligentsia; and we hear the rather worse than not-quite-veritable pipes of Pan. Our young heroine is kissed by a young man named George. After the fashion of heroines, she nevertheless engages herself to another, quite unsuitable, young man; and it takes coincidence and other fantastic works to break the engagement and land her in the properly unconventional arms. In particular we are shown that as she could play Beethoven's less popular pieces she has some core of superiority to common young women; and as for the men, they all return to nature by stripping and taking a bathe in a muddy pool. A rather

Meredithian scene, this; but the book as a whole, though often delicious in phrase and satire, will not, in its composition, bear looking into. If we were to peer, we should see that just as Meredith's novels owe nearly all to their treatment (and little but ill to their mechanism), so this book is no more than a novelette with a sentimental invocation of faunishness and eccentricity and momentary nudism to carry the graver message about Truth which the author has in his heart. Convention is still the enemy; despite the fact that Unconventionality thus applauded is but an inversion of the hideous foe. I doubt if a naturally unconventional person is ever conscious of the vileness of convention. He is more like the little girl who was told the story of the Golden Calf. She remarked, thoughtfully: 'And God was angry?' 'Terribly angry.' 'H'm. Funny. Of course, anybody else would only have laughed.'

In many of its details and assumptions, *Howard's End* is much the most mature and richly diversified book Forster has written. If I say that it is a puzzling book, that is because I think that here, above all, Forster's invention is entirely arbitrary. I am not, as I hope it has been made clear in earlier chapters, a stickler for neatness in the novel; to me each book is to be judged accordingly as its author's aim (as I understand it) has been a worthy aim and well executed. What is called 'richness' has its artistic value no less than scrupulous observance of the unities and other pseudo-classical technical devices. I do not ask of a book that it should be pellucid. In a sense, also, I realize that probability, as the French historian said, 'is not a scientific notion; there was a King of Siam who refused to believe in the existence of ice.' But over *Howard's End* I am in a quandary. I only believe it here and there.

In this book there are two half-German orphan sisters named Schlegel and their brother. The brother may be eliminated; he is but an adjunct. There are also a family called Wilcox, father, mother, two sons, and a daughter; the children for the time being may be set aside, excepting that the younger son and one of the two Schlegel sisters, Helen, for a few moments at the beginning of the book are engaged to be married. The sole point of the engagement is to show that Helen is amorously impulsive. And there are a young uneducated Cockney clerk and his wife (at first his mistress). It is this uneducated Cockney clerk, as you may recall, whose happiest hour has been given him by a decent-mannered undergraduate; and he and his wife, so far as the

intrigue is concerned, are the dominating characters in the novel.
They are not the chief characters; but their actions precipitate
the moral crises of the book.

What am I to do with two persons, in a class well known
to me, who, though they are apparently seriously offered as
portraits, never say or do a single thing which I find credible?
Is it I who am so besotted with the realistic method that I
cannot appreciate essential truth? Or are these two incred-
ibles indeed taken seriously by the author as persons? Or are
they symbols? Or merely instruments in his plot? Let me
tell you what happens, and then let me explain what troubles
me.

At the beginning of the book occurs the abortive engagement.
It is quite an impossible engagement, and is broken off the
morning after. It is also beautifully handled by Forster, who
in the treatment of the whole episode shows himself to be a distinguished novelist: nothing in that respect could be finer. But
shortly afterwards the sisters go to a classical concert at Queen's
Hall, where they sit next to the uneducated Cockney clerk—
there to *improve* himself. One of the sisters accidentally takes
his umbrella; the other, when he suspiciously and accusingly
announces the abstraction, first gives him her card and then
takes him home to recover what proves to be a tattered relic.
Subsequently the Wilcox family, hitherto resident in the country,
at a house called Howard's End, rent a flat immediately opposite
the home of the sisters, and, as Helen (the emotional) has gone
to Germany, and her quondam fiancé to Nigeria, Margaret,
the elder Schlegel, makes friends with Mrs Wilcox, the mother.
From this friendship springs the curious fact that upon her
death shortly afterwards Mrs Wilcox leaves a note asking that
Howard's End shall be given to Margaret. Since the note is
unsigned, and has no legal significance, the Wilcox family ignore
this wish. However, Mr Wilcox, the widower, presently falls
soberly in love with Margaret, proposes to her, and (quite
appropriately and explicably) is accepted. The two marry.

Meanwhile, however, the sisters have had further encounters
with the uneducated Cockney clerk and his wife. Both turn up
rather oddly at the Schlegels' home; the wife because her husband has mysteriously absented himself, the husband to explain
that, having heard the call of the wild, he has been for a week-end
walk. He quotes poetry; the Schlegel sisters patronize him,
learn that he is a clerk in an insurance company, and, as Mr
Wilcox tells them that this particular insurance company is

unsound, advise the clerk to find another job. The clerk finds
another job—in a bank!—but is dismissed from it for incompetence; also his insurance company is proved to be sound. He
and his wife are therefore brought by Helen, the emotional, to a
country house from which Mr Wilcox's daughter has just been
married. Helen Schlegel is beside herself with panic fury, and
insists that Mr Wilcox shall find the clerk work in his own business. Unfortunately the clerk's wife has been Mr Wilcox's mistress in a former incarnation, and as she is drunk she accosts him
familiarly, arouses disturbance, and brings about an estrange-
ment between the Schlegel sisters. Helen, having tried to give
part of her fortune to the clerk, who declines it, goes abroad;
Margaret is married to Mr Wilcox, and goes down to Howard's
End, where she finds that an insane woman has unpacked all her
belongings, and Helen's belongings, in a house which for some
time has been unoccupied. Time passes. Then, very mysteriously, Helen turns up again, shunning her family, and is only
trapped in Howard's End—hunting up her books—by strategy.
She is eight months gone with child; and it appears that this is
the result of another emotional moment in which the Cockney
clerk has been involved. When Mr Wilcox's elder son, who is
not the one who has been engaged to Helen, attacks the Cockney
a bookcase falls over; the clerk dies, the son gets three years for
manslaughter. Thereafter nothing remains but to gather together the fragments, and the sisters share Helen's trial—'the
supreme agony of motherhood, which is even yet not a matter of
common knowledge.'

Forster must not be blamed for my shortcomings as a sum-
marizer, and I do not ask that the story as told by me shall be
regarded as the story as told by him. All I ask is that we should
quietly discuss the question whether the inconsecutiveness of
this story is precisely the inconsecutiveness of life. In so far as
Margaret and Mr Wilcox are concerned, I think it is. There
seems to me no incongruity at all in their relation, which is
entirely reasonable, though not untouched by emotion. In the
same way, Helen's performances could I think have been made
credible; although as the book stands they are to me not credible.
She fluctuates between hardness and emotionalism (not an uncommon mixture), and is only unconvincing because both her
passionate scenes occur 'off' the stage, when probability as
well as pruriency demands that they should be witnessed in
order that they should be understood. We are presented with
the after-facts only: no wonder we are surprised. As for the

uneducated Cockney clerk and his wife, my knowledge of clerks is very extensive, and I have never met one who would be over-whelmed by decent behaviour on the part of an undergraduate, or one to whom such decent behaviour would seem less than his due. A consciousness of condescension would seem rather to belong to the undergraduate. How can I possibly believe in a being so uncouth, when I am told that he springs from a class which I know to be above all others decent, well behaved, and self-respecting?

This is far from being an idle point as to Forster's portrayal of life. Here is another instance. In *The Longest Journey* the irrational half-brother arrives one night, drunk, at the cripple's home. His sister-in-law wearily notes his condition and states it; the cripple greets him cordially, but receives no answer, because the visitor has become insensible. And a third sober conventionalist exclaims on the spot: 'Good gracious me! My advice is, that we all go to bed.' I do not know precisely what *can* be said when a relation tumbles into the house drunk quite late at night; but I am absolutely positive that nobody says: 'Good gracious me! My advice is, that we all go to bed.' All might wish to say it, hoping that the disfigurement would dis-appear by morning; but such complete washing of the hands at the first moment of contemplation is inconceivable to me. After all, the speaker was a busybody, strong in the sense of con-ventional duty.

Well, I shall be told that Forster is not a realistic novelist, which is true; and that brings me to *A Passage to India*, which is the most coherent of his later novels, sacrificing no brilliance as a result of that coherence. This is a picture of Anglo-Indian relations, drawn with much sympathy and beautifully presented. But the book turns upon something that happened in a cave. A young woman believes herself to have been assaulted in this cave by a Moslem doctor, and brings a charge against him which might have ruined his life. He is clearly innocent, and the young woman, when in the witness box, retracts her charge. We are not told what did happen, whether the young woman had a hallucination or whether she was in fact assaulted by a guide. We should like to know. Forster will not tell us. In his quiet way he sighs: 'Yes—oh dear yes—the novel tells a story.' He is interested in expressing by means of fiction—it could be done as well by no other means—what he feels to be the truth about the British in India, and the Indian reaction to British rule. For him the story, such as it is, is but a vehicle for the ideas. As a result of this, *A Passage to India* is less interesting as a novel than as a presentation, a crystallization, of Forster's thoughts and emotions after two long exploratory visits to the East. He does not like British rule; it is in the hands of Conventionalists. However, he has some doubts as to the consequences of its abandonment. In this conclusion, having been a Liberal, he becomes a philosopher, and leaves everything where he found it.

'Yes—oh dear yes—the novel tells a story.' In his study called *Aspects of the Novel* Forster imagines the problem whether a novel should tell a story being posed to three persons. The first doubtfully admits that perhaps a novel *should* tell a story; the second bluffly demands a story; the third, who, Forster says, is himself, very unwillingly agrees that the novel does in fact tell a story: he wishes it did not. He would so much rather it concerned itself with melody or perception of the truth. I should like to discuss this question at length, but that would take time and space. Having, however, been turned from the story-less novel by much experience of the story-less novel as written by others, I am inclined to think that the novel which tells a story is a much purer form of art than the novel which regards story as factitious. Unfortunately there are fewer artists than teachers; and as between the explicit and the implicit, explicit will always seem to persons of culture more immediately important than anything in which the object is not stated. That is by the way. I only introduce the point now for two reasons: one, that it illustrates the attitude of many very intelligent and respectable writers of the present day; the other, that it illuminates the nature of Forster's talent as well as the greatness of his gifts.

By some fatality, which we have all noticed, we bring, perhaps responsively, to any author of exacting mind a similar exactingness of demand. Forster is an instance of such exactingness in an author. I consider his work full of faults—faults of exaggeration, inventive perfunctoriness, property babies, tiresome insistence upon the virtues of irrationality and unpreparedness, and so on. I think it deficient in emotion, though strangely complaisant towards emotionalism. For a man who preaches the need of kindness he seems to me to show very little kindness towards those men and women in his books who suffer from the deadly illness of conventionality; in early books his attitude sometimes, even to unconventional characters, is detached to the verge of distaste; in all his work (but he regards it as a fortune, not a virtue) there is a half-reluctant hint: Some of us were at

King's; the rest, oh dear yes, not. But in spite of these accidents,
which many will think falsely charged and many others unneces-
sarily mentioned, he is as far above the generality of novelists
as, in another respect, he is above the generality of the intelligentsia. He has not only exceptional brains; he has exceptional
honesty. He is not only deft and perceptive; he is original.
While, when he is serious, he is sometimes, to me, displeasing,
harsh, excited, he has a glorious sense of comedy in which over
and over again everything rises as by the most delightful leger-
demain into glittering, many-coloured absurdity. In the case
of Margaret Schlegel, in *Howard's End*, where his sympathy is
never at fault, he achieves great subtlety of understanding and
communication. In *A Passage to India* one believes that he
has truly penetrated some of the disguises and evasions of the
oriental mind. In all his novels he adroitly suggests *milieu*,
mental attitude, conversational skill, and the difficulties of social
and personal adjustment as no other novelist could do with comparable brilliance. There may be life, movement, rich laughter,
eccentricity, accident, or gloom in his books, all of them presented with the greatest possible economy and precision. And
there will be something else, too.

That something is the ethical preoccupation of the author.
'Ought,' 'ought not.' We have our responsibilities. We guard
and are cautious, when we should be unprepared. We are
hypocrites and liars, when we should at all costs tell the truth
and do what is right; live freely and in harmony with Nature.
Tyranny is abhorrent to him; both tyranny and sham. He will
show a pleasant girl slipping from candour into conventionality,
to a lie or obedience to a lie; but always there is somebody across
whose face (though it be his own) a warning shadow of disappointment passes at that moment, and, if she is a good girl,
she recovers her self-respect and plays some lesser-known
Beethoven and so scrambles back to—not safety, but truth,
sincerity, awareness of the best, pursuit of the unconventional.
Just how positive a faith that is, we may doubt; it is at least a
faith which is very fit for those who do not manage the world's
affairs, and so modest a man as Forster would not wish in any
way to urge human beings beyond their capacity. For that
reason, while we may not share his particular enthusiasms, we
can all value his integrity, and can delight in the fact that it only
occasionally obscures his very genuine imaginative gift. Let us
continue to do so! The gift is a rare one.

III. DAVID HERBERT LAWRENCE

God, that I have no choice!
That my own fulfilment is up against me
Timelessly!
The burden of self-accomplishment!
The charge of fulfilment!

D. H. LAWRENCE, *Humiliation.*

Younger than Forster, and younger than the talented young novelists of the 1883–4 generation—Mackenzie, Cannan, Walpole, Brett Young—D. H. Lawrence stands out from them all. He stands out in the first place by his genius; but he occupies more accidentally and less enviably a place of his own in contemporary literature. If we here glance back to the beginning of the Georgian era, and recall what Henry James thought of him, it will amuse us to find that phrase—toiling 'in the dusty rear'—as the first comment of age to seal him an original; and he was an original, or 'sport,' in several unfortunate respects as well as in the all-important one of genius. He was, for example, one of the few writers ever to be threatened with prosecution for obscenity; one of the few painters to have the exhibition of their works closed by police order and the works themselves taken in charge; one of the few poets to have a packet of poems stopped in transit through the English post. He might well claim to have been the victim of persecution: he might well feel hatred and misery at thought of his country and its laws; he might well feel himself a rebel with nowhere to rest his head. Since his death he has had an equally strange fate in being made the subject of biographies and counter-biographies and replies to counter-biographies, and books and books of memoirs, letters, selections, collections, and every kind of analysis. His life, both private and secret, has been published abroad, first by himself either in the disguise of the novel or the passionate candours of poetry, and then by his friends and enemies and those who have axes to grind and those who hope to gain a little publicity for themselves from his posthumous fame. His work and his personality have evoked such emotion that any breath of adverse comment upon one of them or both has been met with fury from one class, while every word of praise has aroused in another class such shocked and repulsive surprise that protests have passed into paroxysms of the most alarming kind. His effect upon the young has been great; his effect upon the old has often enough been that of nausea. It is difficult to foresee his future; it is even more difficult in such an atmosphere calmly to assess his genius.

For one thing, much of the fuss about Lawrence has been of a purely temporary order. It was bound to be so. Psycho-analysis has been a new hobby for thousands of people, and Lawrence is a writer who lends himself—only too readily—to psycho-analysis. He asks for it; demands it. His work was full of autobiography; his poems can be made plainly to tell the story of a life as Shakespeare's sonnets have only been made to do by force; his illustration of the Œdipus complex is terribly timely; the accounts of him which have been published have all dealt in matters of which, concerning nearly every other writer, nothing, or very little, is known. His private life has been turned inside out, not because he was a genius but because he is ready material for such disclosure. There he is: the man, the author; compare this with that, his own words. Was he sexually impotent, was he mad, was he a good friend, an ungrateful biter of the hand that fed him? Are his works obscene or fiercely moral? It has been a really extraordinary situation. If ever man was made for moment, it was Lawrence. But must one accept the verdicts of the moment? Is there something yet more true to be said of him? Are not these disciples by way of being ghouls or unconscious misrepresenters of the man? Was he, as they say, a great man; or was he a weakling? Some of them, while saying he was a great man, depict him as a weakling. He himself said that, as compared with the people who wrote about him, 'nice, well-behaved dogs,' he was a giraffe; and the Lawrence who wrote letters to his friends bears no resemblance at all to the Lawrence who has been described by others.

He was born in Eastwood, Nottinghamshire, on 11th September 1885, the fourth child of a coal-miner. He was what is known as a 'mother's boy,' and was his mother's pet, com-panion, and confidant. When he was thirteen, he won a scholar-ship to Nottingham High School, and later went to Nottingham University College to obtain a teaching certificate. He was a teacher for several years; but after the publication of his first novel, *The White Peacock*, in 1911 (it was advertised in 1910) he abandoned teaching and gave himself wholly to writing. The beginning of his literary career was marked by the active interest of two men, Ford Madox Hueffer, who published some poems in *The English Review*, and Edward Garnett, who told him to submit *The White Peacock* to Heinemann, the London publisher, and in other ways gave him encouragement of the most valuable kind. For a long time Garnett was his chief contact with the book world; later he disappears altogether from among Lawrence's correspondents. Then Lawrence made the acquaintance of Middleton Murry and Katherine Mansfield, and contributed to their journal, *Rhythm*, and embraced them with a full heart of friendship, while at the same time he steadily increased his half-friendships with others who were either producing what was thought to be advanced literature or cultivating the society of the artists and *littérateurs* of the day. His feelings for Murry were more emotional than they seem to have been for any other man; but having thought of him as a John the Baptist he came to regard him as a Judas, so that although the friendship lasted long, and flared up again, it was in the end a failure and a cause of pain and disillusion. Having spent his boyhood among midland workers, Lawrence became through Murry and Garnett and Edward Marsh (another early enthusiast) the associate of the cultivated few in London, bringing to that association a whole body of experience quite alien to the experience of his companions. He was thus from the outset a critical stranger in middle-class aesthetic society.

Middleton Murry, in his curious, rather powerful, and distressingly emotional story of Lawrence's character called *Son of Woman*, delves far into the Œdipus complex for his explanation of Lawrence, and I think convincingly attributes to the relation subsisting between Lawrence and his mother a share in that conflict to which in poems and novels he again and again returned. Aldous Huxley, always fastidiously repelled by the profuse (and therefore by Murry's literary manner and the mind which it expresses), will have nothing to do with any such notion, and truly remarks that Lawrence would have been Lawrence if his mother had died when he was a child. The two views are compatible. We are all agreed (I mean, in this case, Murry, Huxley, and myself) that Lawrence was a genius, and that his genius would have found expression: what is still possible, nevertheless, is that the note of horror prevading all those passages from his writings which Murry quotes might have been mitigated if as a boy he had not lived so constantly in his mother's company. Huxley has had no personal experience of the nearness with which poor people live together, and of the steamy mother-son intimacy, almost identification, which such a life can produce. It is indicated well enough in Lawrence's autobiographical *Sons and Lovers*, where the relationship is underlined but not, as yet, mystically analysed into those terms which Lawrence was later forced to repeat *ad nauseam* owing to the poverty of the English language.

Paul would be built like his mother, slightly and rather small. His fair hair went reddish, and then dark brown; his eyes were grey. He was a pale, quiet child, with eyes that seemed to listen, and with a full, dropping underlip.

As a rule he seemed old for his years. He was so conscious of what other people felt, particularly his mother. When she fretted he understood, and could have no peace. His soul seemed always attentive to her. . . .

. . . When she was quiet, so, she looked brave and rich with life, but as if she had been done out of her rights. It hurt the boy keenly, this feeling about her that she had never had her life's fulfilment: and his own incapacity to make up to her hurt him inside with a sense of impotence, yet made him patiently dogged inside. It was his childish aim.

.   .   .   .   .

Paul was now fourteen, and was looking for work. He was a rather small and rather finely made boy, with dark brown hair and light blue eyes. His face . . . was extraordinarily mobile. Usually he looked as if he saw things, was full of life, and warm; then his smile, like his mother's, came suddenly and was very lovable; and then, when there was any clog in his soul's quick running, his face went stupid and ugly. He was the sort of boy that becomes a clown and a lout as soon as he is not understood, or feels himself held cheap; and, again, is adorable at the first touch of warmth.

.   .   .   .   .

These quotations (they are telescoped here, but are from two early chapters of *Sons and Lovers*) give us the close relationship of mother and son, and they explain Lawrence's character better than much elaborate exposition can do. He was sensitive as few men are sensitive; sensitive, clever, an artist; 'so conscious of what other people felt, particularly his mother.' (I mean, by 'clever,' mentally agile.) In those days his only ambition was to 'earn his thirty or thirty-five shillings a week somewhere near home, and then, when his father died, have a cottage with his mother, paint and go out as he liked, and live happy ever after.' But in *Fantasia of the Unconscious*, if Murry is to be believed, Lawrence has himself in mind when he speaks of a woman 'seeking, seeking the fulfilment in the deep passional self . . . seeking whom she may devour.'

And usually, she turns to her child. Here she provokes what she wants. Here, in her own son who belongs to her, she seems to find the last perfect response for which she is craving. He is a medium to her, she provokes from him her own answer. So she throws herself into a last great love for her son, a final and fatal devotion, that which would have been the richness and strength of her husband and is poison to her boy.

Since Lawrence is an exceedingly personal writer, and since he spent the greater part of his literary life in explaining the relations between himself and his mother, his wife, and two other women whom he knew in youth, I incline to Murry's view. It is only important in an account of Lawrence's life; and I shall not again refer to it.

He was twenty-five when his first novel was written, and this was published in 1911, when it was widely assumed that any author who used initials instead of a Christian name and who wrote as emotionally as Lawrence did of a hero named Cyril must be a woman. In *Sons and Lovers*, which was published in 1913, he told with tremendous force and sincerity the story of his life as it had been up to his mother's death. In the following year, after his wife had been divorced by her first husband, he was married; and in August the European War broke out. The War, to Lawrence, was a merely horrible stupidity. He refused to have any part in it, believing that each man's responsibility was to himself and not to his fellows, and that at bottom the War was waged by England no less than by other countries on behalf of property, trade, and empire. He was already desperately agitated when, in 1915, his new novel, *The Rainbow*, was attacked as filth and the publishers ordered to withdraw it from circulation and destroy the remaining stock.

Lawrence then wrote another novel, *Women in Love*, and for this he failed for another five years to find a publisher. According to my recollection of the time, hesitation on the part of publishers to make themselves responsible for this book was due less to fear of prosecution on grounds of indecency than to another fear altogether. This I must explain. In his simplicity, Lawrence put real people into his books. He put himself over and over and over again; his mother, his wife, the two other women many times; his acquaintances as he needed them. If he was there, naked but splendid, why should they object to a lesser splendour? And there was a portrait in *Women in Love* as to which it was believed that proceedings for libel would be taken if the book were published. I suppose that nobody objects to a favourable portrait: Lawrence's were usually unfavourable. He would meet somebody, take a liking or a disliking, see very intensely whatever he liked or disliked, meditate upon the person, see more and more and more, and, then at white heat, would put that person into a story. The story would often be quite invented; only the person vividly portrayed as if by forked lightning. The consequences were painful. At least one person began proceedings against a Lawrence novel, and had to be soothed by a present from the publisher. Many others were wounded and unsoothed. For those in whose company Lawrence had been uncomfortable (though they had intended nothing but kindness) punishment was exemplary and inexorable.

What with his horror of the War, the humiliation he felt at successive medical examinations by the army authorities (for he was by no means a conscientious objector, and would have fought for any cause of the spirit which he approved), the persecution which he suffered through the suspicions of neighbours in Cornwall, who believed his German wife to be a spy, the prosecution of *The Rainbow*, the publishers' dread of *Women in Love*, and the desperate poverty in which—even with the aid of gifts and loans of money from those who could ill afford to lose what they had—the Lawrences lived, this period must have been enough to send so extraordinarily sensitive a man insane. I believe he did feel the bitterest hatred of England and the English—not the people, but the whole organization of the life of the people. When he wished to leave the country, although he had no longer any fear of being forced to serve in the army (he was obviously unfit for military training), he was refused a passport. He could not go until after the War, in 1919, and from that time to the end of his life, though he paid at least three brief visits, he could not again bear to live in England.

He lived in Italy, Sicily, Germany, Sardinia, Ceylon, Australia, the United States, Mexico, in Italy again, and in the South of France. He travelled extensively and almost incessantly, looking for some part of the world which had not been—in Lawrence's view—demoralized by civilization. He wrote a great deal. He must have been among the most prolific of all modern English writers. Wherever he went he took a readiness to be delighted with what he saw, an enthusiasm, an eagerness; but it always failed him, so that he was forced to haste away to farther and farther places of exile in order that he might set down some account of the horror he had just escaped. He was in this way the first of the moderns, for the materialism of contemporary life was too much for him; and he sought horrified escape from it. But he was greater than any other of the moderns, because he brought to life an extraordinary sweetness of nature, a belief in the virtue of self-knowledge which in his case and in no other known to me was passionate, a peculiarly simple and original genius which no accumulation of dross can conceal, and a power which I believe nobody will deny of attaching to himself as admirers the most diverse body of people that can be imagined. I have not met anybody who knew Lawrence who did not love him.

Perhaps I have been lucky; for it is clear that Lawrence felt himself to be a very lonely man. Nor do I think he always showed good judgment in the choice of those whose company he must have endured. He was largely cut off from the class from which he had come; literary people and amateurs of literature were his only friends. Common literary interests, in my view, provide a false basis for true friendship; and I believe Lawrence knew it. He did not want literary friends. Unfortunately, admirers were necessary to him; in particular, women admirers. He was in this difficulty, that he had exceptional intellectual powers, and yet detested intellectualism. Though he quarrelled with many of the tenets of Christianity, and developed a kind of jealousy of Christ, he was more nearly a Christian mystic than anything else. Therefore he had no patience with the scientific obsession of so many intellectuals. He could be friendly with Bertrand Russell, but he was forced to tell Russell that a synopsis of some lectures which they were to give together was 'pernicious,' and while the acquaintance continued it was seen by both parties to be an impossible alliance. He astonishingly maintained friendship with Middleton Murry (astonishing, I mean, in view of their constant breaks), with whom he at one time seems to have felt himself so much a sort of soul-mate that only Murry can do justice to the relationship. But what he needed above all, and what he never found, even in Catherine Carswell, whom he liked and respected, was the perfection of understanding which could only have been given by a man of his own origins who, like himself, had genius. He was a giraffe among other animals (not only dogs, as he thought), and had a giraffe's high head as well as a giraffe's shyness and disconcerting speed. Has a giraffe any retaliatory weapon? Lawrence had one.

What, actually, were his qualities and his defects? One has to make up one's own mind, I feel sure, as to these; for if one reads what those who knew Lawrence say one finds a hundred contradictions — Murry, Catherine Carswell, Huxley, David Garnett, all say different things about him. As a man, it seems that he would never be rude to anybody when face to face. He could destroy such a person in a tale; but he could not be impolite. This seems to me to be a remarkable trait in one so fearless in condemnation. Then, as one sees his letters thrown together, one realizes that he *was* affected by the wish to placate or maintain the friendship of some for whom he felt qualified regard. One catches piercing criticisms of friends as well as of books; much kindness to individuals coupled with scathing comments upon groups. Was there a cowardice in him? For he greatly disliked compromise: 'I do like plain outspokenness.' He would say very harsh things about his fellow-novelists, especially his seniors; but was oddly anxious to know that they thought of *him*. What did James, Bennett, Forster, and others, think of *The Rainbow*? He did not care; and yet what *did* they think? All writers should admire him; and if they did not do homage they were no good. They were no good, anyway. He could not stand James Joyce; Mackenzie ('the dashing Monty'), who was very kind to Lawrence and had a share in bringing about a resumption of his novel-writing, though 'I get on with' him, was 'a fool not to know (in 1914) that times are too serious to bother about his *Sinister Street* frippery'; even Aldous Huxley, praised in a letter on *Point Counter Point*, suffers later from a cool belittlement: 'No, I don't like his books: even if I admire a sort of desperate courage of repulsion and repudiation in them. But again, I feel only half a man writes the books—a sort of precocious adolescent.'

The explanation lies in Lawrence's feeling that he is an original genius, and the others for the most part fakes or imitators of the dead. He believes that in their hearts all other writers hate him and deny him. That faith in Lawrence is what his intense admirers experience. They are not critical; they *believe*. It is an extraordinary circumstance, and it prevents one who did not know him from criticizing the novels of Lawrence by any except special standards. He was a prophet. His novels, so full of lifeless passages, dull dialogue which when it is not urgently expressive of his own beliefs is no more than echo, and terribly monotonous use of words such as 'dark' and 'obscene,' are charged with spiritual intimations. His beautifully simple *Fantasia of the Unconscious* (which should be read by all who still suppose him to be a wallower) is a gospel. Even *Lady*

Chatterley's Lover, which he says is symbolic, although it reads to the uninstructed as the merest pornography, is a passionate plea for purity. To write of such a man as one would do of one of his contemporaries, and to say that his novels are 'good' or 'not so good,' is to go away from faith into blasphemy, and not to appraise with admired discriminatingness. How impossible, then, to speak of the work apart from the man!

Murry says that Lawrence was never an artist; Huxley says he was an artist above all. They are using the word in different senses. What Murry means is that Lawrence had none of the Jacobean picture technique and subordination of the part to the whole; Huxley, that Lawrence is describable by no other word than 'artist.' I agree with both. To Lawrence a novel was not a work of art, but a new reading of life, an exhortation, a picture of soul-states. He wrote novels as poems, by a sort of spontaneous imaginative energy; and while he rewrote some of them more than once it was never with the object of reducing them to lozenge-shape, only with that of giving more emphatic form to his argument. I do not think he would ever have produced a book to please the technicians; nor do I think he shows a real talent for the creation of character, as distinguished from the creation of mood and passion or the reproduction of idiosyncrasies. Such creation of character for its own sake would have seemed to him artificial, a playing with serious things, an abdication of moral purpose. I don't agree with the view; but the point thus made against the 'artistic' novel is much more than an arguable one: it is crucial. I cannot argue it here, though I suggest an answer to Lawrence's claim for his own method may be found in work written in imitation of Lawrence. Bereft of his passion, and composed by young men and women who have never felt a stronger emotion than dislike, it is both tedious and ludicrous, a peppering of the commonplace with lurid verbs, adverbs, and adjectives. Lawrence's books were apocalyptic visions: unless one has such visions, a tamer and finer technique is quite a virtue.

Just how excellent Lawrence's visions were, time will show. They were produced by the impact upon an original genius of modern conditions and a particular crisis in the world's affairs, and the kind of society to which Lawrence was condemned. That the momentary vision itself was vehement is undeniable. No author has ever pictured a scene with comparable passion. One cannot read such chapters as the 'Water Party,' 'Mino,' and 'Crème de Menthe' in *Woman in Love* without realizing that the author is a great writer. But the books as wholes are lacking in momentum; intrinsically, apart from minors and superficial traits in the principals, all the characters are the same. All are torturers and self-torturers, absorbed in the foulnesses of hatred and disgust. At times, especially in such books as *The Rainbow* and *Women in Love*, Lawrence seems to be obsessed by the passion of gloating, malignant cruelty; and his people have thick, ugly darknesses of soul which cause them to become, not humans, but pagan and terrible creatures. His language in describing them is equally extravagant. The dictionary does not contain adjectives enough for him, and he falls back upon 'obscene' for all purposes. He returns again and again to the emotion of hatred, until the hatred his characters feel moves us no more than does the indifference of our neighbours. With every strong word to describe strong feeling, he produces a loss of value in the word and the emotion. That he felt this hatred himself, and that he attributed it to others (unless he found them, as I am sure he found the intellectuals, bloodless and false), I do not doubt. That such vehemence is a true sign of strength it is hard for one temperamentally indisposed to vehemence to admit. I do not accept the Lawrentian psychology; if I were to pretend to do so I should stultify my own experience, and as Lawrence said once: 'Excuse me if I want to get out of the train.' He came from a poor, opinionated, and outspoken section of the community; and he entered a half-rich, opinionated, and intensely reserved section of the community. He had to do this, for nowhere else could he find intellectual companionship; but he was never at home in it, as a hundred malicious portraits in his books testify. When he offered his soul, these people looked down their noses. No wonder he hated them. But they were not all the people, even in England.

Another fact is that, remaining poor, and having in fact no wish to have that agglomeration of goods and responsibilities which we call a home, he lived nomadically, and always very much alone and at close quarters with his wife. His relations with her were an absorbing topic for thought. When he was not in her company, he was turning over in his mind what had happened between them, what she felt and thought—it was so different from what he thought and felt—how uncontrollable she was, how bent upon her own will, her own self, and so on. He had much time in which to think, really to brood; and out of his intensities of feeling and thought he drew poems and generalizations and novels (or rather, scenes in novels) which were of a kind never previously attempted in English. There is a nakedness of honesty, as well as a fierceness of emotion, in his writing for which the reserved English were unprepared. Only those who in some degree shared his independence of mind were able to appreciate them; the curious were another matter, and at once collected him and his writings for their own diversion. Lawrence knew that: the knowledge explains some of his exasperation, his hatred for the admirers who were so necessary to him. He sometimes hesitated about publication. But his simplicity was so great that he did not, for any consequences to himself, fear the results of disclosure. He returned over and over again to the same theme, with its inevitable variations; mother, wife, self:

> . . . ultimately, she is all beyond me,
> She is all not-me, ultimately.
> It is that that one comes to.
> A curious agony, and a relief. . . .
> When she has put her hand on my secret, darkest sources, the
>   darkest outgoings,
> When it has struck home to her, like a death, 'this is *him*!'
> She has no part in it, no part whatever,
> It is the terrible *other* . . .
>> What should I do if you were gone again
>> So soon?
>> What should I look for?
>> Where should I go?
>> What should I be, I myself,
>> 'I'?
>> What would it mean, this
>> 'I'?

The need for sincerity, for sincere explanation, for the dispelling of all non-comprehension, was ever urgent with him: 'I do like plain outspokenness.' And his wife the only person in the world with whom he could thus speak plain and true:

> How quaveringly I depend on you, to keep me alive,
> Like a flame on a wick.

> Suppose you didn't want me! I should sink down
> Like a light that has no sustenance.

Is it any wonder that his work, though thought ranges wide, is at its best so intense and in general so monotonous? It was all from within; given coherence and meaning by its relation to his own life. I think the growth of appreciation for Lawrence's genius has come very much from an increase in knowledge of Lawrence himself. That seems to be so in Catherine Carswell's case, although she always admired him; I myself, having read his Letters, which, like the *Fantasia of the Unconscious*, are the work of a man supremely sane and sure, have realized better than ever before Lawrence's strong personal charm, and clearness of thought.   Many others must be in the same position.   For his hatred and his flights and eager affections and disillusionments, his insistence upon John Thomas and Lady Jane, his mysticism and revivalistic summons to abandon the sense of sin, we may have fluctuating sympathy (in my case, none for hatred, pity for such magnificent ingenuousness as to intellectual friends, distaste for mysticism, but entire support for the abandonment of the sense of sin, which I have fortunately escaped); but for his genius warm admiration and for his character new esteem are the inevitable result of any dispassionate inquiry.   I have said that I think *Lady Chatterley's Lover* is pornography: it was not intended as such, and there is no harm in its common little story or the silly use of common terms for copulation and the generative organs; but so far as it finds readers at all it will be on account of its aphrodisiac character.   I do not think *The Rainbow* pornography, but a great bad book, full of wonderful beauties and truths, beside which every other novel of its immediate age seems timid, neat, and at least upon the verge of banality, if not over the verge.

Lawrence's appeal is really to the heart, and not to the head. For this reason 'precocious adolescents' and unimaginative elders, desperately chewing the husks of physical science, now cultivate and misunderstand him as a demi-god.   They will continue to misunderstand, but will cease to cultivate him, when a newer fashion arises.   Meanwhile, since they can no longer believe in salvation or the divine adequacy of Jesus Christ, and since they must have faith in something or else fall into abject despair, they clutch at Lawrence as a new Messiah, and are as emotional about him as their own frigidity allows.   It is not as a writer that they value him; but as a teacher: 'Verily, verily, I say unto you . . .'   They search his work for meanings.   'Very gnomic,' as Mr Barbecue-Smith would say.

There is something pathetic and grotesque about all this, for so many of Lawrence's disciples are men and women whom he would have run thousands of miles to avoid—from whom he did run thousands of miles, only to find that, like God, they were everywhere.   That is to say, the people who arouse distaste in such as myself aroused furious horror in Lawrence.   They are Lawrentians.   They chatter about 'otherness' and 'darkness';

they are serious about sex, and worry about it, finding Lawrence an advanced and esoteric Marie Stopes; they assume Lawrence's arrogance, which does not fit them; and they are consciously 'free' and at the same time self-analytical, which is as near as they can get to the Lawrentian insistence upon candour. But they have no true connection with the Lawrentian idea. His cry was for innocence, for purity ('unless ye become as little children'), for a clear distinction between the sexes; theirs is for a different sophistication, a psychologized faith from which they can get what Americans call a 'kick' no longer obtainable from Christianity. Either sophisticates or cranks are Lawrence's followers; genuine Lawrentians are to be found only among those to whom much of Lawrence's work is a tortured nightmare, a writhing, sweating struggle to express personal truths and give them by the use of mystical terms a general application. My belief is that the reputation of this author will decline. As men and women learn more about their own minds, his remarkable pioneer work will fall in importance; as the history of mankind pursues its course his beliefs will be either absorbed or rejected, and will no longer obtain loyalties. We shall be forced back upon his books as literature; and this test, without considerable reservation, they will not pass. He was a product of his day, a portent, a noble-minded man of strong personality, a begetter of faith, a sort of latter-day Carlyle rather than a latter-day Blake, as he has been called. In a hundred years or less he may, I think, be found a little fervid. The defiant faith of a Catherine Carswell will seem slightly 'period,' the exegetical destructions of a Murry altogether irrelevant. He will be seen as a poet, an impressionist; not as a rival to Christ, and not as a great expert in the *psyche*. Let there be no mistake, however, in a hundred years he will probably still be on the literary map, while I, and those like me, will have sunk without trace from every record of the Georgian age.

IV. JAMES JOYCE

My God, what a clumsy *olla putrida* James Joyce is! Nothing but old fags and cabbage-stumps of quotations from the Bible and the rest, stewed in the juice of deliberate, journalistic dirty-minded-ness—what old and hard-worked staleness, masquerading as the all-new!
D. H. Lawrence to M. and A. Huxley.

If Lawrence was unsophisticated, Joyce is the reverse. One can trace his steady progress in sophistication from the close

realistic studies contained in *Dubliners*, impressions mostly
of squalid life in a city, through the quickened reminiscence of
Portrait of the Artist as a Young Man, to the extended and
often very brilliant display of *Ulysses*. Only hard-headed
Irishmen and cosmopolitan Jews are as sophisticated as he, or
could have written anything in such an idiom as that of *Ulysses*.
They are the men, journalists, entrepreneurs, and the like, who
take a professionally knowing view of everything that goes on in
the world, turning like lightning from one subject to another,
and summing each in an expert phrase which is like a password
and which still leaves the soft world rolling unconsciously
through eternity.

They know the argot of every language, the drinks and by-
words of every nation, the 'shop' of every profession, the sewage
of every mind. They are without reverence, hard as stone,
proud of their knowingness and exhibitionary of it, but at
heart wearied to death because they are without illusions. They
automatically and professionally notice and remember for ever
headlines and solecisms in newspapers, the clichés of barmaids,
slips made by common, genteel, and ridiculous persons, smells,
lingerie, betrayals of vulgarity, scandals about well - known
persons, and the *faux pas* of *ingénues*. It is their business to
notice and to know these things. It is a part of the professional
training. At will, these men can run all their observations together in a never-ending patter of expert talk. Their note is
a hard, bright cleverness, a knowingness regarding the baser
aspects of humanity; but for the good and the pure, since they
believe in neither, they can feel nothing but contempt.

Joyce has some of the traits of the sophisticated journalist or
entrepreneur. Being an Irishman, he is master of an inexhaustible pen. His knowledge of the life of back streets, of
saloons, the lewd thoughts of maidens, the doings at Catholic
seminaries in Ireland, of foul old men, and a thousand other
disagreeable matters, is extensive and peculiar. He rarely soars
above the base; but the base is known to him without mercy.
He can lay his hand upon its heart and feel the very beat of it.
He can imaginatively enter it and be of it, so that the reader of
what he writes may well feel that this is at that moment the
whole of life. And as he has progressed in sophistication he has
also progressed in his own quite special technique, which has
not yet reached its end, although it has long passed the instantly
intelligible. He carries a kind of literary post-impressionism as
far as any man has yet done—farther than any other writer

except Gertrude Stein.   Sometimes he writes in a series of jotted shorthand notes; sometimes as if he overheard and recorded a dialogue between strangers; sometimes in wild fantasy; sometimes in a jumble of disconnected thoughts.   The jumble is his mainstay in some of the best passages in the book called *Ulysses*.

Might manage a sketch.   By Mr and Mrs L. M. Bloom.   Invent a story for some proverb which?   Time I used to try jotting down on my cuff what she said dressing.   Dislike dressing together.   Nicked myself shaving.   Biting her nether lip, hooking the placket of her skirt.   Timing her.   9.15.   Did Roberts pay you yet?   9.20. What had Greta Conroy on?   9.23.   What possessed me to buy this comb?   9.24.   I'm swelled after that cabbage.   A speck of dust on the patent leather of her boot.

Rubbing smartly in turn each welt against her stocking calf. Morning after the bazaar dance when May's band played Ponchielli's dance of the hours.   Explain that morning hours, noon, then evening coming on, then night hours.   Washing her teeth.   That was the first night.   Her head dancing.   Her fansticks clicking.   Is that Boylan well off?   He has money.   Why?   I noticed he had a good smell off his breath dancing.   No use humming then.   Allude to it.   Strange kind of music that last night.   The mirror was in shadow.   She rubbed her handglass briskly on her woollen vest against her full wagging bub.   Peering into it.   Lines in her eyes. It wouldn't pan out somehow.

Evening hours, girls in grey gauze.   Night hours then black with daggers and eyemasks.   Poetical idea pink, then golden, then grey, then black.   Still true to life also.   Day, then the night.

Now to a quick mind, self-observant, ready to catch notes and take them, to sight contradictions in mood and response, and to explore memory, the concoction of such a jumble is not difficult. The method is familiar enough in scraps of impressionist fiction. What gives Joyce's jumble its peculiar merit is his wit and the frequent malicious precision of his exposure, which goes deeper into soliloquy than the work of any other writer.   He has an extraordinary ear for words (he is a singer, and well understands the art of phrasing and enunciation), and an intricate mind of which the sensitiveness jumps out like flame to kindle significant associations.   He has a strong taste for Irish slang and idiom (in *Work in Progress* that has been a chief obstacle to understanding for those who have not the Irish voice and vocabulary), a memory as long and exact as any man's, and a wide range of reading to which Stephen Dedalus's mother once objected, as she did to his 'queer mind.'   He has not, I think, a truly creative imagination, but abnormal cleverness, in which he takes a virtuoso's delight.   Those words of Lawrence's which I have quoted put the matter over-strongly.   Though they are so

amusing, they represent the puritan's point of view. But they
have a penetration natural to Lawrence's literary criticism.
Lawrence, though it was his way to see the defects of other
authors, rather than their qualities, made no mistake in the
nature of the defects, and in a phrase summed up what most of
us would take pages to express, even if, at the end of them, we
reached the same conclusion.

Joyce was born in Dublin in 1882, and was educated at
Catholic colleges and the Royal University, Dublin. He has
lived for most of his manhood in various continental cities,
Vienna, Trieste, Zurich, and Paris (where he now is), giving
lessons in the English language, translating, and, it is possible,
though of this I am not sure, doing some journalistic work. In
person he is fairly tall, some five feet nine and a half, but is so
slim that he seems taller. He is dark, his hair dark brown, his
beard a lighter brown; and his eyes, with which he has had great
trouble for years, are blue. His manner is quiet; he will sometimes, to please a host, spend an entire evening at the piano,
singing and playing old Irish airs in a very sweet tenor voice;
but at other times will be wholly silent, though never *farouche*.
And he works very slowly indeed; for those odd phrases, which
seem to us to be such rapid shorthand, often take him a very
long time to compose, so packed are they with meanings and
peculiar appropriateness.

Ulysses, for example, which seems to be as much of a jumble
as some of the reflections contained in it, is an elaborately
constructed work upon the model of Homer's *Odyssey*. A long
book has been written pointing out every parallel between the
Odyssey and *Ulysses*. It is made a point of by all those who
highly esteem Joyce as a writer, that his longest book is a
modern work, based upon the *Odyssey* but dealing with only
eighteen hours in time. Just why a book should be important
because it is based upon another book, I do not know. I
suppose the point is that Joyce is a great scholar who has studied
the *Odyssey* whereas other people might suppose him to be
merely a novelist. In the same way, there is said to be some
magic in its concern with eighteen hours of time. I do not
understand that, either. The time stunt is no better than any
other stunt; it may need some ingenuity for its employment, but
it is not essential for art or meaning. It is a convenience, an
attractive condensation; nothing more. I should know this,
for it was a book of my own which began the time-stunt fashion.
Far too often, nowadays, some ingenuity of technique is given

the blessed name of art. So, as far as I can tell, neither the time scheme of *Ulysses* nor its debt to the *Odyssey* gives the book any special claim to attention. It must stand upon its more positive merits.

Those merits, as I have suggested, are the merits of virtuosity. Nobody has ever presented the thoughts of a vulgar woman such as Mrs Bloom with such terrible convincingness. They have the air of being complete and unerring. In a lesser degree, the thoughts of a cheap girl, earlier in the book, a girl who leans back and shows her knickers for the sake of exciting a stranger, have amusing and edifying precision. There is a wild scene of great length and orgiastic obscenity which shows Joyce to be a master of extravagant invention. On the whole, however, when one abstracts one's admiration for performance, there is little enough in the book which can justify the adjectives of its admirers. It is quite empty of idea, although it is packed with ideas. It is also packed with the most brilliant mimicry known to me; mimicry and impersonation. If mimicry and impersonation made great literature, *Ulysses* would be a great book. It seems to me to be a hotch-potch. The fact that its publication in England has been delayed, and the fact that it is only now available in America after being pirated there, have given it adventitious attractions for the amateur of letters. It has, in the same way, been something of a key book for rebel authors in both countries; and while many of those who applaud it have never read it through, and could not with understanding read it through, they have taken their position as defenders of courage against the squeamishness of mankind, and cannot withdraw.

What Joyce has is this great knowledge of the seamy side of life and character. He has unrivalled power to represent the thoughts and feelings of some very odd people. He has a literary manner which ranges from the Rabelaisian to the Meredithian, and has between those extremes a large area of clever, ingenious, sophisticated impressionism which at its best is of amazing virtuosity and penetration. If he had remained the realist of *Dubliners* (but he could not do that, for his is essentially an egotistical talent), he might have had high standing as an objective realist. He now has high standing as a psychological realist. I should not, however, rate him higher than that; and it will be understood that I am commenting solely upon the claim made by respectable critics that *Ulysses* is a great book, and the author a fixed star. To my mind he is a very able man, but not different in kind from other able men; only more brilliant and ruthless than they, and with a preference for what H. G. Wells has styled the cloacal. In that field he is a past master.

As to his latest experiments, I can say nothing. I do not find them entirely unintelligible; indeed, the words seem to me to swim at times into great vividness of picture or communication. But the ultimate meaning of such writing escapes me.

CHAPTER XV: A POST-WAR SYMPTOM

The art of self-tormenting is an ancient one, with a long and honourable literary tradition. Man, not satisfied with the mental confusion and unhappiness to be derived from contemplating the cruelties of life and the riddle of the universe, delights to occupy his leisure moments with puzzles and bugaboos.

DOROTHY L. SAYERS, Preface to *Great Short Stories of Detection, Mystery, and Horror.*

I

WHILE the idealisms and disillusions of the War had charged the newer poetry with a mixture of horror and flippancy, and while psycho-analysis and metaphysics had drawn a number of novelists into abnormal paths, and pacificism into the considered defence of weakness, other influences were affecting public taste and producing a demand for entirely different ingenuities. There was, in the years immediately following the War, an intense desire for easy reading. That the easy reading should since have become subtilized and sophisticated, until nowadays what was easy has become complicated and difficult, is but a sign of the times: the first call, and the first effort, were both simple enough.

Those learned in the matter have demonstrated that tales of crime and detection were written by early scribes. They track them to the Apocrypha, in the tale of Susanna and the Elders, and to Herodotus. The most simple-minded of them demonstrate that Voltaire, in *Zadig*, had the whole matter of logical deduction from clues at his command. But whether in fact he was anticipated by the ancients or by Voltaire, it is quite clear that Edgar Allan Poe invented for himself the formula later so successfully used by Conan Doyle; and that most subsequent stories devoted to the detection of crime have been variants or avoidances of the Poe-Doyle method. Interest in crime itself gives place in such stories to interest in the conduct of those who investigate the crime, or rather (since that loose definition would apply equally well to Gaboriau) to interest in the acute reasoning by which these investigators convert otherwise insignificant pointers into conclusive proofs of guilt or innocence. That the reasoning, for the greater part of the tale, is as mysterious as the crime itself matters nothing. When Sherlock Holmes found the wax vesta at the scene of John Straker's death, the inspector, annoyed, exclaimed: 'I cannot think how I came to overlook it'; to which Holmes rejoined: 'It was invisible, buried in the mud. I only saw it because I was looking for it.' And again, in the same story, a favourite with lovers of Holmes (*Silver Blaze*), when the inspector says to Holmes: 'Is there any other point to which you would wish to draw my attention?' and Holmes answers: 'To the curious incident of the dog in the night-time.' 'The dog did nothing in the night-time.' 'That was the curious incident.'

Just how much the early tales by Conan Doyle owed to the fact that Sherlock Holmes was a character will never be known. He was so great a character that he trembled upon the borders of farce—never over them, of course: I speak as a fan. His vanity, his eccentricities, his nettling rebukes to Watson, all made him, much to his creator's annoyance (for Doyle thought he had better books, more sober, laboured books, to his credit than the Holmes tales), a character in the full tradition of the Victorian novelists. He stands for all time as a warning to those who think the way to produce immortal literature is to take oneself very seriously.

Imitators perhaps invented better mysteries for their detectives to unravel, as indeed it was their duty to do; but none of them invented a Sherlock Holmes. But what Doyle had done caused a rush of imitations. Most of them are forgotten, or would be forgotten if the post-War spiritual drouth had not already produced for detective stories (as for other writings) a host of Dryasdusts, scholars, and (ghastly, deadening accompaniments to the capture of literature by the uncreative) fixed canons. Because of these scholars certain phosphorescent corpses of old mystery have been propped up, post-mortemed, and bottled and labelled for ever. And because of these scholars, a definite view has been adopted regarding what does or does not make one kind of book superior to another kind of book. The detective mystery story has been given a certificate of quality; the story which has a longer tradition, the story in which crime plays its part as a leading interest, and in which criminals are shown in action, is reduced to the ranks. As E. M. Wrong says, 'the crime story has on the whole been a failure as compared with the tale of detection . . . In fact, the tale of crime is best seen from the detective's angle.'

I wonder if Wrong is right? I wonder this canon does not merely represent the cultivated point of view? If one has been elaborately educated, so that one's brains must be given some problem to chew, any *naïveté* will seem jejune, and one will despise very readily whatever does not supply this necessary fuel. But I am by no means sure that a highly cultivated mind is a mind essentially critical. It brings to the consideration of art a machine, or at least a system of laws and principles acquired with pains and perhaps with devotion. But the application of acquired principles to particular books and kinds of books always strikes me as being as arbitrary as the purely instinctive judgment of those who are less cultivated. In the present case, my own sympathy is with Wrong; in the sense that I personally prefer the detective story to the story of crime. But I think the modern worship of ratiocination may be a fault; and there is something too summary in his decision that the crime story has been a failure as compared with the tale of detection. Perhaps the crime story only fails to interest Wrong.

It has not failed to interest others. Scholars of a different kind, for example, have given many years to the study of Dickens's incomplete *Mystery of Edwin Drood*, begun when the Master, in Gissing's terrible words, 'casting about him for a new story, saw murder at the end of every vista.' I hazard the guess that Oliver Onions's short novel, *In Accordance with the Evidence*, is more important to its readers than many detective stories, although the commission of an undiscovered crime is its central interest. The adventurous histories of John Buchan and others of his type may be as engrossing, and certainly as imaginative, as the majority of detective stories. Dostoevsky's *Crime and Punishment* is without doubt a greater book than Gaboriau's *Mystery of Orcival*. I suggest that the mind which requires a problem is not necessarily superior to the mind that rejoices in its freedom, but only a mind that prefers pencil-and-paper games to pure sport.

This is by the way; and I must not dally. There would be no question as to the fact that vulgar people, never wholly subdued by the few, have always preserved a curious interest in sensationalism for its own sake. In 1905 they bought or otherwise acquired 38,000 copies of a short, vigorous, and highly sensational novel about the conscientious removal of a wicked Cabinet Minister. The book was called *The Four Just Men*, and for the

solution of one point in it which had been left unsolved by
the author a prize of £500 was offered. Whether entrants for the
prize numbered 38,000 nobody now can say. I think the public
read *The Four Just Men* for much the same reason as that which
had led them to patronize in the course of the previous century
such works as *The Woman in White, The Mystery of a Hansom
Cab, Called Back, Lady Audley's Secret,* and *Lost Sir Massing-
berd*. That is because it told a thrilling story, in which time,
troubles, and tedium were annihilated. The author's name was
unfamiliar to readers of novels, and it remained so, apart from
this one book, for a space. But later on, after the War was over,
news began to creep about of this book and that by a single
writer, and it was found that he had produced a number of such
books; and then, as the demand for them grew, more and more
books came tumbling out with his name on the title-page, so
that one name was known to all who read books, from Pall Mall
to Penzance and from Chester to Chicago, and Berlin to Buda-
pest and Buenos Aires.

In England, formerly, two men had held the throne of popularity with masses of their fellow-countrymen. One was Nat
Gould, whose racing novels were said to have sold two million
copies; the other was Charles Garvice, whose novelettes, contributed as serial stories to a women's paper, and republished by
himself, swept the land. We had had startling successes, such
as those of Hall Caine and Marie Corelli, and latterly Ethel M.
Dell and Florence Barclay. We had had our conjunctions of
quality and popularity, such as Wells. But there had not previously been quite such universal reading of a single author as
occurred in the case of Edgar Wallace in the years immediately
following the War. There were sufficient reasons for this.

II. EDGAR WALLACE

I shall be broke again and rich again; but broke or rich, I shall, if
the Lord keeps me in good health, be grateful and happy for every
new experience, for every novel aspect which the slow-moving circle
of life presents to me. I have made many big friends and provoked
a few little enmities, which will clear up some day. And I am here!
Newspaper-boy, cabin-boy, soldier, journalist, writer—what next?
Whatever it is, I'll bet it is interesting.

EDGAR WALLACE, *People*.

Edgar Wallace, who was born in 1875, was the son of an
actress who abandoned him; and at the age of nine days he

was adopted by a Billingsgate fish porter. When he was very small, much against the wish and without the knowledge of his adoptive mother, he began to sell newspapers at a pitch near Ludgate Circus at the bottom of Fleet Street. He then took a number of jobs in factories, which he did not keep, had a single voyage at sea, and joined the army. While in the army he wrote a comic song which was bought by Arthur Roberts, and composed a number of doggerel verses; and when his regiment was sent to South Africa he formed by degrees so persistent a journalistic connection that he got into trouble with superior officers, was persuaded to buy his discharge, and set up in Cape Town as a journalist. When the Boer War began he acted as correspondent, at first for Reuter's, and then, through an accident, directly for London newspapers; and he was the first to transmit to England news that peace was signed. When he eventually left South Africa for home, he acted as reporter for *The Daily Mail*, was for a brief time editor of the London *Evening News*, and as a special correspondent for a year or two knocked about all over Europe.

While all this was happening to Wallace he published several books of verses—most of them admittedly written in imitation of Kipling, who was his idol. And in 1905, as I have said, he wrote and personally published from a room in Temple Chambers *The Four Just Men*, upon which he lost money. He also published at least one other book, the author of which was a Durham schoolmaster named Ian Hay Beith. But publishing and the writing of stories were both unremunerative; and as that was the time of E. D. Morel's denunciation of atrocities on the Belgian Congo Wallace returned to Africa to investigate matters on behalf of *The Daily Mail*. His experiences on the Congo gave him a new theme; and although the literary world did not realize the fact until long afterwards he began his first successful fiction-writing with a series of stories which had the Congo as a background. *Sanders of the River, People of the River, Bosambo of the River* were all in this vein. He now had at his command first-hand experience of the life of London's respectable poor (with sidelights on those less respectable which arose from the police-bashing habits of his step-brothers), army life, War, South African life and politics, journalism, the Congo; he had taught himself with a good deal of labour how to write with a fair semblance of grammatical accuracy; he was adventurous; and when the European War came, as he was too old for military service, he wrote from home, for *The Birmingham Daily Post*, articles commenting on the progress of operations, and a number of very popular short stories for an American magazine about a Scottish mechanic and airman known as 'Tam o' the Scouts.' After the War, he settled to the writing of sensational stories, serials, detective mysteries, and the like; and then indeed his success verged upon the incredible.

The time was propitious, because men and women were crying for distraction from the misery, disgust, and boredom which the War and the peace had produced. Most people were weary; they were in no mood as yet to adore those later loves, erudition and ingenuity; they wanted a writer who could tell a story, and whose invention was equal to the task of keeping them agog for three hundred pages. Smack, crash, bang: 'For a second only the old man stared spellbound, and then his pistol jerked up and he fired twice.' Wallace was their man. He says in his really excellent autobiography, *People*, speaking of an earlier time:

I had learnt the habit of early rising and early working, and always I worked at top speed.

He worked at top speed. He could deliver the goods. More; his invention was inexhaustible, and he could and did—without the smallest help from a 'ghost'—supply with gusto what everybody was waiting for In that period, and for that period, he became the best-known writer in the world.

Edgar Wallace's appearance is known to all through many photographs in which his long cigarette - holder always pro - trudes from a pair of thin lips set in a mask-like white face. A plump face, the flesh about the eyes slightly swollen and the eyes themselves cold and steady; the face of a card-player of steady nerve. He was a man of good size, but not above middle height. His head was clear; he was modest but self-assured, a good public speaker, a fluent talker and tale-teller. He knew what he knew, and never went outside that knowledge in his talk and writing. It is a remarkable fact that the success of his tales owed nothing whatever to salaciousness or suggestiveness, and that his conversation was entirely free from any of the prevailing coarseness to be found in more intellectually ambitious circles. He drank little, if at all, besides copious draughts of tea. He worked and gambled, worked and gambled, from morning to night. He was typical of the respectable poor of England; and was only unlike them in the fact that he had a highly remunerative talent, of which he made full use to the last days of his life.

It is quite true that the most successful novels he wrote were of a disconnectedly sensational kind, and that he never was an artist or a polished *littérateur*. It is also true that some of his books are not very good books, and that the best of them do not bear re-reading. But the qualities which were in the man are in the books. He knew the criminal world better than most of his rivals; he knew the racing world (but apparently not the horses, for he was a poor tipster) to the extent that he could make it an effective background for fiction. And his aim was the continuous excitement and entertainment of his readers, in which aim he was successful. As an ever-afterwards-quoted reviewer once said: 'It is impossible not to be thrilled by Edgar Wallace.' There were times — now past — when nobody but Edgar Wallace could supply just that unsuggestive, plain diet of crime that a world in lassitude needed as tonic or anodyne. Wallace was a superlatively honest, capable, strong-willed, shrewd man of the people who had taught himself to write and who was an inveterate gambler. He did not bother about readers who might prefer Flaubert (and, of course, being a wise man, he did not decry Flaubert); but followed his own bent and did his work as a craftsman. I claim no more for the work than that. But Wallace himself was more original, and he had greater talent, than many much more pretentious writers; and as a sign of the times, as one exalted by the post-War period of relaxation after stress, he is distinctly a figure in the Georgian literary scene.

III. DOROTHY LEIGH SAYERS

The mental features discoursed of as the analytical are, in themselves, but little susceptible of analysis. We appreciate them only in their effects. We know of them, among other things, that they are always to their possessor, when inordinately possessed, a source of the liveliest enjoyment. As the strong man exults in his physical ability, delighting in such exercises as call his muscles into action, so glories the analyst in that moral activity which *disentangles*. He derives pleasure from even the most trivial occupations bringing his talent into play.

E. A. POE, *The Murders in the Rue Morgue.*

The inevitable invidiousness of such a book as this leads me to omit reference to many excellent writers of tales of crime and tales of the detection of crime. If I were seriously to attempt an exhaustive study of each school of writers in every genre, my task would be unending, and each chapter in this book would be a book in itself. So just as I have taken Edgar Wallace as something more than himself, as in fact the archetype of his kind of writer, I shall skip all sorts of interesting composers of detective novels—from A. E. W. Mason to Agatha Christie, and from Ronald Knox to Crofts and the Coles, for the sake of reaching one who represents the farthest point yet reached in the development of detective stories towards complete sophistication. The contrast between Edgar Wallace and Dorothy Sayers is as the contrast between a walk in Chicago and an inquest at Oxford. In the first one is still alive, but apprehensive; in the second apprehension is past but one has become extremely interesting only as a specimen. The coroner talks a good deal, from A to Z.

It is not surprising that Dorothy Sayers should be erudite; for she graduated at Oxford University round about the end of the European War period. In those days she was less sophisticated than she now is; and after beginning cheerfully enough in 1916 with a diminutive collection of poems called *Op. I* she became graver two years later with a second volume entitled *Catholic Tales and Christian Songs*. These little prepared their readers for a later embarkation into the sea of crime. And yet within half a dozen years *Whose Body?* revealed an addition to the ranks of those who ask such disagreeable questions and proceed to deliver the answers at length.

From the first, Dorothy Sayers insisted upon being humorously informative. She has that inconvenient readiness of comment which flows from a mind lively and in good order. She knows a great many things which ordinarily would not find a place in the tale of crime and its detection; she has a number of opinions, also, which no respect for the wooden tradition of Dick Donovan and his peers can cause her to repress. From her mental encyclopaedia, accordingly, come all these richly spiced thoughts and views; and all in turn are stirred into the mystery, or mysteries, until one really feels as if Aldous Huxley himself had taken to lethal weapons. Dorothy Sayers decorates the corpse with jovial detail; she then produces quite a dozen persons whom, as it is shown with Socratic cunning, one must suspect of committing the crime. These persons are all exceedingly tortuous in character and movement upon essential days; and they have peculiar occupations or hobbies which need to be explored and dilated upon. She is a mistress of complications, a perfect fisherwoman of red herrings; and complications and herrings are of Brobdingnagian size and detail. When, as sometimes happens, Lord Peter Wimsey views the body and illustrates his love of *incunabula*, wines, and haberdashery, everything assumes so facetious and fantastic a turn that from being a light diversion the detective mystery novel becomes what has been described to me as 'deep.' It becomes, that is, very intricate, and for adult intellects only.

This is because the scholastic or scholarly mind is never content with the simple. For Dorothy Sayers, the plots of Doyle are thin; she knows all about Aristotle and his unities and E. M. Forster and his dislike of 'story.' And as she finds the Aristotelian unities well observable in the modern detective story it is clear that in spite of her admission that the detective story may never hope to rise to the extremest heights of art she can approve as well as write tales in which form is of more significance than emotion. On the subject of the detective story she is a scholar *facile princeps*. Her preface to the collection she first made of *Great Short Stories of Detection, Mystery, and Horror* is the best and most authoritative survey of the whole ground yet written. And her novels are increasingly and impressively the work of a scholar to whom every formula and every possible deviation from formula is already a sentence in single syllables. Can one who has passed the sixth standard be content with child's play?

If I dwell for a moment longer, as I fear I must, upon the weakness of too much scholarship in the arts, it is because I think scholarship is nowadays excessively valued as a necessary preliminary to creative writing. Much as I admire Dorothy Sayers, it is my suspicion that she is leading the detective story into dust. She writes with distinction; she invents with ingenuity. But in the same way that modern composers consciously and deliberately serve out music representing the acme of musical scholarship and little else, she, it seems to me (like equally accomplished workers in other literary fields), by her very virtuosity is killing the thing she has loved. To write according to the Aristotelian formula, or according to any formula, is to give oneself lockjaw. I agree that Dorothy Sayers as yet gives no sign of personal lockjaw; for she playfully decorates her surfaces with innumerable quips and modern instances. But the supply of mathematically minded persons is not unlimited, and a dreadful fate awaits all who tempt destiny with intellectual pride.

CHAPTER XVI: POST-WAR PESSIMISM

I

I HAVE shown in previous chapters how, during the War, the imaginations of the young poets soured as the result of their experience, and how the intellectual protesters against the futility of war gradually came to have a voice in the popular ear, and how, when men and women at home were severely tried, they escaped as they could by means of a different kind of violence from that of which they had been reading for four years in their newspapers. I must now mention certain writers whose literary reputation is almost wholly post-War, and whose work is a direct outcome of the mood of dissatisfaction, even despair, by which honest and thoughtful young people were seized as they saw the consequences of four years of slaughter.

I have chosen four writers who represent different and highly significant aspects of the post-War literary movement. They have not escaped other literary influences, of course, and I am far from satisfied that their work would have been seriously unlike what it now is if there had been no war at all. The War, I should say, hastened and heightened a tendency which would in any case have manifested itself. But for convenience I have called the chapter 'Post-War Pessimism,' and have ventured to regard the writers named in the chapter not only as individuals but as typical of the age.

There is no doubt that all these writers, and others, take views of life which were not apparent in the generation which was young in 1914. The young of 1914, however false their ex-pectation may have been, could contemplate a stable future. Nevertheless, Lawrence was young in 1914; Joyce was young in 1914; and Gilbert Cannan, who, more than any other of his immediate contemporaries, had what might be called a post-War mind, was young in 1914. You could not print, in those days, what you can print now; but could say the same things in a different way. You could not speak in so many words of homo-sexuality and Lesbianism, the Œdipus complex or casual forni-cation; but you were not prevented from the portrayal of abnor-mal people, and if there had to be greater discretion in language

I am not sure that some feeble little books which have seemed
bold by their use of vulgar words have after all done a tremendous deal for literature. The authors of them, while using some
common words, shrink from the use of others, and are often
enough guilty either of bravado or simple ostentation of knowledge. I say nothing at all about that wonderful new freedom
between the sexes of which we read in the newspapers; for I
think it but a further stage in self-consciousness.

But, as I have used the word 'self-consciousness' it is time
that I should explain in what way the post-War writers differ
from the pre-War writers. It is, in one of its more noteworthy
aspects, by virtue of painfully increased self-consciousness. We
are all so self-conscious now that some are paralysed in their
animal spirits (you see how the old reticence affects my pen!),
and some have carried narcissism to a point at which it has
become an extravagance. As between inhibition and exhibition, I must confess that I am for inhibition every time: it is
less tiresome to others. And the self-consciousness of the post-
War generations has infected letters to a most extraordinary
extent. Half our writers are defending themselves against disapproval of their abnormality; and half are making self-conscious
fun of the self-consciousness of others (or of their abnormality). Nearly all are showing off. If there are exceptions,
they are individuals. For the most part all are doing what I
have said; attacking or defending the most preposterous posi-
tions, and exhibiting their own imaginative poverties.

They all feel that the world is a revolting place, and a hopeless
place. They all want to do as Omar Khayyám wanted to do so
long ago, and smash the world to bits so as to remould it nearer
to the heart's desire. They are nearly all politicians, taking
sides in the fight between tyranny from the Right and tyranny
from the Left. But while they take sides, and chalk up their
newly learned bad words and their anti-Marx or anti-Douglas,
anti-Banks or anti-Capitalism or anti-Communism, they are all
in a condition of gloom and disapproval regarding the world
into which they have been flung. It is a world in a mess. They
know it; we all know it. Some think, therefore, that writers
have no business to sit down and write what they want to; that
they ought to struggle for something, no matter what, even if it
be only peace or war, a new currency or sterilization of the unfit.
Others that writers should mercilessly criticize and condemn the
old, or the young, orthodox or unorthodox economics, or graft
or political intrigue. And if there are some whose ways, moral

or immoral, do not please the majority, so that they are said to be diseased or criminal, they feel themselves to be personally involved in all condemnations of the age, and they, too, rise up into defensive polemics and assertion. 'I 'm right, and you 're wrong.' 'Every man for himself.' 'Punish, persecute, destroy.' 'Why shouldn't we be abnormal, if we want to? Poor things! Instead of bullying us, you should realize that we 're *different*. Not only different, but *better*.' As in the international sphere, so in the literary; everywhere distraction and hostility, one towards another. Barriers, pretensions, threats, fear, and misery. The air is full of criticism and bad words.

With some justification, but not the justification of art. Some say (following the lead of the Soviet Government) that there can now be no art which is not propagandist. They say we must choose to be either for Communism or for Fascism; never above party, never for disinterested truth. Others, contemplating our frantic anthill, knowing that the universe is finite and moving unrescuably towards its end, knowing that every phenomenon is reducible to statistics and scientific laws, seeing around them only the disheartening manifestations of corruption, a furious paroxysm of nullity, are appalled by realization of the littleness of man. They are the idealists, bereft of hope. Man is no more man; only a bundle of atoms, strutting, mouthing, functioning, one of so many thousand millions of his kind, an insect with no God to guide, no heaven to promise. Nothing is of any importance; what we are we have been for ages and shall be until the earth ceases to be able to support life. There is no virtue in us.

There are the quacks and the egotists, the former with nostrums and the latter with grievances. 'I haven't had a fair deal from Society. Damn Society!' 'Everybody 's mad; but I 'm sane.' 'Look out! The bogies will get you!' 'Ladies and gentlemen, if you will only buy this little pill, it will transport you to better trade or better morals or better art. But if you don't buy it, you 're doomed.' 'We're all doomed; for everybody 's against me, and always has been, and always will be. They don't like my face, or they 're brutes, cads, bitches . . .' Lawrence thought there was too much tolerance in the world; he wanted to destroy tolerance, because he believed that it was softness and the enemy of light. But he justifiably complained of intolerance towards himself; intolerance rising to what seemed like persecution. His successors, who have not Lawrence's genius, complain before anything has happened to them, and are so intolerant of each other that the literary world is full of faction. It is a kind of hysteria, perhaps. Their cries fill their polemics; they write, they say, from the standpoint of genius; genius has always been persecuted; and so, just as Captain Hook made his dying speech when he had an opportunity, in case the moment of death should give him no opening for it, they retort upon persecutors who really have been quite innocently wondering what they will have for dinner that day and have no other mischief in mind at all.

No wonder the pessimists, looking upon this scene, and deafened by the row, the tub-thumping and the squeals, are depressed. They shudder again at one more illustration of the increasing vulgarity of life; they criticize yet more stringently. They are used to hypocrisy and stupidity in the mass of people (of whom they know little, and want to know nothing at all); but to find noise and rottenness even in men who are supposedly of some intellect is a fresh horror to them, and one they can ill endure. They can only endure it if they have a power seldom found in company with pessimism or with intellectual prowess —the power of tumultuous laughter. And with that laughter they can ridicule the absurd. Said Elizabeth Bennet, in *Pride and Prejudice*: 'I hope I never ridicule what is wise and good. Follies and nonsense, whims and inconsistencies, do divert me, I own, and I laugh at them whenever I can.' Apart from the fact that he has grave doubts as to whether there are such things as wisdom and goodness, Aldous Huxley could echo Elizabeth's words. He is the one considerable intellectual of his generation who has a great heart and a great humour; who is as fastidious as a maiden aunt, as bawdy as a highbrow, and as unaffected in his amusement as a common man.

II. ALDOUS LEONARD HUXLEY

He handed Burlap the drawing. It was in ink touched with coloured washes, extraordinarily brilliant and lively. Curving in a magnificently sweeping S, a grotesque procession of monsters marched diagonally down and across the paper. Dinosaurs, pterodactyls, titanotheriums, ichthyosauruses walked, swam, or flew at the tail of the procession; the van was composed of human monsters, huge-headed creatures, without limbs or bodies, creeping slug-like on vaguely slimy extensions of chin and neck. The faces were mostly those of eminent contemporaries.

ALDOUS HUXLEY, *Point Counter Point*.

Like other celebrated and less celebrated writers of the day, Huxley, who was born in 1894, published poetry as his first step towards self-expression. He was a contributor to *Wheels*, the Sitwell rival to *Georgian Poetry*, published a book of verses of his own, *The Burning Wheel*, in 1916, and the same year was one of the editors of an annual called *Oxford Poetry*. Unlike some of the others, he has in spite of everything else remained a poet. He is now a poet in revolt against the planned scientific world of the future; and accordingly he has been read and condemned as the author of a book about bottled babies and other abominations. Such condemnation is not new to Huxley; it has helped him to a wider public than that enjoyed by any other writer of similar intellectual preoccupations; but it is regrettable.

Aldous Huxley is the grandson of Thomas Henry Huxley (to whom, according to H. G. Wells, who was T. H. Huxley's pupil, he has a facial resemblance), and on his mother's side is of the family of Thomas Arnold, the famous headmaster of Rugby. Schoolmasters, scientists, poets, and novelists (Mrs Humphry Ward was Huxley's aunt) have been among the notable assembly of his relations: if one were to picture them as fairy godfathers and godmothers, gathered about his bed in 1894, one could trace in his character a benevolent gift from each. He set out thereafter upon a road full of distinguished fingerposts, all pointing to fame by way of the intellect and the pen. It must be a blessing, but a doubtful blessing, to have such famous relations; pleasant to think 'my aunt' or 'my grandfather,' difficult, nevertheless, to ignore a certain imperiousness in the fingerposts.

However, although it is true that few great poets have been more assailed of late than Matthew Arnold, who is of his family, Huxley is not to be envied or commiserated with over his heredity. He is more properly to be discussed on account of his own performance. And first of all, I must say for those who are interested in such things (I have been encouraged all through this book to add notes on personal appearance and traits by reading that such details would be invaluable to writers of biographers for the *D.N.B.*) that he is the tallest English author known to me. He is so tall (and thin, so that he seems to stretch to infinity) that when, years ago, he lived in Hampstead, ribald little boys in that neighbourhood used to call out to him: 'Cole up there, guv'nor?' Naturally this great height has given some of those who encountered him the impression that he lives remote from the world, wrapped in distant hauteur. That is not the case. Expecting conscious superiority in him, casual observers have recorded an excessively lofty manner; whereas the truth is that Huxley converses easily, and is full of gleeful high spirits. He uses long words, because he thinks in long words; and not because he is aware that they are long words. The words he uses most often in conversation (or at least in narrative) are 'fantastic' and 'incredible.' They are appropriate words; for the narratives, made credible by his skill, are more fantastic than anything he has written, and they are also true. He has a happy knack of meeting odd people and seeing odd sights; and while this does not mean that he is himself odd it does mean that he is prepared for every oddity.

As a boy, Huxley suffered greatly in the matter of his eyesight, which it was feared that he would altogether lose. He spent many days alone, in a dark room, unable to read, unable to see: the introspective results of that time are plainly to be found in the nervous gravity—he does not like the word 'morbidity'—of his work. But the fear passed; though it would never be normal, his sight was saved, and he now enjoys it. He was able to go to Oxford. At Oxford he published some poems, as I have said; and when he came down he found work on *The Athenaeum*, under Middleton Murry's editorship. Over the name 'Autolycus' he contributed a regular essay to *The Athenaeum* (a number of these essays are to be found in the volume entitled *On the Margin*), and subsequently he collected several stories in a volume, called *Limbo*, which provided an auspicious opening to his literary career.

After *Limbo* was published, Huxley used to speak of a 'Peacockian novel' which he was writing, and I mention this fact, otherwise nowhere noted, because it is so interesting to realize that his impulse towards fiction came from a scholar-satirist, Thomas Love Peacock, rather than from a novelist. Huxley has never been a novelist in the ordinary sense: always a scholar-satirist. He can tell a story when he wishes to do so (it is usually a short story); but he is a man who uses the fiction form as a vehicle for his ideas, and not a man who writes novels because he must do so or remain sterile.

At the present time, when the 'modns' are all scientific intellectuals, this causes him to be what is called a fashionable writer; but Huxley does not command the suffrages of Bloomsbury, because his ideas are not quite those of Bloomsbury, and because, to the disgust of the exclusives, he has become a popular and very widely read publicist. His interests are multifarious. He is the only man I ever heard of (my informant was his brother, Julian, so I assume the story to be well founded) who, on setting out to go round the world, caused a special packing case to be made for his *Encyclopaedia Britannica*. He is likewise the only man who, with the *Encyclopaedia Britannica* ever to hand, takes an even greater interest in the world of flesh and blood.   Though a bookworm, he is a human being: the combination is a rare one.

First of all in *Limbo*, but more markedly in his first, or Peacockian novel, *Crome Yellow*, he gave evidence of those remarkable high spirits which have made him laugh wholeheartedly at the prigs, smugs, and snobs of the aesthetic world. The novel seemed to be full of portraits, all full of jovial irony; and I think it must have been the portraits which first roused a doubt of Huxley in the minds of really first-rate people.   He dared to laugh at first-rate people:

'What are you reading?' She looked at the book. 'Rather second-rate, isn't it?' The tone in which Mary pronounced the word 'second-rate' implied an almost infinite denigration. She was accustomed in London to associate only with first-rate people who liked first-rate things, and she knew that there were very, very few first-rate things in the world, and that these were mostly French.

That was War, you know.   Because if one laughs at first-rate people, and at the same time shows that one may not retaliatively be called illiterate, one is at once an enemy.   However, Huxley did not care.   He has gone on laughing at first-rate people ever since, and has succeeded in making them what they never seek to make themselves—amusing.   Laughter at every affectation, indeed, for a long time was his lighter strain: he still laughs at the ridiculous.

But in that same book, *Crome Yellow* (a very slight book by comparison with some that he has written since, though a delightfully amusing one), Huxley announced what has been the major problem of all his work:

One entered the world, Denis pursued, having ready-made ideas about everything.   One had a philosophy and tried to make life fit into it.   One should have lived first and then made one's philosophy to fit life. . . . Life, facts, things were horribly complicated; ideas, even the most difficult of them, deceptively simple.   In the world of ideas everything was clear; in life all was obscure, embroiled. Was it surprising that one was miserable, horribly unhappy?

You see there the reverse of the academic adherence to 'principles,' i.e. rules made by dons and rigidly applied in advance of practical knowledge.   Huxley, although almost boastfully an intellectual, is not an academic intellectual.   He is ready, able, and even eager to learn by experience. For this reason his books have provided a most interesting library of modern ideas. I take it that he arrived in town from the university, as Denis did, full of system; and found, as Denis and many others have done, that the system which looks so secure in cloistered calm does not quite deal with the urgent immensities that follow. That is, a tutor's room has its simplicity; but there are more things in heaven and earth than are dreamt of —or at least are demonstrable—in any system of philosophy. Huxley, coming to London, and going among other, older men, found his ideas not completely satisfying. When, a little later, he became a hard-working practical journalist, and began to discover how men and women behaved, and how work was done, although he remained, as he was bound to remain, a very cultured man in the academic sense, he learned a thousand and one things which had not been in the university curriculum.

There were some things he could not learn, but could only glimpse. He was born in the middle, not quite perfectly leisured, class, and not, as Lawrence was, in the class of what Gissing used to call 'the ignobly poor'; it has been almost impossible for him to get out of the class in which he was born. He could see the ridiculousnesses and affectations of the aesthetic sets, and the ugly little round of their squirrel-cage life; but he could not help feeling that fastidious recoil from lower classes which is a part of the middle-class breeding. Very few people of that breeding can make the journey into another type of mind; and Huxley has still much to learn of the world. In the same way, the ignobly poor, to which Lawrence had in childhood belonged, are never at ease in newer surroundings, and never do justice to those of different breeding from their own. You can see the contrast by reading the scornful but not quite vivid descriptions of flannel-trousered intellectuals in *Lady Chatterley's Lover* and comparing the account of squalors and fashions, given at first hand, which Huxley supplies in *Point Counter Point*. But Lawrence and Huxley could be, and were, friends towards the end of Lawrence's life; and there is no doubt in my mind that in spite of his *Encyclopaedia Britannica* Huxley has been better able than any other man of his generation to take a comprehensive view of society. He has book learning and some practical acquaintance with men's actions; when he perfectly synthesizes the two kinds of knowledge he will have achieved the highest of which he is capable. He does not like the ignobly poor in mass; but for the individual he has an invincible sympathy. It is for life he cares: he only looks in the *Encyclopaedia* for information.

This view of Huxley is one which I have come to hold in later years. At first I was delighted and amused by his wit and the fun which he innocently (and yet naughtily) levelled at the vulnerable prigs of the arts. I then felt that in his sincere search for truth by way of further and further disillusion, still confining himself to the aesthetic and intellectual few, he had come to the end of his power to range more widely or to believe in anything at all. He seemed without hope, and therefore without philosophy, without anything but horror at the futility of all things; and obviously drying up. Even the brilliance of *Point Counter Point* did not reassure me, for that book only did with more mature elaborateness what he had done before. It might have been written, as Lawrence said it was written, by a 'precocious adolescent.'

But Huxley himself had been realizing, I think, that he had reached a dead end; that the intelligentsia had amused for the last time, and that they were in such a state that to deal with them longer would be a cruelty and a boredom. He went right away from his pictures of Chelsea bedrooms and drawing-rooms, and leapt into the future of the scientists. The emotion which had been gathering in him as he realized with his imagination what such a world would mean to real men and women gave him new power. In *Brave New World* he wrote a book which, whatever may be its ultimate place in literature, is once again a step in advance of the general consciousness of Huxley's time. It is the work of a poet. It is full of thought and feeling.

The book is that of a man who has had the courage and imagination to envisage the Utopia of scientists in the full horror of being. All those accepted visions of a hygienic and sterilized future, from which emotion, poetry, and beauty have been eliminated, are synthesized in *Brave New World*. Everything is mechanical. Everything planned, bottled, dehumanized, and frightful. And Huxley, of all living writers, is the only man who could have illustrated with such address the consequences of the scientists' dream. Others could have been indignant; they would have been vague. He is specific. He is both scientist and poet. The result is an astounding picture, from which one recoils with loathing, even as the author, in painting it, has done.

My criticism of this book, as of all Huxley's writing, is that it is negative. He was first of all in the small world of the aesthetes, and he found it damnable. Every shoddy pretence in it, every silly and ugly piece of sophisticated futility, aroused his dislike and contempt. From ridicule he passed to deliberate exposure. From the views of life which that world stood for he dissented with energy. But he could offer instead of those views only his own disgust of the people who accepted them. If he went to the cinema, he saw films which caused him loathing; the people crowded into the cinema were reekingly cloddish and foul, mind and body; their conceptions were stupid, and their self-deceptions beastly. If he read books, they were wretched and full of base ideas. If he travelled, he found—always with a sort of jovial gusto—that the new human beings he met were morons and cretins similar to those he had left at home. If he looked into politics, he found them corrupt; into morals, he found them libidinous and sanctimonious; into spiritualism, he found it nothing but telepathy; into the animal kingdom, he found it sniffing and raising its legs and blindly procreating without a thought for the *psyche*. And it is the same with the scientific Utopia; for that, too, is the imagining of men in whom spirit burns feebly and the rationalizing impulse thrusts with busy-body strength.

I say this is negative; for nowhere does Huxley show us, save by implication, what is his own ideal. He does it in some degree in *Brave New World*; but what he does in *Brave New World* is to cry for the old simple earth, the old simplicities of relation, motherhood, mother-tended babies, the unsullied countryside, as if, having scorned the Chestertons and Bellocs, he had mysteriously found himself in their army and on the staff with these two stout generals. The picture which the mind conjures up of Huxley between his two seniors is as amusingly fantastic as anything in the work of the three. It is quite incredible. Nevertheless, something has gone wrong, it seems to me, with the Huxleyan alignment.

That is an exaggeration. Huxley is not a Chestertonian or a Bellocian. He is not really for the natural man who had that wonderful imaginary heyday in Merrie England. He stands for intellect in a world of scientists and hedonists. He believes as strongly as any Bloomsbury aesthete that Demos is a devil which threatens culture. Whatever happened, he would always be on the side of the fastidious. But you see what difficulties arise when, being an intellectual, one courageously ceases to be a pedant. It is impossible for Huxley or anybody

else with generosity of mind and humour to be solely an intellectual; it is equally impossible for a man pledged in his being
to a reverence for culture to be a democrat. One can imagine
him crying:

> The time is out of joint: O cursèd spite,
> That ever I was born to set it right.

That he was born, not to set right the dreadful time in which
we live, but by a process of successive loathings to reach some
positive philosophy, I believe. He would shrink from pro-
mulgating a positive philosophy, perhaps; for all his reachings
out to truth are tentative, lacking in self-confidence, in the
modern manner, and so far have been expressed in the ques-
tionings of his sceptical heroes; but he has the integrity to attain
and to hold a view of life which shall be satisfying to more than
himself. That brief passage which I quoted a few pages back,
in which one of these characters explained the modern note as
one of perceived multiplicity, shows that he is still baffled by the
number of entries in the *Encyclopaedia Britannica*. He is still
overwhelmed by the sense of ignorance before many-faceted
modern knowledge. He wants to know everything about everything. Until he knows everything, he thinks, how can he ever
make up his mind? You might suppose that he would lose
himself in those immense tomes. That is not so. He will one
day do as Beresford's Hampdenshire Wonder did; he will turn
from the *Encyclopaedia*, a full man. *Brave New World* shows
that he is still learning; but it shows just as clearly that there
is a single mind, which is Aldous Huxley, busily transforming
multiplicity into unity and so into wisdom. He has a greater
capacity for wisdom than any encyclopaedia-stuffed man of
this era; and may yet lead his generation, and the younger
generation, into a state of grace out of which great things
will come

III. NOEL COWARD

The fact that this *is* an age of scientific enlightenment does not
yet appear to have penetrated into the minds of those placed by fate
and birth and circumstances on pedestals of authority, from which
it is their duty to decide what is, and what is not, conducive to
corruption of the public morals.

NOEL COWARD, in a Preface.

Having been born in 1899, Noel Coward probably heard the
songs of the Boer War period as he lay in his cradle. *Dolly
Grey, The Soldiers of the Queen, Bluebell*, those haunting tunes

of which he made such tear-drawing use in *Cavalcade*, must have nourished the young heart as infant food fattened the young body. He was hardly out of the cradle when he appeared upon the stage (that was in 1910); and had hardly appeared upon the stage before he became a dramatic author. I seem to remember walking up St Martin's Lane when I was not so very old myself, and observing that Winifred Emery, a celebrated actress of those days, was appearing at the New Theatre in a play by a marvellous boy named Noel Coward. But perhaps I am wrong. Certainly there was a play called *The Young Idea*; and certainly something in the nature of a play called *Women and Whisky* in which our author was concerned was produced in 1919, when Coward had not attained his twentieth birthday. He was precocious enough, full of the theatre from boyhood.

He wrote and he acted. Later, when he entered into association with C. B. Cochran, he wrote the text of a revue, wrote the lyrics for it, and wrote the music too. I am not sure that he did not produce. He could have produced. He is said to be a very good producer. I can testify that he is a very finished actor. His music has been played by innumerable dance orchestras. His plays have been booed (Coward facing the boos with every appearance of dignity) and extolled. He has been billed, in the cinemas of England, as the greatest living dramatist. He has been inaccurately reported as marooned upon a desert island; plays of his have been banned by the censor in England; he has written prefaces (and they have been printed) in italics. He knows all the smart people, and he neither drinks nor stays up late. He is liked wherever he goes; and might at any time, if it has not happened already, be mobbed by those outrageous harpies who molest actors and actresses at stage doors in London. His plays are denied wit by the dramatic critics, and yet in their way are wittier than most other smart plays except those by Frederick Lonsdale.

It would appear that exception has been taken to some of Coward's work on the ground that it directly encourages immorality. That is very strange. His plays are among the most moral plays ever written. Unfortunately all sorts of very odd people insist upon going to the theatre; and while, if these same people read a book, they may complain to the library about it, and have it put under the counter for those who ask for it, even bring about a wide demand for that same book at the bookshops, if they go to the theatre (or if they stay away from the theatre) and make complaints about the morality of a play, they can rarely do it anything but harm. One can read a banned book on the sly; but one may jib at the idea of being seen at an immoral play. Unless one is an intellectual rebel; but then the support of intellectual rebels makes little difference to the box-office. The theatre is a target for all those moral busybodies who like to denounce the stream of filth poured forth by the novelists and playwrights of the earth. However, not all Coward's plays have been banned, even when they showed young ladies drunk or young men hysterical; and it may be that he exaggerates the sufferings he has endured at the instance of Mrs Grundy and her official cousins. He has been one of the most successful playwrights of modern times, and he has had much applause.

Why should he be banned? The answer is, according to Coward, that the Middle Classes impose the weight of their 'massed illiteracy' upon the theatre. He says: 'I do resent very deeply, on my own behalf and on behalf of those young writers who are sincerely attempting to mirror contemporary life honestly and truthfully . . . that this weight of bourgeois ignorance and false sentimentality should not only be allowed to force those in authority to crush down rising talent for the sole reason that its outlook doesn't quite conform with the moral traditions of twenty-five years ago, but that it should be encouraged in every possible way by the press.'

One can tell from this protest that Coward, though a writer supposedly frivolous, has a serious purpose. It is his object to mirror contemporary life. Not all contemporary life, but a section of it. And the part he mirrors is a part given to promiscuity, drunkenness, drugging, and fighting. There can be no question that there is such a part; the part that lives always upon the verge of emotional crises, which either earns money by painting or writing or does not earn money at all and has a great deal of time upon its hands. If it is competent for a dramatist to bore us for three acts with the tale of two young men who miss a boat or a bank cashier who goes on the loose with the bank's cash, then it is quite legitimate for Coward to tell us amusingly about some of the equally boring people who have affairs and quarrel, who get tipsy, who leave their wearisome spouses for lovers, or who divorce each other and remarry, only to feel the old sentiment when they meet by chance at an hotel.

The only trouble is that these plays about neurotics do not quite satisfy us that neuroticism is a completely valuable theme; or that (assuming it to be a valuable theme) Coward has seen it more than superficially. The plays are written with much verve, and many lively sallies adorn them. The chit-chat they contain is insulting, irreverent, cheeky, and full of surprise. They are less good when Coward is serious; for then he gropes a little in the profundities, and his long theatrical experience does him an ill turn by making him specious. Therefore his lighter plays, or the lighter moments in his less frivolous plays, are best. There is no mistaking the success of such a play as *Private Lives*, where Coward's spirits are at their highest throughout and his sense of stage tableau irresistible. Some of the other plays, the ones which may not be produced in London (I do not know why they may not be produced, and Coward's complaint is legitimate enough), are less amusing. He is quick rather than wise; when the characters are shallow, and he knows they are shallow, he is master of them, and has lovely fun; when he over-estimates their significance the audience misses the fun.

That is the problem with Coward. If he may laugh, he has such a light touch that we must laugh, too. Whenever the people talk nonsense—the significant use of the word 'yours' in *Private Lives*, by which we are made at once to know that although they are now married to others the protagonists still feel intimately proprietary towards each other; the young man in *Home Chat* who arrives at a moment of crisis, finds he has not said 'How d' ye do' until it is too late to do so; and so on—the author's glee shoots high. But when he expounds Life and Freedom he does not quite satisfy us. The play *Design for Living*, for example, is interesting in theme, but it is about people who are not made interesting, and we are left indifferent to the future of the four chief characters. Coward wishes to establish the theory that if people are Bohemian they ought to be Bohemian, and do as they like, without being blamed for their Bohemianism. He causes one young woman to have two lovers and then a husband, from whom the lovers at last jointly remove the young woman for what apparently will be a perpetual interchangeable spree. That play is not particularly bad in moral, and parts of it are very well written; but as a piece of mirroring it is restricted in scope. Coward, though he pictures one kind of life with great honesty, is not justified in believing it to be of social or aesthetic importance.

His quality lies in his fun. He has great sense of the stage, and can picture the effect of pyjamas, dressing-gown, a fight, a hotel balcony by night with the band playing an old song. He has a sense of dramatic surprise, which he shows in *Cavalcade*

as well as in his character pieces.   These three excellences have
made him a much-admired and I think a loved dramatist.   His
wit, though it is not of the most subtle and distinguished kind, is
fresh and amusing; his characters do 'toss the ball lightly to one
another,' and rarely drop it.   Having tossed the ball, they have
done all that in the theatre can be expected of them; and for my
part I should like them to go on doing the same thing all the
evening.   When, however, they sozzle or fight or go into bedrooms they cease to be interesting to myself; and when they are
the mouthpieces of Coward's morality my heart sinks.   I grow
uncomfortable, not because (like the massed illiteracy of the
Middle Classes) I am shocked, but merely because smart sentimentalists talk just like that, and the author of *Private Lives*
should give us something a little better than life in intellectual
quality.   Of his ability to do so I make no question.

IV. RICHARD ALDINGTON

The great English middle-class mass, that dreadful squat pillar of
the nation, will only tolerate art and literature that are fifty years
out of date, eviscerated, detesticulated, bowdlerized, humbuggered,
slip-slopped, subject to their Anglicized Jehovah. . . . So, look out,
my friend.   Hasten to adopt the slimy mask of British humbug and
British fear of life, or expect to be smashed.

R. ALDINGTON, *Death of a Hero.*

Long, long ago, before the War, Richard Aldington was an
Imagist poet.   He said that 'the poetry of the nineteenth century—from Shelley right down through Tennyson and Swinburne and Arnold and all the rest to Francis Thompson—is
turgid and boresome and sloppy and wordy to an almost incredible extent. . . . In the poetry of those days there was very little of
the clear precise writing with which the young poets of to-day
are in love; there was nothing hard or marble-like about it.'
That was said in 1914.   It might be printed to-day in a 'modn'
periodical as the view of one newly arrived at the conception of
'modn' first-rateness.   Aldington is a pre-War 'modn.'

He was also, in those days, a somewhat iconoclastic critic,
writing as one may see thinly disguised in *Death of a Hero* for,
among other papers, *The New Age.*   It must have been a very
difficult time for him, because he had no popular wares; only
none too accommodating literary criticism, and poems for which
he had difficulty in finding a publisher.   He lived at Hampstead
or in the country, and translated from the Greek of Meleager and
Anyte of Tegea.   As late as 1916 he was busy with the work of

introducing lesser-known Greek and Latin writers to those unfamiliar with the dead languages. The series of small booklets
or leaflets called *The Poets' Translations* owed much to his enthusiasm, and it was admirable pioneer work. Unfortunately
for us, its publication was suspended in War-time, and as far as
I know it has never been resumed. Aldington, instead, has
published his *Collected Verse*, and he has taken to writing long
novels in the post-War manner.

It is as a novelist that he appears in this chapter, for if ever
there was a post-War pessimist it is he. He tries to laugh off
his pessimism; but (like that of Jack Point) 'his laughter has an
echo that is grim,' and he makes a hollow job of it. The world
and that frightful British middle class, which is likewise Noel
Coward's bugbear, are too much for him. He is indignant with
both. Being by temperament serious, he covers his seriousness
with a crust of merriment. In print the crust wears off.

I explain this fact to myself by thinking that Aldington is not
really a humorist at all, but one who unfortunately, when he is
holding forth with grandeur, hears the sound of his own voice,
and so cannot continue with his address. He 'laughs it off,' as
they say. His indignation over the bourgeoisie has the same
righteousness as bourgeois indignation over backsliding, and a
similar irrelevance. Having embraced, for some reason unknown
to me, a contrary view of life to that of the ultra-respectable,
he sees all who are not happy in their environment as in some
way victims of mass cruelty and as individually defensible upon
moral grounds. This, I need hardly point out, is the attitude
of sentimentality. 'You brute! Leave the poor child alone!
What if the dog did bite you? A great strong creature like you,
to attack somebody or something smaller——'

Accordingly nobody can be surprised if I say I think Aldington
a sentimentalist. I think Coward a sentimentalist. They have
this much in common, that they are driven by their sympathy
for the misfits into a general arraignment of all who are wise or
lucky enough to make successes of their lives upon normal lines.
It is a simple view of life. Far too simple, and too emotional, to
be a profound one. Aldington cannot see a spinster as anything
but one thwarted by a damnable society of prudes; Coward cannot see a temperamental harlot as a harlot, but—how the familiar
euphemism rises to the lips!—as an 'unfortunate,' and must
defend her as one who, whatever the world may say, is as God
made her. His sympathy, like that of the populace, is never for
the murdered person, the victim (he must have been a beast,

anyway, because his love was not that noble thing, extra-matrimonial attachment), but always for a pretty woman or an 'unconventional' egoist. It is the prudish inside out, and not a new morality.

Now it does not, or should not, affect the critic that this rather than another moral attitude is adopted by any author. But a feeling that indignation is too easy and too obvious to be a valuable literary method must arise in him. Aldous Huxley is quite as little satisfied as Aldington or Coward with the world as it is; but he begins with the mental capacity to distinguish good from pseudo-good and unco' guid; and when he satirizes he is not morally indignant over smugness, but aesthetically revolted by whatever is ugly and useless in the life of mankind. It is his taste that is offended; not his facile moral judgment. Both Coward and Aldington react emotionally to the problem of conduct. They are unconsciously distorting an echo of the bourgeoisie Where the respectables say, with Mr Growser of Toytown, 'Disgraceful! It ought not to be allowed!' and, self-righteously, 'Thank God I at least am above such vice or such weakness or such stupidity!' they retort, with equal feeling: 'Why shouldn't she? Poor thing! It 's *natural* to her to misbehave; or it 's *unnatural* that she should be made to behave as you think she ought to!' In Aldington's case the gospel of Lawrence, that one should not be tolerant of the intolerable, but should Crush the Infamy, has played havoc with the native gentleness of a mind never too speedy or light-witted. He does not mean to be rude; but is nervously exaggerative and his hand sometimes weighs as much as a brick. The dazzle of satire, or irony (I can never distinguish between them in modern writing), has been too much for him, and he struggles to translate what has been bewildered pain into a frolicsome comment from the heights of worldly wisdom. Thackeray did the same thing with more successful archness. Aldington's satire, unsweetened and unsalted by strong humour, remains too often as rudimentary as the back answers of an adolescent.

V. PERCY WYNDHAM LEWIS

'I am a pessimist, Hobson. But I 'm a new sort of pessimist. I think I am the sort that will please! I am the Panurgic-pessimist, drunken with the laughing gas of the abyss.'

PERCY WYNDHAM LEWIS, *Tarr*.

Before I deal with Wyndham Lewis, the author of *Tarr* and other works of fiction, I must detach him from all possible confusion with his namesake, D. B. Wyndham Lewis, the humorist and Catholic biographer. They are not the same person. D. B. makes many jokes about popular novelists and lives in the great world from which humorists draw their inspiration; Percy is constantly at war with the smaller fry of the aesthetic world and writes, he says, from the standpoint of genius. He is also an original and very striking draughtsman; but his drawings have no place in the present book, much as they would adorn it, and must now pass from our notice. It is with the written word that we are concerned.

Wyndham Lewis began writing character sketches long before the War, brief and vivid ironic studies: those are his forte. If one could pick them out from among the verbiage of his longer books and bring them together in series, they would reveal better than anything else could do the strength and liveliness of his talent. Just before the War began, he was at work upon an ambitious novel of which all sorts of people heard and of which several people had glimpses; but the War arrived, Lewis was ill, and it was July 1918 before *Tarr* was published by a firm (calling itself after the name of a short-lived periodical) known as The Egoist Ltd. The same firm first published in England Joyce's *Portrait of the Artist as a Young Man*. *Tarr* had its great admirers, mostly among young artists and writers from Chelsea and the Café Royal, who were personally acquainted with the author; but outside these it made little stir, and the larger public never heard of it. The larger public never hears of anything until it has a united push behind it, and Lewis has always missed the united push, for a reason which I shall give in a moment.

Tarr remained an only visible child for some time. Then, on the wings of the newer modernism Lewis shook a little shower of works upon the public, from *Time and Western Man* to the first part of *The Childermass* (so far uncompleted), at last publishing *The Apes of God* under his own supervision, and a number of smaller pamphlets, polemics, and diatribes attacking individuals, abuses, political theories, and venality. All these works were written with the utmost freedom and ebullience of style, and were either greatly and properly admired as invective or shunned as tiresome vehemence or set aside as incomprehensible nonsense. They were mostly in the nature of denunciations, in the expression of which the author excels; and while, following Joyce, he frequently abstains from the use of punctuation he has never been designedly gnomic, and as a rule becomes incomprehensible only when one misses the point through ignorance of the people he is lambasting.

The people themselves, no doubt, understand only too well who is portrayed and what is intended. Some of them, in obscure sheets or in counterblasts, hit back. Most of them ignore what has been said of them. That is their best offensive weapon; for if Lewis is unanswered he has to pass on to another subject, which is distinctly hard on one who means no harm but who must fight or sink into gloomy inaction. I think he has a genuine grievance against those best able to appreciate his great gifts, in the fact that too often, perhaps offended, perhaps ungenerous, they have for personal reasons cold-shouldered him and his writings.

They have not liked him. He has not been of the right colour or the right tone. The standpoint of genius is apt to make a man egotistical and aggressive, and Lewis is egotistical and aggressive. He is afraid that if he were otherwise he would be overlooked. As it is, he is looked at askance. The only time I ever met him he pretended to think I was a doctor; and as we were doomed to sit next to one another throughout dinner I should no doubt have had to defend myself if Richard Sickert had not taken it into his head to play on Lewis the tricks Lewis had purposed playing on me. Yet Lewis, like every other author, needs praise, lashings of praise. He hungers and thirsts for it. Because he sees all sorts of other men scratching each other's backs and rolling each other's logs, he shouts in holy horror at the spectacle. However, he is so much concerned with himself that it never occurs to him to hand the same gross flattery to any friend; and so he remains a lonely figure in the little Café Royal, Chelsea, and Quartier Latin nests of pseudo-artists. Having in himself the coterie temperament, he can never cordially snuggle up to anybody else, and so is forced to do his own scratching. If one took away from Lewis the consciousness of being a genius, he would be a forlorn figure, and a very pathetic one.

I have not the heart to attack any man's belief in his own genius. If so modest and at the same time so comparatively prosperous a writer as myself has his anguishes and humiliations, such as no man who has never written a book can understand, one who has constantly to be his own blazoner, who faces the coldness of those he would tickle to fury or enthusiasm, and who is still outside the (financially essential) sympathy of the library public, needs some support from within if he is to endure life at all. Besides, I am not sure that Lewis is quite wrong about himself. If egotism and ebullience, a multitudinous vocabulary and a capacity for the grotesque which (among moderns) only Joyce surpasses, are enough to make a man a genius, he is one. He certainly has extraordinary talent. He has a furiously energetic brain, full of fire and odd knowledges and scraps of profundity which bob among the general gas; sometimes he can quite brilliantly execute a scene in a book or tear the inside out of a man in a polemic. But he must all the time, so tiresomely, melodramatize everything, enlarge it to the proportions of sensational intrigue or monstrous perversion, proclaim a betrayal or a disaster, and denounce all who are not of his party. Since that party consists of Lewis alone, he is never done with mares' nests.

CHAPTER XVII: SOME LATER NOVELISTS

He will be the most popular artist who gives that view with which the world in general sympathize. A merely professional reputation is not very extensive, nor will it last long.

W. HAZLITT, *Conversations with Northcote*.

I

As I approach the end of my long task, which was undertaken so lightly, and which is now somewhat of a nightmare, I am filled with consternation. I do not wish to beg forgiveness from readers: Pardon me, as Mrs Cluppins said, I would scorn the haction. But I do deeply feel the fact that I must have omitted from my panorama the figures of many excellent men and women writers now living. To have included all would have been impossible; and I have chosen to speak of those whom I regard as most typical. Nor has it seemed to me to be good policy to run hastily through a list of omissions, handing a few words of comment to each, although I might have done this. The truth is that there are at the present time large numbers of writers of talent, and if all were included (as they deserve) the book would be endless. Moreover, many of the younger writers have still to reach their maturity, and they will figure in later and better books written by others than myself. I have purposely confined my record to men and women whose reputations have been established for a number of years.

Now I do not wish to suggest that the only interesting writers were those whose work appealed to small and select audiences. I am not one of those who think that when a book is popular it is bad; on the contrary, I think that if a book is a failure it is because it has some intrinsic defect—generally deficiency of interest. Those who disagree with me in this will feel for me some of the slight distaste I feel for them. We shall both survive the distaste, which I regard as decidedly a point in my favour. And, having said so much, I think fit, as Oliver Cromwell used to say, to speak for a chapter upon one novelist who has not quite come within the scope of any of my earlier chapters and three novelists who have been quite uncompromisingly popular. If I can suggest a reason for their popularity, or for the popularity of any one of them, I shall do so. But first let me speak of a writer whose originality has been both emphasized and cloaked by his use (I have no doubt a quite natural use) of a style which seems to be compounded from equal parts of Defoe and Jonathan Swift, and whose ingenious maiden effort in fiction was hailed by one critic as being 'as aesthetically important as a carved coconut.' I mean, David Garnett.

II. DAVID GARNETT

David Garnett comes of a distinguished literary family. His great-grandfather, Richard Garnett, became Assistant-Keeper of Printed Books in the British Museum and helped to found the Philological Society. His grandfather, Richard Garnett the second, was the author of scholarly, ironic, and fantastic tales collected into one volume as *The Twilight of the Gods*, and besides being an able literary historian also became Keeper of Printed Books in the British Museum. To his father and mother I have already paid tribute. And David Garnett himself, who as a boy was a devoted student of nature, and whose first work was a manual on the management of a kitchen garden, has been a bookseller and publisher as well as author of *Lady into Fox* and its successors.

There are some who see in David Garnett's work no more than a stylistic exercise; but I do not agree. He uses, it is true, an elaborately simple style which at times echoes *Robinson Crusoe* or *Gulliver's Travels*, and which suggests that he is deeply influenced by a reading of eighteenth-century authors. If there were nothing in the books but their manner of writing, as some say, these books would be less than important. But the demureness of such a book as *Lady into Fox* (which is much superior to its successor, *A Man in the Zoo*, despite the fact that *A Man in the Zoo* has moments of great excellence) is proper to the theme, which is nothing less than the sudden transformation of a young and loving wife into a real female fox, her life thenceforward with her husband, her desertion of the husband for a vulpine mate, and the final tragedy in which both husband and lady are killed by hounds. I said 'demureness,' and that implies a criticism, for it is quite true that Garnett did not really believe that a lady had been changed into a fox and that she had gone on as he related, and he was telling her story with a false gravity which amused himself and his friends less because they believed what he wrote than because they thought it very ingenious of him to write in that way.   On the other hand, while I personally do not believe that the lady changed into a fox (though many ladies are said after marriage to be perfect vixens, which some people imagined was Garnett's meaning), I am astonished and delighted by the art with which Garnett tells the extremely beautiful story of what happens after the mishap.   There is in my mind no doubt that *Lady into Fox* was virtuosity, the result of a twist of queer humourless humour; but it is exquisitely told, and has its far deeper virtues of imagination and feeling.

Since that book was written and published, Garnett has extended his range; but he has never yet been ambitious enough, or mentally supple enough, to shake himself free of the shackles of style.   All his books, so quietly and slowly told, are cramped, or they end before they have developed their full growth, or they make a demand upon credence by being odd to no apparent purpose.   They are like engravings upon very small surfaces (I do not mean the Lord's Prayer upon a threepenny piece, but rather that they are intaglio).   They do not quite achieve artistic importance.   And yet what a hand Garnett has for a picture of wild life or the countryside, where in a few words he can give the reader a true experience.   With how much taste does he refrain from every brutality in *Lady into Fox*, while he indicates the progress of the lady's first transformation through her interest in the dove, and her new rough habit of eating, to the moment when she allows her mate to be seen.   How lovely is the monotone of *The Sailor's Return*.

How extraordinarily fine, too, the description of the situation of those stranded aviators in *The Grasshoppers Come*.   How intently we turn the pages, devout and eager—and find that the book has stopped!

III. PELHAM GRENVILLE WODEHOUSE

'For some little time I have been endeavouring to instruct you in the principles of pure English.   My efforts seem to have been wasted.'
The policeman blushed.
'I beg your pardon, Mr Beamish.   One keeps slipping into it. It's the effect of mixing with the boys—with my colleagues—at the station-house.   They are very lax in their speech.'
P. G. WODEHOUSE, *The Small Bachelor*.

For some years now, P. G. Wodehouse has been endeavouring to instruct the world in the principles of what is not so much pure English as the language of pure nonsense. He began when he and the world were both lads, 'he and self having been at private school, Eton and Oxford together,' as Bertie Wooster would say. Not perhaps quite Eton and Oxford, but at least private school, and in Wodehouse's case Dulwich College. And years ago, at the very beginning of time, when boys were boys and boys would be boys, there was published under the editorship of one R. S. Warren Bell a monthly magazine for such boys which was called *The Captain*. It was a good magazine, and there was nothing pious in it about prayers and such disagreeables, but stories and articles fit to be read by the self-respecting of tender years. I do not know when there first appeared in this magazine something very unusual indeed; but I do know that just as I was beginning to feel very learned in eighteenth-century literature as the result of making an index to Boswell's *Johnson* somebody called Psmith fled like a meteor through the pages of *The Captain*.

Psmith? you say; how is that spelt? I must refer you to P. G. Wodehouse. For Psmith was one of his earliest attempts at world instruction in pure English; and it must be said at once that the readers of *The Captain* were so entranced by their lessons that they went without the common necessaries of life in order to satisfy this greater need. They saved their pennies, and denied themselves extra food (such as I see the present degenerate race of schoolboys munching from paper bags) in order to buy this wonder-filled magazine and learn more of a language new and irresistible to them.

As Wodehouse was born in 1881, and as he took England in hand with a first book, *The Pothunters*, published in 1902, it is fair to assume that he was slightly precocious; but you would never suppose from his present fair, bland, highly innocent appearance that he had been born longer ago than 1904, or that there was behind that ingenuous façade a capacity for verbal gymnastic second to none in England at the present time. As Bertie Wooster would say, again illuminatingly:

> I don't know that you would call me an irascible man. I rather think not. Ask them about me at the Drones, and they will probably tell you that Bertram Wooster, wind and weather permitting, is as a general rule suavity itself.

Wodehouse (Pelham Grenville), suavity itself, is less like a humorous author than any man I have ever met. He is not funereal, and he is not laboriously funny. He does not tell comic anecdotes until the dawn breaks or look as if his poor heart

never rejoiced. On the contrary, he is quiet, orderly, and
benign. He is like a young English sportsman, a good friend
and a sympathetic listener. You could tell him your troubles.
You could picture him streaking for the corner flag with an oval
ball under his arm, or making what an erudite young woman
once described to me as 'a crisp cut to leg.' You could imagine
him driving an automobile or pushing a garden-roller, and doing
all these things with good temper. But you would never
imagine him educating the world, as he has done, in a new lingo.
And yet he has educated the world, and the world is still learning
the Wodehouse tongue as rapidly as it can wolf it up. Not only
that part of the world which is England and America, but that
part which is Europe and Asia; although what the Asiatics,
reading his work, as they must do, in Chinese, can gather of that
magnificent vocabulary of new words I do not know. He has
been a world benefactor (without, as Bertrand Russell would
say, 'any feeling of superiority such as is sometimes associated
with the word') for thirty-two years and may well continue his
benefaction for as long again without losing a hair.

And yet Wodehouse is not deliberately a reassuring author;
he does not seek to cheer and console. He is neither prig nor
buffoon. He merely creates merriment—for fun. In a period
when laughter has been difficult, he has made men laugh without
shame. He has done it less by means of his comic invention,
although it must be the comic invention that carries his books
into other lands than our own, than by means of his vocabulary.
He will show you exactly how young men of the brainless class
might talk and think if they had been struck with the lunacy of
genius, will phonetically record the speech of a man who has
had pepper thrown in his face, will as readily give you the
speech of a prize-fighter or a country policeman in pain or delight
as the shrewd interchanges of a dashing young woman and the
man of her heart or the subterfuges of a supposedly reformed
character trying to turn an honest penny by means of begging
letters. Whatever he does, he will make you believe that he
does it upon the spur of the moment. His books have an
irresistible air of improvisation. They continue from scene to
scene as if there were nothing in life but preposterousness.

For this last reason, the long books of Wodehouse are less
satisfactory than his short stories, where the effects are instant
and unquestionable. In the long stories the reader may find
attention wandering; reason (and not cheerfulness) may keep
breaking in; actions may appear to have some fortuitousness;

that significant form to which Clive Bell attaches such importance may vanish under scrutiny and the whole book turn out to be a series of episodes. But significance of any kind is not Wodehouse's object, any more than the portrayal of a shadow of the real world is his object. The world in which his characters move and exchange speech is a world of his spontaneous creation, a fantastic world resembling the scene of an irrational dream. It is a gravely consistent world, like that of a drunken man; all the people who live in it are ready to play the game so concisely invented by Wodehouse. They will black their faces or run amok or scramble upon all fours, will change their minds or their whiskers, will fly from their sweethearts or take charge of wild-living dipsomaniacs without serious qualm. But they will not change their terse manner of conversation (sometimes, as in Jeeves's case, it is orotund), their use of the exclusive Wodehouse vocabulary, the Wodehouse idiom, the Wodehouse lunatic lightness of wit and mood. And as they perform all their antics with the same charming viceless simplicity which is a feature of the Wodehouse world, they never soil nonsense with vulgarity. For this reason, if for a time we tire of them, and set down the book in which their adventures are unrolled in the candid Wodehouse fashion, we always resume their acquaintance with the same delight in the familiar breezy greeting. They advance upon us, removing the lid with as much courtly grace as they can muster and crying: 'Hullo-ullo-ullo'; and we, similarly responding 'Hullo-ullo-ullo' (though we should use that greeting with no other creatures ever invented), grab the old hand warmly and pack ourselves for a happy hour. Who among us, that are not curmudgeons, could resist such pleasantness and pleasantry as this author offers?

IV. JOHN BOYNTON PRIESTLEY

'I nivver knew there were so many folk wandering about. Once you 've fairly set off, you come on 'em all over t'place.'

J. B. PRIESTLEY, *The Good Companions*.

There have been other Yorkshire novelists, besides J. B. Priestley, as for example Halliwell Sutcliffe, Oliver Onions, Winifred Holtby, and Storm Jameson; but of all these Priestley has made the biggest stir in the world, and has been most attacked. He has been attacked, in chief, because he was a brusque Yorkshireman; only secondarily because he has had the greatest success that any novelist in England has had for many years.

He was born in Bradford in the year 1894, and is the son of a schoolmaster. He was educated at Cambridge University. Before he began to write novels, he was a reviewer and essayist; and when he first wrote a novel all the critics said that it was the novel of an essayist, just as when he first wrote a play all the critics said that it was the play of a novelist. But the critics, although they attacked this play of Priestley's, gave one the impression (which perhaps they did not intend) that it was really an interesting piece of work; and as far as I am concerned the play, *Dangerous Corner*, aroused an interest in Priestley which I had not felt as a the result of reading several of his essays and his novel, *Angel Pavement*. Subsequent plays have demonstrated the fact that he is one of the most exciting of all living dramatists.

The novel with which Priestley made his reputation was, as the world knows, *The Good Companions*, the long and ingenious narrative of the adventures of several people who, setting out from different parts of England, were brought together by accident and formed a concert party. That book, rapturously received by nearly all who read it, was in my opinion a great blow struck on behalf of the normal and the large scale in fiction. It was a work showing exceptional talent, boldness, and self-confidence. It succeeded because it was original, very varied, and very entertaining. It was full of natural homeliness, and readers felt that they could like the people in its pages, whom they recognized as being very similar in nature to themselves. Those who did not care for the book did not wish to recognize themselves in persons so commonplace; but that was because in their daily lives they were all pretending not to be commonplace.

The opening of *The Good Companions*, which recalls the work of Arnold Bennett, although it is freer and more copious than Bennett, is full of invitation, especially to those who have any familiarity with scenes similar to those depicted. It is all true, and well and clearly visualized. The conversation is very natural; easy and amusing. In its way it is as good as any conversation of a realistic character that modern times have seen. Everything is recognizable. But Priestley did not make the mistake of writing, as he might have done, a merely realistic novel. He was in pursuit of something else—something which I regard as important—the creation of a large-scale roving tale such as we have not seen (apart from *The Pickwick Papers*) since the eighteenth century. He had his conception, and he had the confidence to aim at its fulfilment.

I think there is no doubt that the first part of *The Good Companions*, besides being admirable in its own way, was an excellent beginning to any tale of length. I think that what follows is equally well handled; all true, copious, interesting; but that while Priestley has tried to give variety by means of differences in scene and character and class he has been unable to bring to each difference that subtle difference of method which would have made *The Good Companions* continuously interesting to those who have read a great deal of fiction with some exactitude. That is, I think the book suffers from a monotony which prevents it from standing as high in modern literature as it might have done. I do not think the positive interest flags, or the quality of the work declines; but only that one can have too much of a good thing.

When a similar fault is found, as I believe it is found, in *Angel Pavement* and its not very satisfactory successor, *Faraway*, the limits of a technique seem to be indicated. In *Angel Pavement* there is again a gathering of characters, none of whom is very profoundly seen, but all of whom are suggested excellently by means of some one or two traits and habits of speech and thought; and there is a more deliberately told story. But whether it is that there is less novelty in the plan of the book, or whether the copiousness which helped one to relish the opening of *The Good Companions* is a fault, a fault of improvisation, *Angel Pavement* is not, in my judgment, a satisfactory book. It is not greatly different in tone (although it is much longer than any of them) from the novels of Pett Ridge. That does not mean, naturally, that it is a bad book, for Pett Ridge was an able writer; but it does mean that it is lacking in just that distinction which would make it important.

However, Priestley's plays, which began with *Dangerous Corner*, are the work of a man whose gifts are altogether superior to those of many who would insist upon regarding the author of Priestley's novels as a second-rate writer. *Dangerous Corner*, which turns inside out half a dozen apparently happy and agreeable people, has such force that for a time it completely dominates the mind. That upon after-consideration it becomes less striking may be due to two causes: one of which is that one realizes how 'arranged' the disclosures have been in their progress to climax, and the other that we have been harshly taken to the sight of ugly things which remain in the end merely ugly.

This would be my expression of Priestley's shortcoming as a writer. He has clearly a vigorous and courageous intellect; his writing, although not so distinguished as to place him high among the stylists of our literature, is fluent and sincere; he has marked intelligence and integrity. But is it a practical intelligence, a practical courage, rather aggressive in the Yorkshire manner, without quicksilver and without subtlety, or with subtlety only as the result of a severe effort of the will. In his novels, as far as I can see, he does not make the effort; his aim is rather to present a generalized picture from which one can pick humours and scraps of nature as one pleases. In his plays he is forced to discipline (possibly to distil) his copiousness, and in that way he discovers how excellent the concentrated statement can be; he also slips into a quickness which might be accounted subtlety. If, with the experience gained in writing plays, he brings intensity as well as broad narrative power into his novels, he will do wonders.

V. ALAN PATRICK HERBERT

A. P. Herbert was born in 1890, was educated at Winchester and Oxford, and is president of the Black Lion Skittles Club. He served in Gallipoli and in France during the War, has been called to the Bar, is on the staff of *Punch*, has written comic opera, revue, much light verse, a novel about divorce, a thriller, a novel about a hero who was shot for cowardice, and *The Water Gipsies*, the tale of a young woman who lived on a river hulk and had as strange a series of adventures as any man might dream of. He sails a barge, assails the licensing laws, wants to see the river Thames used once more as a thoroughfare, and is a thorn in the side of every proletarian humbug in England. Being a humorist, he is deadly serious. Sometimes he is so serious that his humour is lost and buried. He speaks a great deal in public, and makes his audiences laugh tumultuously; for he is a good speaker, and has this power of speech because he so well knows what he wants to say that he is never at a loss for eloquence or wit.

Now one advantage of having certain definite ideas about life is that you know where you are with yourself; and Herbert knows where he is. But one disadvantage is that you may be considered a crank. I am not, indeed, sure how I ought to describe him, whether as a Reformer or a Conservative, a Humorist or a Bargee. He is all these things, a champion skittles player, a believer in the working man's beer, a defender of the middle class, and a satirist of all that intellectuals consider irreproachable. And as a member of Parliament, after a start which caused shaken heads, he has had an extraordinary triumph with a much-needed Divorce Act. I am told by an expert that his light verse is not completely excellent in technique; and I am convinced that he suffers from what is for me the defect of moral indignation. But his novel, *The Secret Battle*, is the best account of the War on two fronts that I have ever read, and *The Water Gipsies*, although it has defects of construction, is a very delectable panorama or peep-show of London life, which combines all Herbert's views of that life with his own delightful kind of nonsense. It is the epitome of Herbert's talent.

But Herbert has not been content to be a good novelist. Nor has he ever been content, as Wodehouse has, to make fun alone. Having as ready a power as James Stephens to make an aura of enchantment about a Cockney girl, he can show her surviving every vulgarity of surrounding and remaining a Cockney girl; but all through *The Water Gipsies*, with its happy descriptions of the Derby and barge life, he is watching for the chance to interpret in his own sense all that happens. He wants to change the hearts of men by defending liberty and condemning both libertines and Labour leaders. He has so much wisdom in his nature—that sagacity which is superior to all the knowledge of facts admired by Bertrand Russell—that he excessively dislikes seeing his possession shared by so few. Confronted by complacent folly and pretentiousness, by the solemn egotism of defeated Socialists and the puritanism of those who want to manage the poor, he brings cold fury to his ridicule of their absurdity. Such a man cannot be only a novelist; and since he cannot be only a novelist I doubt whether he will ever write a first-class novel. A first-class entertainment, yes; he has done it.

CHAPTER XVIII: LATER VISIONS

I

Sainte-Beuve, as he grew older, came to regard all experience as a single great book . . . and it seemed all one to him whether you should read in Chapter XX, which is the differential calculus, or in Chapter XXXIX, which is hearing the band play in the gardens.

R. L. Stevenson, *An Apology for Idlers.*

It will have become clear to readers of this book that my interest is in common phenomena rather than in aesthetic principles. To scholars this will seem a fault. I do not write for scholars. To me, as to Sainte-Beuve as reported by Stevenson, all experience is a single great book; and every form of knowledge, the domestic as well as the biological and astronomical and psycho-analytical, is capable of enriching the mind and imagination and increasing the interest of life. I represent the ordinary unlearned reader. He has few friends among the modern literati.

This is for the reason that literary fashion constantly changes. When it was first the rule to condemn such writers as Zola (I do not mean upon the ground that we have quite enough of the ugly in real life, etc., but more reasonably) because their work was not pastoral in character, it was pointed out that men had taken to living in cities, and that the novel and the play had both become urban. Where rural realism had its compensations of open-air liberty and beauty, urban realism was bounded by walls and a smoky sky. In the same way, this simple realism lost its importance as the general life became more and more complex. You could no longer suppose that men and women led an entirely animal life; but were forced to allow that they had thoughts and emotions which did not immediately reveal themselves. Subtlety entered the realistic novel, which dealt with emotional suffering, and not only with social conditions. But while the realistic attitude satisfied some writers, others pressed on to still further developments in the art of writing. They were struck by the discovery that the individual life is affected by all sorts of apparently unconnected but simultaneous events (Jules Romains is now illuminating this view in a tremendously

long novel called in the English translation *Men of Good Will*)
and by the rhythm of life. Some of them, no doubt influenced
by the scientific and psychological ideas of the time, realized that
there is an incessant activity of jumbled thought in every individual at every moment of the day. Endless emphasis upon
this is the contribution of James Joyce to the novel. Others,
such as Proust, found that one thought can be made to open a
great pathway into memory, or that clever persons of low vitality
enjoy, as Virginia Woolf's characters enjoy, a sort of twittering
reverie which they suppose to be vivacious contact with life.
With all these steps, authors have believed that they were
approaching nearer to the essential, to the heart of man.

I have not hidden my conviction—I hope I have not been too
sturdy, but one does what one can—that the later developments
have over-subtilized the novel and taken it past reality into
confusion. I mean that I think the objective novel capable of
greater subtlety, and greater variety, than psychological ex-
plorers, infatuated with their own ingenuity, would allow. But
even if these developments have done what I suggest, they have
done it without doubt in obedience to the spirit of the hour. I
happen not to approve: to me, these experiments, which are not
entirely outside the range of my intelligence, are calculated
clevernesses which those less clever than myself suppose to be
works of genius. That may be mere jealousy on my part; if
not personal jealousy, then jealousy for my own conception of
the nature of originality, which to me has nothing whatever to
do with purposeful novelty:

> Originality is any conception of things, taken immediately from
> nature, and neither borrowed from, nor common to, others. . . . It
> is feeling the ground sufficiently firm under one's feet to be able to
> go alone. Truth is its essence; it is the strongest possible feeling
> of truth; for it is a secret and instinctive yearning after, and approxi-
> mation towards it, before it is acknowledged by others, and almost
> before the mind itself knows what it is. Paradox and eccentricity,
> on the other hand, show a dearth of originality, as bombast and
> hyperbole show a dearth of imagination; they are the desperate
> resources of affectation and want of power.

Deliberate originality, that is, can only be a contradiction in
terms, both for Hazlitt and myself. Whether, in these self-
conscious days (I use the word 'self-conscious' without implicit
blame), any writer can fail to know what he is doing before he
does it, I cannot say. We are too much cluttered with aesthetic
theory for most men to be other than dilettanti; but genius finds
its own ways, no doubt.

These remarks, as I hope it has been clear, have their relation to modernity. The world is a very different place from what it was in the nineteenth century; and, in spite of Chesterton's claim, it is not possible to put the clock back. We have great speeds, great complexities, many new knowledges or at any rate theories concerning our bodies, our minds, the universe, light, and the future life. We are—still in the good sense—much more self-conscious than our fathers were. Inevitable that the self-consciousness and the complexities should fly together and provoke literary explosions! It could not have been expected that either would refrain. And although I have chosen to speak of the novel, because that is the form of art which most interests me, parallels—not exact, but relative—could be found in painting and poetry; in all knowledge and all human activity. Some men hate the fact, and would resist it; others exult, not so much in a sense of new life, as in a sense that they are offending the old boys; others, like myself, half-echoing E. M. Forster on another occasion say: 'Yes—oh dear yes—nothing stands still. I wish it would.'

Now it will not be forgotten that the Post-Impressionists, who were introduced into England at the beginning of the Georgian age, derived from those Whistlerian Impressionists who claimed to deal in Pure Art. They went much farther away from representational painting than the Impressionists; and in turn they were succeeded in France by painters who became more and more and more primitive, until the very nadir of human intelligence seemed to have been reached. These painters were reaching down below mind, down below the recognizable, down, down—they said—to purity. We thought, to the inane. And just as the symbolist poets—also of France—had sought to find pure poetry, unalloyed by ideas or worldly concepts, these painters tried to suggest the simplicities of nature by the simplest of means. The paradox of such activity seems to me to lie in the fact that the effort after nullity is made deliberately; that it arises, not from impulse, but from a plan consciously formed by the intellect; while the aim is at something outside intellect.

In thus reaching for the unknown, it has followed that poets and artists alike have discovered the incommunicable. Some of them, accordingly, have made a virtue of necessity, and have announced that they abjure communication. They are like the little boy in one of Talbot Baines Reed's school stories who said that in future he was going to mark his exercises 'Private,' for the master had such a vulgar habit of looking to see what he was doing. This seems to me to be another paradox; for I see no reason to publish what cannot be understood. However, there are always critics who can elucidate the meaningless in the finest phrases; and these have not been wanting.

But what has happened is that old-fashioned people (I use the phrase without approval or disapproval) have been inclined to snort. The gnomic offers such opportunity for the charlatan! And those of us who stand four-square for Life As It Is have a certain kinship with the stupid bird in Andersen's tale who, because she could not understand something, said 'That's the fault of the thought.' Feeling has run a little high. It has been retaliatively suggested that all who are not modern are what Aldous Huxley's girl called 'rather second-rate.' Just as if they were wearing last season's clothes at a smart party.

Some of this insistence that the modern writer, being not quite easily intelligible to others, is somehow of better *class* than they, is probably defiant. But not wholly so. Nor is the matter solely one of fashion, although fashion plays a strong part. There is certainly a world-wide dissatisfaction with everything that was admired by older generations—including democracy. Everywhere, younger men and women are agitating for dictatorial government (either by an individual or by *camarilla*); everywhere they are conscious of a new and, they think, improved morality, a new and threatening fear of the future, a disbelief in stability of any kind. And, since the world is topsyturvy, everything rushing at headlong speed to the unknown, many voices shouting, shouting in conflict, life really presents itself to the modern mind in the form of a kaleidoscopic terror.

To older people, who have the mental and spiritual anchor of habit and order and quietness of mind (however sensitive they may be to the chaos about them), the bits and pieces of the newer art can give little satisfaction. To myself, many of them give no satisfaction at all. The pace of life neither stimulates nor terrifies me; I do not wish to set on paper anything about my inner self, because I was born without the introspective habit; I write according to impulse, and not in accordance with elaborate modernist theory. But I feel decidedly doubtful about condemning out of hand what is unintelligible to me. For this reason I will only say that modern poetry, which I have particularly in mind in this chapter, seems to me to be altogether too literary in everything except its language. It is self-conscious in a bad sense, as well as in a not so bad sense. It is also arrogant in tone, and I am inclined to think pretentious in object.

Moreover, while aiming at the expression of what is called

the modern mind, it expresses only the thoughts of an approved small circle of modern minds, so small, and so exclusive, that this circle tends to crystallize itself into a new arbitrary mandarinate.   Being satisfied that the only knowledge worth having is within its grasp, this circle claims to care solely for the best in art and literature; it claims personally to represent the best artistic and literary effort of the time, high above the town and the mob, high above sense and sympathy, enthroned in the first-rate.   I doubt if the claim is justified or justifiable.   We can all see the slight ridiculousness of E. M. Forster's Cockney clerk whose happiest hour arose from contact with a decent-mannered Cambridge undergraduate; some of us can see the similar ridiculousness of Rosamond Lehmann's story of two young creatures who dazzled some frumps with their wonderful modernity; but are not the severely elaborate scrutineers of genius who bring out their test-tubes and crucibles in order to discover that Swift was possessed of great power equally absurd?   Are they not taking themselves, I mean, altogether too seriously?   Because anybody who had ever read a line of Swift would have reached the same conclusion by a less pretentious route, and said nothing about it.

It is against this assumption that what the moderns are interested in—and that the way in which they are interested—is the only good that I should protest.   Many things interest me which do not interest the more academic students of literature; many things interest them which do not interest me.   Our ways have been different; our minds are different.   If it is suggested that my ways and my mind are contemptible, which no man will admit when charged by another, is it not open to me also to despise the ways and minds of others?   That, put crudely, is the general problem.   If the moderns will make no concessions to the non-moderns (the contrary cannot possibly arise, for the great complaint of the moderns is that the non-moderns have conceded everything for the sake of shekels), but persist in remaining exclusively obscure, they will inevitably remain a faction.   They show signs of remaining a faction. They show signs of losing such power as they have had.   Already some who worshipped are coming to the conclusion that obscurity is a mask for impotence, and that arrogance is a part of elaborate humbug.   Already others are feeling that this particular modernity has reached its farthest point, and that the time is ripe for a still newer modernity.   Since a newer modernity is usually a swing to reaction, I look to see a great revival in critical esteem for the unpretentiously explicit.

Would that be a bad thing? If the world could settle down to peace and goodwill, most of us think it would be a happier place for all. But in order that it should settle down, understanding would have to be the order of the day. Not exclusiveness, but at least a little cordial expansiveness. Tolerance, in fact. It will be said firmly that in art there must be no paltering. So say the fire-eating militarists in politics. Do we think them the wisest of men? My own view is that as the economic difficulties from which we now suffer gradually disperse (as according to orthodox economists of distinction they will do when the world inevitably resumes its normal swing), the pessimism of our day will give place to something more hopeful. Young poets will not write sentimentally about the unemployed and about vermin-haunted slums (of which they know nothing), and will take a more optimistic view of life, even finding once again material for sonnets in some personal emotion stronger than self-righteousness. Older poets will no longer be content to be cloistrally cryptic, but will 'come forth into the light of things,' as Wordsworth bade, and with Nature as their teacher find that there are other things in life than their own disconnected images. And in return for these blessings, the general public, which now regards all 'modns' as matter for slightly exasperated merriment, will begin to appreciate what at present seems to be an elaborate hoax, levelled at simpletons by those with more wit than conscience.

Before parting from the moderns, let us glance for a few moments at the one of them who has not yet been discussed in this book; whose poetry and criticism have alike had the strongest possible influence upon juniors, and whose influence is now seriously declining. I mean, of course, T. S. Eliot, who is, he says, 'classicist in literature, royalist in politics, and anglo-catholic in religion.'

II. THOMAS STEARNS ELIOT

That critical discernment is not sufficient to make men poets is generally allowed. Why it should keep them from becoming poets is not perhaps equally evident; but the fact is, that poetry requires not an examining but a believing frame of mind. Those feel it most, and write it best, who forget that it is a work of art.

T. B. MACAULAY, *Essay on Dryden.*

T. S. Eliot was born in St Louis, Missouri, in 1888. He was educated at Harvard, the Sorbonne, and Oxford University. When he first began to write I do not know. It is said by Alida

Monro in the preface to her anthology, *Recent Poetry, 1923–1933*, that *The Love Song of J. Alfred Prufrock* was first published in the *Catholic Anthology* in 1914; I first saw it in 1917, as a small book which was a sensation among those who watch for literary dawns. Then after the War Eliot contributed to *The Athenaem* when that paper was edited by Middleton Murry, and when Murry and Eliot seem to have been involved in curious argument of which the merest echoes found their way into Murry's *Athenaeum* reviews of Eliot's early books of poems and which are referred to in Eliot's essays upon critical principles. It was in 1922 that *The Waste Land*, which is not a single poem, but a collection of shorter poems woven into a whole, was published; and from that time others besides the eager young knew that a poet of powerful influence was abroad in the world. *Prufrock* and *The Waste Land* have had a greater effect upon the course of modern English poetry than any other poems.

It is said that these poems are obscure. I think they are obscure. But long ago I was presented with poems by Robert Browning and George Meredith which were absolutely unintelligible to their readers; and so it does not seem to me to be a damning charge against Eliot as a poet that his poems are obscure. What is of importance—far greater importance, I think, than the line-by-line gloss of those enthusiasts who exclaim at profundities—is that in these poems there is a lovely and secret melancholy music to which the ear responds with rapture. I know of nothing quite like this in English poetry; it has great beauty. Some of the shorter poems by Eliot have their similar extraordinary attractiveness—for example, *Gerontion*. Others have what for me is an adolescent touch; several are elongated epigrams; one, *Hysteria*, which is a prose piece, is no more than a clever cruelty—'I concentrated my attention with careful subtlety to this end.' 'Careful subtlety!' A terribly revealing phrase. A phrase into which the whole of an adverse criticism of Eliot's poetry might be condensed. But the enchantment of the poems under the three titles I have given is perfect.

One can understand quite well even now with what a shock of joyous discovery young poets who were already experimenting for themselves with the object of escaping from over-familiar rhythms and verse forms seized upon *Prufrock* and *The Waste Land*. And it should be said punctually that Eliot is as far as possible from the further eccentricities of many who derive from him. He must often enough have sighed over both his imitators and his expositors. But two points arise from our reading of his poems. Such is the concentration of their form and the fewness of their numbers that in the midst of our admiration of a new and very striking talent we are called upon by some impulse to reflect upon the extremely meagre material given us for any estimate of the poet's full powers. We know that he is much lauded, and that books have been written about him; but we wonder (in the absence of consultation) how the authors of the books ever managed to make a great man of Eliot. A hint, a suggestion, yes; but the perfect picture? Not wholly, perhaps, in the poems, save by act of faith. At any rate, the poems, so few, so small (I mean, most of them so essentially small, unambitious in theme, little versicules in which banalities such as 'the damp souls of housemaids' occur as if they were jewels), are surprisingly, however compact, trivial. Ah, but I have missed, you say, the notes to *The Waste Land*. I have missed the profound significance of that poem, or that series of poems, so expressive of the mind and temper of the age.

No; I have not missed those notes, and I am conscious of the fact that they must have been a subject of controversy of which I have remained unaware. There are ten pages of them, and their object is to gather together, in comment upon line by line of *The Waste Land*, all the literary sources of the poems, from Jessie L. Weston's *From Ritual to Romance* to Dante, Ovid, and St Augustine. It is of their significance and therefore, perhaps, of the significance of *The Waste Land* that I am in doubt. You remember that I did not understand why it was of such artistic importance in the case of *Ulysses* that Joyce had built his book on the framework of the *Odyssey*; and something of the same difficulty arises here. It is of course interesting, or it would be interesting if the notes seemed to add anything to the poem, to know why certain associations occurred to Eliot's mind when he was creating a poem, or after he had created it, and as he came to read it with a cooler mind. It is true, also, that Coleridge and other poets have in a similar way annotated their poems, showing sources and meanings which might have been missed by readers unacquainted with a variety of considerations peculiar to the poet's nature. But is there not, in these notes of Eliot's, some ostentation of learning and reading? Would it not be open to you, or to me, both of us so widely read, likewise to annotate our works with impressive references? We, too, could proudly say of certain collocations that they are 'not there by accident.' But we should only do this if we wished to gain credit for erudition, if we wished to *impress*. I fancy that many have been

affected by knowledge of Eliot's scholarship who might otherwise have found the poems rather commonplace, in the same way
as those admirers of the form of *Ulysses* have been prevented by
knowledge of Joyce's scholarship from finding that book a performance; and that they have brought an irrelevant awe to the
study of the actual works. What a mistake! It is the works
that are of importance; not the sources of inspiration. And
Eliot's annotations suggest that he is not quite aware of the
quality in his poetry which is of value. It is the music, and not
the literary association, which gives these poems their beauty.
They should have been left to speak for themselves.

But Eliot, besides having great influence as the most remarkable innovating poet of his day, is also a critic; and his criticism
has had as great an influence in forming the judgment of other,
younger, men, as his poetry has had in arousing them to the
possibilities of highly complex modern verse. That they have
gone beyond his word, which is always interesting and deeply
sincere, may be allowed. That does not concern us. It is not
the purpose of this book to deal with the writing of critics; and
I must reluctantly pass over a very important aspect of Eliot's
work without detailed examination. Criticism of criticism, save
in the most general terms, is impossible. Eliot is one who
affirms the need of critical method, as opposed to the person who
claims to be able to judge all things by an inner light; and he can
be extremely sarcastic at the expense of those who believe in
the inner lights of both artist and critic. He also has a strong
belief in the craftsman-critic ('the critics who have practised,
and practised well, the art of which they wrote'), providing
always that such critic has what he calls a highly developed
sense of fact.

Setting aside a first doubt of the precision of that cautious
'practised *well*,' I should agree with him in this respect for the
craftsman-critic, whose even wrong words often have interest if
he has given his mind to the subject in hand. But when Eliot
pins his faith to fact I think he rides off without providing us with
a definition of the essential principle from which criticism must
start. The nature of fact may be perfectly well understood by
Eliot; and I think I grasp what he means. But I greatly doubt
whether what Eliot regards as a highly developed sense of fact is
anything more than what I regard as imaginative candour. That
is, he has a respect for his own integrity, and can perhaps appreciate the integrity of another critic, even though he may disagree
with him; but he does not provide any common basis for judg-

ment which shall be intelligible and acceptable to all parties. Having, as is the way of critics with a metaphysical bent (e.g. Coleridge), roused us to a belief that he is going to develop a great general theory of aesthetics, Eliot seems to tire, or to shrug his shoulders, and his wisdom remains fragmentary. He is better in his inquiries into specific talents; for here he gives chapter and verse, we can follow him and agree or disagree with the facts presented.

However, what I wished to say in this connection is that just as Eliot's reputation is partly based upon his criticism, so he is in his character quite half critic. He is so much a critic that his poetry is the poetry of a critic. I mean, not that it is deficient in poetry, although I think it deficient in ardour, but that his critical sense is too active to allow of his poetry being other than meagre in quantity and restricted in range of emotion. In this respect he is of his age. Admirers of the age will say, properly; doubters will question contemporaneity as a virtue. Eliot argues for it as a virtue. The age is not, for the sincere, an age of fluency. Is it, possibly, an age, for poets, of costiveness?

I use that word in relation to something more than quantity. I use it as an adverse comment upon what some modern poets claim as a peculiar excellence. We all justify ourselves. It may be true that Swinburne and Tennyson would have done well to blot a few thousand lines of their writing; but if it was true, as a number of dramatic authors said in evidence before the Dramatic Censorship Committee, that awareness of the censorship prevented them from writing with a sense of proper and dignified freedom, I think it is quite as true that respect for his own judgment has prevented Eliot from giving his poetic inspiration its complete fulfilment. He has done much to discipline modern poetry, as well as to give it a new direction; and he has done much to lead younger poets to explore their own minds with what I hope is scrupulous exactitude, although I fear otherwise. But as his power over young poets declines, as it has already begun to do, he will himself become conscious, I think, that between over-fluency such as we have seen in certain modern poets whom I will not name and the small—Aldington's 'hard or marble-like' —potatoes which comes from poets of the too self-conscious school of to-day, there is a valuable mean which still requires a prophet. Eliot, more than any other man, has been responsible for the justification of literary frigidity (he has been but a leader in the direction taken by all the most elaborately cultured poets and critics of the age); and if I am right in thinking this I fear it is not as good an example as he might have set.   Indeed I wonder whether, the lovely rhythm of his best poems apart, he has not done more harm than good by encouraging a tribe of arid sciolists to imagine themselves *esprits supérieurs*.

INDEX

MADE AT THE
TEMPLE PRESS
LETCHWORTH
GREAT BRITAIN

EVERYMAN'S LIBRARY

A LIST OF THE 942 VOLUMES
ARRANGED UNDER AUTHORS

Anonymous works are given under titles.
Anthologies, Dictionaries, etc. are arranged at the end of the list.

4

8

NOTE—The following numbers are at present out of print:
89, 109, 110, 111, 146, 147, 228, 244, 275, 346, 350, 376, 390, 418, 432, 480, 493, 540, 541, 574, 597, 641-52, 664, 679

LONDON: J. M. DENT & SONS LTD.
NEW YORK: E. P. DUTTON & CO. INC.